MEDIATING THE TOURIST EXPERIENCE

Current Developments in the Geographies of Leisure and Tourism

Series Editors:

Jan Mosedale, University of Applied Sciences HTW Chur, Switzerland and **Caroline Scarles**, University of Surrey, UK and on behalf of the Geographies of Leisure and Tourism Research Group of the Royal Geographical Society (with the Institute of British Geographers)

Tourism and leisure exist within an inherently dynamic, fluid and complex world and are therefore inherently interdisciplinary. Recognising the role of tourism and leisure in advancing debates within the social sciences, this book series, is open to contributions from cognate social science disciplines that inform geographical thought about tourism and leisure. Produced in association with the Geographies of Leisure and Tourism Research Group of the Royal Geographical Society (with the Institute of British Geographers), this series highlights and promotes cutting-edge developments and research in this field. Contributions are of a high international standard and provide theoretically-informed empirical content to facilitate the development of new research agendas in the field of tourism and leisure research. In general, the series seeks to promote academic contributions that advance contemporary debates that challenge and stimulate further discussion and research both within the fields of tourism and leisure and the wider realms of the social sciences.

Mediating the Tourist Experience
From Brochures to Virtual Encounters

Edited by

JO-ANNE LESTER
University of Brighton, UK

CAROLINE SCARLES
University of Surrey, UK

ASHGATE

Published by
Ashgate Publishing Limited
Wey Court East
Union Road
Farnham
Surrey, GU9 7PT
England

Ashgate Publishing Company
110 Cherry Street
Suite 3-1
Burlington, VT 05401-3818
USA

www.ashgate.com

British Library Cataloguing in Publication Data
A catalogue record for this book is available from the British Library

The Library of Congress has cataloged the printed edition as follows:
Lester, Jo-Anne.
  Mediating the tourist experience : from brochures to virtual encounters / by Jo-Anne Lester and Caroline Scarles.
      pages cm.—(Current developments in the geographies of leisure and tourism)
  Includes bibliographical references and index.
  ISBN 978-1-4094-5106-8 (hardback) — ISBN 978-1-4094-5107-5 (ebook) —
ISBN 978-1-4724-0184-7 (epub) 1. Tourism—Social aspects. 2. Advertising—Tourism.
3. Visual communication. 4. Mass media and business. 5. Social media. I. Title.
  G155.A1L4346 2013
  659.19'91—dc23

                                                                      2013011977

ISBN 9781409451068 (hbk)
ISBN 9781409451075 (ebk – PDF)
ISBN 9781472401847 (ebk – ePUB)

Printed in the United Kingdom by Henry Ling Limited, at the Dorset Press, Dorchester, DT1 1HD

Contents

List of Figures

List of Tables

Notes on Contributors

David Airey is Professor of Tourism Management at the University of Surrey where he has also served as Head of School and Pro-Vice Chancellor. His academic career in tourism dates back to the early 1970s and his research interests have included tourism education, policy and policy making, heritage tourism and economic issues related to tourism.

Constantia Anastasiadou is a Reader and Postgraduate Programme Leader in Tourism, Hospitality and Festival and Events Management in the School of Marketing, Tourism and Languages at Edinburgh Napier University, UK. Previous to this appointment she had worked as a qualitative social researcher on tourism, festivals and employability projects and held various posts in the tourism industry. She has published extensively on various aspects of tourism policy in regional trading schemes but was also involved in collaborative projects on tourism marketing technologies. She holds an MSc and PhD from the Scottish Hotel School, University of Strathclyde, UK and a BA (Hons) in Economics from the University of Macedonia, Greece.

Sue Beeton is Associate Professor in Tourism at La Trobe University and Editor-in-Chief of *Tourism Review International*. As well as producing numerous academic papers and book chapters, she has published four books, *Beeton's Guide to Adventure Horse Riding*, *Ecotourism: a practical guide for rural communities*, *Community Development Through Tourism* and *Film-Induced Tourism*, with a fifth book, *Tourism and the Moving Image* due in 2013. Dr Beeton is the founder and President of the Asia Pacific chapter of Travel and Tourism Research Association, Editor-In-Chief of *Tourism Review International* and co-convenor of the bi-annual International Tourism and Media conference (ITAM).

Kathryn Bell is a Lecturer in Travel and Tourism at University College Birmingham and has previously worked in marketing roles within the tourism industry. More specifically, Kathryn has had a variety of experiences using social media in the marketing of tourism products and this continues with her position as lecturer. From this, her research interests have evolved to include tourism and destination imagery with a specific interest in the use of social media in the creation, modification and communication of images.

Susanna Curtin has been working in the field of 'animals and tourism' for ten years and has published research on tourist experiences with animals, sustainable wildlife tourism, the emotional and psychological benefits of taking a wildlife holiday, memorable wildlife encounters, how wildlife tourists attend to and perceive wildlife, and the importance of tour leaders in the responsible management of wildlife tourism. She has also been involved in a large study for the Scottish Government to assess the strengths, weaknesses, opportunities and threats of wildlife tourism in Scotland. Her current interests concern tigers, tourism and conservation, and wildlife tourism volunteering.

Ann Fletchall recently received her PhD from Arizona State University and is currently a lecturer at Western Carolina University. Ann is a cultural geographer whose primary research interests lie in media geographies, especially television. Her research addresses the creation and experience of televisual place.

Leon Hoffman has worked as a strategic analyst at the former Waitakere City Council. He recently completed a MA thesis in Geography at The University of Auckland on the experience of the coast on Great Barrier Island. His fieldwork involved an investigation into local perspectives of the natural, social and cultural landscapes while living on the island during 2010.

Robin Kearns is Professor of Geography at The University of Auckland, with interests in social processes and cultural landscapes, particularly as they relate to human wellbeing. He is an editor of the journal *Health & Place* and has published two books as well as articles in journals including *Tourism Geographies*, *Geoforum* and *Transactions of the Institute of British Geographers*.

Sangkyun (Sean) Kim is a Senior Lecturer and the Honours and Postgraduate Coordinator in the Department of Tourism at Flinders University, Australia. His research interests stem from four main themes: tourism and popular culture, experiential aspects of tourist experience and emotion, tourism and cultural heritage and research methods in tourism including qualitative, quantitative, mixed, and visual research methods. His recent research interest relates to multicultural festivals and special events associated with ethnic minorities and diaspora communities. He currently serves as a member of the editorial boards of *Journal of Tourism and Cultural Change* and is also on the Academic Board of Le Cordon Bleu Australia.

Ralph Lessmeister is Senior Lecturer in the Department of Geography at the University of Bayreuth, Germany. His research interests include the governance of global value chains in tourism and the medial construction of tourism destinations.

Jo-Anne Lester is a Principal Lecturer in Tourism for the School of Sport and Service Management at the University of Brighton, UK. Her research interests encompass visuality and tourism, the relationship between travel and photography, visual methodologies and the consumption of tourist space with a particular interest in popular film as visual data. With an industry background in the cruise sector she maintains a keen interest in cruise tourism. Her doctoral research focused on cruise ships and their uniqueness as spaces of both work and leisure as mediated through popular film. She teaches across a range of subject areas including travel and visual culture; cruise tourism; and research methods.

Chris Lukinbeal is an Assistant Professor of Geography at the University of Arizona. He has been conducting research in film and media geography for the last two decades and is the Co-Editor of *Aether: The Journal of Media Geography* (www.aetherjournal.org <http://www.aetherjournal.org>) and Co-Editor of the book: *The Geography of Cinema – a Cinematic World.*

Stephanie Merchant is a Research Assistant in the faculty of Health, Education and Society at the University of Plymouth. She recently completed her PhD thesis titled 'Submarine Geographies: technology, the body and the mediation of tourist experience' in Geography at the University of Exeter.

Nikos Migas is the Managing Director of SimpleSoft LTD, a consultancy firm that specialises in application for the NHS and the digital print industry. Prior to this appointment he has worked as a researcher in ad-hoc wireless networks, cross-media communications, and intelligent software agents in applications for the telecommunications and tourism industry. He holds a PhD from Napier University in software agents, an MSc from Liverpool JMU in interactive multimedia systems, and a BSc (Hons) in Computer Science from Lancaster University.

Noëlle O'Connor is a Senior Lecturer in Tourism and Hospitality Studies and the Course Director for the Bachelor of Arts (Honours) in Business Studies with Event Management Programme in Limerick Institute of Technology, Ireland. Noëlle is also a MBA Online Tutor at Glion University, Switzerland. She has a wide range of industrial experience, having worked in the Irish, British, French and Austrian hospitality industries. Noëlle edited the book, *Tourism and Hospitality Research in Ireland* (2007) and also published *A Film Marketing Action Plan for Film Induced Tourism Destinations - Using Yorkshire as a Case Study* (2010) and is presently on the Editorial Review Board for many of the leading tourism journals such as *Annals of Tourism Research* and *Tourism Management.* Her research focuses is in the areas of film induced tourism, celebrity endorsement of tourism destinations, social media in tourism, destination branding/management and tourism education.

Catherine Palmer is a social anthropologist in the School of Sport and Service Management at the University of Brighton, UK. She is a Fellow of the Royal Anthropological Institute and secretary to the institute's Tourism Committee. She is also a member of the Association of Social Anthropologists. Her research interests encompass identity and belonging; embodiment and the senses; culture of the coast/seaside; material/visual culture. She is published in leading journals such as *Annals of Tourism Research*, *Tourist Studies* and the *Journal of Material Culture*. She teaches courses on social anthropology and tourism and on research methods. She also supervises PhD research.

Peter Robinson is Principal Lecturer and Head of the Leisure Department at University of Wolverhampton. Peter has a background working in tourism and events management in the public, private and voluntary sectors, and his research interests include tourism management, tourism technologies, community-based and slow tourism, events management and event motivation. Peter has published a number of edited textbooks, including *Operations Management for The Travel Industry (CABI)*, *Events Management (CABI)*, *Research Themes for Tourism (CABI)*, together with journal articles, industry publications and presentations at international research and industry conferences.

Michael Salmond is a digital designer, new media artist, writer and educator. He is currently assistant professor of Digital Media Design at Florida Gulf Coast University, Florida, USA. His art and design work focus on videogames, travel and hybrid culture. His book, *The Fundamentals of Interactive Design* published by AVA/Bloomsbury came out in April 2013 in the UK, USA and Australia and has subsequently been translated into French

Caroline Scarles is a Senior Lecturer in Tourism in the School of Hospitality and Tourism Management, University of Surrey. Her research interests lie in the field of visuals and visualities in tourism, as well as ethics and sustainable tourism. In particular, her research addresses the visual as a means of actively producing and consuming place through negotiations of agency, power and ethics. She is the Chair of the Geographies of Leisure and Tourism Research Group for the Royal Geographical Society with the Institute of British Geographers and is a founding member of the International Network for Visual Studies in Organisations (inVISIO). She is also a resource editor for several journals including *Annals of Tourism Research*.

Nicolai Scherle is Senior Lecturer in the Department of Cultural Geography at the Catholic University of Eichstätt-Ingolstadt, Germany. His research interests include tourism entrepreneurship, tourism and intercultural communication and tourism media. In 2000 his monograph on the presentation of cultural aspects in German-language travel guides was awarded a research prize by the International Tourism Fair (ITB) in Berlin.

Philip Seaton is a Professor in the International Student Center, Hokkaido University, where he is Director of the Modern Japanese Studies Program. His research focuses on memories of war and representations of Japanese history in the media. Major publications include *Japan's Contested War Memories* (Routledge, 2007) and 'Reporting the 2001 textbook and Yasukuni Shrine controversies'

(Japan Forum 2005), which won the Daiwa Japan Forum Prize from the British Association for Japanese Studies.

Maltika Siripis is a Lecturer in Tourism Management in the Faculty of Management Science at Silpakorn University, Thailand. She holds PhD in Tourism Management from the University of Surrey. Her research interests include film and tourism, with a specific interest in the use of popular media in destination marketing, and government intervention in mediating destination image.

Karen Wilkes holds a Ph.D. in Cultural Studies from Nottingham Trent University. She has most recently held the position of Senior Lecturer in Cultural Studies at the University of East London. Her research interests include representations of gender, sexuality, and race in visual culture, post-colonial studies and tourism promotional material.

Takayoshi Yamamura is Professor of Center for Advanced Tourism Studies at Hokkaido University and one of the pioneers of 'Contents Tourism' and 'Anime Induced Tourism' studies in Japan. Since 2008, he has published books and articles focusing on this new concept of 'Contents Tourism' as well as served as the Chair of several governmental advisory boards such as the Meeting of International Tourism Promotion through Animation Contents of The Japan Tourism Agency, Screen Tourism Project of The Japan Tourism Agency, and the ANIME-Tourism Committee of Sitama Prefecture.

Acknowledgements

The editors would like to express their sincere gratitude to the Royal Geographical Society with the Institute of British Geographers (RGS-IBG) and the Geographies of Leisure and Tourism Research Group (GLTRG) for hosting the Mediating the Tourist Experience conference sessions at the 2010 Annual Conference in London. The presentations and discussions from these sessions provided the genesis for initial ideas for this collection. Thanks also to Valerie Rose and Katy Crossan, and all the editorial and production team at Ashgate, who have kept us on track with the publishing process. We also extend our gratitude to Mercedita Hoare, for her generosity and administrative support in compiling this manuscript. We would also like to thank all the contributors for their creativity, patience and resilience in the production process. Thank you all. Caroline would like to thank Ian and the little people for their support, patience and always being able to make me smile. Jo-Anne would like to thank Noel for his unquestioning and continued support, which enables her to achieve the things she does.

Chapter 1

Mediating the Tourist Experience: From Brochures to Virtual Encounters

Caroline Scarles and Jo-Anne Lester

Introduction

Traditionally, tourism media has predominantly referred to the image of destinations constructed through media texts, in particular tourist brochures (see Dilley 1986, Urbain 1989, Dann 1996) and postcards (see Mellinger 1994, Edwards 1996, Markwick 2001, Waitt and Head 2002, Moors 2003), with increasing attention towards other mediascapes (Jansson 2002) such as films and television (see, for example, Beeton 2005, Hudson and Ritchie 2006a and 2006b). Yet, with the prolific advancements and ever-increasing technologies of media communication, such traditional formats and manifestations of mediated representations of destinations have experienced a shift in purpose both in terms of production as well as the consumptive practices of tourists. The possibilities of production and subsequent consumption are unequivocally changing the ways in which tourists imagine, understand and engage with destinations. Indeed, the on-going technological advancements in the creation and transmission of static and moving images to mass audiences manifests itself in concepts such as 'virtual reality', 'cybertourism' and '2nd life' (see Prideaux 2002, Guttentag 2010, Wearing et al. 2010) as tourists and tourism exist in an ever-fluid and hypermobile world (see Sheller and Urry 2004, Urry 2007). Such advancements in both printed and virtual spaces of mediation, contribute to the continued development and power of such media in post-modern societies. Tourism media and the outputs they mobilise, become powerful products infused with political, cultural and social discourse and motivation. Thus, mediation within the context of this edited collection, emerges as a series of nonlinear, dynamic and immanent practices and processes as both producers and consumers come together to negotiate the purposive and performative enactments and experiences of the tourist experience. Indeed, it is not the intention to assume a causal, nor direct, relationship between media and tourists as the complexities of such relationships deny the possibility of such simplistic understanding. Rather, this collection aims to deconstruct such assumptions and highlight the plurality of interplays, practices, processes and performances that exist in mediating tourist behaviours, engagements and connections with place. The notion of directly mediated encounters becomes replaced by a series of messy, unpredictable and diverse practices as both those involved in producing and consuming destinations come together in a series of complex, multifaceted ways (see Coleman and Crang 2002, Crouch et al 2005).

Moving away from the understanding of mediation (traditionally within the context of destination marketing) as a series of highly skewed place perceptions created and mobilised by industry (see, for example, Urry 1990, Selwyn 1996), we propose that mediation and subsequent associated media do not simply manifest via a one-way process of producers offering insight into places and other that are subsequently consumed without question by tourists. Rather, each manifestation of mediated practices and processes holds the possibility of becoming a vehicle for mobilising discourse and discursive interpretation of the interrelationships and affiliations between place, space, self and other by both producers *and* consumers of mediated texts. As Scarles (2004) suggests, in portraying dominant discursive understandings, producers create scenes through which consumers enter imaginative touristscapes and personally connect with place by creating performances through mindsets where consumer and product unite.

Therefore, while mediation and resultant media remain infused with negotiations of authenticity (see, for example, Jansson 2002, Buchmann et al 2010, Rickly-Boyd 2011), myth-making (Barthes 1973, Morgan and Pritchard 1998, Selwyn 1996), and constructed realities, as Crang (1999), Edensor (2001), Osborne (2000) and Scarles (2009) suggest, tourists are now understood to play an active role in the mediation of their own tourist experience as well as the experiences of other tourists. They are not simply passive observers. Rather, experiences are mediated to make the viewer dream into the picture (Urry and Larsen 2011). Tourists become co-producers of their experiences, as they too mediate that with which they engage imaginatively or experientially (Löfgren 1999, Robinson and Picard 2009, Tussyadiah and Fesenmair 2009, Reijnders 2011, Gao et al. 2011). Thus, mediation and the construction of media products becomes a dynamic co-construction of transitional spaces of visualities: the practices and processes that enable the material objectivity of destinations and experiences to transcend their physical boundaries (Franklin and Crang 2001, Scarles 2009). Indeed, a multiplicity of visual and non-visual practices permeate visual devices as mediated representations of other embrace not only that which is seen, but which is performed via political, embodied, ethical, reflexive and imaginative encounter (see also, for example, Veijola and Jokinen 1994, Pons 2003, Pritchard et al. 2007, Scarles 2009).

As co-producers or indeed, co-mediators, of tourist experiences, tourists negotiate not only the other, but also the self, as mediation influences social identities and how these are subsequently expressed and shared by tourists. Further deconstruction of traditional linear communication structures emerges as mediation arises through tourist-to-tourist knowledge exchange of interpretations, expectations and experiences of place and other. Emergent technologies of social media mobilise spaces (Moreno 2007, Wearing et al. 2010) within which tourists are professionalised as authoritative voices in the mediation process as tourists draw upon multiple medias to generate hybrids of knowledge that rely on subtle blends of real and virtual spaces. Yet, such power of voice subtly shifts simultaneously to the tourist-as-receiver as mediated realities themselves become vulnerable to the multiplicity of receiver interpretation. The power of tourists as both producers and consumers of tourism media is undoubtedly further stimulated by advancements in technology as the productive capacities afforded through the virtual spaces of social media and image-sharing erode reliance on commercial images and bestow an authority on the tourist voice as providing an insight to place that is not veiled by politics of selling (Scarles 2004). However, while the politics of selling as a commercial practice may not underpin tourists' mediation of experience as shared with other, subsequent exhibitions remain inherently selective in nature (Hirsch 1981, 1997, Rose 2003) as tourists mediate their experiences according to preferred social, cultural and political ideological manifestations of self.

As Scarles (2009) suggests, in negotiating anticipations and/or experiences according to embodied reflectivity and reflexive remembrances as they negotiate self and the other as presented in order to make sense of and create a connectedness with that presented. Mediation becomes infused with embodied, haptic performances as both producers and consumers rely upon kinaesthetic connections with, and interpretations of, that presented (see Aitken and Zonn 1994, Rodaway 1994, Bruno 1997, Horton 2003). Practices and processes of mediation and the consumption of mediated interpretations become infused with emotion and feeling as tourists connect, react and respond to that with which they encounter as they dwell temporarily in the mediated space of other (Bruno 2002, Moreno 2007). Indeed, as spaces of real and virtual, commercial and personal fuse together, the responses elicited by media are no longer confined to imaginings associated, for example, with relaxing on the tropical island pictured in tourist brochures or on tour operator websites. Rather, alternative mediations of place and other force disjuncture between imagined and real, or realise confrontation with less aesthetically desirable elements of place from unappealing tourist behaviour through to poverty, unsanitary living conditions, political unrest and suchlike.

The Chapters

This book draws together a collection of 16 chapters that explore a range of theoretical and empirical frameworks that mobilise new understandings of media, mediation and mediatisation in particular touristic contexts (Jansson 2002, 2007, Lagerkvist 2008, Tussyadiah and Fesenmaier 2009, Månsson 2011). In varying ways, they examine their influence on the emergent relationships and connections between media practices and tourism practices, everyday experiences and encounters of place. Collectively, the chapters address a range of media and technologies from brochures, television, video, film and maps to mediated virtual spaces, such as e-brochures, Internet cultures, social networks, and photo-sharing websites. Overall, the contributions to this publication highlight the continued significance of media in tourism contexts, recognising both traditional and newer technologies, and the non-linear, continuous cycle of mediated representations and experiences. The collection therefore brings together a group of scholars from a range of disciplinary approaches to tourism and media in order to prompt reflection upon emergent forms and practices of mediation as they influence and direct the tourist experience.

The chapters initially focus on the production and consumption of popular place discourses as a key element of image construction of place; drawing upon some well-established concepts of stereotypes and identity, authenticity, myth-making and the mediation of 'realities' of destinations. In Chapter 2, Noëlle O'Connor and Sangkyun Kim critique the role of media-related tourism in shaping current and future tourism patterns and trends. Using the context of Ireland, they further develop conceptualisations of authenticity by reflecting upon issues of displacement and motivation and propose a renewed attention to authenticity in accordance with personal and symbolic meanings attached to media-related tourism experiences.

In Chapter 3, Karen Wilkes explores issues of identity and cultural values that pervade image construction. In particular, Wilkes challenges the representations of the exotic other in the context of luxury tourism products offered by Sandals Resorts. Politicising the processes of representation, she offers a post-colonial critique of the rhetoric and narratives that dominate image construction processes, thus deconstructing the politics of representation and the elevation of western discourses within image construction. This chapter offers an insightful account of the importance of socio-historical stereotyping in relation to gender and post-colonial relations, and the subsequent interpretations of place that continue to underpin contemporary touristic understanding of, and engagement with, place as mediated by producers (e.g. resort owners and tour operators). Therefore, by questioning the very need for touristic images as representations of place, Wilkes significantly critques the politics of image construction as embedded within contemporary interpretations of socio-historical identities and displayed through popularly consumed visual texts such as tourist brochures.

In Chapter 4, Leon Hoffman and Robin Kearns, further develop such critiques by offering an insight into the 'necessary glamourisation' of destinations in tourist brochures. This contribution focuses upon the power and politics of image construction as mediating the identities of locals and their home environments. Therefore, Hoffman and Kearns use the context of Great Barrier Island in New Zealand to further understanding of mediation through brochures beyond that of the product-tourist relationship to embrace the effect of such discourse and narrative on residents; identifying the potential gap between the image promoted and the realities experienced by locals living in the destinations. The complexity of their critique is further compounded by the emergent politics and power relationships that exist within the constructed realities of place presented in brochure images.

Finally, Chapter 5, by Susanna Curtin, bridges the first and second thematic pathways of the collection by exploring the use of technologies and their mediating power in the construction of contemporary relations with non-human agents. Using the example of natural history programmes, Curtin explores the inter-relationships between increased wildlife tourism demand and the increase in emotive images and supporting narratives offered to viewers of natural history programmes. In doing so, she offers a reconceptualisation of the complex relationships between media representations of the non-human as a series of social representations of animals and animal performance. The central thesis of the chapter is that television media create a series of anticipatory, highly emotive virtual encounters with the exotic otherness of the animal kingdom. She argues that through selective interpretations and the associated media production practices and processes, the discourse of such mediated narratives are heavily orientated towards hyper-sensationalism and the emotional responses that are provoked in the audience decoding process. Curtin therefore argues that what is offered becomes reminiscent of the circle of representation (Hall 1997) as tourists embark on a cyclical journey from the production of programmes and associated anticipatory imaginings of wildlife to the in-situ experience of close animal encounters that are subsequently reproduced through tourists' own recollections to reinforce popular social representations that pervade popular culture. As such, narratives are instrumental in reasserting popular discourse of anthropomorphistic intention rather than offering insights founded within the arguably, less accessible, ecological science.

Key conceptualisations of power and politics are further developed as attention then moves to the second key theme of the collection that identifies a significant shift in the productive capacities of tourists within the mediating practices and process of the tourist experience. With the emergence of new technologies and the hypermobility of communication in the twenty-first century, tourists are now placed at the forefront of the mediating process (see Jansson 2002, 2007, Månsson 2011). Therefore, in subsequent chapters, advances in technologies, together with their mediating and performative power, provide a platform to examine the repositioning of tourists as co-producers in the mediation process as opportunities arise for temporal dwelling in virtual spaces, tourist-to-tourist mediation through virtual spaces, and the politicised construction of self identities.

In Chapter 6, Nicolai Scherle and Ralph Lessmeister provide an insight into the rhetoric on the Internet, Internet cultures and what this means for tourism. Reflecting upon the significant technological advancements that have taken place over recent years, they critique the role of new forms of communication within the mediation processes of tourism; identifying a range of responses to these advancements of virtual technology and the contemporary spaces of virtual mobility that emerge as new spaces of touristic encounter. In doing so, they first outline digitisation as a historical process, before exploring the influence of the Internet as shifting societal expectations and public discourse, and finally critiquing the significance of this on the emergence of touristic Internet cultures as a series of negotiated identities through ever fluid, and increasingly mobile relationships.

In Chapter 7, Kathryn Bell uses the case study of Gloucester in the United Kingdom to address the interplays of promoted images and the role of virtual images of tourist destinations. She examines the utilisation of user-generated content and new technologies to project and construct an image of place exploring notions of tourists as co-producers in relation to third party image contributions. Drawing upon examples of social media and photo-sharing, Bell offers an insightful account of the image consumption practices of tourists; drawing out the increasing influence of technology in producing a multiplicity of realities of place and critiquing the linear trajectory of the circle of representation as she explores the role of new media technologies in mobilising a power knowledge shift from the projector to the receiver. As she suggests: 'it is no longer the power and knowledge of the tourism professional or academic that directs knowledge and understanding of tourism, but a reciprocal process with the tourist of joint knowledge mediation' (118).

In Chapter 8, Constantia Anastasiadou and Nikos Migas recognise that technology has now become intrinsically layered into the tourist experience. As consumers are increasingly positioned as co-creators in the image construction process, Anastasiadou and Migas offer a negotiation of mass customisation in product promotion to explore the opportunities afforded by new and emerging technologies for personalising and individualising the tourist brochure. Using the example of the Edinburgh Festival, they highlight the potential for brochures to be extended beyond status as a static, informative tool, to dynamically adapt to user preferences as information is reconfigured in ways that allow tourists to select the type and volume of information they receive. This chapter therefore offers intriguing accounts of the interactive, real-time production of selective insights to destinations as directly negotiated by destination marketing organisations and event organisations, and tourists. Reflecting the multiplicity of individual interpretation outlined by Bell in the previous chapter, tourists engage in the interactive consumption of destinations and tourism products that facilitates new ways of imagining and subsequently experiencing a destination as each customisation holds the potential to revolutionise how destinations are packaged, marketed and consumed.

In Chapter 9, Sue Beeton, Takayoshi Yamamura and Philip Seaton draw upon the concept of 'contents tourism', or film-based tourism, in Japan to explore the role of tourist as mediator and producer of tourist experiences. However, building upon contributions of existing research in this field (see, for example, Hudson and Ritchie 2006a and 2006b, Croy 2010, Hudson, Wang and Gil 2011), Beeton et al., renegotiate the classic tourism binary of 'host' and 'guest' to critique virtual spaces of tourist created media. In this context, it is argued that tourists, in generating online material focusing on particular characters, films or genres, become 'prosumers' as they create the very contents that stimulate their own and others' desires to visit the sites in question. As mediators of experience, prosumers become trusted sources of information as they actively construct and perpetuate mediated discourses of place. However, while Beeton et al. propose a centring of tourist-as-producer, they also suggest that the emergence of virtual spaces of touristic encounter and the associated prosumers communities, render the media itself, rather than the geographical locale of the destination, the tourist site to be visited.

In Chapter 10, Peter Robinson further develops the interplays and connectivity between producers and tourists as end users in the context of new media technology. Robinson considers the role of technology in the development of the tourist gaze; reflecting upon the relationships between visuality and tourism, the geo-spatial nature of images and the ways in which they are accessed and understood in order to mediate, or rather, e-mediate, the construction of place in relation to tourist destinations. In doing so, he identifies the complex relationships that exist within and between new technologies and end users. He therefore introduces the reader to the democratisation of tourism images through technological advancements as tourists come to know place through temporal dwelling in virtual spaces as the Internet provides opportunity for the transient inhabitation of spaces of other. Such conceptualisations of togetherness arise as the human and non-human come together in virtual spaces to make up landscapes and places through embodied performances that are further explored through the shared, aerial and e-mediated gazes.

Finally, the reconceptualisation of tourist-as-producer should not be assumed to exist solely within the virtual spaces of touristic encounter. Rather, drawing upon theoretical developments on performance as manifest in and through off-line technologies, the final set of chapters identifies the opportunities afforded by media such as souvenir DVD construction, film and television to empower the tourist within the mediation of imagined and experiential encounters. Such conceptualisations lead discussions of the embodied tourist and inevitable disjunctures of practice and imagination.

In the first of this final set of chapters (Chapter 11), Stephanie Merchant explores the transformative role of video and other mediating technologies in the construction and dissemination of tourists' experiences of underwater space. It explores the practices, performances and processes through which tourists engage with visual media formats in order to re-present their self according to experiential encounters with other. Using the example of souvenir videos of diving trips, Merchant renders visible the often unconsidered aspects of visual media production that results in not only the visual images (in this case short souvenir DVDs), but the opportunity for tourists to reinterpret experiences through alternative realities of place, performance and identity as constructed on the editing room floor. Building upon work by authors such as van Dijck (2007), Merchant suggests memories become lived experiences and recollections mediated as stimulants for recollection. As such, mediation provides a professional (re)contextualisation of experience and memories where space exists for discontinuity between the DVD as souvenir and the DVD as economically driven, artistic production. Merchant reflects upon politics of selectivity, aesthetics and production as selected remembrances emerge as produced through recollections of both tourists' personal encounter and the professional ethics of skill in constructing the mediated memories of self.

In Chapter 12, Michael Salmond explores the opportunities afforded by video technologies to mediate identities of self in relation to the other as experienced. He argues that tourists employ media as vehicles for defining and constructing both personal and cultural identities, with new technologies bringing new opportunities for mobilising alternative possibilities of self. In doing so, through the process of digitisation and remediation, tourists-as-producers create simulacra of people and/ or places that are subsequently distributed as forms of reality. Tourists therefore adopt a range of roles from scribe, documentarian, and film-maker to director and producer as well as end-viewer as they audience their experiences and mediate memories through 'hypermediacy' (Bolder and Grusin 2000) as they are produced and consumed through interrelated media tropes and cultural norms.

In Chapter 13, Maltika Siripis, Caroline Scarles and David Airey, seek to explore the influence of film mediation on tourist performances at destinations. Using the example of Thailand and the film, *The Beach*, this chapter examines the relationship between popular film and the enactment of tourism as a series of embodied performances as tourists move through spaces of anticipation to experiential encounter whilst on holiday in the destination itself. The chapter therefore challenges existing research that suggests tourists simply enact that which they see in films on arrival at destinations. Rather, through inherent awareness of self and other that finds genesis in post-modern interpretation, Siripis et al. suggest tourists become active participants in the mediation of place as experienced as they negotiate professional productions of place with self-awareness of personal experience and identity as they perform destinations.

In Chapter 14, Christopher Lukinbeal and Ann Fletchall take inspiration from concepts such as hyperreal places and thirdscapes of the virtual, in order to explore the embodied performances of place as mobilised by cinematic engagement. Presenting haptic, kinaesthetic performances of virtual spaces, this chapter critiques the disjuncture between imagined and real places, where the site filmed is not the place that one has emotionally inhabited. In doing so, it questions the emotional engagement and affiliations tourists are able to develop to place that are not always manifest through experiential encounter. Thus, touristic encounter in this context arises through the blending of actual and virtual spaces to mobilise an indexical relationship between image and reality. Spaces therefore remain open within cinematic spaces through which viewers engage imaginatively; enacting performances of self and other through embodied, haptic instances as places are forged on hallowed, rather than hollowed, ground.

In Chapter 15, Catherine Palmer and Jo-Anne Lester adopt an autoethnographic approach to explore the multiplicity of ways in which tourists mediate their own experiences through a series of encounters with materialities of place. Their exploration of mediation in this context is situated in the use of images in the form of maps as a means of way-finding. It is through our encounters with the materialities of destinations that allow us to come to know and experience our surroundings. Using the example of The Big Egg Hunt in London, Palmer and Lester offer an alternative set of interpretations of place set in the context of a personal journey and narrative as they renegotiate the tourist encounter through a series of interjections, encounters and disjunctures of navigation. In doing so, the human and non-human intertwine through a series of emergent, embodied performances of self and other.

Finally, in Chapter 16, Jo-Anne Lester and Caroline Scarles draw together the key theoretical contributions that have emerged throughout the preceding chapters and, in doing so, will outline avenues and opportunities for future inquiry in the area of media and mediation in the tourist experience.

References

Aitken, S.C. and Zonn, L.E. (Eds) 1994. *Place, Power, Situation and Spectacle: A Geography Of Films*. London: Rowman & Littlefield Publishers.

Barthes, R. 1973. *Mythologies*. London: Paladin.

Beeton, S. 2005. *Film-induced Tourism*. Clevendon: Channel View Publications.

Bruno, G. 1997. Site-seeing: architecture and the moving image. *Wide Angle*, 19 (4), 8–24.

Bruno, G. 2002. *Atlas of Emotion: Journeys in Art, Architecture, and Film*. London: Verso.

Buchmann, A., Moore, K. and Fisher, D. 2010. Experiencing film tourism: authenticity and fellowship. *Annals of Tourism Research*, 37 (1), 229–48.

Coleman, S. and Crang, M. 2002. *Tourism: Between Place and Performance*. Oxford: Berghahn Books.

Crang, M. 1999. Knowing, tourism and practices of vision, in *Leisure/Tourism Geographies, Practices and Geographical Knowledge*, edited by D. Crouch. London: Routledge, 238–56.

Crouch, D., Jackson, R. and Thompson, F. 2005. *The Media and the Tourist Imagination: Convergent Cultures*. London: Routledge.

Croy, W.G. 2010. Planning for film tourism: active destination image management. *Tourism and Hospitality Planning & Development*, 7(1), 21–30.

Dann, G. 1996. The people of tourist brochures, in *The Tourist Image, Myths and Myth Making in Tourism*, edited by T. Selwyn. Chichester: Wiley, 61–82.

Dilley, R. 1986. Tourist brochures and tourist images. *Canadian Geographer*, 31 (1), 59–65.

Edensor, T. 2001. Performing tourism, staging tourism: (re)producing tourist spaces and practice. *Tourist Studies*, 1 (1), 59–81.

Edwards, E. 1996. Postcards-greetings from another world, in *The Tourist Image: Myths and Myth Making in Tourism*, edited by T. Selwyn. Chichester: Wiley, 197–221.

Franklin, A. and Crang, M. 2001. The trouble with tourism and travel theory. *Tourist Studies*, 1 (1), 5–22.

Gao, B.W.; Zhang, H. and Decosta P.L. 2011. Phantasmal destination: a post-modernist perspective. *Annals of Tourism Research*, Article in Press.

Guttentag, D.A. 2010. Virtual reality: applications and implications for tourism. *Tourism Management*, 31, 637–51.

Hall, S. 1997. *Representation: Cultural Representations and Signifying Practices*. Milton Keynes: Open University Press.

Hirsch, M. 1981. *Family Photographs: Content, Meaning and Effect*. Oxford: Oxford University Press.

Hirsch, M. 1997. *Family Frames: Photography, Memory and Post-narrative*. Oxford: Oxford University Press.

Horton, A. 2003. Reel landscapes: cinematic environments documents and created, in *Studying Cultural Landscapes*, edited by I. Roberson and P. Richards. London: Hodder Arnold, 71–92.

Hudson, S. and Ritchie, J.R.B. 2006a. Promoting destinations via film tourism: an empirical identification of supporting marketing initiatives. *Journal of Travel Research*, 44, 387–96.

Hudson, S, and Ritchie, J.R.B. 2006b. Film tourism and destination marketing: the case of *Captain Corelli's Mandolin*. *Journal of Vacation Marketing*, 12(3), 256–68.

Hudson, S., Wang, Y. and Gil, SM. 2011. The influence of film on destination image and the desire to travel: a cross-cultural comparison. *International Journal of Tourism Research*, 13(2), 177–90.

Jansson, A. 2002. Spatial phantasmagoria: the mediatization of tourism experience. *European Journal of Communication*, 17 (4), 429–43.

Jansson, A. 2007. A sense of tourism: new media and the dialectic of encapsulation/ decapsulation. *Tourist Studies*, 7 (1), 5–24.

Lagerkvist, A. 2008. Travels in thirdspace: experiential suspense in mediaspace – the case of America (Un)known. *European Journal of Communication*, 23 (3), 343–63.

Löfgren, O. 1999. *On Holiday: A History of Vacationing*. Berkeley: University of California Press.

Månsson, M. 2011. Mediatized tourism. *Annals of Tourism Research*, 38(4), 1634–52.

Markwick, M. 2001. Postcards from Malta: image, consumption, context. *Annals of Tourism Research*, 28 (2), 417–38.

Mellinger, W.M. 1994. Toward a critical analysis of tourism representations. *Annals of Tourism Research*, 21 (4), 756–79.

Moors, A. 2003. From 'women's lib' to 'Palestinian women': the politics of picture postcards in Palestine/Israel, in *Visual Culture and Tourism*, edited by D. Crouch and N. Lubbren. Oxford: Berg, 23–40.

Moreno, C.M. 2007. Affecting and affective social/ media fields. *Aether: The Journal of Media Geography*, 1, 39–44.

Morgan, N. and Pritchard, A. 1998. *Tourism, Promotion and Power: Creating Images, Creating Identities*. Chichester: Wiley.

Osborne, P. 2000. *Travelling Light. Photography, Travel and Visual Culture*. Manchester: Manchester University Press.

Pons, P.O. 2003. Being on holiday: tourist dwelling, bodies and place. *Tourist Studies*, 3(1), 47–66.

Prideaux, B. 2002. The cybertourist, in *The Tourist as a Metaphor of the Social World*, edited by G.M.S. Dann. New York: CABI, 317–39.

Pritchard, A., Morgan, N., Ateljevic, I. and Harris, C. 2007. *Tourism and Gender: Embodiment, Sensuality and Experience*. Wallingford: CABI Publishing.

Reijnders, S. 2011. *Places of the Imagination: Media, Tourism, Culture*. Farnham: Ashgate.

Rickly-Boyd, J.M. 2011. Authenticity and aura: A Benjaminian approach to tourism. *Annals of Tourism Research*, 39(1), 269–89

Robinson, M. and Picard, D. 2009. *The Framed World, Tourism, Tourist and Photography*. Farnham: Ashgate.

Rodaway, P. 1994. *Sensuous Geographies, Body, Sense and Place*. London: Routledge.

Rose, G. 2003. Family photographs and domestic spacings: a case study. *Transactions of the Institute of British Geographers, New Series*, 28 (1), 5–18.

Selwyn, T. 1996. *The Tourist Image: Myths and Myth Making in Tourism*, Chichester, Wiley.

Scarles, C. 2004. Mediating landscapes: the processes and practices of image construction in tourist brochures of Scotland. *Tourist Studies*, 4, 43–67.

Scarles, C. 2009. Becoming tourist: renegotiating the visual in the tourist experience. *Environment and Planning D: Society and Space*, 27, 465–88.

Sheller, M. and Urry, J. 2004. *Tourism Mobilities: Places To Play, Places In Play*. London: Routledge.

Tussyadiah, I.P. and Fesenmaier, D.R. 2009. Mediating Tourist Experiences: Access to Places via Shared Videos. *Annals of Tourism Research*, 36 (1), 24–40.

Urbain, J. 1989. The tourist adventure and his image. *Annals of Tourism Research*, 16 (1), 106–118.

Urry, J. 1990. *The Tourist Gaze*. London: Sage.

Urry, J. 2007. *Mobilities*. Cambridge: Polity Press.

Urry, J. and Larsen, J. 2011. *The Tourist Gaze 3.0*. London: Sage.

Van Dijck, J. 2007. *Mediated Memories in the Digital Age*. California: Stanford University Press.

Veijola, S. and Jokinen, E. 1994. The body in tourism. *Theory, Culture and Society*, 11, 125–51.

Waitt, G. and Head, L. 2002. Postcards and frontier mythologies: sustaining views of the Kimberley as timeless. *Environment and Planning D: Society and Space*, 20, 319–44.

Wearing, S., Stevenson, D. and Young, T. 2010. *Tourist Cultures: Identity, Place and the Traveller*. London: Sage.

Chapter 2

Media-Related Tourism Phenomena: A Review of the Key Issues

Noëlle O'Connor and Sangkyun Kim

Introduction

Månsson (2011) suggests that media products are ever-present in our society and impact people in many ways, namely through newspapers, magazines, television programmes, films, digital and web-based media, and the emerging social media including Facebook, FourSquare, Twitter and YouTube. Initially, they influence how the world is seen because media provides a continuous movement of images and information about people, places and events (Couldry and McCarthy 2004, Moores 2005). Additionally, this is a universal process whereby both the destination portrayed, featured, or depicted in the media and the consumption of that destination is linked to each other through people's participation with the media products (Moores 2005). Consequently, the media has a great transformational power, particularly when it comes to people's imagery and imagination, in addition to their usage of space (Couldry and McCarthy 2004, Jansson and Falkheimer 2006). As the media infuses our society, it also has a major role in tourism (Månsson 2011).

According to Riley and Van Doren (1992), the media acts as 'pull' factors for prospective tourists by generating awareness, interest and appeal in the geographical locations and imaginations in which they feature. It also plays a vital role in shaping tourist motivations and influencing destination image and tourist visitation patterns (Butler 1990, Kim and Richardson 2003). Furthermore, Kim (2012) suggests that consuming visualised images and representations of a place or a country through popular media forms some basic perceptions of an individual's understanding of the place, and thus creates expectations and imaginations of what he or she would experience at the place when he or she actually becomes a tourist.

In recent years, there has been an increasing academic consideration of media-related tourism research, especially related to popular cultural media products such as films and TV series (Beeton 2005, Buchmann et al. 2010, Connell 2012, Kim 2012, O'Connor and Bolan 2010, Roesch 2009). Despite no data about its exact extent, the influence of the popular media on the tourism sector is evident. For example, Jewell and McKinnon (2008) state that Thomson Holidays in the United Kingdom (UK) estimate that approximately 80 per cent of Britons plan their holidays particularly after viewing a film (Jones 2002), hence creating a new class of tourist, the 'set jetter' (Linge 2006, Richardson 2006). Many films have gained unprecedented demand for internationally renowned tourism destinations such as the *Lord of the Rings* (2001–2003), which emphasises the unique and picturesque beauty of New Zealand; *Crocodile Dundee* (1986) highlighted Australia as an adventurous and attractive destination; and Bollywood themed films, such as *Slumdog Millionaire* (2008), have increased the popularity in the filmed destinations in India. As such, the influence of the *Lord of the Rings* on tourism in New Zealand has been examined in great detail in the tourism literature (e.g. Beeton 2005, Buchmann et al. 2010, Carl et al. 2007, Connell 2012, Tzanelli 2004). Rejinders (2011) identifies comparable studies that have been carried out on *The Da Vinci Code* in Paris, London and Rosslyn, Scotland (Karakurum 2006), *Bladerunner* in Los Angeles (Brooker 2005), the *X-files* in Vancouver (Brooker 2007), *Braveheart* in Scotland (Edensor 2005), *Harry Potter* in the United Kingdom (Iwashita 2006), *The Beach* in Thailand (Tzanelli 2007), and *James Bond* around the world (Reijnders 2010). Several studies have also looked at media-related special tours, among them the *Sex and the City* Tour in New York, the *Inspector Morse* Tour in Oxford (Reijnders 2009), the Manhattan TV Tour in New York (Torchin 2002) and *The Sopranos* Tour in New Jersey (Couldry 2008). More recently, media-related tourism studies in non-Western cultural and linguistic settings have been highlighted. Two Korean TV series *Winter Sonata* and *Daejanggeum* and the popularity of their filmed locations exemplify the media-related tourism phenomena in Asia (Kim et al. 2009, Kim and O'Connor 2011, Kim 2010, 2012).

Tourism researchers refer to such media-related tourism phenomena as 'media induced tourism' (Hudson and Ritchie 2006a, 2006b, Law et al 2007), 'film tourism' (Connell 2012, Kim 2012), 'film induced tourism' (Beeton 2005), 'movie induced tourism' (Busby and Klug 2001, Riley et al. 1998), 'teletourism' (Aitchison et al. 2000), and 'screen-tourism' (Kim 2010, Kim and O'Connor 2011). In the meantime, researchers in media, cultural and fan studies have labelled the same phenomena 'symbolic pilgrimage' (Aden 1999), 'media tourism' (Couldry 2000), 'cinematic tourism' (Tzanelli 2004), and 'cult geography' (Hills 2002). As varied as the terms used above, a range of useful definitions has been provided in previous studies and film tourism is considered as a widespread and broad-brush term for such media-related tourism phenomena (Connell 2012). Beeton (2005: 11) defines *film tourism* as 'visitation to sites where movies and TV programmes have been filmed as well as to tours to production studios, including film-related theme parks'. Despite this inclusive definition, the term *film tourism* seems to downplay the impact of TV programmes and other media products on tourism relating to screened outputs (Kim 2010, Kim et al. 2009). Thus, a more generic term *media-related tourism* is adopted in this chapter to describe tourist visits to a destination or location at least in part as a result of the destination being featured or portrayed as background or foreground of media productions on big or small screen.

Despite anecdotal evidence of media-related tourism around the world, there are some critical gaps in the way the phenomena have been approached to date. First, previous studies in this area primarily investigate the roles and impacts of films and TV series, including soap operas, on the pre-visit stage of tourist experiences in relation to destination image, travel intention, and destination choice (Croy 2010, Hahm and Wang 2011, Iwashita 2006, 2008, Kim and Richardson 2003, Kim et al. 2008, O'Connor et al. 2010, Shani et al. 2009, Tasci 2009), as well as the motivations of media-related tourism (Macionis and Sparks 2009). Secondly, and related to the above, there is relatively little research on the on-site tourist experiences associated with media-related tourism destinations, and consequently there is little understanding of how those tourists perceive, interact and experience media-related tourism destinations (Kim 2010). Thirdly, although there are some exceptions (Beeton 2005, Buchmann et al. 2010, Couldry 1998, Kim 2012, Roesch 2009), there is a dearth of research that aims to theoretically and conceptually understand, answer and discuss how to explain and examine tourist experiences in the context of media-related tourism. However, Crouch et al. (2005) attempted to place the tourism and (popular) media relationship into a more theoretical frame with the focus on the (tourist) imagination that is utterly central to previous viewing experience of TV series or films. Given that previous viewing experience and its subsequent actual touristic experience with locations depicted in TV series or films is considered as one that is highly personalised, subjective and unique to each individual based on their own pleasure, emotion, imagination, interpretation, and memory (Kim 2012), film tourism experiences are constructed and contextualised by televisual and cinematic narratives and mediated representations of other lands with embedded signs, myths and symbolic meanings (Couldry 1998, Kim 2010, 2012).

Media-related tourism can also fall under the same umbrella as cultural tourism. Both film and TV can be hugely influential on its audience. The amount of exposure a film (Hudson and Ritchie 2006a) can give a city or country such as Ireland can be a massive advertisement for that area as the potential for millions of people to see new destinations becomes increasingly apparent (O'Connor et al. 2006). Kim et al. (2009) maintains that the acknowledgment of these gaps forms a useful context and starting point for this chapter which examines, within an exploratory case study mode, the significance of media-related tourism in Ireland and how it is contributing to the shaping of tourism patterns in that country. Also, this chapter attempts to incorporate, integrate and theoretically discuss three key issues and/or concepts that should be taken into account in order to advance our understanding of tourist experiences associated with media-related tourism destinations. These three concepts are displacement, authenticity and motivation. The chapter could benefit destination managers, film and TV stakeholders, academics and students who have an interest in media-related tourism destination development, planning and marketing.

Media-related Tourism in Ireland – A Case Study

Jewell and McKinnon (2008) argue that media-related tourism offers film and tourism stakeholders the opportunity to influence tourists to visit a destination. It would appear that popular films which sequentially motivate tourists to the films' location settings were initially in novel form. As perceived by Herbert (2001), literary destinations are no longer just the location of a writer's birthplace, burial site or of historical fact; rather these locations are social constructions, generated in order to attract tourists. A novel based film and/or television series can raise awareness from a tourism perspective about a destination whether it be a country, city, town or rural site. It could also be seen that media-related tourism is based on a type of imagined nostalgia which symbolises an idyllic olden time, a romantic philosophy or longing to return to what life should still be like (Goulding 2001, Grabum 2001, Jones 1993, Lowenthal 1993, 1996, McKercher and du Cros 2002).

Ireland has attracted many audiences globally with highly successful films such as *The Quiet Man* (1952), *Michael Collins* (1996), *My Left Foot* (1989), *Evelyn* (2002), *Saving Private Ryan* (1998) and *Angela's Ashes* (1999). TV series also play a big role in the growth of media-related tourism in Ireland. Ireland is a host country to many successful Irish television series including *Ballykissangel* (1996–2001), *Glenroe* (1983–2001), *Father Ted* (1995–1998) *Showbands* (2004) and *Aifric* (2006). These dramas play a major role in attracting tourists to the country. The TV series *Ballykissangel* (1996–2001) is a prime example of this. The success of the series made Avoca, County Wicklow one of the main media-related tourism destinations in Ireland. Another example of the consumption of a destination TV series which has encouraged visits to Ireland is *Father Ted* (1995–1998). The series lasted just three years but proved to be very popular worldwide, particularly in the UK. *Father Ted* depicts a remote parish off the West Coast of Ireland and was set on Inishmore (Aran Islands) and the North Clare parish of Kilfenora. The show still attracts a large number of tourists every year. Craggy Island Parochial House in County Clare is a popular media-related tourism attraction even though it is private property. This led to the creation of a hugely successful event called 'Ted Fest' that is a unique celebration of the *Father Ted* (1995–1998) phenomenon, which generates a large amount of tourist interest annually. Whether they are real life documentaries or the fantasies of fictional tales, films have always been a way for audiences to encounter other places (Beeton 2005).

Tourism continues to be a major shaping force in Irish society. The film industry is constantly growing and provides a way of showing international countries an insight into Irish heritage and culture. Ireland is portrayed to other countries as a friendly nation, full of history and traditions with imagery of leprechauns, green landscapes, shamrocks, folk music, castles and beer, but is this how Ireland really is, or is it giving out a false image? In one way the strong image of green Ireland portrayed in films is a massive selling point to other countries, giving out a relaxing and friendly image. Myths and traditions are also a great way to attract tourists into visiting, such as leprechauns and pots of gold at the end of the rainbow, but it is worth noting however, that not all Irish films are seen in a positive light, such as *Song for a Raggy Boy* (2003) or *The Magdalene Sisters* (2002). These films visualise part of Irish history that Ireland's Catholic Church did not want publicised as they portray the unhappy lives of young people in their institutions.

As such, media-related tourism in Ireland is a growing trend in recent years. Ireland is even becoming a firm favourite among filmmakers for its beautiful scenery and colourful cities. Some of the films shot in Ireland include *Educating Rita* (1983), *The Tudors* (2007–2010) and *King Arthur* (2004). The world-wide phenomenon of the *Harry Potter* film series also include scenes shot in Ireland. The country has a lot to offer to filmmakers in terms of landscape, small towns and cities. The first ever film to be made in Ireland, *The Lad from Old Ireland* (1910) was shown nationwide. The film industry has grown enormously since then, and now attracts a lot of attention with films being shot in various locations around the country and distributed globally.

With the huge success of the films mentioned above, tourists are enticed to visit the wonderful scenery they see in the films for themselves and this has led to the recent growth in inbound tourist numbers. The Irish Film Board[1] (IFB), an organisation set up in 1980 as the potential of the film industry was realised, is the backbone of the success of the industry to date. Not only does the organisation provide essential resources to Irish filmmakers but it also promotes the entire island, with everything it has to offer, to filmmakers across the globe and provides them with all the necessary information they require. Essentially, due to the IFB generating so much interest in recent years in the quality of Irish film locations, there were major tax cuts in the industry, again making it even more enticing for potential filmmakers to come to Ireland. A ten year strategic plan was developed and instilled in the organisation, by the Irish Government in 1998. This plan was introduced to further develop the industry, in order for it to reach its full potential, and to remain viable and competitive. Apart from the organisation's studios in the country, they opened an office in Los Angeles to further market Ireland to the USA in 2006. Martin Cullen, the former minister for Arts, Sport and Tourism (2008–2010) said that the huge success of the Irish film industry brings with it many benefits including 'the development and projection of the Irish culture and the promotion of tourism'. Mainly due to the success of the internationally acclaimed films set or shot in Ireland, the tourism industry has experienced a massive boost. A recent survey, conducted in 2010, by Failte Ireland[2] found that 34 per cent of tourists who came to Ireland were hugely influenced by a film or television series they had seen. Tourism Ireland[3] now works closely with the film board to fully

---

1   The IFB is responsible for developing the industry as well as marketing Ireland as an attractive film location to outside producers (IFB 2010).

2   Fáilte Ireland are the state body responsible for domestic marketing in Ireland.

3   Tourism Ireland is the government agency responsible for the marketing of Ireland (both north and south) abroad.

maximise the success of this emerging tourism trend. It is the collaboration of these bodies that has led to the growth of the media-related tourism trend in Ireland.

Displacement

Displacement is an evolving factor and plays a crucial role in understanding media-related tourism experiences from a strategic and operational perspective for both tourism and media practitioners. Bolan (2009) defines displacement as when a film is shot in one place but in reality is representing somewhere completely different. Similarly, Buchmann et al. (2010) identify the concept of displacement as destinations which do not represent themselves in the film but are physically substituted for other locations. Displacement is used when the production is meant to be set in a particular area but the film crew could not find an appropriate location within that area, so they filmed it elsewhere. There are anecdotal evidences of displacement occurring. The Boston bar used in the phenomenally successful TV series *Cheers* (1982–1993), attracts many tourists yearly even though the series was not filmed there at all. Many major American blockbuster films have been made in Canada due to their low production costs, but the issue of displacement arises as these films were actually set in the USA. *Twilight* (2008), *X-Men* (2000), *Lethal Weapon* (1987–1998), *Tomb Raider* (2001–2003), and *Speed* (1994) are some examples to name but a few.

Ireland is not an exception from the issue of displacement in this context of media-related tourism, given the fact that many filmmakers choose Ireland as the ideal location due to its vast scenery and low film tax. These incentives give a boost to the local areas while filming is taking place, but at what cost in the long run? Ireland has played home to films set in England, Scotland, and Normandy in France; for example, the opening scenes of the impressive *Saving Private Ryan* (1998) were filmed in Curracloe Strand, County Wexford, but set in Normandy. The film *Braveheart* (1995) was set in Scotland but again filmed in Ireland where many Irish landmarks were portrayed, such as Trim Castle in Ireland as York Castle in the film. In the film *Barry Lyndon* (1975) the German military encampment scenes were filmed in Cahir Castle, County Tipperary. The book *PS I Love You* (2005) was set in Ireland but the film version of this story which was released in 2007, was set and filmed both in Ireland (Counties Dublin and Wicklow) and the USA (New York).

As with the above examples of displacement associated with media-related tourism locations, there are several future threats and issues that face the media-related tourism concept, the primary one being 'do tourists visit the location where the film was set or do they visit the actual site it was filmed?' In some cases, consideration should be given as to whether the tourist is actually aware of where the film was really set or whether they think that they are visiting the actual location. Previous studies conducted by Tooke and Baker (1996) and Frost (2010) suggested that tourists were more influenced by the places where films were set rather than where they were filmed. In comparison, other previous studies noted that tourists were disappointed when they did not see exactly what they had experienced on the screen (Beeton 2005, Carl et al. 2007), which indicates that those tourists want to experience the places where the films were actually made. This can be seen in the case of *Braveheart* (1995), *PS I Love You* (2007) and *Saving Private Ryan* (1998).

Although it is noted that visitation to media-related tourism locations is an incidental tourism experience (Di Cesare et al. 2009, Macionis and Sparks 2009), there are still specific or purposeful media-related tourists who actively seek out locations portrayed and featured in film or on TV as well as their personalised and symbolised meanings and values (Kim 2012). For those tourists, the main purpose of visiting media-related tourism locations is based on what they have seen, experienced, imagined, and interpreted on screen. They may, therefore, feel disappointed and disheartened, and may not fully enjoy their time there and leave with disgruntled views, when they come to what they thought was the film location when in fact it is not. Consequently, it could have a detrimental effect on the credibility of the market, and have an adverse effect on the tourist's perception of that area, and lead to negative word-of-mouth that is a highly important aspect of tourism, and in turn may lead to a decrease in tourist numbers to that destination (Bolan 2009). This could also have a knock-on effect to the actual location of the film, as the tourists already made the accomplishment of going to what they thought was the actual filmed location and therefore may not have the resources to travel again for some time. Thus the actual film location is losing out as well as the setting location. There is, however, no single and simple explanation or answer for the question, 'who will benefit as media-related tourism locations – set versus actual filmed location?'

In short, both setting and actual location, together, cannot equally benefit from displacement. Yet, research has shown that it would be possible for the two destinations (set and actual filmed location) to benefit, albeit to different degrees. This is exemplified by the fact that both Ireland and Scotland have gained tourists since the release of the academy award winning film *Braveheart* (1995). The reason for this being that the audience fantasise about the place (being the set of the location), but they also want to visit the location where it was filmed. To avoid detrimental effects of displacement, both tourism and media sectors, as media-related tourism stakeholders, need to effectively cooperate. When displacement occurs potential tourists should be educated and given full knowledge with regard to the issues involved. For example, when a film is made it should highlight where the film is shot. Also if a film is released on DVD, it could have an advertisement at the start conveying where the film was shot. At film premieres, the shooting location could be showcased before the film though this may not benefit both the destination where the film was set and filmed.

Authenticity

MacCannell (1999) highlights the fact that the grandiloquence of tourism is full of the indicators of the importance of authenticity between tourists and what they see. In the context of media-related tourism, many, if not most filming locations, are in one way or another closer to MacCannell's (1999) 'pseudo' sites than to his concept of 'true' or 'authentic' attractions, because many filming locations 'stand in' for sites physically located somewhere else. This is what this chapter discussed above in relation to the concept of displacement. Beeton (2005: 31) states that such substitutions 'can create a situation where people are basing their knowledge on false information as well as developing false expectations of sites they choose to visit, resulting in dissatisfaction with the experience'. Some locations, in science-fiction films such as *Star Wars* in particular, are overtly fictitious and graphically enhanced, often, in both temporal and spatial contexts. Butler (2011) comments that the location(s) portrayed in those films are seldom memorable and appealing enough to induce visitation (although *Star Wars* locations in Tunisia are recognised to an extent by aficionados of that film series) because of lack of authenticity embedded within those locations. Thus, there is often, if not always, an apparent conflict in the relationship between authentic location and its subsequent experience and this highly artefactual production process in the field of media-related tourism (Buchmann et al. 2010).

The issue of authenticity emphasises the objective attributes of the toured objects/artefacts and their authenticity, this so-called 'object authenticity' is a means of understanding tourist experiences with a particular focus on the cognitive dimension of unbiased authentic status of objects and activities (see MacCannell's (1973) notion of authenticity). However, Buchmann et al. (2010) suggest that such object authenticity is problematic to examine and understand. The authenticity of a film or a TV series inherently deals with fictional places which influence viewers into believing the story is real, or of reminiscing sentimentally of an idealised past representation aimed at consumerism (Jinhua and Chen 1997) or, as in the case of *The Man From Snowy River* (1982), demonstrating the fictional perceptions of Australia and Australian values to a potential tourist market (Beeton 2001). This can create a desire to visit the destination of a film's setting or location so as to become part of this cultural landscape. Furthermore, the destination, as seen with the *Lord of the Rings* trilogy, may not essentially be 'true', but to tourists and their collective community, the actual location is real and consequently allows their imagination to be swayed by the film's trilogy to complete the missing pieces. Sometimes, the destination is real such as can as seen with the *Star Wars* films (1977–2005) in Tunisia. Tourists can travel to Tunisia and see the city of Tataouine, that is depicted in the film as Luke Skywalker's home planet. Tourists can even stay in Luke Skywalker's home which is in reality a hotel (Jeffery 2004). Possibly, these new cultural landscapes, produced by films and the consequent media-related tourism industry, can be in part a new form of authenticity and identity among the global film public (Jewell and McKinnon 2008).

As such, the authenticity of media-related tourism experience is highly important but complex. This might not be fully understood by a rather simplistic assessment of object authenticity associated with media-related tourism locations. In this regard, Buchmann et al. (2010) highlight that subjective, symbolic or even the constructed nature of media-related tourism locations and experience does not necessarily downplay its own authenticity by suggesting an urgent need for increasingly sophisticated understandings of authenticity in the context of media-related tourism. This is well exemplified by a study on visitors of Granada Studios Tour (GST) in Manchester, associated with an ever popular British soap opera, *Coronation Street* (Couldry 1998). Couldry (1998) identified that tourists' experiences go beyond the obvious cognitive dimension of the locations as their fictive but authentic status in the dramatised world and are appreciated as a memory structure and various symbolic dimensions of these spaces as ritual places (Couldry 1998), or even as 'sacred places' (Roesch 2009). Buchmann et al. (2010) also identify that the very moment of embodied interaction with the filmed locations and other tourists was the highlight of authentic media-related tourism experiences. Furthermore, a number of studies have established the significant role that re-enacting actions or scenes from film or TV series has in creating authentic, memorable and meaningful media-related tourism experiences (Carl et al. 2007, Kim 2010, 2012, Roesch 2009). Buchmann et al (2010: 232) stated that the basis of this authenticity is akin to Wang's (1999: 159) notion of 'existential authenticity': 'Existential authenticity, unlike [the] object-related version, can often have nothing to do with the issue of whether toured objects are real. In search of [a] tourist experience which is existentially authentic, tourists are preoccupied with an existential state of being activated by certain tourist activities'.

O'Connor (2011) suggests that closer collaboration between film and tourist stakeholders should take place in order to help maximise the selling potential of a destination. In turn, this will also reinforce their film-induced tourism brand. This could possibly recreate or sustain a film set, therefore making it more authentic for tourists. In relation to Ireland, a destination marketing organisation could be introduced to target film makers.

Motivation

Media-related tourism motivation is the last, but not least important, issue for this chapter to highlight and discuss in order to advance our understanding of media-related tourism experience. Tourist motivation is one of the most prevalent research topics in the existing tourism literature. As there is a growing body of media-related tourism literature suggesting that films and TV series may have become fundamental to what people base their travel decisions on, studies on motivation associated with media-related tourism have increased (see Macionis 2004a, 2004b, Macionis and Sparks 2009, Singh and Best 2004). Visiting the sets and locations of favourite films and TV series is becoming more popular among tourists. The ever increasing 'need' among tourists for an incomparable holiday is one of the reasons behind this emerging trend. The entertainment industry is growing and has an increasing influence on consumers' everyday travel related decisions. Many of today's films are not produced with the intent to lure people to visit certain destinations. Nevertheless, in a sense a destination depicted in a film can be seen as a form of product placement. Film and TV series have been broadly acknowledged as being able to create representations of global destinations. The audience can look at destinations at home or in the cinema.

It is indeed evident that media-related tourism is one of the key motivations for travel in Ireland. Bolan and Davidson (2005) examined the different types of media and investigated the degree of influence they have on a purchaser's destination choice when booking a trip to Ireland. They carried out a survey (n=150) at various tourism related locations in both Northern Ireland and the Republic of Ireland.

Many respondents confirmed that media had been a motivating factor in their choice of destination to visit. Respondents were also asked which media type had influenced them most. The results demonstrated that the three forms (film, radio and TV) of media dominate respondent choices. It is worth noting that TV (29 per cent) and film (27 per cent) were the most important media influences. Simply, Bolan and Davidson's (2005) findings reveal that media does have a strong influence on respondents choice of tourist destination and TV in particular can be a strong motivating factor to visit such destinations, at least in Ireland (Bolan and Davidson 2005). Regarding the trend of media-related tourism motivation studies, Beeton (2010: 3) states that: 'While the previous research of film-induced tourism focused primarily on the more superficial, passive viewing of a scene when discussing the motivation of tourists to a film site, this moved into more complex discussions regarding private and personal motivations'.

The initial emphasis lies in spectacular scenery and splendid landscape to be a major motivational driver for media-related tourism in earlier studies (Riley and Van Doren 1992). However, further academic studies have identified a wider range of motivational drivers. For example, Riley et al. (1998: 924) articulate that 'if some part of a movie is extraordinary or captivating, it serves as an icon which viewers attach to a location shown in the movie...a movie's symbolic content, a single event, a favourite performer, a location's physical features, or a theme can represent all that is popular and compelling about a movie' (Riley et al. 1998: 924).

Later, Macionis (2004a, 2004b) adopted a push and pull framework and conceptually developed a simple and intuitive model of media-related tourism motivation. The pull factors are categorised by place, personality and performance, whilst the push factors include ego enhancement, status, fantasy, vicarious experience and search for self-identity. This is ultimately a method of classifying how or why tourists may visit a destination due to its association with films or TV series. Furthermore, Macionis (2004a) proposed three categories of media-related tourist typology depending on the level of significance of film or TV series as a main motivational driver: (1) the serendipitous media-related tourists, who happen to be visiting a location conveyed in film or TV series; (2) the general media-related tourists, who are not attracted to a location by media-related tourism alone but who participate in tourism activities in the location; and (3) the specific media-related tourists, who are actively seeking to visit locations they have seen in film or TV series. Such media-related tourism motivators include; novelty, nostalgia, enjoyment, memory, success and exposure of film, romanticised views, celebrity and commercial prowess, and otherness:

- if people are in the area at the time, they may feel it would be a novelty to visit a film location nearby;
- it can create nostalgia for people and create that fantasy world that people dream of when they see films;
- people who are generally film fans enjoy visiting places where films were located;
- some people are motivated by childhood memories e.g. watching *Dirty Dancing* (1987) and visiting the Virginia Lake House hotel where it was filmed;
- the success and exposure of the film can motivate the tourist;
- tourists can get a romantic view of a certain film location e.g. *Love Actually* (2004) and London;
- tourists may like the celebrity factor and the commercial prowess that the area exuberates. In New York, there is the *Sex and the City* (1998–2010) tour which brings feeling of celebrity to them;
- when people see the scenery in a film or a certain place they are automatically drawn to it if it is appealing and something that they have never seen before.

As such, people visit filming locations for a variety of reasons. To some people certain films evoke something special for them such as having watched a film as a child, a feel good film or a film that they associate with a person they know. 'Feel good' films that have a love story for example, may entice viewers to visit its film location so they can experience what the characters did in the film. Escapism is an underlying motivation here, as more and more tourists want to relive the film's theme for themselves. Reeves (2001) argues that to become a popular tourist attraction, a location should arouse the feel good factor linked with romance/ escapism (Buchmann et al. 2010). The study on *Winter Sonata* conducted by Kim (2010) is one of the examples to demonstrate the significance of a love story and the filming location as a metaphor of an embodiment of Korean courtship and passion toward true love. It's filming location, Nami Island in South Korea, became a shrine to passionate love in the minds of many young and old tourist couples (Kim 2010). Similarly, tourists may be enticed to experience what the characters in the film *PS I Love You* (2007) did when they went to Ireland. After watching the film, viewers may associate Ireland with the theme of the film, love, and may be enticed to go and visit Wicklow and Dublin, where some of the film was filmed.

Some may travel to a film site because it is an iconic location; the Empire State Building in New York has been featured in many films, such as *Sleepless in Seattle*. Some others may travel to a film site to fulfil a fantasy they have about a place, whereas other motivations include the novelty of being in the place a famous actor stood. It may also be so they can feel like they have been in a film. A key example, that is globally renowned, is the sensational TV series *Sex in the City*. This TV show was shot in Manhattan, New York. It showed a wonderful positive side to the city, and how exciting life in the Big Apple could be. Most of the famous landmarks in the city where shown at one point throughout the life time of the show giving potential tourists watching at home an appetite for the big city.

In the Irish context, the key motivations of tourists who visit filming locations are triggered by the powerful images used in films, which tend to show Ireland's beautiful scenic areas that almost act as an advertising opportunity. For example, tourists may be motivated to visit places like Northern Ireland where the scenery was used as an inspiration for the mythical film of *The Chronicles of Narnia: The Lion, the Witch and the Wardrobe* (2005) (O'Connor and Bolan 2008). History lovers may visit the film locations of war films so they can relive past times and events, for example people may be enticed to visit the Wicklow Mountains as some of the scenes from the film *Michael Collins* (1996) were filmed there. Tourists may also have more than one motive for visiting a destination, for example a tourist may want to visit a destination that featured in a film but they also may want to feel real authenticity of a scene that was shot in the film. An example of this would be visiting *Michael Collins* (1996) home town in West Cork, but also visiting Béal na mBláth where he was assassinated. Tourists who are interested in tracing their ancestral routes, a huge market, may be enticed to visit Limerick for example after seeing the film *Angela's Ashes* (1999). Other tourists are curious to see the film location of their favourite film or TV series, for example visiting *Father Ted's* house in County Clare.

Summarising Insights

Central to this chapter, was the significant role media-related tourism plays in shaping current and future tourism patterns and trends in Ireland. It also attempted to conceptually understand the media-related tourism phenomena and its associated tourism experiences. In doing so, the chapter drew on three important key issues, these being displacement, authenticity and motivation. These issues are closely related to each other, and play equally important roles in understanding the media-related tourism experiences. As media-related tourism is a complex and diverse product which relies on viewers' personal and subjective experiences of a film or TV series through both simultaneous production and consumption, there is no single agreed approach to understand and examine media-related tourism experiences. The audience and touristic appeal of media products' representations and images are themselves complex and cannot be reduced to some single (Kim et al. 2009) motivational driver. Furthermore, despite the welcomed concept of authenticity in tourist experience studies, the notion of 'object authenticity' has a limitation in better explaining authentic experiences and personal and symbolic meanings attached to media-related tourism experiences. Consequently, an urgent need for a more sophisticated understanding of authenticity was highlighted through Wang's (1999) notion of existential authenticity related research.

Indeed, it is also evident that media-related tourism is growing in Ireland and its relevant stakeholders, namely Fáilte Ireland and Tourism Ireland, are beginning to realise the market potential of such related tourism in their destination promotion of Ireland. While critics might argue that many media productions present a romanticised view of Ireland, Tourism Ireland (2011) sees this as another tool with which to sell holidays to the island. Many of the films or TV series shot in Ireland highlight the qualities which are attractive to the potential target market of media-related tourism – the warm, witty, welcoming people; rich history and heritage; green unspoilt landscapes; vibrant contemporary culture and lively cities. What might seem overly-stereotypical to the critical Irish eye, might fulfil the dreams of, and tick all the boxes for, an overseas tourist and motivate them to book their holiday in Ireland (Tourism Ireland 2011).

However, it is clear that many destinations in Ireland have not yet fully realised their full tourism potential as there has been very little research, interest and investment placed on the sector within the Irish context. In this regard, Lam and Ap (2006) argue that it is imperative to recognise what the present literature has to say, ascertain gaps in the literature and look at future directions for such research. If media-related tourism as a field of research is not focused on, our appreciation of it will continue to be inadequate and its promise to mature as a tourist product in many destinations may not be fully understood, resulting in lost opportunities for destinations like Ireland (O'Connor et al. 2010); to strengthen their ever-diminishing pull factors. Yet, films are a huge part of the Irish economy, and in turn promoting Ireland through film is an innovative way of advertising as it is viewed by a potentially massive audience which, arguably, could never be reached by normal promoting methods and it is significantly cheaper. Given the fact that 11 *Bollywood* feature films have been shot or partially shot in Ireland since 2004 and that the top South African soap *Isidingo* (1998–present) aired a week-long storyline shot in Ireland, there is another strong rationale why the key stakeholders from both film and tourism industries should develop the media-related tourism locations and prioritise destination marketing.

As discussed, the impacts that media-related tourism bring to the country would be both positive and negative, and would create both opportunities and threats in the future. Therefore, sufficient time needs to be spent researching this field in order to fully understand this concept and its future possibilities. More importantly, the key tourism and film stakeholders need to work collectively to ensure that Ireland benefits in the long run, as Macionis and O'Connor (2011) suggest that in order for the film locations to be a 'standalone destination brand' key stakeholders in an area must work together. They also need to make potential tourists aware what films are shot in Ireland (through promotion with Fáilte Ireland and Tourism Ireland). Tours of film and TV sets and particular landmarks depicted in a film should also be set up and a brand for Irish film should be developed and used to promote Ireland. Furthermore, media-related tourists should be given full, truthful information so as to meet their expectations especially if they are a specific film tourist. Through this process displacement can benefit both locations, where the film was filmed, and where it was set, as is evident from the film *Braveheart* (1995). The stakeholders also need to realise that having any film shot in their locality can yield free advertising and it should be utilised in order for the media-related tourism concept to be used as a tourism planning and sustainable development tool.

As demonstrated earlier, the film-induced tourism concept can be applied to Ireland (both North and South) but the displacement phenomenon needs to be considered. It is worth noting that *The Chronicles of Narnia: The Lion, the Witch, and the Wardrobe* (2005) was filmed in New Zealand but the Northern Ireland Tourist Board used it to boost their tourism industry through a re-branding campaign (e.g. movie maps) (O'Connor and Bolan 2008). To avoid displacement occurring, media-related tourism stakeholders need to come together, cooperate effectively and work towards exercising their market to its full potential. This could be achieved, by the collaboration of the media-related tourism stakeholders, such as the IFB, Fáilte Ireland and Tourism Ireland working together to create an effective strategic plan.

References

Aden, R.C. 1999. *Popular Stories and Promised Lands: Fan Cultures and Symbolic Pilgrimages*. Tuscaloosa: University of Alabama Press.

Aitchison, C., Macleod, N.E. and Shaw, S.J. 2000. *Leisure and Tourism Landscapes: Social and Cultural Geographies*. London: Routledge.

Beeton, S. 2001. *Cyclops and Sirens – Demarketing as a Proactive Response to Negative Consequences of One-eyed Competitive Marketing. TTRA 32nd Conference Proceedings: A Tourism Odyssey*, TTRA, Fort Myers, Florida, USA, 10–13 June.

Beeton, S. 2005. *Film-induced Tourism*. Clevedon: Channel View Publications.

Beeton, S. 2010. The advance of film tourism. *Tourism and Hospitality Planning & Development*, 7(1), 1–6.

Bolan, P. 2009. *Displacement Theory: Probing New Ground in Media Induced Tourism. The 6th Annual Tourism and Hospitality Research Conference – Current Challenges and Future Opportunities*, Shannon College of Hotel Management, Shannon, County Clare, Ireland, 16–17 June.

Bolan, P. and Davidson, K. 2005. *Film Induced Tourism in Ireland: Exploring the Potential. University of Ulster Conference Proceedings: Tourism and*

Hospitality Research in Ireland: Exploring the Issues. Portrush: University of Ulster.

Brooker, W. 2005. The *Blade Runner* experience: pilgrimage and liminal space, in *The Blade Runner Experience*, edited by W. Brooker. London: Wallflower, 11–30.

Brooker, W. 2007. Everywhere and nowhere: Vancouver, fan pilgrimage and the urban imaginary. *International Journal of Cultural Studies*, 10(4), 423–44.

Buchmann, A., Moore, K., and Fisher, D. 2010. Experiencing media-induced tourism. *Annals of Tourism Research*, 37(1), 229–48.

Busby, G. and Klug, J. 2001. Film-induced tourism: the challenge of measurement and other issues. *Journal of Vacation Marketing*, 7(4), 316–32.

Butler, R. 1990. The influence of the media in shaping international tourist patterns. *Tourism Recreation Research*, 15(2), 46–53.

Butler, R. 2011. It's only make believe: the implications of fictional and authentic locations in films. *Worldwide Hospitality and Tourism Themes*, 3(2), 91–101.

Carl, D., Kindon, S., and Smith, K. 2007. Tourists' experience of film locations: New Zealand as *'Middle-Earth'*. *Tourism Geographies*, 9(1), 49–63.

Connell, J. 2012. Film tourism – evolution, progress and prospects. *Tourism Management*, 33, 1007–29.

Couldry, N. 1998. The view from inside the 'simulacrum': visitors' tales from the set of Coronation Street. *Leisure Studies*, 17, 94–107.

Couldry, N. 2000. *The Place of Media Power: Pilgrims and Witnesses of the Media Age*. London: Routledge.

Couldry, N., and McCarthy, A. 2004. Orientations: mapping media space, in *Mediaspace: Place, Scale and Culture in a Media Age*, edited by N. Couldry and A. McCarthy. London: Routledge, 1–18.

Couldry, N. 2008. Pilgrimage in mediaspace. Continuities and transformations. *Etnofoor*, 20, 63–74.

Croy, G. 2010. Planning for film tourism: active destination image management. *Tourism and Hospitality Planning & Development*, 7(1), 21–30.

Crouch, D., Jackson, R. and Thompson, F. 2005. *The Media and the Tourist Imagination: Converging Cultures*. London: Routledge.

Di Cesare, F., D'Angelo, L., and Rech, G. 2009. Films and tourism: understanding the nature and intensity of their cause-effect relationship. *Tourism Review International*, 13(2), 103–12.

Edensor, T. 2005. Mediating William Wallace: audio-visual technologies in tourism, in *The media and the Tourist Imagination: Converging Cultures*, edited by D. Crouch, R. Jackson, and F. Thompson. London: Routledge, 105–18.

Fáilte Ireland. 2010. *2010 Tourism Facts and Figures – Tourist Attitudes Survey*. Dublin: Fáilte Ireland.

Frost, W. 2010. Life changing experiences: film and tourists in the Australian outback. *Annals of Tourism Research*, 37(3), 707–26.

Goulding, C. 2001. Romancing the past: heritage visiting and the nostalgic consumer. *Psychology & Marketing*, 18(6), 565–92.

Grabum, N.H.H. 2001. Learning to consume: what is heritage and when is it traditional?, in *Consuming Tradition, Manufacturing Heritage*, edited by N. Alsayyad. London: Routledge, 68–89.

Hahm, J. and Wang, Y. 2011. Film-induced tourism as a vehicle for destination marketing: is it worth the effects? *Journal of Travel & Tourism Marketing*, 28, 165–79.

Herbert, D. 2001. Literary places, tourism and the Heritage Experience. *Annals of Tourism Research*, 28(2), 312–33.

Hills, M. 2002. *Fan Cultures*. London: Routledge.

Hudson, S. and Ritchie, J.R. 2006a. Promoting destinations via media induced tourism: an empirical identification of supporting marketing initiatives, *Journal of Travel Research*, 44(4), 87–96.

Hudson, S. and Ritchie, J.R. 2006b. Media-related tourism and destination marketing: the case of *Captain Corelli's Mandolin*. *Journal of Vacation Marketing*, 2(3), 256–68.

IFB. 2010. About the Irish film industry. [Online]. Available at: http://www.irishfilm board.ie/irish_film_industry/About_the_Irish_Film_Industry/44 [accessed: 9 February 2011).

Iwashita, C. 2006. Media representation of the UK as a destination for Japanese tourists. *Tourist Studies*, 6(1), 59–77.

Iwashita, C. 2008. Roles of films and television dramas in international tourism: the case of Japanese tourists to the UK. *Journal of Travel & Tourism Marketing*, 24(2/3), 139–51.

Jansson, A. and Falkheimer, J. 2006. Towards a geography of communication, in *Geographies of communication: The Spatial Turn in Media Studies*, edited by J. Falkheimer and A. Jansson. Goteborg: Nordicom, 9–25.

Jeffery, F. 2004. Wishing on a star. *Travel Weekly*, 1731, 15.

Jinhua, D. and Chen, J.T.H. 1997. Imagined nostalgia, *Boundary 2*, 24(3), 143–61.

Jewell, B. and McKinnon, S. 2008. Movie tourism—a new form of cultural landscape? *Journal of Travel & Tourism Marketing*, 24(2–3), 153–62.

Jones, M. 1993. The elusive reality of landscape: concepts and approaches in research, in *Heritage: Conservation, Interpretation & Enterprise* (The Robert Gordon University Heritage Convention: Aberdeen, Scotland), edited by J. M. Fladmark. Wimbledon, London: Donhead Publishing Ltd., 17–41.

Jones, M. 2002. *Tourism: Keeping up with the Indiana Joneses*, United Arab Emirates: TRI Hospitality Consulting.

Karakurum, D. 2006. *Cracking The Da Vinci Code: An analysis of The Da Vinci Code Tourist Phenomenon*. Unpublished doctoral dissertation, Breda: NHTV Breda University, The Netherlands.

Kim, H. and Richardson, S.L. 2003. Impacts of a popular motion picture on destinations perceptions. *Annals of Tourism Research*, 30(1), 216–37.

Kim, S. 2010. Extraordinary experience: re-enacting and photographing at screen-tourism locations. *Tourism and Hospitality Planning & Development*, 7(1), 59–75.

Kim, S. 2012. Audience involvement and film tourism experience: emotional places, emotional experiences. *Tourism Management*, 33(2), 387–96.

Kim, S., Long, P., and Robinson, M. 2009. Small screen, big tourism: the role of popular Korean television dramas in South Korean tourism. *Tourism Geographies*, 11(3), 308–33.

Kim, S. and O'Connor, N. 2011. A cross-cultural study of screen-tourists' profiles. *Worldwide Hospitality and Tourism Themes*, 3(2), 141–58.

Kim, S.S., Argusa, J., Chon, K. and Cho, Y. 2008. The effects of Korean pop culture on Hong Kong residents' perceptions of Korea as a potential tourist destination. *Journal of Travel & Tourism Marketing*, 24(2/3), 163–83.

Lam, S. and Ap, J. 2006. Review and analysis of the media-related tourism literature, in *The International Conference on Impact of Films and Television on Tourism Conference Proceedings*, edited by K. Chon and A. Chan. Hong Kong, China: The Hong Kong Polytechnic University, 166–181.

Law, L., Bunnell, T., and Ong, C.E. 2007. *The Beach*, the gaze and media induced tourism. *Tourist Studies*, 7(2), 141–64.

Linge, N. 2006. Set jetters follow Scot Da Vinci trail. *Daily Star Newspaper*, 15 April, 4.

Lowenthal, D. 1993. Landscape as heritage: national scenes and global changes, in *Heritage: Conservation, Interpretation & Enterprise* (The Robert Gordon University Heritage Convention: Aberdeen, Scotland), edited by J.M. Fladmark. Wimbledon, London: Donhead Publishing Ltd., 3–15.

Lowenthal, D. 1996. *The Heritage Crusade and the Spoils of History*. England: Penguin Group.

MacCannell, D. 1973. Staged authenticity: arrangements of social space in tourist settings. *American Journal of Sociology*, 79, 589–603.

MacCannell, D. 1999. *The Tourist: A New Theory of the Leisure Class*. Berkeley: University of California Press.

Macionis, N. 2004a. *Understanding the Film-induced Tourist: 1st International Tourism and Media Conference Proceedings.* Melbourne: Monash University, Tourism Research Unit.

Macionis, N. 2004b. *Media Induced Tourism – The Tourist in the Film Place: Placing the Moving Image, Symposium Proceedings* Brisbane, Griffith University, Griffith Business School.

Macionis, N. and O'Connor, N. 2011. How can the film-induced tourism phenomenon be sustainably managed? *Worldwide Hospitality and Tourism Themes*, 3(2), 173–78.

Macionis, N. and Sparks, B. 2009. Film-induced tourism: an incidental experience. *Tourism Review International*, 13(2), 93–101.

Månsson, M. 2011. Mediatized tourism. *Annals of Tourism Research*, 38(4), 1634–52.

McKercher, B. and du Cros, H. 2002. *Cultural Tourism: The Partnership between Tourism and Cultural Heritage Management.* Binghamton, New York: The Haworth Hospitality Press.

Moores, S. 2005. *Media/theory: Thinking about Media and Communications.* New York: Routledge.

O'Connor, N. 2011. A conceptual examination of the film induced tourism phenomenon in Ireland. *European Journal of Tourism, Hospitality and Recreation*, 2(3), 105–25.

O'Connor, N. and Bolan, P. 2008. Creating a sustainable brand for Northern Ireland through media induced tourism. *Tourism, Culture & Communication*, 8(3), 147–58.

O'Connor, N. and Bolan, P. 2010. *To Identify the Future Viability of Using the Media-related Tourism Concept to Promote Ireland as Tourism Destination: 4th International Tourism and Media Conference Proceedings.* Prato: Monash University.

O'Connor, N., Bolan, P. and Crossan, M. 2006. *Film and Television Induced Tourism in Ireland: A Comparative Study of* Ryan's Daughter vs. Ballykissangel: *Proceedings of the 5th DeHaan Tourism Management Conference – Culture, Tourism and the Media.* Nottingham: University of Nottingham.

O'Connor, N., Bolan, P. and Crossan, M. 2008. *An Investigation into the Film and Television Induced Tourism Phenomenon in Ireland –* Ryan's Daughter *and* Ballykissangel: *The 4th Tourism and Hospitality Research Conference – Reflection: Irish Tourism and Hospitality – A Success Story*, Tralee Institute of Technology, Tralee, Co. Kerry, Ireland, June 10–11.

O'Connor, N., Flanagan, S., and Gilbert, D. 2010. *A Film Marketing Action Plan for Media-related tourism Destinations: Using Yorkshire as a Case Study.* Germany: Lambert Academic Publishing.

Reeves, T. 2001. *The Worldwide Guide to Film Locations.* Chicago: A Capella.

Reijnders, S. 2009. Watching the detectives: inside the guilty landscapes of *Inspector Morse, Baantjer* and *Wallander. European Journal of Communication*, 24(2), 165–81.

Reijnders, S. 2010. On the trail of 007: media pilgrimages into the world of James Bond. *Area*, 42(3), 369–77.

Rejinders, S. 2011. Stalking the count: Dracula, fandom and tourism. *Annals of Tourism Research*, 38(1), 231–48.

Richardson, D. 2006. Film locations draw 'jet setters'. *Travel Trade Gazette UK and Ireland*, 2709, 60.

Riley, R. and Van Doren, C.S. 1992. Films as tourism promotion: a 'pull' factor in a 'push' location. *Tourism Management*, 13(3), 267–74.

Riley, R., Baker, D., and Van Doren, C.S. 1998. Movie-induced tourism. *Annals of Tourism Research*, 25(4), 919–35.

Riley, R.W. 1994. Movie-induced tourism, in *Tourism. The State of the Art*, edited by A.V. Seaton et al. New York: John Wiley and Sons, 453–58.

Roesch, S. 2009. *The Experiences of Film Location Tourists*. Bristol: Channel View Publications.

Shani, A., Wang, Y., Hudson, S., and Gil, S.M. 2009. Impacts of a historical film on the destination image of South America. *Journal of Vacation Marketing*, 15(3), 229–42.

Singh, K. and Best, G. 2004. *Film-induced Tourism: Motivations of Visitors to the Hobbiton Movie Set as Featured in* The Lord of the Rings. *Proceedings of international tourism and media conference 2004.* Melbourne: Tourism Research Unit, Monash University, 98–111.

Tasci, A.D.A. 2009. Social distance: the missing link in the loop of movies, destination images, and tourist behaviour? *Journal of Travel Research*, 47(4), 494–507.

Tooke, N. and Baker, M. 1996. Seeing is believing: the effect of film on visitor numbers to screened location. *Tourism Management*, 17(2), 87–94.

Torchin, L. 2002. Location, location, location: the destination of the Manhattan TV Tour. *Tourist Studies*, 2(3), 247–66.

Tourism Ireland. 2011. Bollywood Film to Provide Tourism Boost. [Online]. Availableat:http://www.tourismireland.com/Home!/About-Us/Press-Releases/2011/BOLLYWOOD-FILM-TO-PROVIDE-TOURISM-BOOST.aspx [accessed: 23 February 2012].

Tzanelli, R. 2004. Constructing the 'cinematic tourist': the 'sign industry' of the *Lord of the Rings*. *Tourist Studies*, 4(1), 21–42.

Tzanelli, R. 2007. *The Cinematic Tourist. Explorations in Globalization, Culture and Resistance*. London: Routledge.

Wang, N. 1999. Rethinking authenticity in tourism experience. *Annals of Tourism Research*, 26(2), 349–70.

Chapter 3

From the Landscape to the White Female Body: Representations of Postcolonial Luxury in Contemporary Tourism Visual Texts

Karen Wilkes

Introduction

In the context of contemporary global media, the sophisticated and high quality tourist images of the Caribbean provide us with representations of gendered and racialised consumer utopias (Mclaren 1998) without reference to their historical or political origins. Tourism images continue to be important for their contributions to the construction of meanings around the notions of identity and belonging to different social categories those of, race, class, gender and sexuality.

There is a significant tradition of analysing tourism images (Dann 1996, Selwyn 1996, Cohen 1992) and this chapter adopts a postcolonial approach to explore the mediating practices underpinning contemporary representations in tourist brochures, which have an increasingly broad reach through online technologies. The case study examples of Jamaica and Sandals' Internet and brochure images are used to explore the constructions of the white female as the epitome of beauty which have been specifically positioned within the discursive formations of the Caribbean region as a luxury destination in which to host white weddings.

Media representations of identity continue to be important in the contemporary context as they disseminate the dominant version of beauty; taking its cue from the fashion industry and celebrity culture is the thin torso, long hair and pale Caucasian skin (although usually tanned in tourist brochures to connote luxury and wealth), in which whiteness is displayed as the normative category (Dyer 1997). One of the potential consequences of the continued use of whiteness as the ideal is the marginalising effect that it has on subjects who cannot or do not wish to subscribe to a narrow prescription of femininity (Butler 2007, Walter 2010, Stone 1995 cited in Cole and Sabik 2009). However, centring whiteness in representations of the Caribbean is significant as they allude to a continued disavowal of non-white identities, and also point to the existing and enduring hierarchies of global power through the operations of tourism 'after the formal end of colonialism' (Shohat and Stam 1994: 2).

The Politics of the Visual in Tourism Studies

Rakić's and Chambers's (2012) text, *An Introduction to Visual Research Methods in Tourism*, demonstrates the wide range of applications and theories of the visual in tourism studies. The edited collection is one text in the Routledge series entitled, *Contemporary Geographies of Leisure*, which incorporates analyses of the visual and representation within 'cognate areas such as anthropology, cultural studies…policy studies and political economy' (Hall 2012: ii, see also Scarles 2012, Haldrup and Larsen 2012, Crouch et al., 2005).

This chapter is concerned with the politics of representation and discusses how 'the visual' tend to adopt a Eurocentric perspective (Shohat and Stam, 1998 cited in Rose 2001: 8). However, scholars in the field of tourism studies (Scarles 2012, Haldrup and Larsen 2012) have broadened the discussion of the image and culture in relation to tourism and identified the importance of examining the components of images in the tourism process (Dann 1996, Cohen 1992, Selwyn 1996, Urry 1990). Such scholarship has provided analyses of tourism to include the cultural dimensions as well as the economic factors which affect the tourist industry. My aim here is to draw on these analyses by using a multidisciplinary approach of semiotic and discourse analysis, to explore the meanings and cultural values that underpin the way images are constructed (Morgan and Pritchard 1998) and to examine where such representations position the Caribbean in the contemporary global world order.

The chapter provides an analysis of how people in the Anglo-Caribbean are represented in Sandals' images, and in particular the perspective from which the viewer is encouraged to respond to those representations of the world and the power relations within it. It can be argued that images may not be received in the way that the producer of the image intended, nevertheless, there is a specific (class, race, and cultural) position from which tourism images tend to be produced and such representations, if not critiqued, are in danger of being taken at face value and applied universally. Images are a signifying practice. They carry meaning because they operate as symbols or signs, which stand for or represent the meanings we wish to communicate. In themselves they do not have a clear meaning, yet the messages and interpretations are achieved by those who share the 'same cultural codes' or language (Hall 1997: 4, see also Hall 1992). As we shall see, images are significant as they provide a window on how society and the social order are depicted. The chapter aims to contribute to the existing debates regarding whiteness as a neutral category (Bhattacharyya et al. 2002) which forcefully positions the white female body as the beauty ideal for all women to aspire to. This practice is being undertaken in the context of new technologies and online brochures which provide marketing agents with access to wider global markets. The effectiveness of whiteness and related discourses is their ability to remain undetected through the circulation of 'universalising' certain characteristics or values regarded as 'speaking for everyone', yet in practice they represent the concerns or 'interests of a privileged minority' (Fiske 1994, cited in Bhattacharyya et al. 2002: 24).

The Sandals images presented for discussion in this chapter can be located within the discourse of 'contemporary travel representations' (Simmons 2004: 43) which as Simmons (2004: 45–46) argues, 'construct an expectation among tourists that they are a travelling social elite' and are 'elevated above [the] local inhabitants'. Thus, the assumptions that are made regarding the social and cultural positioning of prospective Sandals guests, as already privileged in their Western country of origin (Simmons 2004), facilitates the construction of the 'West and the Rest' binary (Hall 1992: 277) as a standard 'model of comparison' (ibid: 277) in which non-Western places are positioned as 'counterfoils for Western modernity' (Sheller 2003: 1). Sandals have utilised dominant and entrenched 'Western ideas of a romantic other' (Hall and Tucker 2004: 10) to construct a narrative of longing and desire 'for the place of others' (Simmons 2004: 46, see also Hall 1992).

The celebratory displays of heterosexuality in Sandals'[1] images forcefully emphasise whiteness as rightfully entitled to luxury. It is the repetition of these images which encourages the content to be largely viewed as neutral and unanchored to any social or cultural context. However, the ideal white couple's wealth and 'exclusive access to luxury' (Simmons 2004: 45) is framed by colonial discourse, specifically conveyed by versions of whiteness being dutifully served by the disavowed black subject (Hall 1996c). The advantages of whiteness are explicitly connected to the material benefits of possessing the leisure time and the economic resources to take vacations in the Caribbean. Although such privileges derive from an unequal and competitive system, they are expressed through 'Western culture's enduring attachment to romanticism' (Lipsitz 2006: 120) and the discourses of paradise, as displayed in the Sandals images. A historical framework is required to understand these rituals; the history and longevity which gives them substance and legitimacy (Said 1995). Thus, in the colonial context, Jamaican planters were infamous for their hospitality (Burnard 2004), yet were dependent on the labour of slaves to perform the rituals of fine dining and the accumulation of wealth. References to this history are apparent in the visual construction of postcolonial Caribbean states where the black subject continues to be scripted by particular white identities (see Hall 1996a).

The 'tourist-Other relations' (Simmons 2004: 45) that are portrayed in the images are concealed beneath Western generated myths of the 'seductive', 'exotic' (Simmons 2004: 46, see also Sheller 2003) island paradise, thus the Caribbean landscape is presented as a dream-like fantasy, with white beaches and azure blue skies and ocean, which enable tourists to escape the social realities of modernity (Simmons 2004), without reference to the region's urban realities and violent colonial history. Such visual constructions disguise the power relations of the agent constructing particular myths and their intentions for encouraging particular perspectives. Thus, myths need to be examined to reveal their power relations

---

1 Images published in the 2012 Sandals promotional material (both online and hardcopy brochures) and those selected for analysis in previous research, see Wilkes 2008.

(Said 1995) and attention paid to how our understanding of social identities are influenced, and in turn shaped, by what we observe in tourism images. Thus:

> In the contemporary culture the media have become central to the constitution of social identity. It is not just that media messages have become important forms of influence on individuals. We also identify and construct ourselves as social beings through the mediation of images. This is not simply a case of people being dominated by images, but of people seeking and obtaining pleasure through the experience of the consumption of these images. An understanding of contemporary culture involves a focus on both the phenomenology of watching and the cultural form of images. (Angus and Jhally quoted in hooks 1991: 5)

Scholars writing on the subject of whiteness (hooks 1991, Morrison 1992, Dyer 1997, Frankenberg 1993, Bonnet 2000) and scholarship which analyses the colonial representations of the Caribbean landscape (Sheller 2003, Strachan 2002, Taylor 1993, Thompson 2006) have demonstrated in their analyses the resilience of discourses of whiteness and the 'tropicalisation' of the Caribbean, and their ability to operate independently. However, each group of discourses has become more resilient and powerful by forming intertextual relations with associated discourses to 'promote dominant cultural norms' (Bhattacharyya et al. 2002: 7).

This chapter offers analysis which assists in our understanding of the 'conditions of postcoloniality and power relationships' (Hall and Tucker 2004: 6); by specifically interrogating the visual constellation of essentialised categories, images of the white female as a mark of beauty and the carrier of the meanings of entitlement to privilege, and heterosexual romance and white weddings. The discussion that follows examines how the Sandals images are representations of the ideals of contemporary femininity in a post-feminist context, which display representations of class and privilege in the context of a global world-wide recession, yet they are also a reminder of colonial relations and the 'successes' of nineteenth century colonial projects.

Jamaica and the Aesthetics of Tourism Promotions

The establishment of tourism in Jamaica stemmed largely from the desire of the colonial authorities to reverse the decline in the white population and to generate business with the opening of American owned hotels (Taylor 1993, Thompson 2006). Jamaica was represented through the eyes of the local ruling white elite as a tropical idyll (Thompson 2006). Their focus was on developments which portrayed Jamaica as modern and picturesque, thus the emphasis was on 'tourism-orientated locations' (Thompson 2006: 15). The colonial aesthetics of tourism had a tangible effect on the development of the island as the focus was on providing visitors with a luxury experience and modern amenities, yet the ruling authorities neglected to provide an infrastructure for the local population (Thompson 2006,

Taylor 1993). As with all images the promotion of Jamaica as a tropical haven was a process of selection and construction and any representations which did not fit within the framework of Jamaica as bountiful tropic were omitted (Thompson 2006). The way in which the Caribbean is imagined in the West is through the repeated display of the region as a tropical 'island landscape' (Thompson 2006: 42), thus how we have come to understand Jamaica is through visual texts (ibid.: 46). This may explain why contemporary representations of Jamaica in tourist brochures suggest that the scenery is unchanged 'as "natural" as tropical nature itself was made to appear' (Sheller 2003: 62) in nineteenth century travel accounts produced by Anglo-American visitors. The practice of referring to Caribbean nations as principally tropical retreats is an additional discursive strategy which reinforces the binary and positions the region as timeless and pre-modern in comparison to the West. Jamaica could therefore be considered to be pre-modern due to the enduring construction of the island nation as a tropical Eden, and post-modern for its hybrid and diasporic communities.

From the Landscape to the Body

In a post-feminist context where a small, yet significant number of white women have been able to win spaces of independence in the forms of economic emancipation and sexual liberation, the ability and possession of the economic resources to travel to foreign destinations is a key mechanism through which social status can be expressed. White women are imbued with certain amounts of power, such as that of a consumer and possessor of cultural capital (Skeggs 1997). Indeed, the repeated displays of the white female body in Sandals' promotion of the Caribbean are significant for conveying notions of good taste. Alongside the specific use of language: *cute*, *chic*, *classic* and *heaven on earth* and *luxury included* (Sandals 2012), the images signify the exacting standards of the elite and privileged (Craik 1994). White women are displayed as 'symbolically' central (Hall 1996c: 475) to whiteness in the tourism images, yet continue to be socially constructed in relation to white men.

Against the backdrop of the quasi-feminist rhetoric of liberation (Walter 2010), ideals for women to aspire to remain narrow and are largely dependent on prominently projecting a sexualised image which appeals to 'the desires of men' (Lawson 2012: 10). Adopting the identity of a princess bride or hyper-sexed vixen does not entail gaining independence, but conversely, encourages reliance on traditional masculinity which refers back to a key feature of upper-class femininity during the nineteenth century (Skeggs 1997).

The traditional hierarchies of respectability have been subsumed under more liberal cultural attitudes towards the body. Yet, it is still the practice for 'certain bodies [to be] allocated certain values and their access to physical comfort is shaped by the allocation of value' (Bhattacharyya et al. 2002: 38, see also Trepangier 1994 cited in Cole and Sabik 2009). The idealised white female body is encoded within the discourse of marriage and white weddings. Retaining social positions of economic and cultural privilege, they carry the discourse of respectability. Middle and upper-class women are able to use the institution of marriage as a vehicle to attain social recognition and social status through behaviour, language and appearance which continue to 'operate as both social rules and moral codes' (Skeggs 1997: 46).

Although 'an array of "women" are constructed' (Butler 2007: 19) and valorised, respectability is only attainable for those who are located within the predetermined categories of white and middle and upper-class. Contemporary representations of white women as sexual beings appear to be transformative, yet they are constructed within a masculinist framework and female acquiescence continues to be a masculine fantasy (Skeggs 1997, see Walter 2010). Butler (2007) argues that 'a woman only exhibits her womanness in the act of heterosexual coitus in which her subordination becomes her pleasure' (Butler 2007: xiv). Therefore, in this post-feminist context there continues to be stringent parameters for the categories of woman which are produced and reproduced in popular visual culture. This also suggests that although attitudes towards the female body are more liberal, women are dependent on heterosexual relations in order to gain social recognition. Romance continues to be 'the acceptable face of desire for women' (Bland 1983: 9, see also Coward 2011) in Western cultures and within the discursive formation of luxury and self-indulgence, the female is still inscribed as beautiful, gentle and ultimately reinforcing masculinity (Kilbourne 2000, Butler 2007).

The Styling of White Femininity in Sandals Images

The Sandals images rely heavily on 'textually mediated discourse' (Smith 1988 cited in Skeggs 1997: 98) which portray white women as the ideal in consumer culture (Redmond 2003, Coward 1984, Kilbourne 2000). The female subject is an active creative subject, yet her activities are organised and structured by the existing historically determined discourses of femininity which in turn are framed by 'wider global markets' (Skeggs 1997: 98) of consumption.

However, sexism has not meant an absolute lack of choices for white women (hooks 1984), and the suggested message in the Sandals visual texts is that white women are not subject to the 'same respects or constraints' as women from racialised communities (Bhattacharyya et al. 2002: 105). Therefore, the Sandals images are addressing women who have largely benefited from the social changes produced by the feminist movement. Yet articulations of femininity are only successfully performed with the correct 'gendered stylization of the body' (Butler 2007: xv) by conforming to the contemporary beauty ideal as young, white, and thin (Cole and Sabik 2009). As Butler (2007) argues, the extent to which the gender norms are considered to be real depends on the 'ideals and rule of proper and improper masculinity and femininity, as many of which are underwritten by racial codes of purity and taboos against miscegenation' (Butler 2007: xxiv–xxv).

Although rules of 'proper' femininity and Western standards of beauty (in particular the ideal of a slim physique[2]) are narrow and oppressive, they are pursued in 'the cult of thinness' as described by some feminists (Hesse-Biber 2006 cited in Cole and Sabik 2009: 175) and is one feature of the beauty matrix which is reliant on social categories such as sexuality, race and class for its meaning. Thus, to understand these beauty norms, they need to be placed within a historical context, since 'white women's privileged position with respect to beauty is premised, in part, on their [historical] comparison to women of colour' (Collins 2000, Trepangnier 1994 cited in Cole and Sabik 2009: 181).

Thus the racialisation of beauty can be traced back to the travel literature of the late nineteenth and early twentieth century. This period is significant in the history of tourism in the Caribbean as it was during this period that an increasing number of Anglo-American travellers visited the region and recounted details of their visits for the public back home (Sheller 2003). Although the white female is not the identified subject of the travellers' accounts, she is present due to the vehement comparisons that were made between African women and European ideals of beauty. In the writings of colonial travellers, black women were derided for their physiognomic features, as the following comments indicate: 'buxom black negresses, with their thick lips, gay turbans, merry laughter, and somewhat aggressive curiosity' (Brassey 1885 quoted in Sheller 2003: 132), and 'Their faces are almost always repulsive, the thick lips and wide nostrils being fatal to European ideals of beauty...' (Hastings Jay 1900 quoted in Sheller 2003: 135).

Popular visual culture is complicit in promoting the idea that beauty and femininity come in the form of a heterosexual white woman. As a consequence of representations of whiteness being held up as the ideal, white women are best positioned to take advantage of 'their privilege in the domain of beauty' (Hurtado 1989 cited in Cole and Sabik 2009: 181). Therefore, what it means to be a woman is closely linked with the appearance of a woman's body and is mediated by cultural representations (Conboy, Medina and Stanbury 1997 cited in Cole and Sabik 2009: 180) such as those presented in the Sandals wedding and holiday brochures.

The displays of white brides appear to be the ultimate articulation of hyper-femininity, as all the elements that are deemed to identify the white female as the guardian of beauty (Goldberg 1993) are utilised in the Sandals 2012 brochure images. The images feature white brides with slim physiques, long, sleek hair, and [tanned] white skin. All the brides are styled to epitomise delicate femininity and refinement by wearing white wedding dresses made of silk and organza, and decorated with lace and brocade details, which all operate to reference luxury, style and the sophistication of a Sandals wedding.

---

2   For example, Cole and Sabik (2009: 177) refer to 'research that has repeatedly demonstrated the damaging effect the thin ideal may have on body image, eating habits, and feelings of self-worth among young white women (Noll and Fredrickson 1998, Tiggeman and Slater 2001, Tylka and Hill 2004)'.

The Princess Bride

Marriage was the preserve of the wealthy and a mechanism for reproducing the Euro-Creole upper class elite in nineteenth-century colonial Jamaica (Green 2007). In the contemporary context, the Jamaican landscape continues to be used as an expression of white cultural traditions, in particular the visual celebration of marriage and its contemporary manifestation, elaborate white weddings. This is within the contemporary context of American culture in which romance, weddings and marriage continue to be social aspirations (Banks 2011, Ingraham 2008).

The representations of the Caribbean as tropical and the narratives of romance and white weddings are interlocking phenomena; the positioning of matrimonial representations of white femininity to connote luxury, are located within existing discourses of the paradise landscape (Sheller 2003). Both discursive formations work in tandem to sell Jamaica and the wider Caribbean as a destination for self-indulgence and pampering,[3] thus appealing to the aspirations of affluent white women. It is perhaps the allusion of taking on a new identity – the transformative qualities of becoming a princess bride for one day, and the ability to reinvent oneself through marriage that is so appealing to white female audiences. This is within the context of the popularity of body enhancement practices and plastic surgery in Euro-American cultures.

The recent royal weddings in Europe (Katherine Middleton and Prince William, and Charlene Wittstock and Prince Albert of Monaco) are particularly significant for the ways in which wealth, power and privilege are disguised by broader media and public discussions of 'perfect princess brides' and the myth of happy-ever-after marriages. Such public displays of commoners marrying into royal dynasties suggest that 'hereditary monarchy' is 'democratic and accessible' (Coward 2011: 38). In truth, such displays demonstrate the extent to which 'physical attractiveness work[s] as a form of capital' (Skeggs 1997: 102), and can be utilised/exploited to climb the scales of the social hierarchy. In order to be fully accepted into the royal fold, the princess bride must renounce her individuality and commoner identity by undergoing a transformation, signalled by wearing a couture wedding gown and becoming an ambassador and public face of elite power and their institutions so that they do not appear to be anarchic or socially irrelevant. The royal princess bride's role is to produce heirs and to socialise them into the norms and values of the aristocratic realm (Ingraham 2008).

Lower down the social hierarchy the elaborate white wedding is also a visual display of traditional femininity; the ultimate form of public recognition which gives the feminine subject legitimacy and social acceptance. This celebration is a public pronouncement of social achievement, a performance, and a 'spectacle of wealth' (Ingraham 2008: 150) which is the climax of the accruement of white

---

3   Sandals have introduced the Red Lane Spa product at their resorts. The video playlist online features semi-naked white women being attended to by black subjects and receiving spa treatments – see http://www.sandals.co.uk/media/.

social privileges and consumerism and 'sets up in [sic] dichotomies of Otherness and power hierarchies between women' (Davis 2006: 566).

The images forcefully display the enjoyment of luxury and visually establish distinctions between individuals who have the economic resources to spend, on average, £15,000–£20,000 on one day (Anonymous 2010: 2) and individuals who do not. In the contemporary context, the white wedding appears to have become 'a marker of social distinction' (Cole and Sabik 2009: 179). As Ingraham (2008: 35) states, 'Wedding marketers are aware that white middle-class women are more likely to consume wedding products than any other group, and so they target their marketing campaigns to white women'.

Sandals Weddings

The prominence of white women in the Sandals 2012 wedding booklet[4] promotes the message that by conforming to beauty norms, some white women have an avenue through which 'to claim power' (Hurtado 1989, Wolf 1991 cited in Cole and Sabik 2009). However, more significant is the way in which these messages are contained within a constellation of intertextual and overlapping themes and ideas which contradictorily position the white wedding as an exclusive preserve, yet attainable luxury, within the packaging of a Sandals wedding. By perpetuating the myth that the white wedding is every female's ultimate fantasy, Sandals present their audience with wedding packages which suggest that the dream of a white wedding can be a reality in the Caribbean.

> Every little girl grows up excitedly imagining her perfect day, from the time she pretends to walk down the aisle in her mum's high heels and a curtain veil, to the magical moment when he pops the question. So how do you decide on the ideal style for you? Luckily Sandals Weddings by Martha Stewart™ makes the job a whole lot easier, as you can choose one of these charming wedding ceremonies in an amazing choice of romantic Caribbean locations. (Sandals 2012)

The discourse of white weddings which epitomises the romantic utopia is salient as it links and overlaps with established fantasies, myths and tropes of the colonial utopia of the Caribbean as an earthly paradise. The effect is that the performative nature of tourism enhances the performative display of white weddings. Already familiar with the 'desire' for individuals to perform in Western cultures (Illouz 1997), vacation weddings appear to satisfy this appetite. The transformation of the postcolonial island state into a vacation wedding site permits uncomfortable truths regarding colonialism and slavery to be rewritten by 'tightly

---

4   Sandals' wedding package details can also be viewed online http://www.sandals. co.uk/weddingmoons/weddings/collections/wedding-themes.cfm.

scripted' (Hollinshead 2004: 28), 'multiple representations' (Hollinshead 2004: 26) of modern day princesses in apparently neutral displays in 'paradise'.

Whiteness has been bolstered by the discourses of white weddings, the commodification of the message of second wave feminism, and notions of entitlement to luxury that are propagated by the cosmetics industry and celebrity culture.[5] All of which are a complementing mix of discourses which reinforce the narrative that white women are 'special' (Davis 2006: 566) and their prominence in the promotion of the Caribbean as a holiday/wedding destination ensures that the white female body is not out-of-place.

Sandals weddings are framed by the recurring use of white in the montage of images used in the Sandals brochures and the ceremonies featured on Sandals Video Playlists (which can be accessed via the website's Weddings Items Catalogue[6]). The heterosexual white couples wear white wedding attire, stroll along white sandy beaches and in the 2012 Sandals brochure the promotion of the white wedding experience continues to overwhelmingly feature white couples (there are three images of black couples; one head and shoulders close-up and two pictures taken at a distance). There are no ethnically mixed couples featured on the website or in the brochures.

The discussion here draws on wider research into Sandals' promotion of white weddings and holidays in the Caribbean for heterosexual couples (Wilkes 2008). 'In the commercialised environment of the contemporary wedding' (Coward 2011: 39) Sandals' white weddings all-inclusive experience offers the materially affluent the opportunity to live out the fantasy of being a princess for one day, within the context of a location which once produced the wealthiest colonialists in the British Empire and was infamous for high and extravagant living (Burnard 2004). It is the excess in terms of overabundance, lavishness and extravagance which is inscribed in whiteness and celebrated in the Sandals images. There are no references to modernity, in particular the urban landscape, and representations of the local population are absent (Wilkes 2008). The brides' white wedding gowns encapsulate the idea of luxury and displace any obvious requirement to undertake employment to support such extravagance.[7]

---

5   L'Oreal's long running 'Because You're Worth It' campaign which has been fronted by high profile female actors and celebrities Beyoncè Knowles, Eva Longoria, Jennifer Anniston, Scarlet Johannson is one example of this practice.

6   http://www.sandals.co.uk/weddingmoons/weddings/wedding-catalog/.

7   Sandals declined permission to publish the images used in their promotional material for this chapter, and despite initially gaining permission from Kuoni to publish the image entitled 'a groom carrying his bride', they subsequently requested the image should not be published. Readers can view the Sandals wedding images by accessing the Sandals website at: http://www.sandals.co.uk/, and the image entitled 'a groom carrying his bride' (image reference: 77993028) can be viewed by accessing the Getty archive at: http://www.gettyimages.co.uk/Search/Search.aspx?contractUrl=2&language=en-GB&family=creative&assetType=image&excludenudity=true&p=77993028#.

The 'West and the Rest' binary is exemplified by the use of the Caribbean region as a destination appropriated to display the 'refinement of white civilisation' (Barker 2012: 272) and perpetuates the idea that the Caribbean, as a 'Third World' region is reliant on the West for its 'development' (Caton and Santos 2008). There are indeed 'large disparities in wealth between tourist-generating and tourist-receiving societies' (Caton and Santos 2008: 8), however, it is the tourist-generating societies that define the terms of the tourist/host interactions by the dissemination of images which are used to woo Anglo-American tourists by revering their cultural traditions. The imbalance in the tourist/host relationship in the Sandals context is obscured by celebrating the conventions of heterosexual love and romance with American advertising style taglines which have a direct and personalised address. For example, in phrases common across Sandals' promotional material, such as *love is all you need*, *luxury included* and, *discover your wedding style*.

The use of the 'hard sell' in the form of hyperbole and overstatement (De Mooij 1998) in phrases such as *the best all-inclusive*, may be intended to distinguish Sandals from the competition and directly appeal to the target audience of American tourists. This is perhaps an indication of the extent to which Jamaica, via the prominence of Sandals in the region (World Travel Awards 2011) is 'entangled in a relationship of dependence on the economies and industries of the United States' (Pertierra and Horst 2009: 103). Thus the 'dominant images of the Caribbean' demonstrate how they are 'products of Euro-American perspectives' (Pertierra and Horst 2009: 104) and convey the perennial need for the structures of the social hierarchies of marriage and gender norms to be maintained and reproduced.

The spectacle of the white wedding and the accompanying trappings of the event are the window dressing for a lucrative American and international industry (Ingraham 2008). One of the ways in which the Euro-American perspectives can be identified is in the commodification of the Caribbean as almost belonging to the Sandals company as noted in the comment made by Darcy Miller, editing director for *Martha Stewart Weddings* that 'they have Sandals all over the Caribbean' (Martha Stewart Show, n.d.). Sandals have collaborated with the American lifestyle guru and media magnet, Martha Stewart to create six themes for a Sandals wedding; *Flutter With Romance, Seaside Serenade, Tropical Island Paradise, Vision in White, Chic and Natural* and *Beautiful Beginnings*. The available themes offer a generic and commodified package for a luxury wedding at a Sandals resort. *Vision in White* features white eyelet and lace decorations on white linen tablecloths, with white pillar candles and white orchids to provide a traditional setting, whilst *Island Paradise* references ideas of the tropical by using bright pink orchids, tropical fruit and brightly coloured cocktail umbrellas. Such representations do not reference the dynamic cultures of the Caribbean. Sandals' styling of the resorts – of which they have 23 across the Caribbean – are generic and there is nothing to differentiate the photographs of the Jamaican resorts from the resorts in Antigua. In the images, the Caribbean appears as an undifferentiated homogenised tropical playground.

Sandals' marketing of the Caribbean to American audiences is assisted by the endorsement of a well-known American entrepreneur, Martha Stewart. American audiences would easily recognise the entrepreneur who has a business empire encompassing *Martha Stewart Weddings*, home wares, best-selling books, and radio and television programmes.

The six signature wedding themes were introduced to viewers during an episode of the *Martha Stewart Show* where details of three of the weddings were laid out in the television studio to a live female audience. A recording of this feature can be accessed via the Sandals video playlist on its website[8] and marthastewartweddings. com. During the promotion of Sandals weddings by Martha Stewart and Darcy Miller, the audience were reminded of how they could book a Sandals family holiday through *Beaches*, the Sandals sister company which caters for groups and family holidays. Martha Stewart's partnership with Sandals is an example of the 'convergence culture' where brands/companies reference each other so that consumers are 'courted across multiple media platforms' (Jenkins 2006 quoted in Ingraham 2008: 133). Globalisation and new media technologies have ensured the proliferation of neo-liberal free market strategies and 'privileged American styles and tastes' (Jameson 1998, Lomnitz 1994, Trouillot 2001, cited in Thomas and Clarke 2006: 7). It has enabled Sandals to carry out its 'global marketing initiatives by accessing untapped markets in Russia, Eastern Europe and the Far East', and it claims to be the 'largest private sector employer in the Caribbean' (YouTube video of the World Travel Awards 2011).

The Essentialised Black Subject

The Sandals website provides accounts of 'real' Sandals weddings and testimonials. For example, 'Nothing was too much trouble', and 'The staff were ever so gracious', 'Sandals is the place to go if you want to experience luxury in paradise!' These testimonials, taken from the Sandals website, construct the tourist-receiving destination as servile and principally present to meet the desires of foreign visitors. Indeed, one of the claims that Sandals makes is that they aim to exceed the expectations of the tourist by '*giving you far more than you ever dreamed of is something you'll only experience at Sandals*' (Sandals 2012), thus drawing on the idea that the Western tourist is a member of the travelling elite and is naturally deserving of such treatment.

The displays of flawless, slim white couples being attended to by 'dedicated' black waiters in the Sandals images serve to encourage the tourist to identify themselves as special, and reproduces colonial relations by positioning the West as a superior elite and Caribbean nations as the compliant Other (Simmons 2004,

---

8   (http://www.sandals.co.uk/weddingmoons/weddings/). Videos featuring Martha Stewart and Darcy Miller discussing Sandals weddings can be accessed at: http://www. youtube.com/watch?v=gLeh_o24kME&feature=relmfu.

Caton and Santos 2008). Thus, alongside drawing on the historical references of the Caribbean as a tropical paradise, Sandals adopts the tradition of appropriating the black male to signify service[9] by using images of traditionally attired black waiters in the 2012 brochure. This could be described as a dispersal of colonialist discourses into more modern forms in contemporary visual texts, which, through Sandals' marketing of Jamaica, power relations between the largely white guests and black hosts are portrayed as being 'based on nostalgia for the plantation era of black servitude...' (Thompson 2006: 305). Thus, the relevance and significance of tourism images in the contemporary period is the connections that the images have to wider systems of meaning within constructions of racialised power relations, paradise and concepts of luxury which appear to support the subordinate and often marginal positions occupied by black people located throughout the African diaspora (Hall 1996c, see Gilroy 1993). The images are a cue or insight into this positioning as dependent on, an auxiliary to, but not in the West (Sheller 2003). The focus on the tropics and white beaches keep the countries of the Caribbean as examples of island paradise in the Western imagination, represented as being outside of modernity (Sheller 2003) with no active part in the era of globalisation. However, 'Jamaica currently has one of the world's highest levels of mobile phone ownership' (Pertierra and Horst 2009: 102) and the multi-ethnic population resulting from the activities of European colonial regimes suggest that the region is more modern than the static representations of the urban-free tropical landscape would have us believe. The region's 'economy is based on transnational capitalism' and bears the 'hallmarks of a globalized, (post) modern society – such as transnational flows and diasporic populations, multi-ethnic communities and the hybridisation and appropriation of cultural forms' (Pertierra and Horst 2009: 108). However, 'the images communicate a weak essentialising moment as they naturalise and dehistorise difference, mistaking what is historical and cultural for what is natural, biological and genetic' (Hall 1996c: 472).

> ...certainly, blacks are as ambiguously placed in relation to postmodernism as they were in relation to high modernism: even when denuded of its wide-European, disenchanted Marxist, French intellectual provenance and scaled down to a more modest descriptive status, postmodernism remains extremely unevenly developed as a phenomenon in which the old center peripheries of high modernity consistently reappear. (ibid: 466)

Hall (1997) argues that contemporary Western ideas about race have been shaped by the fateful history of the slave trade, colonisation, and imperialism and as

---

9   Round Hill Hotel and Villas in Jamaica used an image of a smiling black waiter standing in an empty white furnished restaurant in its promotional material in 2002.

In *Paradise and Plantation* Ian Gregory Strachan (2002: 118) discusses the significance of an image used by the Bahamas Ministry of Tourism in which 'Adrian' a black waiter stands in an empty restaurant to convey the 'pride and joy' in providing service to tourists.

discussed earlier in this chapter, the current trend for images to be presented as though they are without any historical origins, allows the gaze of whiteness to be the 'unacknowledged norm' (Apple 1998: xii). One of the aims of this chapter has been to make explicit the connections between the portrayals of whiteness in contemporary tourism visual culture in Sandals brochures, and the history of colonialism in the Caribbean region. Thus by recognising that 'global developments' include the creation of new technologies and new tourism products, this chapter has aimed to demonstrate how these phenomena 'have helped to reconfigure old patterns of ethnic relations and create new forms of racial privilege and politics' (Bhattacharyya et al. 2002: 8). Indeed, the international news media largely portrays the 'urban Caribbean as almost entirely represented as a site of danger' (Pertierra and Horst 2009: 104) yet such representations are temporarily suspended when the discourses of white weddings and heterosexuality are enlisted to sell the region.

Postcolonial scholars can be credited for 'winning' limited spaces for difference and articulating the way in which colonial and postcolonial discourses operate, however the narratives and representations in the tourism images appear on a global stage, displaying blackness as unproblematic-ally simple, deformed, inauthentic and grossly commodified (alongside a particular version of whiteness). The black serving subject is central to conveying modern-day luxury in the Caribbean, as noted in the emphasis on butlers who provide service with a smile and deliver the 'wow' factor to their guests. As Morgan and Pritchard (1998: 232) suggest, '…in black destinations the local people rarely figure and if they do it is largely in a service capacity or as an attraction…the Caribbean appears as an almost exclusive white, heterosexual playground'.

In order for the positioning of the tourist as superior and modern elite to be effectively maintained in the postcolonial context, there needs to be a continual and repetitive signification (Bhabha 1994) of the black serving subject on which it is dependent. The black subject is regulated and disciplined; conveyed by their uniformed attire and identified by white gloves and bow tie. Whilst the serving black subject appears as a 'partial' presence (Bhabha 1994: 86), they are indeed central in the brochure images which communicate power and privilege in the form of a racial dichotomy where the white subject is encouraged to indulge in the excessive attention made available by what Bhabha (1994) argues is 'a visibility to the exercise of power; [which] gives force to the argument that skin, as a signifier of discrimination, must be produced or processed as visible' (Bhabha 1994: 79).

The fixing and the essentialising of the black subject produces a sense of continuity with the past and a reminder of the power relations as they were under colonial regimes, where slaves served and planters were famed for their hospitality. The images suggest that whilst the Western world continues to change and globalisation produces uncertainties, Sandals are able to offer tourists a return to tropical nature and the notion of colonial successes when 'everyone knew their place'. For example, 'The Riviera Great House, reminiscent of Jamaica's historic plantations offers a rich sense of timelessness and hospitality' (Sandals 2012).

The end of the essential black subject (Hall 1996c) has been extensively debated by postcolonial scholars (Bhabha 1994, hooks 1996, Gilroy 1993, Mirza 1997, Spivak 1988), yet the binary positions as they are displayed in the Sandals images suggest that the black subject is continually scripted by particular white identities (see Hall 1996a) which are engaged in 'the ultimate in luxury – personal butler service' (Sandals 2012).

The following descriptions of images in the Sandals 2012 brochure demonstrate the articulation and expression of luxury through the representation of the black subject as an essentialised black waiter.[10]

The first image is of a slim white couple being approached by a black waiter. The couple are reclining on a beach lounger beneath a palm tree, which is located on what appears to be an empty white beach. The couple featured have tanned skin. The female subject has long brown hair and wears a short olive green tunic. Her bare legs are stretched out on the white beach recliner. Her male companion is dressed in a loose white shirt with black shorts and white check details. He displays a relaxed pose as his left hand rests leisurely on his bended knee.

Clear blue sea provides a backdrop to the image, and in the background there are white and yellow yachts dotted just beyond the shoreline. The couple appear to be engaged in conversation as the man smiles widely at his female companion, whose face can be just-seen as she is turned away from the viewer's gaze.

In contrast to the couple's attire, the waiter is dressed in a fully buttoned, mustard coloured waistcoat, affixed with a name-badge, along with a white shirt, black trousers and white gloves. He is carrying fruit and drinks on a tray with one hand and is smiling as he approaches the couple.

The second image is a formal setting which features a white couple dining at a table beneath a large cream parasol. The table has been positioned on the edge of an empty pier and the image is framed by the blue sea and blue sky. The table has been dressed with a floor-length, white table cloth, crystal candelabra and wine glasses. The couple are being attended to by a black waiter who is fully dressed in the standard uniform of a waistcoat, white shirt and black trousers. He stands to attention as he places a white plate in front of the female guest.

The romantic displays in the images suggest that there is 'a script of romance' (Illouz 1997: 250) that is only successfully communicated when gendered roles of 'proper masculinity and femininity' (Butler 2007: xxiv–xxv) are enacted. In particular, the females in the images conform to the prescribed beauty ideal by being slim, with tanned skin, and have long, sleek hair. In the first image, the composition of the female's bended knee and direct gaze towards her male companion suggest that she is 'acting appropriately like a woman' (Sherwood 2009: 144) and is displaying 'emphasised femininity' (Sherwood 2009: 144) by being compliant in relation to her male companion. Thus, proper heterosexual femininity is that which supports and emphasises traditional masculinity (Butler

---

10   William Hogarth's engraving entitled *The Industrious Prentice Grown Rich and Sheriff of London* (1753) features a black servant offering a drink to white diners.

2007). The power and status of the white male subjects in the images is conveyed by the visual differences between them and the black serving subject. In the first image, the white male is relaxing on a secluded beach and has the attention of an attractive young woman, whilst the black male is working, and wears restrictive, uniformed attire. The second image invokes the intimate relationship between imperialism and visuality in this 'master-of-all-I-survey-scene' (Pratt 1992: 201) as the white male looks out onto the Caribbean Sea and dines in 'a remote and exotic place' (Illouz 1997: 251) with an attractive young woman. In contrast the black waiter's employee status is visually apparent as he attends to the white diners. As with the displays of elaborate white weddings, the luxury activities portrayed in the images can be defined as 'marker[s] of social distinction' (Cole and Sabik 2009: 179) which symbolically draw attention to 'extraordinary moments in a [heterosexual] relationship' (Illouz 1997: 135).

The Sandals All-butler Service and the Virtual Tourist Experience

The Sandals experience could be described as beginning with viewing its highly sophisticated, interactive website. Viewers are able to access the Sandals video playlist which is a collection of videos providing details on dining, accommodation and its spas. There is also a video montage which promotes the Sandals 'World-Renowned Butler Service'. The virtual tours and talks offer a two-dimensional experience with the use of vision and sound to convince the prospective tourist of the authenticity of Sandals and its services. The video detailing a day in the life of 'Rory the Butler',[11] accompanied by a soundtrack of *Rule Britannia*, which references historical, colonial relations and encapsulates the Sandals concept of *Luxury Included*, as in each scene of the video Rory is occupied with a task in order to provide the 'wow' factor and aims to exceed the expectations of his guests. Rory takes personal responsibility for his guests and echoes the testimonial accounts provided by former visitors, 'nothing is too much trouble' for him. Alongside the use of colonial tropes and white architecture, the All-Butler concept draws on the British working-class profession of being 'in-service' in wealthy households. Sandals have enlisted the Guild of Professional English Butlers to train the butlers at their resorts:

> Giving you more than any other resorts on the planet also includes personal butlers trained by the Guild of Professional English Butlers. This prestigious organization trains the finest butlers and valets in the world, overseen by renowned butler guru, Robert Watson. While our butlers are handpicked for their wonderful, warm personalities, they are never obtrusive so your every request is discreetly fulfilled with a quiet grace (Sandals 2012).

11　www.sandals.co.uk/difference/butler-service.cfm.

Listed in the services provided by dedicated butlers are 'unpacking and packing luggage, attending to every wardrobe detail and catering to your every request'. The representations of the black subject as cook, butler, chambermaid or entertainer in the Sandals images draw together the 'living components of a western sensibility that extends beyond national boundaries, linking America to Europe and its empires' (Gilroy 1993: 159). Thus, America has its own history of racial and colonial oppression, and white and non-white Americans alike would have no difficulty in recognising the racial class hierarchies displayed in Sandals' promotional material which appears to be referencing the so-called legendary dutiful service of black house slaves in the American South. As Hall (1996b: 466) argues:

> ...I remind you of the ambiguities of that shift from Europe to America, since it includes America's ambivalent relationship to European high culture and the ambiguity of America's relationship to its own internal ethnic hierarchies. Western Europe did not have, until recently, any ethnicity at all. Or didn't recognise it had any. America has always had a series of ethnicities, and consequently the construction of ethnic hierarchies has always defined its cultural politics.

The significance of examining the use of the Caribbean as a destination for romantic escapes continues to provide insight into how 'political subjects such as white or black, cannot be treated as if they are mutually exclusive entities' (Brah 2007: 78). The images demonstrate the interdependent relationship between black and white subjects in a constructed paradise setting.

Thus the unthreatening, smiling, dutiful servant has been '*handpicked*' (like fruit) in order to exemplarily treat his guests as though they are nobility or celebrities (*each request is fulfilled with grace*), to know the name of every guest and their favourite drink. The black subject is depersonalised. The representations are dependent on the black subject being scripted as essentially black, yet he must be black in relation to the white man (Hall 1996a). The tourist can feel at ease with the power relations as they are constructed on the website, in the brochures and in the resorts, as the butler's motto is *your wish is my command*, which suggests that they are happy with their subservient position, conveyed in their desire to please and smile at their guests: 'Nevertheless, the whites demand that the blacks be always smiling, attentive and friendly in their relationships with them...' ("L'oncle Rémus et son lapin" by Bernard Wolfe, *Les Temps Modernes*, May, 1949: 888, quoted in Fanon 1986: 50).

The Sandals website offers prospective tourists a stylised, polished and trouble-free perspective of the Caribbean which feeds into established ideas regarding the region as paradise and being 'laid back'. The socio-political concerns in the region are obscured by the repetitive images of pampered white subjects being waited on by uniformed black waiters. Thus all the tourists' needs are attended to within the all-inclusive resort, and the only black people that the tourists meet are the people serving them. Therefore, the constructed reality which Sandals promotes in its brochures and through its website does not inform audiences unfamiliar with the Caribbean and its complex history, or the cultural practices of the different Caribbean nations or their specific social contexts (Pertierra and Horst 2009).

Conclusion

This chapter has discussed the significance and relevance of the visual in relation to the cogent disciplines of tourism studies and cultural studies, and has aimed to contribute to postcolonial debates regarding representation and the end of the essential black subject (Hall 1996c). Using Sandals' brochure images and the Sandals website, this chapter has demonstrated that there is a continual need for inquiries into how representations are constructed with the use of entrenched and established colonial discourses of paradise, racialised service and white subjects as creators and recipients of luxury.

The historical framework that has been used in this discussion has aimed to demonstrate how historically constructed colonial power relations operate in the postcolonial context. In particular, the imperial practices of appropriating foreign lands are reworked clichéd narratives of 'surveying paradise' and are the mainstay of commodified tourism packages promoting the Caribbean.

Despite the marginal economic position that the Caribbean region occupies in the global world order, the role that the region plays in the Western imagination is central to the constructed image of the 'Western self' as modern and superior. As this chapter has demonstrated, the West is dependent on the binary for its superior self-image to be maintained. The details of how this interdependent relationship works in practice is evident in the repeated displays of the black subject as dutiful servant and white subjects as recipients of luxury. Such displays of racialised binary positions are reworked and overlaid with apparently neutral displays of heterosexual romance.

The discussion on the representations of the white female as princess bride has aimed to contribute to the studies on whiteness and in particular, the analysis has detailed how the white wedding, an often taken for granted, yet gendered cultural ritual, intersects with race and class to signify sophistication and luxury as a public declaration of social status and privilege. Such constructions of femininity as displayed in the Sandals images are based on the premise of celebration of conventional femininity as compliant and nonthreatening to traditional masculinity. They are principally dependent on the exclusion of non-white females. Although the princess bride occupies a privileged position within the social hierarchy, the subject positions available for white females to ascribe to are narrow and are ultimately dependent on reinforcing conventional masculine positions.

This chapter has focused on the importance of studying the visual in tourism studies, particularly as the international tourism industry is continuing to respond and adapt to the challenges of globalisation and the development of new media technologies. By using Sandals as a case study example, this chapter has discussed the complex discourses that are utilised to visually construct the Caribbean in Sandals' brochures and via its website, and the need to employ a multidisciplinary approach to critically examine Sandals' particular brand of heterosexual tourism in the Caribbean.

References

Angus, I. and Jhally, S. (eds) 1989. *Cultural Politics in Contemporary America.* London: Routledge.

Anonymous. 2010. Damn this Bridal Froth! *The Guardian*, 22 May, 1–2.

Apple, M.W. 1998. Foreword, in *White Reign: Deploying Whiteness in America*, edited by J. Kincheloe, et al. London: Macmillan, ix–xiii.

Banks, R.R. 2011. *Is Marriage For White People? How the African American Marriage Decline Affects Everyone.* London: Penguin Books Ltd.

Barker, C. 2012. *Cultural Studies. Theory and Practice.* 4th edition. London: Sage.

Bhabha, H.K. 1994. *The Location of Culture.* London: Routledge.

Bhattacharyya, G., Gabriel, J. and Small, S. (eds) 2002. *Race and Power.* London: Routledge.

Bland, L. 1983. Purity, motherhood, pleasure or threat? Definitions of female sexuality 1900–1970, in *Sex and Love: New Thoughts on Old Contradictions*, edited by S. Cartledge and J. Ryan. London: Women's Press, 8–29.

Bonnett, A. 2000. *White Identities. Historical and International Perspectives.* Essex: Pearson Education Ltd.

Brah, A. 2007. Feminism, 'race' and Stuart Hall's diasporic imagination, in *Culture, Politics, Race and Diaspora. The Thought of Stuart Hall*, edited by B. Meeks. Kingston: Ian Randle Publishers, 73–82.

Brassey, S. 1885. *In the Trades, the Tropics, and the Roaring Forties.* London: Longman.

Burnard, T. 2004. *Mastery, Tyranny and Desire. Thomas Thistlewood and his Slaves in the Anglo-Jamaican World.* Chapel Hill and London: The University of North Carolina Press.

Butler, J. 2007. *Gender Trouble. Feminism and the Subversion of Identity.* London: Routledge.

Caton, K. and Santos, C.A. 2008. Closing the hermeneutic circle? Photographic encounters with the Other. *Annals of Tourism Research*, 35(1), 7–26.

Cohen, E. 1992. The study of touristic images of native people migrating the stereotype of the stereotype in *Tourism Research: Critiques and Challenges*, edited by D. Pearce and R. Butler. London: Routledge, 36–69.

Cole, E.R. and Sabik, N.J. 2009. Repairing a broken mirror. Intersectional approaches to diverse women's perceptions of beauty and bodies, in *The Intersectional Approach. Transforming the Academy Through Race, Class and Gender*, edited by M.T. Berger and K. Guidroz. The University of North Carolina Press, 173–92.

Collins, P.H. 2000. *Black Feminist Thought*. 2nd edition. New York: Routledge.

Coward, R. 1984. *Female Desire. Women's Sexuality Today*. London: Granada Publishing.

Coward, R. 2011. A tale of two princesses. *The Guardian*, 9 July, 38–39.

Craik J. 1994. *The Face of Fashion. Cultural Studies in Fashion*. London: Routledge.

Crouch, D., Jackson, R. and Thompson, F. (eds) 2005. *The Media and the Tourist Imagination: Convergent Cultures*. Abingdon, Oxon: Routledge.

Dann, G. 1996. The people of tourist brochures, in *The Tourist Image: Myth and Myth Making*, edited by T. Selwyn. Chichester: Wiley Press, 61–81.

Davis, K. 2006. Beyond the female body, in *The Celebrity Culture Reader*, edited by P.D. Marshall. London: Routledge, 557–80.

De Mooij, M. 1998. *Global Marketing and Advertising. Understanding Cultural Paradoxes*. London: Sage.

Dyer, R. 1997. *White*. London: Routledge.

Fanon, F. 1986. *Black Skins, White Masks*. London: Pluto Press.

Frankenberg, R. 1993. *White Women Race Matters: the social construction of whiteness*. Minneapolis: University of Minnesota Press.

Gilroy, P. 1993. *The Black Atlantic. Modernity and Double Consciousness*. London: Verso.

Goldberg, D. 1993. *Racist Culture*. Oxford: Blackwell.

Green, C. 2007. Unspeakable worlds and muffled voices: Thomas Thistlewood as agent and medium of 18th century Jamaican society, in *Culture, Politics Race and Diaspora. The Thought of Stuart Hall*, edited by B. Meeks. Kingston: Ian Randle Publishers, 151–84.

Haldrup, M. and Larsen, J. 2012. Readings of tourist photographs, in *An Introduction to Visual Research Methods in Tourism*, edited by T. Rakić and D. Chambers. Abingdon, Oxon: Routledge, 153–168.

Hall, C.M. 2012. Introduction to the book series: Contemporary Geographies of Leisure, Tourism and Mobility, in *An Introduction to Visual Research Methods in Tourism*, edited by T. Rakić and D. Chambers. Abingdon, Oxon: Routledge, ii.

Hall, C.M. and Tucker, H. 2004. Tourism and postcolonialism. An Introduction, in *Tourism and Postcolonialism. Contested Discourses, Identities and Representations*, edited by C.M. Hall, and H. Tucker. Abingdon, Oxon: Routledge, 1–24.

Hall, S. 1992. The West and the rest: discourse and power, in *Formations of Modernity*, edited by S. Hall, and B. Gieben. London: Polity Press in association with the Open University, 275– 320.

Hall, S. 1996a. The After-life of Frantz Fanon: Why Fanon? Why now? Why black skins, white masks? in *The Fact of Blackness. Frantz Fanon and Visual Representation*, edited by A. Read. ICA in association with Bay Press, 14–37.

Hall, S. 1996b. New ethnicities, in *Stuart Hall Critical Dialogues in Cultural Studies*, edited by D. Morley and K. Chen. London: Routledge Publishers, 441–49.

Hall, S. 1996c. What is this 'black' in black popular culture? in *Stuart Hall Critical Dialogues in Cultural Studies* edited by D. Morley and K. Chen. London: Routledge Publishers, 465–75.

Hall, S. (ed.) 1997. *Representation: Cultural Representation and Signifying Practices*. London: Sage in association with the Open University.

Hastings, E.A.J. 1900. *A Glimpse of the Tropics, Or, Four Months Cruising in the West Indies*. London: Sampson Low, Marston &. Co.

Hogarth, W. 1753. *The Industrious Prentice Grown Rich and Sheriff of London* (engraving) Museum of London.

Hollinshead, K. 2004. Tourism and new sense. Worldmaking and the enunciative value of tourism, in *Tourism and Postcolonialism. Contested Discourses, Identities and Representations*, edited by C.M. Hall, and H. Tucker. Abingdon, Oxon: Routledge, 25–42.

hooks, b. 1984. *Feminist Theory: From Margin to the Centre*. Boston, USA: South End Press.

hooks, b. 1991. *Yearning. Race, Gender, and Cultural Politics*. London: Turnaround Books.

hooks, b. 1996. *Reel to Real. Race, Sex and Class at the Movies*. London: Routledge.

Illouz, E. 1997. *Consuming the Romantic Utopia*. Berkeley, California. London: University of California Press.

Ingraham, C. 2008. *White Weddings. Romancing Heterosexuality in Popular Culture*. London: Routledge.

Jenkins, H. 2006. *Convergence Culture: Where Old and New Media Collide*. New York: NYU Press.

Kilbourne, J. 2000. *Can't Buy Me Love: How Advertising Changes the Way We Think and Feel*. London: Touchstone.

Lawson, M. 2012. Teenage clicks. Mark Lawson on a gripping moral fable about the decline of privacy. *The Guardian Review*, 11 February, 10.

Lipsitz, G. 2006. *The Possessive Investment in Whiteness. How White People Profit From Identity Politics*. Philadelphia: Temple University Press.

Mclaren, P. 1998. Whiteness is…the struggle for postcolonial hybridity, in *White Reign: Deploying Whiteness in America*, edited by J. Kincheloe, et al. London: Macmillan, 63–75.

Mirza, H.S. (ed.) 1997. *Black British Feminism. A Reader*. London: Routledge.

Morgan, N. and Pritchard, A. 1998. *Tourism, Promotion and Power. Creating Images, Creating Identities*. Chichester: John Wiley and Sons Ltd.

Morrison, T. 1992. *Playing in the Dark. Whiteness and the Literary Imagination*. Massachusetts: Harvard University Press.

Noll, S.M. and Fredrickson, B.L. 1998. A mediational model linking self-objectification, body shame, and disordered eating. *Psychology of Women Quarterly*, 22, 623–36.

Pertierra, A.C. and Horst, H.A. 2009. Introduction. Thinking about Caribbean media worlds. *International Journal of Cultural Studies*, 12, 99–111.

Pratt, M.L. 1992. *Imperial Eyes. Travel Writing and Transculturation*. London: Routledge.

Rakić, T. and Chambers, D. 2012. *An Introduction to Visual Research Methods*. London: Routledge.

Redmond, S. 2003. Thin white women in advertising. *Journal of Consumer Culture*, 3 (2), 170–90.

Said, E. 1978. [1995] *Orientalism. Western Conceptions of the Orient*. London: Penguin Books Ltd.

Sandals 2012 brochure. *'Sandals, Love is All You Need, More Quality Inclusions Than Any Other Resorts on the Planet, Also Featuring Beaches Resorts for Everyone'*. [brochure was requested online]

Scarles, C. 2012. Eliciting embodied knowledge and response: respondent-led photography and visual autoethnography, in *An Introduction to Visual Research Methods in Tourism*, edited by T. Rakić, and D. Chambers. Abingdon, Oxon: Routledge, 70–91.

Selwyn, T. ed. 1996. *The Tourist Image: Myth and Myth Making*. Chichester: Wiley Press.

Sheller, M. 2003. *Consuming the Caribbean*. London: Routledge Publishers.

Sherwood, J.H. 2009. The view from the country club. Wealthy whites in the matrix of privilege, in *The Intersectional Approach. Transforming the Academy Through Race, Class and Gender*, edited by M.T. Berger and K. Guidroz. The University of North Carolina Press: Chapel Hill, 136–53.

Shilling, C. 1993. *The Body and Social Theory*. London: Sage Publications Ltd.

Shohat, E. and Stam, R. 1994. *Unthinking Eurocentrism: Multiculturalism & the Media*. London: Routledge.

Simmons, B.A. 2004. Saying the same old things. A contemporary travel discourse and the popular magazine text, in *Tourism and Postcolonialism. Contested Discourses, Identities and Representations*, edited by C.M. Hall and H. Tucker. Abingdon, Oxon: Routledge, 43–56.

Skeggs, B. 1997. *Formations of Class and Gender*. London: Routledge.

Smith, D.E. 1988. Femininity as discourse, in *Becoming Feminine. The Politics of Popular Culture*, edited by L.G. Roman, L.K. Christian-Smith and E. Ellsworth. Lewes: Falmer Palmer, 37–60.

Spivak, G.C. 1988. 'Can the Subaltern Speak?' in *Marxism and the Interpretation of Culture*, edited by C. Nelson and L. Grossberg. Basingstoke: Macmillan Education, 271–313.

Stone, S.D. 1995. The myth of bodily perfection. *Disability and Society*, 4, 413–24.

Strachan, I.G. 2002. *Paradise and Plantation. Tourism and Culture in the Anglophone Caribbean*. Charlottesville: University of Virginia Press.

Taylor, F.F. 1993. *To Hell with Paradise*. Pittsburgh London: University of Pittsburgh Press.

Thomas, D.A. and Clarke, K.M. 2006. Introduction: Globalization and the transformations of race, in *Globalization and Race. Transformations in the Cultural Production of Blackness* edited by K.M. Clarke and D.A. Thomas. Durham: Duke University Press, 1–34.

Thompson, K. 2006. *An Eye for the Tropics. Tourism, Photography and Framing the Caribbean Picturesque*. London: Duke University Press.

Tiggemen, M. and Slater A. 2001. A test of objectification theory in former dancers and non-dancers. *Psychology of Women Quarterly*, 37, 243–53.

Tresidder, R. 2012. Representing visual data in tourism studies publications, in *An Introduction to Visual Research Methods in Tourism* edited by T. Rakić and D. Chambers. London: Routledge, 187–200.

Tylka, T.L. and Hill, M.S. 2004. Objectification theory as it relates to disordered eating among college women. *Sex Roles*, 51, 719–30.

Urry, J. 1990. *The Tourist Gaze*. London: Sage Publications.

Walter, N. 2010. *Living Dolls: The Return of Sexism*. London: Virago Press.

Wilkes, K.A. 2008. *Returning the Gaze from the Margins: Decoding Representations of Gender, Race and Sexuality in Tourist Images of Jamaica*, unpublished PhD Thesis. Nottingham Trent University.

World Travel Awards 2011. [online, October 2011] Available at: http://www.sandals.co.uk/weddingmoons/weddings/http://www.sandals.co.uk video playlist; Accolades and Awards [accessed: 10 March 2012].

World Travel Awards 2011. [online, October 2011] Available at http://www.youtube.com/watch?feature=player_embedded&v=OCPab1vhW7E [accessed: 12 November 2012].

Chapter 4

A Necessary Glamorisation? Resident Perspectives on Promotional Literature and Images on Great Barrier Island, New Zealand

Leon Hoffman and Robin Kearns

Introduction

For any destination set apart from the daily lives and experiences of potential visitors, a fundamental challenge is to promote and generate interest in visiting. This is especially important for places like islands that are relatively remote and require something of an effort to reach. In the quest to attract tourists, promotional material in the form of brochures have long been a common 'take home' source of information and images that suggest possible experiences (Figueiredo and Raschi 2012, Molina and Esteban 2006). When the consumption of this information is followed by actual visits by tourists, such material serves to mediate the tourist experience. This mediation occurs in the sense of having offered visual and verbal 'promises' that inevitably influence expectations and the way a destination is ultimately regarded. Researchers have discussed and speculated on reactions to advertising on the part of tourists. Scarles (2004: 45), for instance, writes that '...brochures communicate vital messages to potential consumers, influencing consumer destination choice and bringing positive place characteristics to life'. A delicate balance must be achieved in the production of tourist brochures. Images of destinations must be selected to entice visitors, yet they must reasonably approximate the observable place otherwise there may be visitor dissatisfaction, a failure to recommend the place to others and a disinclination to return in the future (Garrod 2009). Other writers have identified discrepancies between the images promoted and the reality of local contexts (Figueiredo and Raschi 2012). Our chapter addresses this potential gap between image and reality, through investigating how 'locals' in a remote island setting regard the promotional material which serves to represent their home.

In the chapter, we examine the alignments and disconnects that exist in the space between the production of promotional images and their reading by local residents. Through this consideration we fill a gap: relatively few studies of island settings examine the way permanent residents regard promotional material. We examine the case of Great Barrier Island, New Zealand's fourth largest island which lies approximately 90 km to the northeast of Auckland, the country's largest city (population 1.4 million) (Figure 4.1). Great Barrier, or Aotea in Māori, is a destination defined by relative isolation and an impressive coastline. The island covers 285km², is nearly 45 km long and rises to a height of over 600m. It occupies a paradoxical space in being jurisdictionally part of the Auckland urban area, yet is a remote and challenging-to-reach location of only approximately 800 full-time residents. The vast proportion of Aucklanders have never visited Great Barrier, knowing the island as only a faint outline on the horizon on a clear day. The key obstacles to visiting are cost, distance and lack of visitor facilities. To those who do venture there, its under-developed character offers what Figueiredo and Raschi (2012: 21) call '…reserves of authenticity and genuineness both in natural and in cultural terms'.

The majority of tourism ventures operating out of Great Barrier Island are owner-operator entrepreneurial activities, often surviving on little capital, and leaving slim margins for any type of promotional material. Most advertising is undertaken through web-based initiatives, either of their own creation or locally

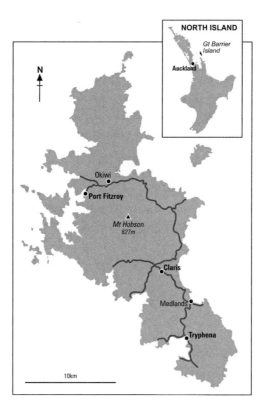

Figure 4.1   Great Barrier Island, New Zealand

maintained tourism marketing websites such as 'greatbarrierisland.co.nz', 'thebarrier.co.nz', and 'greatbarriertourism.co.nz'. In light of this situation, the print material which is available at tourist information kiosks on mainland New Zealand is primarily produced by the main transport operator to the island (Sealink Ferries), local government (the Auckland Council), or central government (the Department of Conservation).

Being rugged and remote, ambivalence characterises the relationship between Great Barrier Island and urban Auckland; tourism is generally valued for its contribution to the island's local economy, but is troubling when it brings visitors from the city with unrealistic expectations to its shores. Great Barrier's location is part of the island's attraction; it is literally a barrier between the Auckland's Hauraki Gulf and the vast Pacific Ocean beyond. This remoteness is central to the island's promotion. While elsewhere in New Zealand, contrived attractions such as bungee jumps and jet boat rides are promoted for their potential to thrill (Cloke and Perkins 2002), Great Barrier is part of a broader reimagining as '…an invigorated, energising destination, which offers (experience of) liminality' (Ateljevic and Doorne 2002: 661). To this extent, and unlike better known tourist destinations in New Zealand like Rotorua or Queenstown, Great Barrier Island can be regarded as a 'pre-commodified landscape' (Cloke and Perkins 2002) in which sites are visited and sights are seen but without direct entry costs beyond the expenses of travel, accommodation and subsistence. Arguably, the inherent sense of adventure and novelty in getting to the island suggests that Great Barrier attracts what Urry (1990) has described as 'post-tourists' – visitors seeking to 'escape', not only everyday life, but also the well-trodden routes that tourists walk.

Tourists are the primary readers and consumers of brochures, but in this chapter we consider the perspectives of an under-examined readership – the 'locals' whose lives may (directly or indirectly) benefit or be disrupted by tourism activity. In the remainder of the chapter we initially examine how the need to represent places for tourists – in words and images – has been considered and the capacity for such material to mediate between not only place and visitors, but also between place and the perceptions of 'locals'. We then examine how Great Barrier Island is represented in three brochures that are widely distributed throughout Auckland, the major 'market' for Great Barrier's tourists.

Representing Place for Tourists

To create a brochure for tourism purposes is to produce a document which has the primary function of marketing a destination to non-locals through text and image representation (Morgan and Pritchard 2000). As Scarles (2004) argues, there are three mediations involved in the making of tourist brochures: market research, photography and design. So too we might classify readership: the primary readers are prospective visitors, but a secondary group are 'locals' who might see such material and find that the content either aligns or departs from how they see their island. We begin by examining ways that places – and especially island places – are represented through tourism brochures, concentrating primarily on the representations of destinations through the images within these documents. Representation involves a strategic selection of texts and images with the result that 'landscapes are formed and given meaning' (Kobayashi 2009: 347). Significantly, landscape can be seen as 'formed' not only by geomorphic and anthropomorphic processes, but also through the influence of perception and perspective. We argue that in literally 're-presenting' places, a process occurs in which a gap can open between visitor expectations and local realities.

The act of representing material places through text and images is a two-way and dynamic process. Jones and Natter (1999: 243) explain the conundrum of representing space: 'What on one hand is regarded as "material" space has almost certainly been made possible by, and is interpreted through, representations. In turn, representations such as "texts" and "images" are materializations of social relations embedded within particular social spaces of production and reception'.

In this light, the representational images found within tourist brochures are produced alongside dominant and positive understandings of a place, but conversely, place might have a particular meaning attached to it due to actors having used these touristic representations as a guide to developing their own sense of the place. This role of brochures as a guide is important for tourists, as people who leave the predictability and familiarity of everyday life, to embrace '...places, practices and experiences which are ephemeral and largely unknown' (Cloke and Perkins 2002: 523). Interpretation is central to the reading of brochures. According to Ateljevic and Doorne (2002: 651), 'producers and consumers negotiate meaning through continuous acts of interpretation by (re)imaging and consuming the (con)text'.

In other words, it may not only be touristic representations which help to construct the way that a place is understood, and they do not always dictate how people/tourists view a place. Their strength depends on how powerful a representation they might be, and if other representations of place, primarily those created by locals, are able to overcome the discourse which tourism brochures offer. The touristic discourse therefore has the capacity to become the norm for the majority of interpretations of that particular place.

Place Production Through Representation

Promotional materials are 'decisive' in projecting a particular image of place (Figueiredo and Raschi 2012: 23). Through tourism promotion 'consumers are tutored to see a particular representation of [their tourist destination]' (Hughes 1991: 34). Hughes writes that representations aimed at tourists build an imagined geography of the places they are promoting, a practice that often has 'fundamental implications for the social and physical shaping of those places' (Hughes 1991: 40, see also Norton 1996). Other writers, such as Jenkins (2003) and Butler and Hall (1998), have labelled the outcomes of tourism promotion as the creation of 'place myths'. One implication is that these mythical constructions invariably generate a static view of places and their associated culture(s). To an extent, these views of places are rendered static because places themselves can offer under-realised opportunities for branding (Morgan et al. 2004). In other words, the destination itself (and – like a photograph – a frozen-in-time image of it) becomes the brand rather than constituent attractions found within it. Tourist destinations can therefore be branded as 'stylized vignette[s] of local history' (Ringer 1998: 2, see also Scarles 2004), thus promoting what might be seen as important to the tourist in experiencing the constructed myth(s) of that place (Hall 1994). In some circumstances, the creation and perpetuation of a static place-myth or 'pseudo-reality' might be valuable in the preservation of a tourism economy, but often 'misleading presentations undermine the sustainability of the destination by arousing antagonism between hosts and their visitors eventually dictating limits of acceptability for the long term' (Saarinen 1998: 158). That is, overly persuasive but unrealistic exhortations and images may, in the short term, attract visitors, but in the long term may be counterproductive, given a dissonance between expectation and reality, and between visitor aspirations and the daily experience of 'locals'.

Two case studies are worth noting. Norton (1996) investigated the difference between represented and experienced geographies of tourism within East African safaris. Interviews were conducted with tourists who had completed a safari in a wildlife park, focusing on what was expected while on tour versus that which was actually experienced. Images found within the brochures promoting the safari experiences were seen to be based upon a broad consensus of popular understandings of Africa as dry and 'sparsely vegetated with yellow grasses' (Norton 1996: 367), but as a number of the interviewees noted, the landscape was found to be highly fertile and very green. Furthermore, 'East African fauna had been depicted in the tourist brochures to be much more abundant and accessible to viewing', sparking debate as to how realistic and representative the images were in light of the visitors' 'disappointment at not having seen the "big five"' animals (Norton 1996: 367).

Elsewhere, Jenkins (2003) adopts a different approach to the study of tourism images, comparing photographs taken by tourists with images most commonly represented in tourism media. Giving disposable cameras to backpackers travelling around Australia, she found that although backpackers are often seen to be 'alternative' in their approach to tourism, they are still 'susceptible to the myths and messages of photographic tourist images' (Jenkins 2003: 323). She found that like other tourists, backpackers seek out popular scenes. Further, the reproduction of these images in the photographs of visitors is part of a 'circular process by which particular tourist images are produced, projected, perceived, propagated and perpetuated' (2003: 324) as affirmation that what they have experienced was the expected reality. Similarly, Markwell (1997) has demonstrated that tourists are likely to take personal photographs of scenes which closely mirror those images found in tourism brochures or depict the destination how they *want* to experience it. Recent work suggests more complex processes may be at play. Haldrup and Larsen (2006), for instance, focus on the interplay between the material objects and human agency, and point to the way technologies like cameras are crucial in making tourism geographies 'happen-able and perform-able'. A question remains, however, regarding how 'locals' regard this shaping of tourism landscapes in the quest to attract visitors.

Representation in Great Barrier Island's Tourist Literature

Great Barrier Island is a popular destination for adventurous tourists looking to breach the comfort of the urban environment and avoid the more frequently visited 'wilderness' areas. In the following section we examine how Great Barrier Island is depicted within promotional material produced for travellers, attempting to discern whether the facilities and opportunities that are provided for tourists elicit similar place interpretations and meanings as they do for those who live upon the island.

In this study, we examined the content of three widely-available tourism brochures designed to promote the island: '*Great Barrier Island: The Official Guide 2010*' published by Tourism Auckland (2010), '*Aotea Great Barrier Island*' issued by the Department of Conservation (2006), and '*Great Barrier Island and Waiheke Island*' by SeaLink Holidays (2009), (the car and passenger ferry company which serves Great Barrier Island). We reviewed both the textual and pictorial aspects of this publicity used to inform visitors about Great Barrier Island. We then examined the way in which interviewees interpret and react to the 'factual' information within the brochures as well as the photographic representations of the island.

Linguistic Analysis

We initially performed content analysis of all text appearing within the three brochures. This analysis revealed five distinct categories: information on activities, qualitative descriptors, portrayal of 'nature', preparatory advice, and 'other' (see Table 4.1). What is most apparent is the overtly positive way in which the island is presented, with the use of superlatives like 'grandeur', 'haven' and 'tranquil', and phrases such as 'adventurer's paradise' and 'last great wilderness area'. The island is thus represented as a place which actualises ideas of paradise and promises an uninhabited, unspoilt and peaceful landscape.

In terms of available activities and recreational engagements, Great Barrier is portrayed as a place with 'endless' possibilities to engage in activities, with statements mentioning that the visitor will never 'be short of things to do'. It is constructed as a place of continual entertainment and adventure, implicitly offering a contrast to the place the visitor has arrived from.

Table 4.1   A content analysis of three Great Barrier Island tourism brochures

	Tourism Auckland	Department of Conservation	SeaLink
Activities	'endless' 'wilderness adventure'	Mentions tramping and camping	'...won't be short of things to do'
Descriptors	'tranquil' 'unspoilt' 'adventurer's paradise'	'rugged' 'last great wilderness area'	'grandeur' 'stunning beauty and sheer remoteness' 'breathe in the peace and tranquillity and enjoy this truly back-to-nature experience'
'Nature'	'golden beaches' 'crystal clear waters' 'vast native forests' 'nature...is king here'	'diversity' 'plants flourish'	'haven for endangered species' 'pristine beaches and native bush'
Preparation	'mobile phone coverage is limited' 'the weather can be changeable' 'no banks' 'boiling [water] or treatment recommended'	Provides information on camping and huts	Suggests bringing a car
Other	'essential information' such as emergency numbers and shop availability	History of land and habitation. Information on birds/lizards/marine animals/plants	Motel and rental property information

The way in which the island is described within these brochures aligns it with a utopian imaginary. This alignment is reflected in adjectives found within the brochures such as 'unspoilt', 'tranquil' and 'rugged', and within phrases including 'breathe in the peace and tranquillity and enjoy this truly back-to-nature experience' as well as 'last great wilderness area'. In combination, such statements assign Great Barrier Island the status of an earthly paradise bearing few signs of any human imprint. They also play upon the ideal of the tropical island with phrases such as 'pristine' or 'golden' beaches and 'crystal clear waters', a set of tropes aligned with Salazar's (2012: 886) remark that 'prospective tourists are invited to imagine themselves in a paradisiacal environment, a vanished Eden'.

Our examination of the brochures found little information about the available infrastructure and realities of what is involved in terms of visiting and getting around the island. Of the three, only one brochure (Tourism Auckland 2010) mentions that there is little, if any mobile phone coverage, no banks and that the weather has the tendency to be changeable and harsh. There is no information provided that notes issues including the lack of public transport on the island or a higher cost of everyday items such as petrol and groceries than on the mainland. This finding reveals that most information provided is focused on stereotypes of an uninhabited tropical paradise and the presence of natural flora and fauna thus providing a vision of the place that is limited at best, and at worst, potentially misleading.

Image Analysis

As might be expected, the images contained within Great Barrier Island tourism brochures depict the island and its coastline in a guise which suggests beauty and a place of paradise. The weather is favourable, dolphins are playing, and the sea is calm. The images used to represent it conjure up a romanticised, paradisiacal, unexplored and utopic place; a place which is seemingly always found in this static, calm and sunny state.

The imagery used endorses an illusion that Great Barrier Island truly is what one brochure claims it to be: the earth's 'last great wilderness area' (Department of Conservation, 2006). Photographs include depictions of empty beaches, dolphins and native birds, and largely exclude people, thus presenting the notion that the island is uninhabited and devoid of any markers of human occupancy. The few people included in the photographs are representations of tourists, and they are arguably included to suggest that once upon the island you and your family or friends will be virtually alone, a trope that contrasts with the inclusion of hosts in tourist brochures as scenic props, as described by Dann (1996).

This lack of evidence of human habitation in the brochures also helps to construct the island as a place of unexplored solace and adventure, and a place where one will be able to find 'peace and tranquillity' (SeaLink Holidays 2009). Furthermore, images that hide evidence of a the resident population serve to reinforce the image of the 'castaway'. Ideas of solace and *de facto* ownership for those who visit are implied, suggesting that one will, at all times, be alone on what could be thought of as a private beach, a representation echoing a dominant motif used in coastal real estate advertisements (see Collins and Kearns 2008).

The imagery is also highly selective in the way it depicts natural landscapes as 'unspoilt' and as a place of 'vast native forests' where 'nature...is king' (Tourism Auckland 2010). The photographs present no suggestion of the island's history of extractive industry (e.g. logging, mining) which once desecrated the island and the concern about which lives on through 'green politics' and environmental activism. This absence of historical representation assists reinforcing the notion of the island as a utopia where the coast acts as a border to 'fend off contamination from

Figure 4.2   Examples of images of Great Barrier Island to be found in tourism literature

Source: Courtesy of Greg Roigard: Akapoua Bay, Michael Field/Fairfax Media: Pitokuku Island and Whangaparapara Harbour.

Note: Due to copyright and permission issues we are unable to include the particular images found in printed Great Barrier Island tourism material. These images are examples that reflect those found in Great Barrier Island promotional brochures, taken by members of the public and used with permission.

the outside world' (McMahon 2003: 191). In a manner not unlike that discussed by Waitt and McGuirk (1996), the imagery used only serves to disassociate the viewer from a harsh history of resource exploitation, reminders of which will likely become evident upon visitation (e.g. the remnants of the highly destructive Kauri tree logging industry, such as disused dams and the foundations of their associated milling operations).

Taken together, the imagery used to depict Great Barrier Island within tourism material appears to constitute a concerted attempt to reinforce Western presuppositions of the tropical island paradise and to underplay any association with a history of resource exploitation. The images also disregard reference to the resident population and appear to suggest that visitors to the island will be able to have an experience akin to that of being on their own private holiday island.

Residents and Tourism Representations

In this section of the chapter we turn to residents' reactions to images of Great Barrier Island found in its tourism brochures. We draw on a thematic analysis of 23 in-depth interviews that were undertaken and transcribed during a period of fieldwork undertaken by the first author in May and June, 2010. To recruit research participants, communication was first established with local shop owners and informational flyers were mailed to affix to their notice boards. The initial participants made contact by email, registering their interest; the remainder were contacted through a snowball recruitment method whereby interviewees were asked who else they know who might be willing to participate. Interviews were undertaken at a local cafe and in the homes of the participants, each lasting between 30 and 60 minutes.

Resident Reactions to the Wording of Publicity

It was often mentioned that although they provide relevant information, the brochures contain omissions pertaining to relatively basic and important information that is needed to enjoy and experience Great Barrier Island. A prime example of this can be seen in Hilda's comment: 'Cell coverage is limited...cell coverage is almost non-existent'.

Another example of the way in which the information is provided, or in many cases, not provided at all, commonly results in issues as highlighted by Mary: 'The first thing a lot of people ask is "where are the banks?". ... they don't realise that you can't just come here and slip down the road to the hole in the wall [ATM].'

As these comments reveal, the brochures do not always prepare people for the visitor experience which is offered on Great Barrier Island. The majority of visitors who arrive are from Auckland and are used to being well connected in terms of access to money and telecommunications. The brochures often convey the impression that as the island is a part of Auckland (which it is politically and administratively), the same or similar facilities will be available. On the one hand, to not address this assumption may be interpreted as shrewd marketing so as to instil a sense of security in terms of connectedness, thus ensuring people were not deterred visiting the island. However, on the other hand, this comment also represents a lack of appreciation by residents about how limited the producers of brochures are in terms of design, cost and content. It further reveals the 'two worlds' of tourism promoters and local residents: for the former the fundamental premise of a brochure is to convey the iconic elements of a place that tourists expect to see; for the latter there is the concern with the 'gritty' details of daily life and encounters with visitors who experience the dissonance between expectation and actuality.

As is previously noted, Great Barrier's tourism marketing invariably portrays the island using positive and lively wording. This portrayal often leads to false expectations for tourists and visitors who are frequently unprepared in terms of what to expect during a stay on Great Barrier Island: 'I think the information they give is limited. I think a lot of people who come here are expecting to be occupied and do things, be entertained if you like, whereas in actual fact there is very little happening in that department' (Elinor).

Unlike a tropical Pacific island resort, there is little activity provided for visitors on 'the Barrier'. Issues such as the profound difference between summer and winter retail opening hours are not made explicit in promotional material. Furthermore, brochures do not assert that having a car (or at least a bicycle) is of high importance if you want to visit parts of the island beyond where you are staying, given that there is no public transport and the island is large.

The omission of information can also be seen in the depiction of facilities. None of the brochures mention what it is like to live without otherwise taken-for-granted 'utilities' on mainland New Zealand, such as reticulated water and sewerage, mains power or gas. Again, people are often unprepared for the experience of foregoing such amenities:

> I think [the brochures are] fairly good in terms of their representation of a fairly wild environment that needs to be protected, but I don't think they really give one an idea of what it's actually like to live…without mains power, and without a bank for example. A lot of people come here and are completely unprepared for that. (Elinor)

The foregoing comments signal that, from the perspective of 'locals', prospective tourists considering Great Barrier as a destination and prompted by brochures, do not necessarily consider how the place 'works'. However, this 'functionality of place' (e.g. banks and phone coverage) is both difficult and unproductive to convey in promotional material.

Resident Reaction to the Images Used

Participants were asked to review the images contained within the tourism brochures mentioned above. Our analysis of their reactions and responses allowed us to assess the degree to which their statements might align with Dilley's (1986) assumption that tourism images portray the destination as the locals perceive it to be.

Many of the interviewees indicated that the images were accurate in terms of how they themselves perceive the island. As Eileen postulated:

> I think they're pretty standard sort of photographs for tourism brochures, I think they're very accurate. We often have dolphins in the bay; the beach more often than not looks like this; we have fabulous amounts [*sic*] of Tui [a native bird]; that is a beautiful walkway; I've stood in that spot – looks exactly like that.

For Gladys, the images contained within the brochures represent the island well but she was quick to note that the tourist might not always be able to experience all that the brochure is offering. However for her, the representations were accurate enough to provide a suggestion of what might be experienced:

> From what I can see, the images are a good representation of the island. They show the parts that I like the best and they certainly give you a good indication of the wildlife. You may not get to see all of it while you're here so at least having some photos telling you the little animals that are protected here, even though you may not get to see them, just knowing that they're extremely rare and being made aware of this is a good thing.

Gladys's comments are suggestive of Urry's (1990) description of the post-tourist as one who plays with the possibilities offered by the producers and providers of the tourist experiences. Such travellers are well aware that brochures present idealised and selective interpretations of destinations and are designed to sell places. Hence, to the knowing post-tourist, they offer possibilities rather than guaranteed experiences and, in the words of Gladys, 'you may not get to see all of it while you're here'.

The accuracy of the images was further endorsed by Rachel who commented that: 'All of these places do exist and do look like that for quite a lot of the time, and even in summer you can walk on to a beach where [there are] no people and no boats, so I think it's pretty accurate'.

Rachel was happy with the images chosen to represent the island and she felt that they are 'pretty accurate'. However, she also noted that the places depicted 'look like that for a quite a lot of the time' revealing that perhaps one will not *always* find the place as the image presents it. This view is similar to the way in which Polly reacted towards the tourism images. For her: '…they are short term. We get people who come here and they're starry-eyed and say "what a beautiful place" and "I want to live here", but I call it the holiday syndrome – you can have a holiday for three weeks, but after that it gets boring'.

In Polly's eyes, the images are accurate in their representation of Great Barrier Island as a physical destination. They work well as a draw card for tourism by presenting the island in a desirable and romanticised light, but these images of the island are unsustainable for the long term visitor or resident. In her concept of the 'holiday syndrome', Polly is not refuting the physical beauty of the natural surroundings as they are presented in the images, but is proposing that the way in which visitors respond to and interact with this environment changes over time. Tuan (1977) would call this change in landscape response the acquisition of the 'concrete reality' of Great Barrier Island. The views of these 'beautiful' landscapes comprise only part of 'the Barrier' experience. As time passes and the island is experienced in numerous and more diverse ways, the 'concrete reality' of Great Barrier Island, as a place, may lose its romanticised appeal as a tropical paradise, giving way to the reality of the 'hard life' that a number of participants alluded to. In other words, what was seen as exotic becomes routine and ordinary over time, hence diluting the experience of the 'other' and highlighting the way time-limited visits maintain a sense of novelty in tourism.

Some interviewees recognised the pictorial representations could be unrealistic and portrayed an overly glamorised version of the island and its coast:

> They obviously show it in its best light, in summertime, but this is how I mentally picture it, so I think it is a good representation because even if you did come here and it was cloudy and overcast and raining, the beaches are still just as beautiful as they are photographed here and I don't think a tourist would be disappointed.

For Gladys, the images are simply depicting the place in its most desirable guise – in summer. In her narrative, Gladys realises that the creators of the tourist literature choose to provide images of the island which are more appealing to the Western imagination of the paradisiacal island. On the other hand, she admits that she feels the beaches of Great Barrier Island are indeed 'just as beautiful' when it is raining and stormy, believing that visitors will also find this experience of the island just as appealing as when the sun is shining.

Willie also agrees that the images within the brochures are obvious glamorisations: 'They're always taken on sunny days, you never see them when the sou-wester picks up and it's rough and rugged and you can't access the beach'. He knows that the beaches of Great Barrier Island are not frozen in a state of static paradisiacal summer, but nonetheless feels that this glamorisation is warranted for at least two reasons: 'It's partly in our interests that they glamorise it a bit so we have, you know, tourism's one of our major industries over here, so we need these pictures to show the better side. And also perhaps they'll help [show] that we hope to keep it this way'.

For Willie, although he is aware of the reality of the island experience, glamorisation of tourism images is acceptable in the way it encourages tourists and their contribution to the island's small economy. Implicitly, he is acknowledging the value of rural and remote areas to urban populations, as reserves of authenticity in natural, cultural and economic terms (Figueiredo and Raschi 2012). Willie also notes that the use of romanticised imagery might help to influence behaviour of those people who do visit the island. He suggests that if people arrive on Great Barrier Island with the preconceived mental image of a pristine and untouched landscape, they will police their own behaviour and not act in a way which might be detrimental to the stability of this image (e.g. leaving rubbish on a beach).

Willie's acceptance of an overt glamorisation of tourism images is shared by other members of the island community, and aligns with Scarles' (2004) account of local residents in Scotland agreeing to appear in tourist advertising (see also Scarles 2012). For instance, another resident, John, postulates that the 'images are pretty accurate if you're looking at the island in a positive way and you want to attract people'. John's view mirrors that of Willie, in that he too feels that the images have been specifically chosen for their utilitarian and conservational worth in terms of tourism marketing.

Interestingly, only one participant took a vocal stance against the glamorisation of the island in marketing images. Philip firmly stated that: 'Nope! No, you can't glamorise beauty. You cannot. There's no way you could glamorise Okiwi Bay, it is just exceptional, an outstanding piece of coastline. So, that's how it is, you've only got to walk there on a sunny day'.

In this narrative Philip refuses to believe that the images within the tourism literature can add to or reflect the natural landscapes of Great Barrier Island. Rather he contends that one simply needs to visit the place in which the photo was taken to find evidence for the fact that these views are in no way glamorised. For Philip, the use of an image showing the landscape in a guise which plays up to the trope of the tropical island paradise does not constitute glamorisation if there is potential for the place to be experienced that way. Ultimately there seems acceptance that a picture can never truly capture a *real* place.

The Notion of 'Comfort Zone'

A final comment on the image representation in Great Barrier Island tourism literature comes from Dennis, who viewed the brochures in a different way to the other participants. For Dennis, the images are not glamorising the natural land/seascapes, but rather they play on the romanticised Western imagination of the isolated and idealised tropical island, showing potential tourists images of what they think, and have been told, they want to experience. This finding resonates with the results found in Jenkins' (2003) study of backpacker photography in which the 'adventurous' backpacking tourists, despite their reputation, were found to seek out and represent known and comfortable experiences. In Dennis' mind, the images within these brochures are promoting the island through depictions of comfort and the known: 'All they're trying to do is show you your comfort zone, and they're familiar things like tuis. Most people have seen tuis and everything else before, so they're trying to keep people in a comfort zone and we should be saying "this is right out of your comfort zone".'

For Dennis, what makes Great Barrier Island a prime tourist destination are the very aspects that make it unique and not a location which provides the same opportunities as any other island destinations. One of these facets is that Great Barrier Island is isolated, and although the brochures do represent this sense of distance, it is not represented in a way that Dennis feels is correct. As Garrod (2009) contends, tourists are motivated to travel to destinations from what they have been led to expect through exposure to visual representations carried in tourism advertisements. Dennis is suggesting the publicity for Great Barrier is too tame and plays to what many visitors have already experienced elsewhere or already know about the island. Rather, for him, the island's isolation can be lonely and uncomfortable and this is what Dennis feels should be promoted as a selling point of the Great Barrier Island experience; it is a location which takes people out of their comfort zone and it should be promoted as such:

> There's nothing really on the Barrier that you can't find somewhere else on the Coromandel or Northland. It's an isolated destination and I think the important part about it is that they start to experience the isolation when they get on the boat or get on the plane, because it's somewhere different, it's somewhere that takes them out of their comfort zone.

Philip similarly has views that concur with those of Dennis. He notes that the experience of Great Barrier Island is often hard for some visitors, especially when they are expecting a place of comfort and ease. But for Philip, this experience is something which will stay with them and encourage self-reflection. It is not a facet that he believes needs to be promoted in the literature, as it is best discovered individually:

> Do we have to anaesthetise everybody? You know, that's the experience. I think that some people might have at the time...they might feel that it was a difficult experience but it'll change them in some way I believe...They may or may not recognise it at the time but it will be with them there, gnawing away at some level. You know, [visitors may feel] "I need to get back to nature a bit more", "I need to change my life", or "I'm really happy, thank God, I don't live there".

In this light, perhaps the omission of any mention of the relative isolation of Great Barrier in promotional material can be viewed positively – once the visitor is upon the island and is able to confront their constructed expectations with the reality of experience. The isolation can potentially provide an unexpected encounter which will spark this self-reflection that Philip posits as an important part of experiencing the island. Although tourists are greeted in the literature with romanticised images of the idealised aspects of Great Barrier Island, it might be the unanticipated experiences that end up providing the foundations for the sense of place that visitors build throughout their stay. However one should proceed cautiously with this speculation. For, as suggested by De Botton (2002), it is the lived expectation of travel desires which most commonly provide a positive experience for the tourist, whereas to find that a place is not how it is *pictured* often becomes the instigator of both physical and emotional stresses. With this view in mind De Botton (2002) writes that getting out of one's comfort zone is indeed uncomfortable, and for many, the practice may not be the instigator of change or self-reflection as Dennis and Philip postulate, but rather one which serves to reinforce the comforts of home.

Conclusion

This chapter has investigated the ways in which Great Barrier Island is represented within brochures aimed at tourists, and whether or not residents of the island feel that the text and images within that literature reflect lived experience on the island. For any tourist destination set at a distance (both literal and figurative) from the everyday routines of potential visitors, there is an acute need to generate and maintain interest in visiting. This is especially so in the case of islands, such as Great Barrier, where transport options are few and there is a need for considerable planning and additional costs to visit. We have shown how publicity images, found in brochures as well as reproduced in newspaper advertisements and elsewhere (e.g. on screens aboard Auckland's commuter ferries), offer visual and verbal 'promises' that inevitably influence visitor expectations. Rather than focus on the way such images mediate visitor experience, we have followed a less travelled route into the perceptions of 'locals' and explored how they regard the depiction of their 'home patch' as a tourist destination.

Generally island residents were sympathetic to the way Great Barrier Island was portrayed to visitors. They indicated that a measure of verbal and visual flattery was warranted, notwithstanding recognition that a carefully chosen photograph can create an illusion of climatic constancy. In terms of the text included within the brochures, interviewees stipulated that although the literature did provide a well-rounded and relevant account of the island, many items considered to be essential information were either omitted, or the explicit nature of the issue was downplayed. Conversely, interviewees found the majority of the images within the literature to be a good representation of how they believe Great Barrier Island to be, although most agreed that the images often glamorised the island or only showed it in its best light.

Of greater concern was the way publicity elided reference to the fact that island life is characterised by a tough simplicity involving, for instance, fickle generators, dependence on roof-water tanks, limited telephone access and few forms of transport. Residents saw the minimal forewarning to largely metropolitan visitors as something of a liability, and a potential source of dissonance between expectation and experience. A paradox is faced however; to dwell more overtly on the privations of a remote, but alluring, place risks publicity that neutralises the quest for difference, adventure and a 'taste of paradise' with the prospect that a comfort zone will be transgressed. In other words, the superlatives and sunny panoramas are a necessary glamorisation to entice the potential tourist into contemplating a journey they might otherwise be dissuaded from. As this chapter has shown, the stakes are high in such fragile and modest tourist economies; the risk of dissonance between expectations of comforts and experience of relative privations is best embraced only when people have already crossed the water and are able to confront the island's grandeur.

References

Ateljevic, I. and Doorne, S. 2002. Representing New Zealand: tourism imagery and ideology. *Annals of Tourism Research*, 29(3), 648–67.

Butler, R. and Hall, C.M. 1998. Image and reimaging of rural areas, in *Tourism and Recreation in Rural Areas*, edited by R. Butler et al. Chichester: Wiley, 115–22.

Cloke, P. and Perkins, H. 2002. Commodification and adventure in New Zealand tourism. *Current Issues in Tourism*, 5, 521–49.

Collins, D.C.A. and Kearns, R.A. 2008. Uninterrupted views: real estate advertising and changing perspectives on coastal property in New Zealand. *Environment and Planning A*, 40(12), 2914–32.

Dann, G. 1996. The people of tourist brochures, in *The Tourist Image: Myths and Myth Making in Tourism*, edited by T. Selwyn. New York: John Wiley and Sons, 61–81.

De Botton, A. 2002. *The Art of Travel*. London: Hamish Hamilton.

Department of Conservation. 2006. *Aotea Great Barrier Island*. Auckland: Department of Conservation.

Dilley, R.S. 1986. Tourist brochures and tourist images. *The Canadian Geographer*, 30(1), 59–65.

Figueiredo, E. and Raschi, A. 2012. Immersed in green? Reconfiguring the Italian rural tourism promotional materials, in *Field Guide to Case Study Research in Tourism, Hospitality and Leisure (Advances in Culture, Tourism and Hospitality Research.* Volume 6, edited by K. Hyde et al. Bingley: Emerald Group Publishing Limited, 17–44

Garrod, B. 2009. Understanding the relationship between tourism destination imagery and tourist photography. *Journal of Travel Research*, 47(3), 346–58.

Haldrup, M. and Larsen, J. 2006. Material cultures of tourism. *Leisure Studies*, 25(3), 275–89

Hall, C.M. 1994. *Tourism and Politics*. Chichester: Wiley.

Hughes, G. 1991. Tourism and the geographical imagination. *Leisure Studies*, 11(1), 31–42.

Jenkins, O. 2003. Photography and travel brochures: the circle of representation. *Tourism Geography*, 5(3), 305–28.

Jones, J.P. and Natter, W. 1999. Space 'and' representation, in *Text and Image: Social Construction of Regional Knowledges*, edited by A. Buttimer et al. Weimar: Gutengergdruckerei GmbH Weimar, 239–47.

Kobayashi, A. 2009. Representation and Re-presentation, in *The International Encyclopaedia of Human Geography*, edited by N. Thrift. and R. Kitchin. Philadelphia: Elsevier Science, 347–50.

Markwell, K.W. 1997. Dimensions of photography in a nature-based tour. *Annals of Tourism Research*, 24(1), 131–55.

McMahon, E. 2003. The gilded cage: from utopia to monad in Australia's island imaginary, in *Islands in History and Representation*, edited by R. Edmond and V. Smith. London: Routledge, 190–202.

Molina, A. and Esteban, A. 2006. Tourism brochures: usefulness and image. *Annals of Tourism Research*, 33(4), 1036–56.

Morgan, N. and Pritchard, A. 2000. *Advertising in Tourism and Leisure*. Oxford: Butterworth-Heinemann.

Morgan, N., Pritchard, A. and Pride, R. (eds.) 2004. *Destination Branding: creating the unique destination proposition*. 2nd edition. Elsevier: Oxford.

Norton, A. 1996. Experiencing nature: the reproduction of environmental discourse through safari tourism in East Africa. *Geoforum*, 27(3), 355–73.

Ringer, G. 1998. Introduction, in *Destinations: Cultural Landscapes of Tourism*, edited by G. Ringer. New York: Routledge, 1–13.

Saarinen, J. 1998. The social construction of tourist destinations: the process of transformation of the Saariselkä tourism region in Finnish Lapland, in *Destinations: Cultural Landscapes of Tourism*, edited by G. Ringer. New York: Routledge, 154–73.

Salazar, B. 2012. Tourism imaginaries: a conceptual approach. *Annals of Tourism Research*, 39(2), 863–82.

Scarles, C. 2004. Mediating landscapes: the processes and practices of image construction in tourist brochures of Scotland. *Tourist Studies*, 4(1), 43–67.

Scarles, C. 2012. The photographed other: interplays of agency in tourist photography in Cusco, Peru. *Annals of Tourism Research,* 39(2), 928–50.

SeaLink Holidays. 2009. *Great Barrier Island and Waiheke Island*. SeaLink Holidays.

Tourism Auckland. 2010. *Great Barrier Island: The Official Guide 2010*. Tourism Auckland.

Tuan, Y. 1977. *Space and Place: The Perspective of Experience*. Minneapolis: University of Minnesota Press.

Urry, J. 1990. *The Tourist Gaze*. London: Sage.

Waitt, G. and McGuirk, P. 1996. Marking time: tourism and heritage representation at Millers Point, Sydney. *Australian Geographer*, 27(1), 11–29.

Chapter 5

The Effect of British Natural History Television Programmes: Animal Representations and Wildlife Tourism

Susanna Curtin

There have been many articles written about tourists' desire to see, enjoy and even interact with wildlife (Curtin 2010a, 2009, Bulbeck 2005, Newsome et al. 2005, DeMares and Krycka 1998). Fifteen years ago wildlife tourism could be considered a niche product aimed at a small and dedicated market. However, it is a mistake to think of it purely in these terms today given that wildlife tourism is thought to be growing by 10 per cent per annum and is attracting growing attention from operators, destinations and governments (Mintel 2008, United Nations Environment Programme 2006).

Tourism commentators propose that greater urbanisation and decontextualisation from nature and nature's processes coupled with an inherent interest in nature, the proliferation of destinations and tour operators, and increased media coverage of wildlife and environmental issues are possible drivers of the increase in popularity (Lemelin et al. 2010, Newsome et al. 2005, Walpole and Thouless 2005). Indeed, British wildlife tour operators and tour guides interviewed by the author frequently confirm an inter-relationship between increased wildlife tourism demand and the increase in emotive natural history programmes; particularly those which depict charismatic, iconic, flagship or disappearing species (Curtin 2010a, 2010c). Whilst reference to this relationship is frequently mentioned, it has yet to be adequately explored or explained.

A study of the wildlife tourism literature, tourism marketing, and the burgeoning number of wildlife tourism products and places is testimony to the fact that wildlife has a wide and growing appeal. Tourists can choose from a myriad of experiences from extended dedicated wildlife tours to short day trips to see iconic and charismatic wildlife, either in its natural setting or in captivity. There is still some debate about what is driving this tourist activity; whether it is an inherent human desire to seek out nature/wildlife experiences or whether it is the proliferation of business opportunities that facilitate it. Nonetheless, tourism destination marketers have been quick to exploit this growing interest (Higginbottom 2004, Moscardo et al. 2001, Tremblay 2002). Any content analysis of the use of animals in tourism marketing reveals the frequent adoption of animal photographs to depict place identities (Turner 2010, pers. comm. The Born Free

Foundation, Tremblay 2002). This culminates in animals being both symbolic of place as well as an added interest or focus for travel.

In his discussion of the use of wildlife icons in tourism marketing, Tremblay (2002) asserts that the social construction of iconic wildlife can be used by the industry to anchor places in tourists' minds. Tourism attractions depend on the demarcation processes that help distinguish them from ordinary places and activities (Shaw and Williams 2004). This process is heavily reliant on well-defined signs or markers in the landscape (Urry 1990). Wildlife, which is symbolic of a country or place, is commonly used as a signifier for the tourist gaze. However in order for something to be an attractive or appealing signifier, it has to already mean something in the minds of the potential tourist. Prior perceptions of wild animals are drawn from a number of media such as art and literature, but more recently natural history television programmes.

The purpose of this chapter therefore is to offer a conceptual contribution to the complex relationship between media representations of the animal kingdom and the demand for wildlife tourism experiences. The discussion will pay particular attention to the types and delivery of natural history programmes, social representations of animals and animal performance, and the role of television media in creating anticipatory images of animals. The chapter argues that the discourse of this mediation is heavily orientated towards hyper-sensationalism and the emotional responses that are provoked in the audience decoding process. The foundation of this argument is based upon the work of Hall (1980), whose encoding and decoding theory has been used to evaluate the construction of public knowledge. Hall adopts the concept of a 'code' which is used by programme makers (or any popular media) as a system of meaning to relay visual and linguistic signs to the different ideological positions by which a cultural order is either legitimised or contested (Philo 2008). The point is that what is being written in to a programme constitutes a 'dominant cultural order', which imposes a 'taken for granted knowledge of social structures' (Hall 1980: 134). This hegemonic viewpoint carries with it the stamp of legitimacy, which is decoded by a passive audience.

In the analysis of natural history programmes, the chapter argues that these codes culminate in a reality based on selectivity, myth-making and storytelling where animals ultimately become interesting and sought after subjects in a tourist's world. The chapter provides a conceptual framework, which illustrates a cyclical journey from the production of natural history programmes and audiences' anticipatory images of wildlife to the ultimate tourist experience and a then-continued popular social representation of the animal kingdom.

Natural History Programmes

Programmes such as the British Broadcasting Corporation's (BBC) *Big Cat Diaries*, *The Bear Family and Me*, BBC *Springwatch/Autumnwatch* and films such as the *March of the Penguins* are gripping, emotional accounts of animal lives. They allow audiences to follow the 'soap-opera' performance as it unfurls and are instrumental in capturing television audiences and tourist imaginings in order to persuade them to visit places to experience wildlife first hand. The lives and performances of animals thus become agents and co-constituents of tourist (consumer) experiences and place-making (Cloke and Perkins 2005).

Television programmes, popular media, art and literature establish how we conceptualise animals and their habitats. Out of all these genres, natural history television programmes are arguably one of the most powerful in determining animal narratives and value-orientations towards wildlife due to their visual, 'up-close' and 'real-time' portrayal of the trials and tribulations of animal life. Wildlife television programming began by capturing the attention of a developed post-war world which at that time still had abundant wildlife. From the 1960s onwards programmes presented an 'expert' vision of nature that stressed the importance of field observation and scientific interpretations of animal form so revolutionised by the 'scientific voice' of Sir David Attenborough and his colleagues. Today, however, many would argue that this narrative has long since gone to be replaced by one which is more anthropomorphic (i.e. transferring human characteristics onto animal behaviours), emotional and hyper-sensational; scripts that reflect societies' changing wildlife value orientations and sensibilities particularly in the light of deforestation, climate change, habitat loss and declining species.

Studies focusing on wildlife tourism behaviour and experiences increasingly acknowledge the role of engaging audience emotions (Balantyne et al. 2010, McIntosh 1999). Wildlife viewing can be both an educational and emotional activity; therefore both affective and cognitive motives underpin and shape the tourist experience. One way of understanding emotional experiences in a wildlife context is as an affective outcome of a relational encounter between self and animal other (i.e. either as an active participant in a natural habitat or as a passive observer of film). Conradson (2007: 103) explains how in coming close to 'other ecologies and rhythms of life', we not only obtain distance from everyday routines but also new perspectives on our own circumstances. There are a number of reasons why time spent watching animals and birds is particularly transformative. Rolston (1987) highlights animals' agency and the fact that they provide movement and life in an otherwise still environment. They are subjects in the environment whereas the mountains, trees and rivers are objects. This spontaneous movement and life in defence of its very survival, he claims 'moves us aesthetically' (1987: 187) and add adventure and thrill. The excitement lies both in the surprise and the anticipation where there is 'intrusion, intimacy and otherness' (1987: 190). Whilst the landscape and topography will always be there to behold; the birds in the trees, the tiger running wild; these are unique moments in time, which are inordinately memorable for us.

According to Ballantyne et al. (2009) the affective domain is particularly important in wildlife tourism encounters because humans generally respond emotionally to animals. Animals have always played a very important part in the human imaginings. Throughout our evolutionary history man has had an extremely complex relationship with the animal kingdom. Animals are uniquely positioned relative to humans in that they are 'both like us, but not us' (Franklin 1999: 9). They have the capacity to represent the differentiations, characters and dispositions of any given society. Indeed human-like characteristics particularly prevalent in mammals often reflect the extent to which mankind can empathise with animal behaviour or attributes, and this in turn affects how worthy species are of the tourist gaze or even of protection or conservation. Given this inherent human fascination with the animal kingdom, it is no wonder that wildlife programmes and films are so popular with audiences.

The wildlife television documentary has a long history and is a major part of the international media industry. The genre sits precariously between education and entertainment and whilst there is little research to determine its global size and reach, it is a highly significant and exportable source of public information regarding the natural world. Discovery Communications claim that their Animal Planet channel is available in 87 million US homes and another 150 million in 160 other countries (Dingwall and Aldridge 2006). With Sir David Attenborough at the forefront of the BBC natural history programmes, many of the most popular wildlife documentaries (see Table 5.1) have been exported to other countries making Sir David Attenborough and his films a global brand.

Table 5.1   Flagship wildlife documentaries from the BBC's Natural History Unit

Programme	Year of Production
Animal Magic	1962–1983
The World About Us	1969–1982
Wildlife on one	1977–2005
BBC Life on Earth	1979
Flight of the Condor	1982
Natural World	1983–present
The Living Planet	1984
Big Cat Diaries	1996
Land of the Tiger	1997
Andes to Amazon	2000
The Blue Planet	2001
Wild Down Under	2003
Annual *Springwatch*	2005–present
Annual *Autumnwatch*	2006–present
Planet Earth	2006

Programme	Year of Production
Saving Planet Earth	2007
Wild China	2008
Pacific Abyss	2008
Lost Land of the Tigers	2008
Big Cat Live	2008
Life	2009
Frozen Planet	2010
The Bear Family and Me	2011

Wildlife programming tends to either be blue chip or presenter led. Blue chip typically focuses on mega fauna in beautiful environments, which are presented with a dramatic 'story-line' set amidst powerful visual images. The cost of production is extremely high and therefore producers must ensure that the product has a long potential shelf-life and a high export value. The human story-teller is often removed from the scene and the commentary is devoid of politics, people or history (Cottle 2004, Bouse 2000). The presenter's monologue draws on a small number of grand and 'universal' narratives such as 'life and death', 'diurnal rhythms', 'the struggle for survival' and the 'universality of family ties'; thereby creating a mixture of 'warmth and jeopardy' (Bouse 2000: 81). Despite being thought of as an informational source by audiences, Bouse (2000) reveals that those working in the wildlife documentary industry regard documentary making as storytelling. In the commercial world in which they operate, they are in direct competition with traditional drama rooted in conventional cinema. Therefore the 'story' they convey must conform to a classic and universal formula.

Commentators as well as audiences would be forgiven for the assumption that blue chip wildlife documentaries present a more authoritative voice regarding the animal kingdom. However Dingwall and Aldridge (2006) suggest quite the opposite in-so-far as they should be better understood for their entertainment value as a spectacle of the natural world rather than as a true representation of it. Their exportable narratives are instrumental in reasserting popular discourses and myths about symbolic and charismatic wildlife rather than providing their viewers with realistic textualisations of ecological science.

In contrast to the blue-chip documentary, the presenter-led programmes tend to include human/animal interaction and are more organic in their production. The story and working-life of the wildlife cameraman is sometimes also included to capture real-time wonderment of nature and to create a sense of outdoor adventure. They tend to have lower production costs and a relatively quick turnaround. More recent programmes such as *The Bear Family and Me* and *Spring/Autumnwatch* are presented by fun, attractive and approachable naturalists who have become 'wildlife celebrities' fronting renowned conservation organisations such as the

Royal Society for the Protection of Birds (RSPB). Indeed, a discourse analysis of *Springwatch* reveals language that is 'cosy', 'caring', 'concerned', 'chatty', 'friendly', 'live and inclusive' (Curtin 2010c). This makes these programmes extremely popular and engaging to a wide audience.

Wildlife documentaries tend to be aired during peak viewing and attract a wide range of audiences. In Champ's (2002) study of wildlife media, he found that wildlife television was perceived as an acceptable, safe-orientated, educational experience for the entire family; one of his study participants claiming that 'in a media world of troubling sex, violence and adult themes, it is a safe harbour' (2002: 278). It is therefore little wonder that audience numbers tend to be high. In the United Kingdom, wildlife programmes are watched by 52 per cent of men and 51 per cent of women (DCMS 2009). For women it is the fifth most watched television genre following the news, films, soap operas and comedy. For men, wildlife programmes are also rated fifth after news, sport, films and comedy. Despite their popularity in the UK and America, there is scant research beyond the American studies of Champ (2002) and Bagust (2008) on how audiences receive or respond to wildlife programmes; particularly how much they inform social representations and values of the animal kingdom and how they might inspire viewers to want to see wildlife for real.

Amongst academic and media critics, however, there is much debate as to whether wildlife media communicate good science, whether the construction of the narrative is appropriate (Dingwall and Aldridge 2006, Mabey 2005, Cottle 2004) and how much they contribute to wildlife value orientations: i.e. what version of the wildlife 'object' are people encouraged to value (Champ 2002)? In particular, producers of wildlife media have been criticised for staging scenes, sensationalising nature, only focusing on charismatic or flagship species and presenting an unbalanced view of life and death. Mabey (2003: 56) sees the natural history documentary as a 'dominionistic, anthropocentric ransacking of wildlife's innermost secrets, distorting sensational portrayals of life in the wild dominated only by the hunt and kill similar to the scenes of human violence that are in the tabloids'. By concentrating on the 'blood, claws and reproduction', it ignores how most creatures spend the majority of their lives, resting, grooming, playing and sleeping. It also has the effect of 'deadening our imaginations of nature'. Mabey (2003:56) likens the wildlife documentary to displaying the natural world as if it were an '18th century cabinet of curiosities' (see also Franklin 1999) rather than a true portrayal of animal life.

Further critique argues that programmes present a 'hyper-real' experience which depict nature as distant, separate from mankind, exotic and remote, and in so doing shield the developed world from examining their own extractive relationship to nature thus protecting dominant Western, capitalist worldviews (Bagust 2008). It also fails to acknowledge how people and nature live side by side. The documentary presenter is typified as a messenger between the ecosystem out there and 'us' over here. Blue-chip documentaries, such as *Planet Earth*, avoid any sense that human beings impinge on the natural world or that wild creatures have any impact upon us. Such portrayals may deeply affect tourist perceptions of the relationship between animal and human interconnectedness; making charismatic mega fauna mere objects of the tourist gaze rather than subjects in a universal ecosystem.

Hyper-reality, Animal Performance and Tourism

Bagust (2008: 213) also reminds us that the 'technologies of screen representations are beaming not just images of unmediated nature but also images of fantastically enhanced and simulated natures as well' blurring the reality of these new 'screen ecosystems' even further by seemingly objective/realist documentary makers in their use of special effects.

As well as these hyper-real images, audiences rarely appreciate the time it takes to achieve the live footage. Neither do they grasp the advanced technology of zoom lenses, which can produce close-up footage of animal behaviour from a long way away. This gives would-be wildlife tourists the misconception that wildlife is a) abundant, b) easy to see and identify, and c) that it is possible to obtain up-close and prolonged views.

Thus Crouch et al. (2005: 5) conclude that 'the active audience or tourist develops utopian aspirations within a reality jointly constructed by the media'. This hyper-reality, they argue, may heighten tourist expectations of what reality should be, for example close-up encounters with charismatic mega fauna or an unmediated and one-to-one wildlife experience. Bulbeck (2005) affirms this 'Attenborough effect' in her description of dolphin tourism where due to the 'hyper-real' rhetoric used to portray dolphins, tourists expect a spectacle of dolphins leaping about and taking an intense interest in humans which of course they do not. Tour operators may attempt to reorganise reality to meet these heightened expectations by orchestrating behaviour using food provisioning, tracking and flushing out wildlife. But often, utopian aspirations collide with the reality of being on a wildlife tour where only fleeting glimpses of wildlife or no glimpse at all is the norm (Curtin 2010a).

Tourism takes place within meaningful spatial contexts. Thus tourist experiences are carried out upon particular 'stages'. For example, on beaches, in mountains, rainforests, coral reefs, national parks or nature reserves. These settings, Edensor (2001: 63) suggests, are 'distinguished by boundedness, whether physical or symbolic, and are often organized, or stage-managed, to provide and sustain common-sense understandings about what activities should take place there'. Tourist experience is thus socially and spatially regulated to varying extents and wildlife tour operators are no different in their construction of the ideal or desired tourist experience; the exception being that the outcome on a wildlife tour is never guaranteed; that animal performances are spontaneous and unpredictable. Tour operators can only lay the foundations of the experience and allow nature to perform the rest. For the tourist this adds to the adventure and authenticity, yet the desire for drama is ever present. For example, Desmond (1999: 188) narrates her experience of watching elephant seals and describes a scene whereby seals and pups lay motionless in a static landscape. For her it is like 'watching a movie'. Despite this there is an expectation of performance when at any moment it could change into a riot where the wildlife watcher is confronted with 'three tons of raging flesh in motion, charging towards them in fury'.

Such animal 'performances' are a key concept of the zoological tourist gaze. Tourist satisfaction is very often related to the performance as well as the presence of focal species, i.e. tourists want to see animals 'doing' something rather than just 'being' something. Wild animal 'performances' tend to relate to behaviour such as hunting, feeding young, nest building and gathering food. By being active participants, animals become 'agents' of the tourist experience (agency is defined as a 'relational achievement involving the creative presence of organic beings in the fabrics of everyday living' (Whatmore 2002: 26)). Nature arguably exerts agency over places; trees, flowers, animals and the topography are active co-constituents of place-making (Cloke and Jones 2001). Similarly focal species, for example, birds, whales and dolphins, the big five African safari animals (elephant, lion, rhino, buffalo and leopards) and animal migrations are enrolled by tour operators due to their predictable presence and ability to perform (Cloke and Perkins 2005). Place, wildlife and tourism thus become inter-related, assembled and marketed.

Davin (2005) therefore suggests that the worlds of tourism and television (and arguably place) overlap as a complex web of texts and hypertexts, and points to the possibility that the boundary between television watching and tourism can indeed become very blurred. When it comes to tourist motivations, Nielsen (2001: 51) proposes that expectations are 'rooted in a weave of preconceptions that have been formed over time from a variety of difference sources', not just television. This 'phase before the gaze' is an incredibly important precursor to tourist experiences and satisfaction. How people assimilate new messages into pre-existing belief structures, and how these beliefs then turn into tourist imaginings and ultimately tourist behaviour, is therefore important for wildlife tourism professionals to understand.

Yet there is much debate as to whether wildlife television creates particular social representations of the animal kingdom or whether it merely reflects existing ones. Dingwall and Aldridge (2006: 140) conclude that the closed, universal structure of wildlife programme narratives means that 'at crucial points, there is an ellipsis allowing viewers to hear the narration without disrupting whatever prior framing they have brought to their viewing'; thus suggesting that programmes do not attempt to challenge dominant societal views. Similarly, Champ (2002: 275) posits that 'prominent contemporary wildlife value orientations prompt media producers to create texts that appeal to (already) existing sensibilities with regards to animals and their welfare'.

How animals are socially represented in programmes, and/or misrepresented, underpins many of the anthropomorphic understandings and imaginings of the animal-other and particularly what constitutes attractive and charismatic species in a tourism setting. Social representations theory is a constructivist approach and comes from the work of Moscovici (1961). It concerns the way knowledge is conveyed by a society and shared by a social group. It explores how a 'reality' is socially constructed, how it is made meaningful and how it is communicated. The end result is that a 'reality' corresponds to the way a society mentally represents it. Animals exist both 'outside' human society and 'inside' human culture (Beardsworth and Bryman 2001: 85). They are presented to us as baby's toys, in stories, cartoons and fables, and appear as symbols for sports teams, brands and trademarks. Cats, dogs, birds, small mammals and even reptiles are accepted into our home environments. We learn to love and take care of them and they allow us insight into a non-human, animal otherness. Television programmes may merely reflect this anthropomorphic empathy with fellow creatures. Given our evolutionary history rooted in nature, it is perhaps no wonder that the animal kingdom outside our doors may hold fascination for us (Kellert and Wilson 1993) and this is why animals are so prevalent in the tourist experience (see Table 5.2).

Table 5.2   Use of animals in tourism

Captive wild animals 'attractions'	Wildlife viewing experiences/use of domestic animals
Zoos and safari parks	Safari game drives
Dolphinaria and marine parks	Walking/riding safaris
Animal sanctuaries	Wildlife viewing by boat
Animals used as photographic props	Scuba/snorkelling
Bird of prey demonstrations	Animal nesting sights
Animal circuses	Elephant riding
Crocodile wrestling	Camel/lama riding
Bear baiting and 'dancing'	Horse/mule/donkey riding
Elephant camps	Pack animals
Elephant/camel polo	Husky dog sleigh rides
Swimming with dolphins, sea lions etc.	Cage diving
Crocodile cage diving	Rodeo
Crocodile and snake farms	Bullfighting
Tiger farms	Hunting
Bear pits	Fishing
Turtle hatcheries	Wildlife souvenirs
Individual animals in hotels and casinos	Animal sacrifice
Magic shows using animals	Swimming with marine mega fauna
Animals in performances	

The relationship between audience and television media is thus a much researched and contested field of study. Early theorists posit that television content determines audience's beliefs; a viewpoint that ignores viewers' agency, preconceptions and prior ideas (Hall 1980). This view was eventually to shift towards the possibility of multiple meanings and an active audience who chooses what to believe (see Hermes 1995). That said, it is still assumed that media remain potentially influential in affecting how audiences see the world and that corporations such as the BBC's Natural History Unit have a high degree of institutional power. Messages, which are repeated, consistent and unambiguous, lack alternatives and come from a known, authoritative source, such as Sir David Attenborough, and the BBC are likely to have a higher impact on audiences' attitudes and beliefs (Clayton and Myers 2009, Dingwall and Aldridge 2006). Beardsworth and Bryman (2001: 86) likewise conclude that media representations 'and the ideological frameworks within which they are organised' come to dominate the ways in which wildlife is construed in contemporary cultures.

This is certainly true when it comes to environmental destruction. Despite the common apolitical commentary there does exist a strong narrative in wildlife programming which depicts declining biodiversity, loss of habitat, climate change and ominous environmental predictions which seemed to have entered the social psyche. In their research of polar bear tourism in Churchill, Canada, Lemelin et al. (2010) refer to the growing social angst about climate change, disappearing species and the subsequent desire to see places and species before they are gone. Indeed, a narrative analysis of *The Blue Planet: Frozen Seas*, (BBC1, 3 October 2001), regarding the lives of the polar bears of Churchill illustrates how programmes shape and reiterate the social representation of the plight of iconic species. Dingwall and Aldridge (2006: 143) describe an edited and narrated story of a single polar bear parent and her 'child' whose survival depends on the outcome of her hunt on the now diminishing pack ice:

> The narrator cannot know precisely what the female bear feels – but after five months without food he would feel hungry. Similarly he cannot know that the cub's tumbling has the same meaning as play to a human infant – but it looks similar and he feels confident in imputing this meaning...The bear's attack on a suspected seal hole is followed by a quick shot of a seal, which we are invited to think of as cowering in its lair, then it's back to the bear, then to the seal, the bear, the cub and finally the seal, diving and escaping. The viewer is told an emotive story which is made even more moving by the indeterminacy of the ending: will these bears live or die?

For the viewer, this represents a continuous story yet these are not contemporaneously filmed images. Instead it is an edited and highly constructed sequence which is determined by a selective choice of imagery that reflects the preferred narrative. The editing is deceptive; a different seal, a different time.

Research on how audiences receive these messages and decode them has yet to be assured. It is interesting that conservation psychologists such as Clayton and Myers (2009) claim that anthropomorphic narratives such as this are a natural human response when witnessing the lives of animals and are essential to conservation values. In the limited research that has been conducted, there is some evidence to suggest that programmes provoke a deeper psychological effect, which counters the purely visual spectacle. Champ (2002), for example, refers to wildlife media as having a 'grounding function' for viewers. 'Grounding' is a term drawn from psychological research on the meanings of objects in people's life-worlds. These objects then become tools to develop and maintain self-identity. In the case of wildlife programming, Champ's participants reveal how watching wildlife on television provides them with a space to reflect on the meaning of life, their own spirituality, the cycle of life, the essence of existence, their connection to Mother Nature and to *Planet Earth*, and most importantly how they feel or connect to animals and the environment.

This finding is akin to Curtin's exploration of the psychological benefits of wildlife tourist experiences (2009) and tourists' self-identity (2010b), where experiencing wildlife for real allowed participants a space to philosophise about themselves and the nature that surrounded them. This similarity suggests a naturally occurring, inherently human interest in the natural world, which is somewhat fulfilled by both virtual and real wildlife experiences. Some studies, however, suggest that our understanding of, and engagement with, nature arises more strongly out of real-life experiences with actual animals than intellectual engagement with them. Bulbeck (2005: xxiii) asserts that passion for nature and wildlife comes from 'physical contact with the "concrete" wild as opposed to mere knowledge of the "abstract" wild', which is produced through social discourse and media representations.

In the concrete wild, Rolston (1987: 187) describes the aesthetic experience of wildlife as 'spontaneous form in motion'. On film there is movement but for the most part it is scripted, therefore planned and programmed; controlling to a degree the audience response to it. In contrast, 'wild lives move themselves, and they move us' (ibid: 187). Excitement lies in the surprise as well as the anticipated. Wildlife 'have eyes that look into ours', and they make sounds; 'something is there behind the fur and the feathers, a centre of experience amidst the movement' (ibid: 187). When we see wildlife for real, there is intrusion into our own existence, intimacy and otherness. These experiences and imaginings are hard to capture by the social sciences as the aesthetic appeal of wildlife runs ahead of, and is deeper than, our cognitive thought process. Moreover aesthetic appeal is ultimately subjective and unknowable. As science often condemns subjectivity, it is little wonder that we do not understand the process of how the emotions and perceptions of nature conveyed in wildlife programmes awaken a desire for real wildlife tourism experiences. Yet they clearly do, as the following case study suggests.

Case study: BBC *Springwatch* **and** *Autumnwatch*

Springwatch *and* Autumnwatch *are annual BBC television programmes which follow the trials and tribulations of British wildlife during the changing of the seasons in the United Kingdom. The programmes are broadcast live from various locations around the country and are transmitted on BBC 2 during primetime television. They involve a crew of 100 and rely on over 50 remote cameras, making them the BBC's largest outside broadcast event. Many of the cameras are hidden and operated remotely to record natural behaviour, for example badgers outside their set, rutting deer, foxes and their cubs leaving the den and of birds in their nests.*

Springwatch *begins on the Spring bank holiday at the end of May and is broadcast four nights* each *week for three weeks. After the success of the first* Springwatch *in 2005, the BBC commissioned* Autumnwatch, *which is also broadcast once per week over eight weeks. The* Springwatch *brand has now expanded to incorporate further TV 'spin-offs' and specials. It also has a strong online presence with the website offering further video content and allows viewers and programme makers to interact through a message board, Flickr photography group and blogs. It encourages conservation and appreciation of British wildlife and has recently begun to encourage viewers to get out and visit locations in order to enjoy British wildlife for themselves (primarily aimed at the domestic/day trip tourism market).*

Research recently undertaken in the United Kingdom (both in-depth interviews and survey data) reveal how this popular, live, twice weekly programme on British wildlife has instilled or reawakened *an interest in trip taking to see Britain's wildlife. Survey data suggested that 30.3 per cent of visitors to Scotland were influenced by wildlife/ nature television programmes such as* Springwatch *(Scottish Government 2010).*

Tourists either decide what wildlife they want to see and choose their destination accordingly; alternatively they select their destination and then see what wildlife there is to see there. Tour operators and accommodation providers refer to them as the 'post Springwatch' *market and cater for them with suggested itineraries, by signposting wildlife hotspots and incorporating hides and webcams into their facilities,* and *in their marketing.*

The use of webcam technology in programmes like Springwatch *has also prompted tourist attractions to incorporate live webcam footage of nest sites and wildlife corridors on their land to offer another tier of entertainment to their visitors. Some attractions such as Scottish Sea Bird Centre at North Berwick are award winning wildlife tourism attractions which are based solely on webcam technology to bring the off-shore nesting seabirds and marine mammals within reach of land-based tourists. Rural based tourism accommodation businesses also use wildlife web-cams to differentiate themselves from their competitors and to provide added advantage for their guests; as do national parks and nature reserves.*

Whilst this is a welcome *market in Scotland, television programmes have been criticised for raising expectations and focusing only on charismatic species such as puffins, seals, dolphins, and whales (Scottish Government 2010).*

Conclusions

Tourist expectations of places and experiences are thus rooted in a web of imaginings and preconceptions that are built over a period of time. Information from social means can be moulded into a media image that can alter preconceptions and/or reinforce pre-existing beliefs (Nielsen 2001). Social representations of animals, their charisma, their behaviours and appeal are communicated through the use of pictures and images which are coded by wildlife programme makers and then somehow 'decoded' by the audience to form anticipatory images of animals and habitats (see Burgess 1990). For some members of the audience, this instils a desire to travel to specific places and habitats to witness this animal performance for themselves. However the information and the versions of reality regarding the animal kingdom, its behaviour and plight are called into question as television media must comply to a requisite formula that will appeal to the mass market. This makes the wildlife programme highly apolitical, scripted to conform to current animal sensibilities and carefully constructed and edited to reveal a strong 'storyline'.

From a wildlife tourism point of view, such programmes are considered highly influential in determining the appeal of focal species and destinations. Destinations, which report declining habitats and/or iconic species, have seen increases in visitation as social angst regarding climate change and declining animal populations take an emotional hold on audiences. Programmes have also reawakened an interest in endemic wildlife and have played a strong part in defining places to go to see charismatic species in the domestic market. Whilst this is a positive force for human engagement, recreation and support for conservation, television programmes have been criticised for creating hyper-real associations with specific animals and for raising tourist expectations with regards to abundance of species, proximity to wildlife and prolonged viewing.

Despite the popularity of these programmes, this genre of media has received little attention from academics and nature commentators. How much, for example, do they underpin knowledge and appreciation of species and how are media representations of wildlife received and assimilated by viewers? There is a wealth of academic tourism literature on the relationship between films, television series and tourism, yet virtually none based upon the connection between wildlife tourism and media representations of animals. This is surprising given the frequently mentioned correlation between television programmes and wildlife tourism demand. There now needs to be a large scale wildlife tourism survey to explore the basis of wildlife tourist motivations in relation to television programmes; particularly with regards to what type of programmes are influential, what messages they convey and how the border between being satisfied with virtual wildlife and wanting real wildlife tourism experiences is eventually crossed.

References

Ballantyne, R., Packer, J. and Hughes, K. 2009. Tourists' support for conservation messages and sustainable management practices in wildlife tourism experiences. *Tourism Management*, 30(5), 658–64.

Ballantyne, R., Packer, J. and Sutherland, L.A. 2010. Visitors' memories of wildlife tourism: implications for the design of powerful interpretive experiences. *Tourism Management*, 32(4), 770–79.

Bagust, P. 2008. 'Screen natures': special effects and edutainment in 'new' hybrid wildlife documentary. *Continuum: Journal of Media and Cultural Studies*, 22(2), 213–26.

Beardsworth, A. and Bryman, A. 2001. The Wild Animal in Late Modernity. *Tourist Studies*, 1(1), 83–104.

Bouse, D. 2000. *Wildlife Films*. Philadelphia: University of Pennsylvania Press.

Bulbeck, C. 2005. *Facing the Wild: Ecotourism, Conservation and Animal Encounters*. London: Earthscan.

Burgess, J. 1990. The production and consumption of environmental meanings in the mass media: a research agenda for the 1990s. *Transactions of the Institute of British Geographers* New Series, 15(2), 139–61.

Champ, J. 2002. A culturalist-qualitative investigation of wildlife media and value orientations. *Human Dimensions of Wildlife*, 7, 272–86.

Clayton, S. and Myers, G. 2009. *Conservation Psychology: Understanding and Promoting Human Care for Nature*. Chichester: John Wiley & Sons.

Cloke, P. and Jones, O. 2001. Dwelling, place and landscape: an orchard in Somerset. *Environment and Planning A*, 33, 649–66.

Cloke, P. and Perkins, H.C. 2005. Cetacean performance and tourism in Kaikoura, New Zealand. *Environment and Planning D: Society and Space*, 23, 903–24.

Conradson, D. 2007. Freedom, space and perspective: moving encounters with other ecologies, in J. Davidson, M. Smith, and L. Bondi (eds) *Emotional Geographies*. Aldershot: Ashgate Publishing Ltd., 103–16.

Cottle, S. 2004. Producing nature(s): on the changing production ecology of natural history TV. *Media, Culture and Society*, 26(1), 81–101.

Crouch, D., Jackson, R. and Thompson, F. (eds). 2005. *The Media and the Tourist Imagination*. Oxon: Routledge.

Curtin, S.C. 2009. Wildlife tourism: the intangible, psychological benefits of human-wildlife encounters. *Current Issues in Tourism: Special Issue on "animals in the tourism and leisure experience"*, 12(5), 451–74.

Curtin, S.C. 2010a. Managing the Wildlife Tourism Experience: The Importance of Tour Leaders. *International Journal of Tourism Research*, 12(3), 219–36.

Curtin, S.C. 2010b. The self-presentation and self-development of serious wildlife tourists. *International Journal of Tourism Research*, 12(1), 17–33.

Curtin, S.C. 2010c. *Watching the Performance: Wildlife Tourism in Britain and the "Springwatch" Factor*. The RGS-IBG Annual Conference, Imperial College, London, 1st–3rd September 2010.

Davin, S. 2005. Tourists and television viewers: some similarities in *The Media and the Tourist Imagination*, edited by D. Crouch, R. Jackson, and F. Thompson. Oxon: Routledge, 170–82.

DeMares, R. and Krycka, K. 1998. Wild animal triggered peak experiences: transpersonal aspects. *The Journal of Transpersonal Psychology*, 30(2), 161–77.

Department of Culture, Media and Sport. 2009. *The National Survey of Culture, Leisure and Sport.* Available from: DCMS.gov.uk

Desmond, J.C. 1999. *Staging Tourism: Bodies on Display from Waikiki to Sea World.* Chicago: The University of Chicago Press.

Dingwall, R. and Aldridge, M. 2006. Television wildlife programming as a source of popular scientific information: a case study of evolution. *Public Understanding of Science*, 15(2), 131–52.

Edensor, T. 2001. Performing tourism, staging tourism: (re)producing tourist space and practice. *Tourist Studies*, 1(1), 59–81.

Franklin, A. 1999. *Animals and Modern Cultures: A Sociology of Human-Animal Relations in Modernity*. London: Sage Publications.

Hall, S. 1980. 'Encoding and Decoding', in *Culture, Media and Language*, edited by S. Hall and the University of Birmingham Centre for Contemporary Cultural Studies. London: Hutchinson, 128–38.

Hermes, J. 1995. *Reading Women's Magazines: An Analysis of Everyday Media Use*. Cambridge: Policy Press/Basil Blackwell.

Higginbottom, K. 2004. (ed.) *Wildlife Tourism: Impacts, Management and Planning*. Victoria, Australia: Common Ground Publishing on behalf of the Cooperative Research Centre for Sustainable Tourism.

Kellert, S.R., and Wilson, E.O. (eds) 1993. *The Biophilia Hypothesis*. Washington, DC: Island Press.

Lemelin, H., Dawson, J., Stewart, E.J., Maher, P. and Lueck, M. 2010. Last-chance tourism: the boom, doom, and gloom of visiting vanishing destinations. *Current Issues in Tourism*, 13(5), 477–93.

Mabey, R. 2003. Shallow wildlife documentaries and sentimental nature writing. *The Guardian*, 15 March.

Mabey, R. 2005. *Nature Cure*. London: Chatto & Windus.

McIntosh, A.J., 1999. Into the tourist's mind: understanding the value of the heritage experience. *Journal of Travel & Tourism Marketing*, 8 (1), 41–64.

Mintel. 2008. Wildlife Tourism International. from Mintel Oxygen Web site: http://academic.mintel.com/sinatra/oxygen_academic/search_results/show&/display/d=349671. [accessed: June 21 2010].

Moscardo, G., Woods, B. and Greenwood, T. 2001. *Understanding Visitor Perspectives on Wildlife Tourism*. Wildlife Tourism Research Report Series, No. 2) Australia: Cooperative Research Centre for Sustainable Tourism.

Moscovici, S. 1961. *La Psychoanalyse: Son Image et Son Public*. Paris: Presses Universitaires de France.

Newsome, D., Dowling, R. and Moore, S. 2005. *Wildlife Tourism*. Aspects of Tourism Series. Clevedon: Channel View Publications.

Nielsen, C. 2001. *Tourism and the Media:* Frenchs Forest, NSW: Pearson Education Australia.

Philo, G. 2008. Active audiences and the construction of public knowledge. *Journalism Studies*, 9(4), 535–44.

Rolston, H. 1987. Beauty and the beast: aesthetic experience of wildlife, in *Valuing wildlife: Economic and Social Perspectives*, edited by D. J. Decker and G.R. Goff. Boulder CO: Westview Press, 187–96.

Scottish Government. 2010. *The Economic Impact of Wildlife Tourism in Scotland.* May 2010. Available from: http://www.scotland.gov.uk/Publications/2010/05/12164456/5. [accessed: 12 July 2011].

Shaw, G. and Williams, A.M. 2004. *Tourism and Tourism Spaces.* London: Sage Publications

Tremblay, P. 2002. Tourism wildlife icons: attractions of marketing symbols? *Journal of Hospitality and Tourism Management*, (9)2, 164–80.

United Nations Environment Programme (UNEP). 2006. *Wildlife Watching and Tourism: A study on the benefits and risks of a fast growing tourism activity and its impact on species.* Bonn: Produced by UNEP/CMS Convention of Migratory Species and TUI. Available from url: http//www.cms.int/publications/pdf/cms_wildlife watching pdf. [accessed: 12 April 2007].

Urry, J. 1990. *The Tourist Gaze: Leisure and Travel in Contemporary Society.* London: Sage.

Walpole, M.J. & Thouless, C.R. 2005. Increasing the value of wildlife through non-consumptive use? Deconstructing the myths of ecotourism and community-based tourism in the tropics, in *People and Wildlife: Conflict or Coexistence?*, edited by R. Woodroffe, et al. Cambridge: Cambridge University Press, 122–39.

Whatmore, S. 2002. *Hybrid Geographies.* London: Sage.

Chapter 6

Internet Cultures and Tourist Expectations in the Context of the Public Media Discourse

Nicolai Scherle and Ralph Lessmeister

Introduction

In the context of recent Internet cultures, especially in the case of Web 2.0, it becomes apparent that technological development often generates repetitive rituals in the public discourse about the media sector. While those in favour of new technologies often present themselves (or let others present them) as the media avant-garde, critical voices, as prophets of doom, are often picked up by the cultural pessimists among our contemporaries. In a discussion of the prevailing discourses, the consequences on the demand side and the supply in tourism are shown. In doing so, two central interests are pursued. First, the text provides a concise insight into recent public media discourses about tourism, and secondly, it develops recent theories in media research to further the existing understanding of tourism. Therefore, in this chapter some critical reflections will be presented, providing an overview of the current situation.

In order to do so, it is first of all necessary to reflect that societies constitute themselves through communication. In this context, communication is not simply understood as interpersonal or medial communication but, in an analogy to Luhmann (1995), as an abstract conception of a three-staged selection of information, messaging and comprehension. This concept can be applied to social groups on the micro or meso level (e.g. political parties, associations, but also companies or families), as well as to the global society of the twenty-first century, where no technological innovations have aroused more hopes in respect of the globalisation process than the Internet (e.g. Castells 2001, Chesbrough 2003, Beinhocker 2006). However, the ongoing process of digitalisation not only holds the potential to overcome obstacles in information and communication. Rather, in this process of cross-linking, conceptions of a new world and a global Internet culture are becoming manifest so much so that one could almost say that everybody is connected with everyone and everything at any time. The circuit boards and processors of today's computer chips become, as Meckel (2001: 61) rightly states, 'the neurons and synapses of a global brain'.[1] Just as neuronal

---

circuits in the human brain do not necessarily result in the production of sense, more digital cross-links do not automatically mean greater comprehension. In the concept of communication outlined above (based upon information, messaging and comprehension), the first two steps (in simple words: sending and receiving information) are similar all over the world. However, comprehension requires a distinct production of sense which depends to a high degree on socialisation and the environment, and therefore the potential for globalisation is increasingly called into question. Kneip (1999: 130) describes this fact metaphorically when he writes: 'The Internet makes the world a global village. But the name of the village is Babylon'.[2] In other words we can talk to each other but it remains rather uncertain if we really understand each other.

In this chapter, the rapid evolution that has occurred in the field of digital media will be reflected upon as it has, without any doubt, revolutionised tourism, at least with regard to its communication structures. The dynamics of this process have increased dramatically, with no end in sight (Hepp 2006). Web 2.0 is certainly the best known, but in no way the only, example in history if we think of the telegraph or telephone or, more recently the increasing importance of Smartphones, which also have revolutionised our way of communication. The increasingly networked global society has complex effects on many contexts of our daily life, for example on the forming of the political will (the most prominent example is probably the Arab Spring), online dating or buying behaviour. Precisely for this reason, one needs to critically examine these processes and their consequences to avoid blindly joining in the digitalisation euphoria, for one thing is sure: beyond all technological innovation, human beings remain the creator and the user of all the options recent technology offers. There are many aspects which support Meckel's idea of all our priorities, structures and differentiations in the analogue world being transferred to the digital world, under different conditions but with similar outcomes (Meckel 2000).

The following section will provide a brief account of the development of digitalisation. This is mainly for two reasons: on the one hand, developments in the field of media are inextricably bound up with societal changes; on the other, a historic-genetic perspective allows the contextualisation of recent structures and processes. In a theoretical perspective, this section will also give an incisive insight into the current public discourse about new media which is strongly characterised by normative aspects. Subsequently, the next section will refer to tourism, as this phenomenon has undergone a true technological revolution due to ongoing innovations in the field of new media. The chapter will be concluded by a problem focused résumé.

---

2   German original text: Das Internet macht zwar aus der Welt ein globales Dorf. Aber der Name des Dorfes ist Babylon. Translation by the authors.

Digitalisation as a Historical Process: A Problem-focused Review

If one tries to explain the ongoing digitalisation of our world solely from a deterministic, technological perspective, the complex interactions between techniques and social transformation processes would be neglected (see Dorer 2006). It is because of various interdependencies that one talks today about a network society or a society of connectivity. The media scientist Krotz (2006: 30) notes in this context:

> The fact that social, cultural and economic contexts and interdependencies, that the entire communicative, medially transmitted, and personal and social relations of people can be described by functional concepts such as networks or connectivity, is not only a consequence of globalization, but also one of individualization, mediatisation and commercialization. It is a general and common tendency of social life. [Translation by the authors]

What Krotz describes is certainly reflected most impressively in the global diffusion of the Internet. Its origins date back to the 1960s, when in the United States computers were cross-linked to form so-called Local Area Networks (*LAN*) or Wide Area Networks (*WAN*). From a historic-genetic perspective, based upon Lovink and Schultz (1999), the central phases in the development of the Internet and their implications on tourism are presented below:

- **Phase 1** (1969–1989) is mainly characterised by an enforced cross-linking of large capacity computers in military, science and big business contexts. Young people appropriate 'secret' technological knowledge, and so-called 'hackers' and 'cyberpunks' argue in favour of open access to the Net – often in a quite unconventional and not always legal manner. At this time, mysteries like disembodiment, hybridisation of man and machine, cyborgs and cybersex – all frenetically commented on by the scientific community – occurred.
- **Phase 2** (1989–1995) is strongly associated with the belief in a 'digital revolution'. It is the time of easy profits, utopias about the Net, but also the time when the Internet is heavily criticised. Diverging interests successively form a 'virtual class'. In this era first attempts to utilise digital media in the tourism industry were made, mainly on the level of national tourism boards, which provided information about their destinations in the form of digital brochures through the Internet.
- **Phase 3** (1995–2000) is the era of the 'dotcom bubble'. Numerous technology enterprises push onto the market and promise lucrative profits and price advantages, but in many cases they cannot meet the expectations. It comes to a necessary shakeout, and the investor's confidence in IT values is badly shaken. Whereas the Internet in this period is generally becoming increasingly important for the tourism industry, which uses it

as an information tool, its relevance for business transactions is still very limited. The market share of e-commerce is still on a negligible level, while bookings via telephone and television have reached a climax.

- **Phase 4** (2000–ca. 2005) involves increasing multimedia capability and interactivity of new media, which is reflected especially in the evolution of Web 2.0. The ongoing digital connectivity accelerates globalisation and concentration processes, while at the same time the question of political influence – for instance with regard to censorship versus freedom of speech or freedom of the press – appears on the agenda. The Internet as a medium for information has become a standard in tourism marketing and online reservation systems have become common practice in tourism Business to Business (B2B) transactions. But unlike in Business transactions, the Internet is still not able to unfold its full potential in Business to Consumer (B2C) transactions or in the relations between Consumer and Consumer, which can be seen as the crucial point in the use of new media in recent years.

- **Phase 5** (2005–today) The recent era sees the evolution of the Web 2.0 and the breakthrough of so called 'social media' as an ongoing process of technological refinement in which the two most important media – telephone and Internet – are combined in a new generation of mobile Internet devices (Smartphones, Smartbooks etc.) and the respective software. The Internet has become indispensable for many people's everyday life and – in contrast to the up to now unidirectional Web 1.0 – it allows for social interactions and relations between its users. Web 2.0 thereby follows the logics of a self-sustaining and self-regulating social system, which is based on references, ratings, comments and discussions of its members (Egger 2005). This crucial step in the media evolution of course brings dramatic changes to tourism as well. While services in tourism before had to be considered as credence goods, and the client as a passive recipient who had to rely on the information given by tourist suppliers, the collective experience of social networks shared in the Internet now empowers clients to estimate tourism offers in a profoundly new way. But although this process has tremendous consequences for the demand side as well as for the suppliers in tourism, there are still players on both sides who do not even utilise the potential of the Web 1.0, while others are already proceeding to a Web 3.0 (Longhi 2008).

While often referred to as a medium, it is perhaps more accurate to talk of the Internet as a 'space of communication' (Wilke 2009) that offers opportunities for many different modes of communication. It only partly fulfils the function of classic distribution media; its main function has become one for direct communication between persons, or the searching for and processing of information (Krotz 2006, Jansson 2007, Scherle and Hopfinger 2007).

In particular, Web 2.0 with its numerous new interactive online offers has given important impulses to direct communication. While people used the Internet in a passive manner some years ago to search and inform themselves, for example about opening hours or listings of hotels or guesthouses, Web 2.0 has meant a profound paradigm shift: following the slogan of a 'participatory Web', it shows the various possibilities of participation, which are mainly used by social networks and virtual communities, such as Internet message boards, online chat rooms or web forums (Amersdorffer et al. 2012).

The evolution of new media technologies is generally closely related to the supporting public discourse (see Dorer 2006). Therefore, it is necessary to further investigate societal expectations and how the Internet, and especially Web 2.0, is related to changes in such public discourse.

Internet Cultures, Societal Expectations and the Public Discourse

Like no other media, the Internet has become related to the idea of a general democratisation in public communication. The theoretic background for this can be found in the Habermasian paradigm of a non-hierarchical discourse (Habermas 1981). This ideal type of human communication implies that societies contribute best to the solving of their political problems by reflection and reasoning. The central premise, however, is that all social actors abandon large parts of their egoistic interests, and the whole communication process is not influenced by political or economic issues (see Mai 2007).

Development and changes in the field of the media are not only part of socioeconomic transformations, but also an expression of specific expectations in our society (see Marr 2005, Zillien 2009). It is a system-immanent phenomenon that not all of these expectations can be fulfilled, and therefore polarised patterns of perception and appraisal can be found. Generally, two diverging points of view in the discussion on digitalisation may be distinguished: on the one hand, euphoria over technology – just think of the hype when a new Smartphone generation is released – associated with the idea of a revolution in human coexistence, and on the other hand there is scepticism and pessimism about the cultural and social consequences. Both perspectives can be considered as phenomena that are inherent to the medial system, appearing every time a newly emerging media is about to outstrip an established one. In connection with the introduction of TV and radio, for example, Dorer (2006: 355) says:

> The introduction and establishment of the Internet was bound up with the same myths which had accompanied the introduction of radio and TV: on the one hand, cultural pessimism which found its expression in restrictive media education and public welfare-orientated media politics, and on the other hand a cultural optimism of the kind we are already familiar with from Brecht's radio theory.

Its credo back then – exactly as for the Internet today – was: every receiver is a potential transmitter. [Translation by the authors]

One of the best-known cultural-pessimistic pieces of literature in the context of media criticism is the polemic book *Amusing Ourselves to Death*. In it, the American media scholar, Neil Postman, describes the transformation from book printing to the television era as a profound cultural change, in which serious content is increasingly displaced by entertainment. As Postman (1985: 8) writes:

> To say it, then, as plainly as I can, this book is an inquiry into and a lamentation about the most significant American cultural fact of the second half of the twentieth century: the decline of the Age of Typography and the ascendancy of the Age of Television. This change-over has dramatically and irreversibly shifted the content and meaning of public discourse, since two media so vastly different cannot accommodate the same ideas. As the influence of print wanes, the content of politics, religion, education, and anything else that comprises public business must change and be recast in terms that are most suitable to television.

Postman (ibid.), who conceives of media mainly as metaphors, assumes the introduction of new technology not only broadens human possibilities, but that along with the diffusion of technology, the cognitive patterns of human beings and the content of their culture will be transformed. Referring to television, he warns especially of an increasing trivialisation, imposed on us by the entertainment industry. Regrettably, media critics are often characterised by distinct polarisation, with only little space for modifying nuances; this can best be explained by the role of the media as the fourth estate, often labelled with normative connotations, and the fact that the vision of an information society is always related to the hope for social and political progress. Against this background, we will highlight in the following section how the intensified digitalisation of our society affects travelling and tourism.

Touristic Internet Cultures

Today's tourism structures would certainly be unimaginable without the recent developments in the field of new media. This is not only true of the structural changes induced by new information and communication media, but also for the journalistic valorisation of the 'travel bug', which increasingly follows alternate and innovative paths (see Scherle and Hopfinger 2007, Buhalis and Law 2008, Kleinsteuber and Thimm 2008). Due to the increased global linking of local information systems and the connection of a huge number of private households – at least in technologically developed countries – the Internet has significantly optimised access to information and considerably lowered search costs for information (Bourreau, Gensollen and Perani 2002, Porter 2004, Amersdorffer et al. 2012). The implications for the supply side, as well as for the demand side, are serious: local travel agencies for instance lose their distribution monopoly for conventional package tours, while at the same time new online agencies gain a place in the market by using the manifold possibilities of the new media, thus responding perfectly to the demands of the hybrid consumer (see Teltzrow, Günther and Pohle 2003, Günther and Hopfinger 2009). Whether booking a flight, accommodation, a rental car, a concert ticket or even thalassotherapy, digital media gives the consumer – depending on the level of experiences with new media – relatively uncomplicated access to the multifaceted holiday world he or she knew previously only through local travel agencies or travel catalogues.

The effects of these transformation processes are that the hitherto mainly linear value chains have been largely replaced by complex value networks, which generate not only new informational and economic transactions between tourism enterprises and consumers (B2C), but also between enterprises (B2B), as well as between consumers (C2C). This results in quite different opportunities and risks for individual actors. In this context Amersdorffer et al. (2012: 180) state:

> Customers receive the same status in the communication process as the previous gatekeepers and transmitters. Communication processes do no longer happen unidirectional but multidirectional between consumers, between consumers and gatekeepers and between consumers and institutions. Communication through media is associated with the social web in a process of individualisation due to the changes. However, the democratisation of the Internet does not lead to a complete equality in the communication context. In traditional communication models, the organisational position of the transmitter decided on the influence of communication processes, though, today this has been substituted by socio-Darwinist patterns: the attention in social networks and social applications as well as the mastery of the principles of communication and technology are the key factors for the domination of communication processes and social networks.

If one tries to describe the influence of E-commerce on value creation in tourism, it first has to point out that in this context territorial borders have significantly lost their importance (see Wynne et al. 2001, Egger 2005). The Internet provides a new distribution channel, in which new virtual value chains have been built up. They mainly comprise online activities like the providing of information about destinations, and making bookings. This enables some tourism actors to reduce costs and to increase their productivity, while at the same time the influence of other players – especially intermediary ones – is waning (see Anderson 2008, Wynne et al. 2001, Zerfaß and Sandhu 2008). Also an increasing trend towards specialisation and the breaking up of established value configurations can be observed, along with the co-option of enterprises, which means that they compete and cooperate at the same time (Werthner and Ricci 2004: 103, Rayman-Bacchus and Molina 2001: 597). Here again, the Internet is an appropriate medium, which allows for the integration of tourism players who serve the customers' demands for quick interaction, transparency, linked offers and low prices.

Against this background, there is one aspect which is likely to be overlooked: for tourism players in developing countries, the Internet is an uncomplicated and inexpensive opportunity to offer their products and services on the global market – presuming that they manage to gain consumer trust and the necessary reputation (see Lessmeister 2009). To name only one example, one may think of small and medium incoming agencies which often do not have sufficient personnel or financial means to participate in tourism fairs, like the ITB (Internationale Tourismusbörse Berlin) or the WTM. (World Travel Market, London). It is right here that digital media can make a huge contribution to the economic integration of these tourism players (see Scherle and Hopfinger 2007).

For quite some time now, the transformation process outlined above has gone hand in hand with another medial development, the ongoing convergence of what were once separately operating media. Media producers combine contents and services, which until recently were marketed in completely different ways. To link converging media services with tourism services in a further step is a consistent one, not only in the light of the resulting synergistic effects (see Kleinsteuber and Lühmann 2001, Pan and Fesenmaier 2006). Concrete examples of this are TV shows in which hotels are presented together with their homepage, so that they can be booked by the potential client online. It is obvious – at least from a critical perspective – that the interests of the media and the tourism industry converge in a way that could, without any doubt, pose a threat to journalistic freedom. While the amalgamation of information and advertising in television is already often criticised, this has become much more virulent in the context of social media, as the case of Facebook demonstrates: a company that is almost paradigmatically criticised for being infiltrated by advertising.

From a consumer's perspective, probably the biggest innovation is the development of the Internet to a 'participatory Net' whose self-conception is primarily based on the participation of its users, or rather on the *customer-generated content*. Here, individual touristic experience is shared through forums, blogs or wikis with a tourism-related *community*. In this context, Web 2.0 basically acts as a soundboard for the exchange of information or travel advice (Molz 2004, Pudliner 2007, Litvin, Goldsmith and Pan 2008).

In this connection there is a clear empowerment of the demand side, as customers have to rely on the information given to them by tourist providers less often. Amersdorffer et al. (2012: 181) note: 'communication through media in the age of the social web is no longer defined by the influence but by the choice of the communication tool and contents. Activities like "self broadcasting", "ego boosting" or "social involvement"…can be understood as experiences with an internal impact of the individual'. This is invaluable, especially if one is not familiar with the encrypted formulations used in travel catalogues. More than one blogger has exposed a supposed bargain for a 4-star hotel as a rip-off in the concrete jungle, and many a paradisiacal and unspoiled beach described in glossy brochures is set in a more realistic light, when forums speak of flotsam that has been lying around for years. It seems to be evident that social media users generally put more trust in their own community than in commercial statements which mainly pursue economical aims.

The consequences of these transformative processes go even further: consumers today have insights into the services market which they never had before; this market transparency leads to a significant quality displacement. Moreover, tourism brands are hard to govern from top down, and the role of tourism intermediaries is likely to change profoundly. Another change-over is seen in the fact that actively searching the Internet – for instance for certain destinations or tourism providers – has largely been replaced by a more passive process in which friends or acquaintances provide hints and information.

Especially among younger people, the so-called digital-natives, the openness of most of these communities is based on an enormous leap of faith, which many tourism providers are envious of. It is therefore not really surprising that more and more tourism providers try to take advantage of digital media by adding their own communities to established Internet portals, or even by creating their own (Pan and Fesenmaier 2000, Katz 2002). Generally, there is nothing to be said against this practice, but it becomes problematic when these online portals are undermined by hidden advertising in the form of subtly placed, unmarked PR messages appearing to be ordinary contributions. When professional marketing interests unduly overlay the actual content of such portals, they will lose their main capital, which is their credibility; these networks live from the idea that people help and advise others without any financial motivation (see Dohler 2008).

There is no doubt that the most fascinating aspect of the ongoing process of digitalisation is that the demand side now has access to formerly unimaginable ways of travelling. In virtual worlds like data highways or chat rooms, which came to life in the 'communication room Internet' (Wilke 2009), physical space has lost its importance. To an Internet surfer at the beginning of the third millennium, travelling has become borderless and free from physico-spatial restrictions, while being localised in global villages. Entering new – virtual – spaces, which – in analogy to artificial worlds – are not to be seen as a 'do or don't' alternative to conventional travelling, but rather as an expansion of previous offers (see Krüger 2001). But in the complex and fragmented virtual world of cyberspace, tourists now have to face one big challenge: increasing confusion about the unmanageable number of offers and possibilities. They permanently have to deal with the question of what to read, listen to, see or visit first, and of deciding which offer best suits their expectations.

Summary

The global diffusion of the Internet and its evolution to Web 2.0 in particular, has changed the tourist world profoundly. With just a few mouse clicks we can (virtually) go from Acapulco to Zaragoza and from Austria to Patagonia, and almost instantaneously, within the 'blink of an eye', we can obtain not only geographical and historical information about any destination, but also tips and tricks and 'secret knowledge', which remain hidden for most of the classic print media recipients. Which travel guide can inform you about the current weather conditions at any given destination, and connect you directly to the booking system of a hotel there? And which travel magazine is able to provide up-to-date information about the program of a cultural festival? These examples show that the Internet has proved its worth, especially when it comes to availability and immediacy of information and services. In this context, it can be considered a useful complement to conventional tourism media.

Especially with regard to the interaction between the supply and demand sides, the new online reality represents a radical change, with the latter experiencing an up to now unknown degree of empowerment. Web-users can for example recommend a website and therefore trigger a wave of interest, while on the other hand competitors or self-proclaimed commentators may appear, claiming to reveal perceived deficits or even false information by presenting their own point of view. It therefore has become crucial for tourism companies to engage in the corresponding development, particularly in the context of a strategic complaint management. In the ideal case, they manage to incorporate clients as 'external collaborators' into their business process in order to expand their own perspective.

Anticipating future developments in the field of digital media is very difficult, but all the signs point to the fact that the Internet will keep its catalysing function in the compression of time and space. The ongoing virtualisation of our lives will blur the media-immanent distinction between 'here and there', and 'past, recent and future' (Virilio 1991, White and White 2006). This process calls for the user not only to act and react within very short time (Menzel 1998), but engage proactively as an ever reflective and continuously information-seeking recipient. Furthermore, as Meyrowitz (2005) or Günther and Hopfinger (2009) state, the above outlined processes of virtualisation evoke an ongoing trivialisation or demystification of far off places, as new technologies extend the familiar surroundings. In the end the whole world could become a global village in the sense of McLuhan (1971) – a village one may enter as a native but cannot leave as a tourist; the established linkage between travelling (in the sense of spatial mobility) and escaping from everyday life is increasingly severing. The oversupply of information, services and offers is probably the biggest challenge for the virtual tourist in this context. In the end, he or she may come to the conclusion that the best thing to do is to shut down the computer and simply stay at home.

References

Amersdorffer, D., Bauhuber, F. and Oellrich, J. 2012. The economic and cultural aspects of the social web: implications for the tourism industry. *Journal of Vacation Marketing*, 18(3), 175–84.

Anderson, C. 2008. *The Long Tail: Why the Future of Business Is Selling Less of More*. München: Carl Hanser.

Beinhocker, E. 2006. *The Origins of Wealth: Evolution, Complexity, and the Radical Remaking of Economics*. Boston: Harvard Business Press.

Bourreau, M., Gensollen, M. and Perni, J. 2002. *Economies of Scale in the Media Industry*. Available at: http://www.gensollen.net [accessed: 22 October 2012]

Buhalis, D. and Law, R. 2008. Progress in information technology and tourism management. 20 years on and 10 years after the Internet. The state of etourism research. *Tourism Management*, 29(4), 609–23.

Castells, M. 2001. *The Internet Galaxy: Reflections on the Internet, Business and Society*. Oxford: Oxford University Press.

Chesbrough, H.W. 2003. *Open Innovation: The New Imperative for Creating and Profiting from Technology*. Boston: Harvard University Press.

Dohler, C. 2008. Der Klick zum Bär. *Die Zeit*, 33 (11 August), 56.

Dorer, J. 2006. Das Internet und die Genealogie des Kommunikationsdispositivs: Ein medientheoretischer Ansatz nach Foucault, in *Kultur – Medien – Macht: Cultural Studies und Medienanalyse*, edited by A. Hepp et al. Wiesbaden: VS Verlag für Sozialwissenschaften, 353–65.

Egger, R. 2005. *Grundlagen des eTourism: Informations – und Kommunikationstechnologien im Tourismus*. Aachen: Shaker.

Günther, A. and Hopfinger, H. 2009. Neue Medien – neues Reisen? Wirtschafts- und kulturwissenschaftliche Perspektiven der eTourismus Forschung. *Zeitschrift für Tourismuswissenschaft*, 1(2), 121–50.

Habermas, J. 1981. *Theorie des kommunikativen Handelns 1*. Frankfurt a.M.: Suhrkamp.

Hepp, A. 2006. *Transkulturelle Kommunikation*. Konstanz: UVK-Verlagsgesellschaft.

Jansson, A. 2002. Spatial phantasmagoria. The mediatization of tourism experience. *European Journal of Communication*, 17(4), 429–43.

Katz, J. 2002. Here come the weblogs, in *We've Got Blog: How Weblogs are Changing our Culture*, edited by J. Rodzvilla. Cambridge: Perseus Publishing.

Kleinsteuber, H. and Lühmann, D. 2001. Reisejournalismus: Phantasieprodukte für den Ohrensessel? *Tourismus Journal*, 5(1), 97–113.

Kleinsteuber, H. and Thimm, T. 2008. *Reisejournalismus: Eine Einführung*. Wiesbaden: Verlag für Sozialwissenschaften

Kneip, A. 1999. Internet: Ein Dorf namens Babylon. *Der Spiegel*, 15 March, 128–34.

Krotz, F. 2006. Konnektivität der Medien: Konzepte, Bedingungen und Konsequenzen, in *Konnektivität, Netzwerk und Fluss. Konzepte gegenwärtiger Medien-, Kommunikations- und Kulturtheorie*, edited by A. Hepp, F. Krotz, S. Moores and C. Winter. Wiesbaden: Verlag für Sozialwissenschften, 21–41.

Krüger, R. 2001. Zwischen Strandurlaub und Internet: Räume des Reisens. *Tourismus Journal*, 5(3), 365–74.

Lessmeister, R. 2009. Why selling dreams brings power, but making dreams come true does not: governance, power and coordination in special tourism value chains. *Journal für Entwicklungspolitik/Austrian Journal for Development Studies*, (25), 129–49.

Litvin, S.W., Goldsmith, R.E. and Pan, B. 2008. Electronic word-of-mouth in hospitality and tourism management. *Tourism Management*, (29), 458–68.

Longhi, C. 2008. *Usages of the Internet and e-tourism. Towards a new economy of tourism.* Available at: http://halshs.archives-ouvertes.fr/docs/00/27/77/67/ PDF/New_Economy_of_Tourism.pdf [accessed: 22 October 2012]

Lovink, G. and Schultz, P. 1999. Aus der Schatzkammer der Netzkritik, in: *Kommunikation – Medien – Macht*, edited by R. Maresch and N. Werber. Frankfurt: Suhrkamp, 299–328.

Luhmann, N. 1995. Was ist Kommunikation? in *Soziologische Aufklärung 6. Die Soziologie und der Mensch*, edited by N. Luhmann. Opladen: Westdeutscher Verlag, 113–24.

Mai, M. 2007. Die Informationsgesellschaft als Utopie und Versprechen. *Die Politische Meinung*, (450), 14–20.

Marr, M. 2005. *Internetzugang und politische Informiertheit: Zur digitalen Spaltung der Gesellschaft.* Konstanz: UVK-Verlagsgesellschaft.

McLuhan, M. 1971. *The Gutenberg Galaxy: The Making of Typographic Man.* London: Routledge & Kegan Paul.

Meckel, M. 2000. Die Medien-Matrix. Konturen und Schnittstellen des Computerzeitalters, in *Cyberworlds. Computerwelten der Zukunft*, edited by M. Meckel and M. Ravenstein. Ottobrunn: Trurnit & Partner, 9–36.

Meckel, M. 2001. *Die globale Agenda: Kommunikation und Globalisierung.* Wiesbaden: Westdeutscher Verlag.

Menzel, U. 1998. *Globalisierung versus Fragmentierung.* Frankfurt: Suhrkamp.

Meyrowitz, J. 2005. The rise of glocality: new senses of place and identity in the global village, in *A Sense of Place: The Global and the Local*, edited by K. Nyíri. Wien: Studien Verlag, 21–30.

Molz, J.G. 2004. Playing online and between the lines: round-the-world-web-sites as virtual places to play, in *Tourism Mobilities: Places to Play, Places in Play*, edited by M. Sheller and J. Urry. London: Routledge, 169–80.

Pan, B. and Fesenmaier, D.R. 2006. A typology of tourism-related web-sites: its theoretical background and implications. *Information Technology and Tourism*, 3(3), 155–76.

Pan, B. and Fesenmaier, D.R. 2006. Online information search: Vacation planning process. *Annals of Tourism Research* 3(33), 809–32.

Porter, M.E. 2004. *Competitive Advantage: Creating and Sustaining Superior Performance.* New York: Free Press.

Postman, N. 1985. *Amusing Ourselves to Death. Public Discourse in the Age of Show Business.* New York: Penguin Books.

Pudliner, B.A. 2007. Alternative literature and tourist experience: travel and tourist weblogs. *Journal of Tourism and Cultural Change*, 5(1), 46–59.

Rayman-Bacchus, L. and Molina, A. 2001. Internet-based tourism services: business issues and trends. *Futures*, 33(7), 589–605.

Scherle, N. and Hopfinger, H. 2007. Tourismus und Medien zu Beginn des 21. Jahrhunderts, in *Tourismusforschung in Bayern: Aktuelle sozialwissenschaftliche Ansätze. München*, edited by A. Günther et al. Munich/Vienna: Profil, 363–70.

Teltzrow, M., Günther, O. and Pohle, C. 2003. Analyzing Consumer Behavior at Retailers with Hybrid Distribution Channels – A Trust Perspective, in *Proceedings of the 5th International Conference on Electronic Commerce*, Pittsburgh, 422–8. Available at: http://public.management.uottawa.ca/~benyoucef/public/OnlineReputation/p422-teltzrow.pdf [accessed 30 July 2013].

Virilio, P. 1991. Das öffentliche Bild, in *Digitaler Schein. Ästhetik der elektronischen Medien.*, edited by F. Rötzer. Frankfurt: Suhrkamp, 343–45.

Werthner, H. and Ricci, F. 2004. E-Commerce and tourism, *Communications of the ACM*, 47(12), 101–5.

White, N.R. and White, P.B. 2006. Home and away: tourists in a connected world. *Annals of Tourism Research*, 34(1), 88–104.

Wilke, J. 2009. Multimedia/Online-Medien, in *Fischer Lexikon Publizistik Massenkommunikation*, edited by E. Noelle-Neumann et al. Frankfurt: Fischer Taschenbuchverlag, 329–58.

Wittel, A. 2006. Auf dem Weg zu einer Netzwerk-Sozialität, in *Konnektivität, Netzwerk und Fluss. Konzepte gegenwärtiger Medien-, Kommunikations- und Kulturtheorie*, edited by A. Heppet al. Wiesbaden: Verlag für Sozialwissenschften, 163–88.

Wynne, C., Berthon, P., Pitt, L., Ewing, M. and Napoli, J. 2001. The impact of the Internet on the distribution value chain: the case of the South African tourism industry. *International Marketing Review*, 18(4), 420–31.

Zerfaß, A. and Sandhu, S. 2008. Interaktive Kommunikation, Social Web und Open Innovation: Herausforderungen und Wirkungen im Unternehmenskontext, in *Kommunikation, Partizipation und Wirkungen im Social Web, Strategien und Anwendungen: Perspektiven für Wirtschaft, Politik und Publizistik, Neue Schriften zur Online Forschung*, edited by A. Zerfaß et al. Köln: Halem, 283–310.

Zillien, N. 2009. *Digitale Ungleichheit: Neue Technologien und alte Ungleichheiten in der Informations- und Wissensgesellschaft*. Wiesbaden: Verlag für Sozialwissenschaften.

Chapter 7

A Comparative Analysis of the Projected and Perceived Images of Gloucester

Kathryn Bell

Research suggests a strong tie between tourism and imagery; a notion supported by Burns (2007) and Feighey (2005), with the former asserting that tourism is image rich. The fact that images are subjective and affected by a range of factors (Camprubi et al. 2008) encounters issues of perception. Within the arena of tourism, the factors affecting perception are based on both the cognitive and affective components of an image (Alcaniz et al. 2009), and the inputs that contribute to these, including organic and induced attributes. Crucial to tourism is the important, if not central role, that destination image plays in consumer decision-making (Alcaniz et al. 2009). Whilst this research does not aim to explore the decision-making process, it does serve to elaborate on the importance of the projected and perceived image, and assess the importance of congruency for a competitive tourist destination. The research will critically examine the important relationship between the tourist and the destination through the images communicated and mediated. The research will discuss how new forms of technology and the continually changing world of web 2.0 and user-generated content mediate tourism spaces and alter the tourist gaze. A need therefore arises to highlight the evolving management challenges and assess how new medias 'give sense to everyday life' (Nogues-Pedregal 2008: 229). The research will utilise the theoretical and conceptual foundations of image production and consumption spanning theories and constructs from marketing, to psychology and sociology. Building upon research by authors such as Garrod (2007, 2008, 2009) and Garlick (2002), and exploring Tribe's (2004) concept of new realities and mediation of tourism spaces and ultimately knowledge creation in tourism, this research intends to critically examine the changing relationship between the projected and perceived images.

In the following chapter, the image of Gloucester, England will be analysed using official marketing material and participant generated photographs, critically comparing its projected and perceived image. Alongside this, an assessment of the importance of congruency between the two will test concepts that the projection and perception of a destination image is changing, due to utilisation of user-generated content and ubiquitous new technologies to project an image. Much of the tourism research based on imagery generally aims to analyse a specific attribute of an image (Dwivedi et al. 2009). However, this research is more pluralistic in its aim, comparatively analysing the complexities of projected and perceived visual images of Gloucester. In particular, this research will concentrate on the visual imagery that contributes to the overall destination image rather than any one specific attribute. Furthermore, whilst visual images include photographs, films or images (Palmer 2009), this research will specifically analyse the visual imagery within photographs. Using the relatively new method of Visitor Employed Photography (VEP) (Garrod 2007, 2008, 2009), also known as respondent led photo elicitation (Stedman et al. 2004), participants in Gloucester will take the lead in the collection of their perceived images of the city to compare to a range of projected images produced by the destination. The research design has utilised a triangulated approach based on a framework of Visitor Employed Photography (VEP), content and semiotic analysis to act as a discourse in order to provide the frame of reference for this research. The use of the visual methods of VEP to elicit perceptions will empower participants in an area vulnerable to subjective interpretation, and is fundamental to the scope of the research and trends in online photo sharing (Xiang and Gretzel 2010) in distinguishing between the roles of industry and tourists in image creation.

Image Research in Context

Image research is well established, with the idea of a destination image coined in the 1970s (Grosspeitch 2006, Pike 2008), and further conceptualised by Gartner (1993). In the decades since, research has generally followed trends to utilise somewhat restrictive researcher-led methods of enquiry such as surveys analysing specific image attributes, and explorative methods of enquiry analysing the holistic image (Mackay and Couldwell 2004). The use of photographic imagery by tourism destinations has resulted in imagery becoming part of normal life, or as Branthwaite (2002: 164) suggests, 'part of everyday experience'. On that point, Scarles (2004) suggests that tourists and destinations have become immersed in a world of non-verbal communication reliant on imagery. This assimilation into everyday life has had an impact on consumer behaviour and the process of marketing a destination. Social media and photo sharing has further led to what can be termed as a 'collective intelligence' (Xiang and Gretzel 2010: 180), and a new age of consumer-led image building. This is compounded due to the interactive nature of the Internet (Govers and Go 2005), which can add new dimensions to a destination image. With the development of Web 2.0 and use of website communities, there is the potential to compound this intelligence further and understand the changing nature of images within destination marketing.

Defining the Image

Whilst the photographic image has become part of everyday western life, there are still issues with the conceptualisation of the image. An image according to Stern et al. (2001) is the outcome of a transaction between a signifier and a receiver, resulting in a perception (image). However, there is little distinction between different types of images. Forrester (2000) and Stern et al. (2001) refer to what is mentally constructed by the consumer and that constructed by the external world. From this, it becomes apparent why defining an image, and in particular a destination image, is an obscure task. Research has endeavoured to define this much-used term (Stern et al. 2001, Tasci et al. 2007), often referring to either the process of perceiving or projecting an image. However, Edwards (1996, cited in Hunter 2008) defines a destination image as a representation of a destination, which can be made up of denotative (the actual image represented) and connotative (metaphorical implications of the image) elements. This provides a distinction between what can be typified as the projected and perceived image, and illustrates the practical issues when communicating an image.

The Formation of Images

How images are formed is well researched with Mackay and Couldwell (2004) discussing the cognitive and affective formation attributes, and Gunn (1988, cited in Pike 2008) and Gartner (1993) distinguishing between organic and induced components. Litvin and Mouri (2009) suggest that research illustrates the development of a destination image is a fluid process. The consumer will encounter the image of a destination through projected and perceived images to create a holistic image of a destination. It is dependent upon whether the consumer receives contrasting or congruent images as to whether one can influence another. Much destination image research suggests that a destination can have a control over the image distributed, from images used in marketing to the perception of actual and potential tourists (Camprubi et al. 2008, Govers and Go 2005). A lack of research into destinations not always in control of image formation exists, with authors such as Jani and Hwang (2011) touching on this concept. This provides scope for this research to discuss further, in an age of Internet photo sharing, the transfer in power from traditional image formers, such as destination management organisations (DMOs), to tourists and opens up concepts of a multi-way process of communication. This communication and online photo sharing led by consumers alters Miguel and Pedregal's (2008) tourism spaces to become virtual spaces online where tourists mediate and develop a place image.

Echtner and Ritchie (2003) summarise the factors that influence the construction of the mental image as functional characteristics that can be observed or measured, psychological characteristics that cannot be measured and individual attributes that contribute to the holistic impression; the destination image. The authors conceptualise the destination image, incorporating both a destination's salient attributes and holistic impressions, providing a succinct overview of the image formation process. Considering this, Alcaniz et al. (2009) argues that the most accepted consensus is that the image comprises two main components; the cognitive and the affective; the mental responses to stimuli. Working together, these dimensions add up to create an overall impression of a destination (Mackay and Couldwell 2004), and more specifically a perception.

The Perception of Images

Barthes's (1977) theory of semiology is fundamental to the understanding of perception of visual images, alluding to the complexity of meanings conveyed through photographic images. When perceiving, a tourist breaks an image down into component parts. As tourist places have become immersed in the language of visuals, tourists have to decode the messages within the images. This decoding of images links to the foundation of semiotics; the concept of a sign, in this case a photographic image, as being the relationship between the signifier and the signified. This, as Urry (2002) promotes, has resulted in the transition from tourists to semioticians. To assess the salient attributes of, and the holistic destination image, Tapachai and Waryszak (2000) propose five characteristics of an image: functional, social, emotional, epistemic and conditional, evaluated during perception.

Perception or 'the gaze' (Urry 2002) of a tourist upon a destination image is created through many mediums, including photography, to provide either a reality or staged reality for consumers to gaze upon, which the consumer believes to be real. Linking back to the concepts of semiological signs, the construction of the gaze through signs, and photographs, are the outcome of capturing the signs. What becomes an issue when a tourist gazes upon a photographic image is that the image may not be realistic, therefore affecting congruency between the projected and perceived image. Thus eluding that projected photographic imagery creates idealised images constructed for the viewer (Scarles 2004) or indeed, as the research tends to neglect, by the viewer. Whilst, historically, photography was viewed as objective (Deacon et al. 2007), the current consensus is that destination images tend to not reflect the reality of a destination (Dewar et al. 2007) and are surrounded by historical, aesthetic and cultural frames of reference. Digital technology has contributed to this with Branthwaite (2002) discussing the normality of images that are selected, cropped and edited, becoming 'proprioception of fragments of reality' (Scarles 2009: 469). Urry (2002: 128) highlights how professional photography actively constructs aestheticised and idealised images 'devoid of cars, people, bad weather, litter'. Although, perhaps as a counter balance to this, the use of social media to share photos online can offer a realistic image, showing litter, grey skies and so on.

Whilst technology can affect the reality and actuality of a destination image, much wider influences can impact upon what is photographed and perceived. This notion is imperative to this research, based on the concept of a hermeneutic circle (Urry 2002) or a circle of representation, as explored by Caton and Santos (2008) and Jenkins (2003), who suggest a cycle by which certain attributes of a

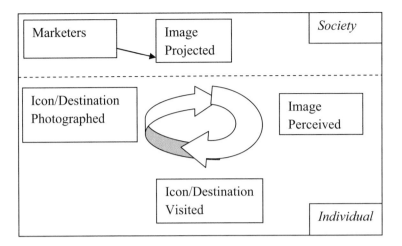

Figure 7.1   Circle of representation

Source: Jenkins, O.H. 2003. Photography and travel brochures: The circle of representation, *Tourism Geographies*, 5(3), 305–328. Reprinted by permission of Taylor & Francis Ltd.

destination image are perpetuated (see Figure 7.1), and as Scarles (2009) defines (re)encountered. In this process, technology can act as a catalyst in changing the dynamics of destination marketing and image communications. The consumer increasingly acts as the (co)producer where the circle embeds images of destination.

Figure 7.1 illustrates both the images that tourists photograph themselves and the images projected by marketers. Jenkins' (2003) model signifies a continuous reproduction of images that results in an everlasting perception of a destination by a consumer. Tourists begin to perceive a destination in accordance with the projected images and generate a mental stereotypic representation of tourists to a destination (Beerli et al. 2007). Jenkins (2003) for example, found that backpackers in Australia captured iconic images in their photographs, perpetuating the images projected by DMO's. Garrod (2007) discusses the circle of representation within the context of Urry's (2002) tourist gaze, whereby tourists feel compelled to photograph what has already been introduced, or projected. Hillman (2007), who still regards the tourist photograph as authentic, highlights the danger that the images projected by destinations are rife with cliché-ridden language. However, based on the concept of the circle of representation, issues of accuracy arise if a tourist is simply replicating the projected marketing images. Both this and notions of postmodernism, such as the tourist as dictator (Garlick 2002) and the post-tourists quest for inauthenticity (Urry 2002), would suggest a break away from the circle of representation, with the post-modern tourist more interested in seeking new things to photograph, rather than the image projected by destination marketers. The post-tourist increasingly holds the power when projecting a destination image, becoming the mediator or co-mediator of the destination and as such the tourist experience. This emphasises the need for congruency between the image projected by a destination and that perceived by a tourist in developing or maintaining a successful destination image.

Methods

This research specifically focuses on a different paradigm of participant-led research utilising the images generated by tourists. Using the technique of Visitor Employed Photography (VEP) the researcher analyses photographs taken by a sample of tourists and is based in the concept that the tourist and photography are intrinsically linked (Garlick 2002). Primary research consisted of both a sample of perceived and projected photographic images. Projected images consisted of the official marketing material of Gloucester as the main projector of Gloucester's destination image. This included the official website http://www.thecityofgloucester.co.uk, a 2010 visitor brochure (Marketing Gloucester Ltd 2010) and an official Facebook group, http://www.facebook.com/gloucester. In total 115 images were identified across all three sources. From this, after excluding images that were not compatible to this research, a sample of 74 images was established.

The VEP study collated the perceived images, with an initial aim for 10 photos each from 15 participants, giving a minimum sample of 150 photographs based on the return rate for VEP cameras in previous studies. Whilst other VEP surveys have been performed on a larger scale (Mackay 2005, Mackay and Couldwell 2004, Stedman et al. 2004, Dorwart et al. 2006) and have reached an 100 per cent return rate, these studies relied on the researcher staying on site and collecting cameras. However, to encourage creativity this research utilised postal collection of cameras. With a 60 per cent response rate, the sample totalled 109 photos. Using random sampling at the Tourist Information Centre (TIC) in Gloucester city centre allowed both residents and tourists to take part in order to distinguish between the perceptions of different visitor types. Participants completed a short form when taking each photograph to highlight the characteristics of each photo. The aim of this was to provide more interpretation on behalf of the participant rather than leaving interpretation solely to the researcher. The participants also completed a short sociodemographic questionnaire to highlight basic demographic and familiarity variables, as Mackay (2005) suggests that these affect how people judge visuals.

Photographing took place over one day, and even though some authors (Haywood 1990) advised against this, it provided control to capture initial perceptions. Each participant used a 27 exposure disposable camera and, as in other VEP studies (Mackay and Couldwell 2004), copies of photographs were offered as an incentive to return the cameras. The procedure for collecting the projected images included obtaining the 2010 brochure from the TIC and images from the website and Facebook group. For the latter, and to maintain continuity, sampling of images from both websites took place on one day. The images were also taken at most only three links deep from the website homepage as recommended by Govers and Go (2005) following website navigation.

Secondly, content analysis provided the basis for analysing all of the visual images collected. A specifically designed coding schedule used clear and mutually exclusive data categories such as Barthes's (1997, cited in Van Leeuwen and Jewitt 2001) photogenia connotations to assess the metaphorical implications of the image (Edwards 1996, cited in Hunter 2008). The images were also analysed based on Tapachai and Waryszak's (2000) five core values of image perception, to both assess the salient attributes of, and the holistic image. Lastly, following initial analysis, the content and composition of the images and the covert and overt messages within, were analysed based on the principles of semiotics. This allowed for distinction between denotative meanings such as whom or what is depicted and connotative meanings, or what ideas or values are expressed (Van Leeuwen and Jewitt 2001).

Analysis and Discussion

Following the VEP study and content analysis, the findings from 183 images (109 perceived and 74 projected) suggested key themes of heritage, shopping and individuality. Characteristics found within the images provide a basis for comparing the two image sets and providing an initial overview (see Table 7.1) of the salient attributes of the projected and perceived image of Gloucester.

Table 7.1   Top ten projected and perceived images

Projected image	No. of images	Perceived image	No. of images
People	20	Gloucester Docks	30
Gloucester Docks	16	Gloucester Cathedral	14
Gloucester Cathedral	8	Gloucester Quays Designer Outlet	7
Abstract	5	Medieval Streets	6
Rugby	4	Southgate Street	6
Food	4	River Severn	5
Gloucester Museum & Art Gallery	2	Individuality	4
Cheese Rolling	2	St Mary's Square	4
Blackfriars Priory	2	Westgate Street	4
Ramada Bowden Hall Hotel	1	Old Fathertime Clock	3

Table 7.1 identifies heritage icons, such as Gloucester Docks and Cathedral as key salient attributes of the projected and perceived image. However, other attributes show less congruency, with suggestions of a more dynamic, city centric perceived image than a generic county wide projected image. People are a key attribute to the projected image, perhaps adding to the staged nature of projected images as suggested by Scarles (2004). Table 7.1 displays comparable numbers of individual, abstract images ranging from close-ups of medieval architecture to views of skylights in shopping centres (see Figure 7.2). This would indicate an imbalance in the level of congruency between the projected and perceived image.

Figure 7.2   Projected abstract images captured via VEP study

The photogenia connotations identified by Barthes (1997, cited in Van Leeuwen and Jewitt 2001) allow judgments and discussion on the emotional linkage between the image and consumer. Results suggest that the image of Gloucester is emotive with an average of 63 per cent of images classed as very close or medium shots. These tended to be abstract in nature with photos from the VEP study concentrating on stonework in the Cathedral or dock buildings, and projected images concentrating on people. The multidimensional phenomenon of the image (Tapachai and Waryszak 2000) provides insight into the salient attributes that comprise the holistic image, with the functional value identifying the perceived utility of the destination and the purpose of what the tourist is viewing. Images of pub gardens, dock walkways and tourist attractions identify Gloucester's core function as a leisure destination, with shopping as a secondary function. The social value of the image of Gloucester is strong and links the destination to a range of cultural groups. Projected and perceived images include the Cathedral and Priory, blue heritage plaques and traditional street furniture and indicate a level of congruency. Following this, the epistemic value of an image can identify a destinations ability to arouse curiosity, provide novelty and satisfy a desire of knowledge (Tapachai and Waryszak 2000). The projected images displayed the epistemic values of learning, knowledge, and discovery, representing knowledge through historic buildings; interpretation and discovery through libraries and museums; and learning through re-enactments and restoration. However, the emotional value of Gloucester's image (the aspects that influence choice of one destination over another) and conditional value are imbalanced. The projected image is mainly one of entertainment, compared to the perceived image of calmness. Using the principles of semiotics (Barthes 1997, cited in Scarles 2004), further analysis will allow for distinction to be made between denotative and connotative meanings (Van Leeuwen 2001), to explore what ideas or values are expressed through representation and thus congruency in the salient attributes of, and the, holistic image.

The Projected Image

Content analysis has identified a constricted projected image, suggesting that Gloucester's image is relying on the popularity of primary tourist attractions such as Gloucester Cathedral and the Docks. Urry's (2002) concept of aestheticised images is evident with the use of images of the surrounding countryside suggesting a green image, with images of the Severn Bore and Cheese Rolling in Coopers Hill. This could be suggestive of a lack of confidence in the projectors (DMO), that the city alone is strong enough an image. Culture is also utilised in the projected image, with images representing knowledge through images of historic buildings, children enjoying interaction at the Gloucester Folk Museum or shopping within the city centre. These images were mainly close shots, which imply an image aiming to create emotional connections with potential tourists suggesting that the image of Gloucester intends to be socially closer to the viewer, as suggested by Van Leeuwen and Jewitt (2001), rather than being perceived as socially distant or detached from the viewer. Gloucester projects multiple destination uses, all suggesting a great ability to fulfil as a leisure destination. As Scarles (2004) discussed, the projected images are representations of a mediated discourse and ultimately aim to maintain the power of the DMO. However, the discourse is constructed and presents only one reality of place. Staged images of people, vistas generally people-free with minimal disruption within the image from construction work or rubbish for example, ultimately project a mediated and highly aestheticised (Urry 2002) image. The image projected through Facebook differs and presents another mediated reality using more abstract and individual images indicating the influence of user-generated content and consumer influence.

The Perceived Image

The connotative meanings reveal a varied destination image of Gloucester, which reflects the individualistic element to, and participant-led method of VEP. The photo logs supported this with creative descriptions of the images. Key to the perceived image of Gloucester is the range of activities on offer, as both a leisure and shopping destination. A high proportion of the images highlight a range of shopping and leisure activities including shopping centres, older traditional shops and Gloucester's primary attractions such as Gloucester Docks and Gloucester Cathedral. The multi-functional perception of Gloucester is evident in a large number of photos of signage around the city (see Figure 7.3) highlighting Gloucester's secondary attractions.

Images of historic buildings such as Robert Raikes House and St Oswald's Priory compounds the perceived image with evidence of knowledge attributes. Symbolic British culture is evident in images of iconic historic buildings and places of worship. The perceived images tend to highlight abstract and creative images and suggest a more contemporary perceived image. This perhaps is also evidence of the popularity of photography (Forrester 2000, Cobley and Haefner 2009) and reflective of the individualistic nature of the VEP study.

The abstract and individualistic nature of the images suggests an emotional connection to the city, with participants in the study taking the time to appreciate the image and not just photograph the iconic tourist sites. The photo logs further support this with many creative and idiosyncratic descriptions of the images. For example, descriptions such as 'What a mess!' when describing a derelict building or 'beautiful stonework' when describing historic stonework in St Mary's Square.

Figure 7.3   Signage captured via VEP study

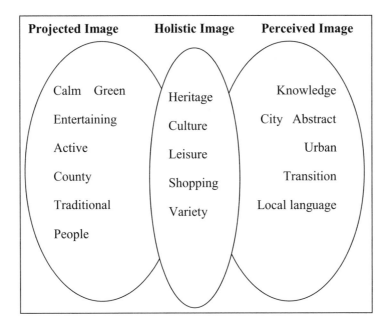

Figure 7.4   Semiotic image set comparison

Together, this could be evidence of Garlick's (2002) post-modern tourist gaze with the less reliant post-modern tourist constructing a gaze and seeking out different images and other realities in order to engage with a destination.

Contrary to the projected image, the VEP study returned very few images of green spaces. Images include pedestrianised shopping areas and of the docks area, with a particular concentration on the historic industrial buildings rather than the water. However, this urban image does capture passive leisure activities such as participants using public benches or casual shopping indicating a relaxed emotional relationship to Gloucester. This denial of the gaze (Urry 2002) illustrates the use of photography as a mediator of place and exploring the plurality (Scarles 2009) of experiences of place, and a rejection of constructed discourses.

The key themes of the projected and perceived image of Gloucester are illustrated in Figure 7.4 and can allude to levels of congruency between the two.

The comparison (Figure 7.4) reflects results of similar research by Andreu and Cooper (2000) and Grosspietsch (2006). The research suggests that heritage, culture, leisure, shopping and individuality are fundamental to Gloucester's projected and perceived image and the holistic image, and suggests evidence of a hermeneutic circle (Urry 2002), or circle of representation (Jenkins 2003), whereby the perceived images are in part reflecting images that are projected. However, the research demonstrates that the congruencies between the images are not solely based on a one way influence in which the projected image influences the perceived. The perceived images offer a more individualistic interpretation of the destination image of Gloucester and, as such, are arguably more authentic (Hillman 2007). Indeed, Gloucester's use of Facebook to some extent emulates the perceived image. The concept of a circle of representation has always acknowledged that the circle can be reciprocal and that the perceived image can affect the projected (Jenkins 2003). However, the power-knowledge relationship between the two has always been unequal with the projected image seen as the more powerful influencer.

The analysis of the images has provided evidence to suggest a power and knowledge shift, from the projector to the perceiver, whereby the tourist is empowered in mediating a destination image. This is evident in the wide range of different perceived images, but also in the difference in the projected image within different medias. The images analysed from the website and Facebook are more creative and distinctive than the images used in the brochure. Whilst the brochure still uses photography to construct a gaze (Urry 2002), the power of the perceiver on an image is beginning to manifest itself in more modern medias. Images within the brochure are ideals as suggested by Urry (2002), with staged images and those without rubbish or grey skies. However, the images on Facebook and the website are less so, particularly on Facebook which utilises a more relaxed style of photography and is more congruent to the perceived image of Gloucester. Tourists are utilising social media and Web 2.0, as tools to assert one's own experiences as part of the mediated tourist experience. Web 2.0 and new technologies such as Facebook are creating the power for consumers to construct alternative discourse through such ubiquitous tools. Such platforms can (re)create multiple realities of place. The research on a small scale suggests that projectors are beginning to take more interest in the perceived reality and embracing user-generated content and interaction. The projected image is being increasingly influenced by collective intelligence (Xiang and Gretzel 2010) and driven by consumer (perceiver) led image building and a new reliance on social media.

The hermeneutic circle has developed alongside changes in methods of communicating a visual destination image. This change has been illustrated in Figure 7.5 whereby the circle first established by Jenkins (2003) and Caton and Santos (2008) continues but it is influenced at various stages by different medias, taking into consideration the impact of the media and changing relationships between producers, tourists and destinations on the resulting destination image.

The changes in the circle illustrate a much wider trend and supports evidence of post-modernisation (Urry 2002). The break away from the conventional circle of representation (see Figure 7.1), to the adapted model above ties in with the individualism of post-modernism, with tourists breaking away from the image projected by destinations and finding alternative images to capture (Garlick 2002). Tourists are exploring the new realities of tourism spaces and in creating an individual image of a destination, become the advocate of the image. Although, with increasing use of social media this could result in the formation of new perceptions of a destination circulated and re-constructed through the tourist gaze. The extent of a shift in the projection and perception of a destination image will be influenced

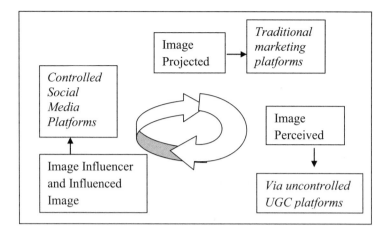

Figure 7.5   Media influenced circle of representation

by the continuing growth of social media and user-generated content, which will create new images and modern myths which are associated with destinations. Essentially, the destination image becomes reflective of individualism and any disconnections between the projected image and the new realities explored by the perceived image can be re-evaluated. The destination marketers can re-evaluate the concept of the destination image and pre-conceived knowledge of a destination using social media to capture perceived images. By utilising this, there is the potential to have greater congruency of a destination image and a greater chance of making a link between an individuals' goals, motivations and preferences, which is the key to success according to Jenkins (2003).

Conclusion

The research highlights the imbalanced congruencies between the perceived and projected image of Gloucester, and the crucial role that new medias play in maintaining and developing a successful holistic destination image. This supports the notion of a circle of representation but in a modified form, based on wider changes in consumer behaviour. The power and knowledge of the projectors of a brand image, not just a destination image, has shifted towards the consumer: empowering the perceiver in the image formation process. Identifying these elements can allow projectors to evaluate the image projected via imagery, clarifying where images are being under or over used, and highlighting new vistas to project. Importantly, rather than projectors dictating an image of a destination this research can offer destinations the opportunity to align themselves with perceptions. As an alternative to using generic or staged images as identified in this research, the use of more individualistic and abstract images could attract more tourists to a destination appealing to both tourists' mental and visual images (Forrester 2000, Stern et al. 2001) of Gloucester.

This research has also gone some way towards clarifying the concept of the image within destination marketing, identifying the image as imbued in a circle of representation between the projector (the destination marketers) and the perceivers (the tourists/residents). Importantly, what this research has established is that previous concepts of a circle of representation developed by Jenkins (2003) and Caton and Santos (2008), require updating with new methods of marketing employed by tourism destinations. As tourists' perceived images of a destination become viewable via new technologies, destination marketers now face the challenge Miguel and Pedregal (2008) highlight in communicating the right image to tourists. The use of new marketing methods such as user-generated content and social media should be embedded within practice, with attention given to the impact of such media on a destination image. The changes in how destination images should be formed by the new model of the media circle of representation (Figure 7.5) goes some way to reflecting these changes, and could be used as a model by destination marketers to maintain or change a destination image with user-generated content impacting upon image formation. Furthermore, the new model clearly identifies the role that social media can play in the projection and perception of a destination image alongside the traditional DMO. Importantly, the model highlights control and power issues and differentiates between the use of social media by a destination, and the use of social media by the tourist. This links back to the earlier conclusion of aligning a destination image with already established perceptions, although this, to some extent, would depend on the nature of the perceptions (whether positive or negative). DMO's should consider the significance of collective intelligence, and the use of social media and user-generated content, on the formation of a destination image as increasingly important when developing and maintaining a successful tourism destination image. What the research identifies is a power and knowledge shift, which on a larger scale can be reflective of a change in the way knowledge is created in tourism studies. With the use and growth of ubiquitous social media tools such as Facebook, it is no longer the power and knowledge of the tourism professional or academic that directs knowledge and understanding of tourism, but a reciprocal process with the tourist of joint knowledge mediation.

References

Alcaniz, E.B., Garcia, I.S. and Blas, S.S. 2009. The functional-psychological continuum in the cognitive image of a destination: a confirmatory analysis. *Tourism Management*, 30(5), 715–23.

Andreu, L.B. and Cooper, C. 2000. Projected and perceived image of Spain as a tourist destination for British travellers. *Journal of Travel & Tourism Marketing*, 9(4), 47–67.

Barthes, R. 1977. *Image-Music-Text*. London: Cape Editions.

Beerli, A., Meneses, G.D. and Gil, S.M. 2007. Self-congruity and destination choice. *Annals of Tourism Research*, 34(3), 571–87.

Branthwaite, A. 2002. Investigating the power of imagery in marketing communication: evidence-based techniques. *Qualitative Market Research: An International Journal*, 5(3), 164–71.

Burns, P. 2007. Six postcards from Arabia: a visual discourse of colonial travels in the Orient. *Tourist Studies*, 4(3), 255–75.

Camprubi, R., Guia, J. and Comas, J. 2008. Destination networks and induced tourism image. *Tourism Review*, 63(2), 47–58.

Caton, K. and Santos, C.A. 2008. Closing the hermeneutic circle?: photographic encounters with the Other. *Annals of Tourism Research*, 35(1), 7–26.

Cobley, P. and Haefner, N. 2009. Digital cameras and domestic photography: communication, agency and structure. *Visual Communication*, 9(2), 123–46.

Deacon, D.H., Golding, P., Pickering, M. and Murdock, G. 2007. *Researching Communications: A Practical Guide to Methods in Media and Cultural Analysis*. 2nd edition. London: Hodder Arnold.

Dewar, K., Li, W.M. and Davis, C.H. 2007. Photographic images, culture, and perception in tourism advertising. *Journal of Travel & Tourism Marketing*, 22(2), 35–44.

Dorwart, C.E., Moore, R.L. and Lueng, L. 2006. *Visitor Employed Photography: It's Potential Use in Evaluating Visitor's and Use in Evaluating Visitors' Perceptions of Resource Impacts in Trail and Park Settings*, Proceedings of the 2006 Northeastern Recreation Research Symposium, Pennsylvania, USA: 9–11 April 2006, Available at: http://www.treesearch.fs.fed.us/pubs/12694 [accessed: 5th October 2009].

Dwivedi, M., Yadav, A. and Patel, V.R. 2009. The online destination image of Goa. *Worldwide Hospitality & Tourism Themes*, 1(1), 25–39

Echtner, C.M. and Ritchie, J.R.B. 2003. The meaning and measurement of destination image. *The Journal of Tourism Studies*, 14(1), 2–12.

Feighey, W. 2005. Negative image: developing the visual in tourism research. *Current Issues in Tourism*, 6(1), 76–85.

Forrester, M.A. 2000. *Psychology of the Image*. 1st edition. London: Routledge.

Garlick, S. 2002. Revealing the unseen: tourism, art and photography. *Cultural Studies*, 16(2), 289–305.

Garrod, B. 2007. A snapshot into the past: the utility of volunteer-employed photography in planning and managing heritage tourism', *Journal of Heritage Tourism*. 2(1), 14–35.

Garrod, B. 2008. Exploring place perception: a photo based analysis. *Annals of Tourism Research*. 35(2), 381–401.

Garrod, B. 2009. Understanding the relationship between tourism destination imagery and tourist photography. *Journal of Travel Research*, 47(3), 346–58.

Gartner, W.C. 1993. Image formation process. *Journal of Travel & Tourism Marketing*, 2(2–3), 191–215.

Govers, R. and Go, F.M. 2005. Projected destination image online: website content analysis of pictures and text. *Information Technology and Tourism*, 7(34), 73–89.

Grosspietsch, M. 2006. Perceived and projected images of Rwanda: Visitor and international tour operator perspectives. *Tourism Management*, 27(2), 225–34.

Haywood, K.M. 1990. Visitor-employed photography: An urban visit assessment. *Journal of Travel Research*, 29(1), 25–9.

Hillman, W. 2007. Travel authenticated?: postcards, tourist brochures, and travel photography. *Tourism Analysis*, 12(3), 135–48.

Hunter, W.C. 2008. A typology of photographic representations for tourism: depictions of groomed spaces. *Tourism Management*, 29(2), 354–65.

Jani, D. and Hwang, Y. 2011. User-generated destination image through weblogs: a comparison of pre- and post-visit images. *Asia Pacific Journal of Tourism Research*, 16(3), 339–56.

Jenkins, O.H. 2003. Photography and travel brochures: the circle of representation. *Tourism Geographies*, 5(3), 305–28.

Litvin, S.W. and Mouri, N. 2009. A comparative study of the use of 'iconic' versus 'generic' advertising images for destination marketing. *Journal of Travel Research*, 48(2), 152–61.

Mackay, K.J. and Couldwell, C.M. 2004. Using visitor-employed photography to investigate destination image. *Journal of Travel Research*, 42(4), 390–96.

Mackay, K.J. 2005. Is a picture worth a thousand words? Snapshots from tourism destination image research, in *Tourism Development: Issues for a Vulnerable Industry*, edited by J. Aramberri et al. Clevedon: Channel View Publications, 44–65.

Marketing Gloucester. 2010. http://www.thecityofgloucester.co.uk/ [accessed: 10 March 2010].

Marketing Gloucester. 2010. *The City of Gloucester: Your Guide. 2010*. Gloucester: Marketing Gloucester.

Nogues-Pedregal, A.M. 2008. A tauromachian controversy over identities. The mediation of tourism space in the negotiation of meanings. *Mediterranean Ethnological Summer School*, 7(1), 221–38.

Palmer, C. 2009. Moving with the times: visual representations of the tourism phenomenon. *Journal of Tourism Consumption and Practice*, 1(1), 74–85.

Pike, S. 2008. *Destination Marketing: An Integrated Marketing Communication Approach*. 1st edition. London: Elsevier.

Scarles, C. 2004. Mediating landscapes: the process and practices of image construction in tourist brochures of Scotland. *Tourist Studies*, 4(1), 43–67.

Scarles, C. 2009. Becoming tourist: renegotiating the visual in the tourist experience. *Environment and Planning D: Society and Space*, 27(3), 465–88.

Stedman, R., Beckley, T., Wallace, S. and Ambard, M. 2004. A picture and 1000 words: using resident-employed photography to understand attachment to high amenity places. *Journal of Leisure Research*, 36(4), 580–606.

Stern, B., Zinkhan, G.M. and Jaju, A. 2001. Marketing images: construct definition, measurement issues, and theory development. *Marketing Theory*, 1(2), 201–24.

Tapachi, N. and Waryszak, R. 2000. An examination of the role of beneficial image in tourist destination selection. *Journal of Travel Research*, 39(1), 37–44.

Tasci, A.D.A., Gartner, W.C. and Cavusgil, S.T. 2007. Conceptualisation and operationalization of destination image. *Journal of Hospitality & Tourism Research*, 31(2), 194–223.

Tribe, J. 2004. Knowing about tourism: epistemological issues, in *Qualitative Research in Tourism, Ontologies, Epistemologies and Methodologies*, edited by J. Phillimore and L. Goodson. London: Routledge, 46–62.

Urry, J. 2002. *The Tourist Gaze*. 2nd edition. London: Sage Publications Ltd.

Van Leeuwen, T. and Jewitt, C. 2001. *Handbook of Visual Analysis*. 1st edition. London: Sage Publications Ltd.

Xiang, Z. and Gretzel, U. 2010. Role of social media in online travel information search. *Tourism Management*, 30(2), 179–88.

Chapter 8

Individualising the Tourist Brochure: Reconfiguring Tourism Experiences and Transforming the Classic Image-maker

Constantia Anastasiadou and Nikos Migas

Introduction

A brochure is a form of printed promotional material designed to communicate with existing or potential tourists (Molina and Esteban 2006). Traditionally it has been used as the main marketing instrument to enhance awareness of destinations, provide information and generate desire to purchase (Chiou et al. 2008, Getz and Sailor 1993, Zhou 1997, Yüksel and Akgül 2006). In addition to the role of the tourist brochure as a mediator of the tourist gaze (Urry and Larsen 2011), the consumption (Jennings and Weiler 2006), staging and visual representation of place (Scarles 2004, Long and Robinson 2009) and image construction (Tressider 2010, Ye and Tussyadiah 2011) have also been debated. Previous research had highlighted the co-creation experience that the consumption of promotional materials generates; that is the expectations and anticipations the consumption of the marketing messages that brochures and other printed materials transmit (Scarles 2004, Ye and Tussyadiah 2011). However, with the advent of the World Wide Web, more emphasis has been placed on electronic media advertising and the impact of the incorporation of moving images in tourist promotion (Gretzel and Jamal 2009). Moreover, electronic media, such as blogs and wikis, enabled consumers to obtain information about holiday destinations from past visitors and communicate their needs and expectations directly to the suppliers (Buhalis 2003). Further technological innovation has enabled consumers to become more involved in the experience building process during the trip planning stage, as well as sharing their own experiences of the destination with other tourists after their visit. Consequently, tourists are no longer passive recipients of induced images from official sources but, by sharing their tourist experiences through social media they become co-creators of destination image (Månsson 2011, Urry and Larsen 2011). Despite the rise in popularity of social media in the creation, exchange and distribution of information, the brochure remains an important marketing medium and new and emerging technologies can update the format and presentation of tourism brochures (PODI 2004).

Technological innovations have enabled the inclusion of consumer tastes and preferences in the product development process through a procedure known as mass customisation (Jiang 2002). Customisation extends the role of images presented in tourist brochures, beyond that of a conventional, static and passive tool, to a position that allows it to dynamically adapt to the user preferences (Migas et al. 2008). The personalisation potential of the tourism brochure, both online and in print, has implications for the way destinations and tourism products are marketed, imagined and consumed as it adds an additional dynamic dimension to the printed brochures but the preferences and attitudes of tourists towards customised brochures are unknown.

This chapter will discuss findings from a research project on the use of customised brochures by attendees of a community festival in Edinburgh. It will examine their engagement with the festival and the personalised brochures, and debate the potential implications of personalisation for tourism brochures. The chapter concludes with a reflection on the theoretical implications of this research and some recommendations for future research.

Importance of Brochures as a Communication Medium

Brochures are highly visual mediums and rely upon images and photographs to sell destinations (Scarles 2004). Getz and Sailor (1993) identified three types of brochures: 'informational', such as directories and travel guides which are mostly descriptive; 'promotional' which aim to sell an attraction or business; and 'lure' brochures which promote a destination area. Most tourism brochures would be described as a mix of promotional and lure brochures, as they present factual information about the destination, as well as trying to create particular images and associations with the destination in the minds of the visitors. To be effective tools for promotion, brochures should influence image formation, destination choice and satisfaction (Molina and Esteban 2006).

Tourism brochures generate images and include text that locate the services they provide, as well as the places and culture in which they are located (Long and Robinson 2009); conjuring up images of the 'Other', the exotic and the authentic (Hillman 2007). In this way, brochures generate expectations and anticipation of the tourist experience and tourist consumption of the place in the minds of the tourists before their visit (Scarles 2004, Urry and Larsen 2011). Due to the intangible nature of the tourism experience, the brochure is a very powerful medium that stakeholders (i.e. tourists, tourist providers and governments) use to capture the tourist imagination of the place and mediate the tourist experience (Wang et al. 2012). The mediation potential of the brochure is thus very important for destinations to manage visitor expectations and anticipate visitor behaviour.

Technological advances have created the opportunity to obtain information about destinations and tourism products from a variety of sources (Álvarez et al. 2007, Buhalis 2003). Electronic media are increasingly allowing tourists to move away from the passive consumption of 'official' tourism media and participate in the co-creation of experiences, sharing tourism images and narratives of place (Månsson 2011). Consumer generated media (Gretzel and Jamal 2009), the online sharing of videos (Tussyadiah and Fesenmaier 2009), the influence of social networking sites (Fotis et al. 2011, Hays et al. 2012) and blogs (Aram 2011), and the use of recommender systems (Ricci and Werthner 2002, Gretzel 2011), that propose activities based on previous tourist behaviour and current preferences (Loh et al. 2004), are just a few examples of how technology has added further layers to mediation in tourism. Studies by Wang et al. (2012) and Gretzel (2011) argue the need to better understand the relationship between information needs, information tools, and the touristic experience, as there is still limited awareness of the engagement of tourists with electronic media and the complex ways they mediate the tourist experience and consumption of place.

In this dynamic and fast changing environment, the relevance of printed brochures has come under questioning. Brochures have been described as a passive, static medium (Wan et al. 2007) that lacks the potential of other media for interaction and communication with consumers (Chiou et al. 2008, Wan et al. 2007). Nonetheless, there is evidence to suggest that printed brochures remain as popular as ever (Scarles 2004, Gretzel et al. 2006, Edelheim 2007). In their study of destination management organisations, Gretzel et al. (2006) discovered that despite the existence of websites, tourists still preferred to receive physical copies of the tourism brochures. Moreover, Scarles (2004) discussed the tangibility of the brochure and the importance of the material presence of the brochure as part of constructing anticipations of a holiday. So ingrained is the tourist brochure in the tourists' psyche, that promotion bodies usually offer the option to request the printed brochures alongside the information that is available on their websites (Scarles 2004). Moreover, for many people the printed brochure is their primary means of making contact with the destination and its attractions. Where package travel is concerned, the brochure can even act as a legal contract between the tour operator and their customer under EU regulations (Holloway and Humphreys 2012). As such, tourism brochures remain widely used alongside more innovative marketing and communication mediums, but there is increasing demand for personalised messages and information (Jansson 2007).

New and emerging technologies can also help improve the personalisation potential of brochures (Migas et al. 2008), which allows them to remain a popular marketing and distribution medium. Jansson (2007: 11) argued 'there is an expectation to provide increasingly personalised information guidance and attractions *within* the market segments – that is, greater opportunities for customisation'. Mass customisation has been defined as 'the use of flexible processes and organisation structures to produce varied and often individually customised products and services at the price of standardised mass produced alternatives' (Hart 1996: 13).

Mass customisation has significant implications for the consumption and production of the tourist destination and may affect the mediation efforts of tourism stakeholders. Whilst strengthening the relationship between consumer and supplier, it provides the consumer with stronger motivation, loyalty and satisfaction (Rowley 2002, Sigala 2006). Customisation reduces search costs, increases the quality and reduces the volume of information that users receive (Rumetshofer et al. 2003). It also presents customers with products that have a higher degree of relevance (Rowley 2002). For tourism suppliers, customisation provides detailed information on consumer behaviour allowing them to adapt their offering to suit the customer's needs whilst reducing packaging and marketing costs (Huffman and Kahn 1998). Customisation could then allow for improved marketing communications, strengthened image construction and brand associations, and the knowledge generated can be applied to further tailor the destination product and marketing messages. Therefore, given the continued popularity of printed brochures amongst other marketing media, the customisation of the tourism brochure would then transform it from a static marketing tool into an original and highly innovative medium.

Moreover, brochure customisation can allow the transformation of the brochure's generic destination image to an individual destination image created through the personalisation of the marketing information (images and text). The personalisation of the marketing message may help address a potential gap between the producer perceptions and presumptions of the tourist information needs and the tourists' actual needs. Personalisation would also allow the visitor to imagine the destination through those images, text and associations that appeal most to them. Whereas in the past tourists relied upon subjective understanding and partial knowledge to create subtleties and anticipations of their holiday experience, through customisation there is increased potential to enliven the individual within the image generating process.

Interactive consumption of the destination would thus be enabled, allowing the brochure users to select their own induced images of the destination, making their own destination image associations and hence, creating a new dimension to the notion of tourist as a co-creator of the tourism experience.

There is evidence to suggest (Larsen et al. 2006, Gretzel and Jamal 2009) that different audiences engage with and respond very differently to technological innovations. Hart (1995) identified 'customer customisation sensitivity' (CCS) as a determining factor for successful customisation. CCS is conditioned by the uniqueness of the customer's needs and the customer sacrifice gap. The bigger the gap between the customers' desired product and the available products, the more customisation becomes desirable. The popularity of dynamic packaging and personalised travel services (Fink and Kobsa 2002, Franke 2003, Norrie et al. 2005) are strong indications of a customer sacrifice gap between the desired and available tourism products, however, the desire for customisation and its potential benefits (and costs) to service providers and tourists alike are unknown (Migas et al. 2008).

This research would first seek to explore attitudes towards tourist brochure customisation to establish whether a CCS gap exists, and secondly to reflect on how the customisation of brochures may affect the mediation process. As such, the chapter makes a distinct contribution to the tourism mediation theory by incorporating the mass customisation perspective. The study concludes that full brochure customisation reconfigures the mediation process but that tourism providers are likely to be resistant in pursuing it; however, partial brochure customisation can facilitate better marketing campaigns and enhance the tourist consumption experiences of the users.

Methodology

Using the brochures from a community festival in Edinburgh as a case study, this chapter empirically tests the information needs and customer customisation sensitivity of tourism brochure users and the willingness of the tourism operators to customise their brochures.

There are some key similarities and differences between tourism and festival brochures. Although festival brochures are primarily informational (Getz and Sailor 1993), similarly to tourism brochures, image and text are used to create associations with the festival and mediate the experience before it takes place. Festival brochures do not need to project place associations and consumption in the same way as tourist brochures because their audiences largely consist of local residents who have their own 'actual' experiences of the location or 'festivalgoers' who wish to disassociate themselves of the 'tourist' tag (Gration et al. 2011). In this respect there is less opportunity to present the 'place' in a positive light, however the festivals are also about repackaging the city by encouraging festivalgoers to break away from the everyday and the mundane; by celebrating local culture, and encouraging 'experiencing' the city in different ways (Prentice and Andersen 2003, Johansson and Kociatkiewicz 2011), and creating festivalscapes (Lee et al. 2008). Moreover, festival brochures create an 'image' for the festival and attempt to convey information about the festival in a stimulating and attractive manner. They are instrumental in conveying the festival image and brand identity which are reflected in the design and presentation of the brochures. The festival brochure will also communicate messages to its intended audience and the type of experiences festivalgoers should anticipate and associate with the festival.

The case study festival is representative of many community festivals of its type in terms of the challenges that it experiences (limited funding, lack of resources and significant marketing costs). The festival had a substantial part of their marketing budget spent on the production of brochures which were mainly physically distributed in several city locations. The organisers wished to better understand how the festival attendees were using their brochures, if the brochures persuaded them to attend events or if alternative media were also desirable.

The festival organisers provided the researchers with a database of individuals who had registered on the festival website to receive news and offers by email. The database contained approximately 1000 email addresses, not all of which were active. A personalised email was sent that asked those registered on the database to indicate their interests and preferences for events on an attached selection mechanism. Once this information was submitted, the electronic brochure was produced and emailed back to them as a follow up email.

In total 110 people clicked the link and produced their personalised brochure; 57 later responded to a brief electronic survey about their experiences of the customised brochure and to test whether the customisation of the promotional material influenced their decision to purchase tickets. This gave the questionnaire a response rate of 51 per cent, which was considered satisfactory. A selection of these findings is presented here; namely the respondent and festival organisers' attitudes towards customisation and the wider implications of customisation for the image and consumption of the festival.

Discussion of Findings

Producer Bias to Customisation

The festival organisers were apprehensive about allowing a full customisation of the brochure, although they were given the option of trying out a fully customised version. Part of their reservations towards the production of a fully customised brochure could be attributed to the innovative nature of the project and the lack of understanding of the associated costs and benefits of the different levels of customisation. It is more likely though that the organisers assumed that a fully customised brochure would be counterproductive in terms of improving ticket sales, as the festivalgoers would only view part of their programme. However, the festival organisers were enticed by a targeted marketing campaign that could substantially reduce their printing costs and offer them further insights into the motivation and purchasing behaviours of the attendees. The customisation campaign generated significant knowledge of the festivalgoers' behaviours and attitudes that had not been collected before. Moreover, the organisers were particularly keen to promote one large-scale event and wished to explore whether the customised brochure would promote the event better and generate more ticket sales.

For these reasons, the customisation that took place was largely cosmetic (Gilmore and Pine 1997), that is the presentation of the brochure rather than the content was customised. The customised brochure presented the festival logo next to a selection of events based on the preferences the users indicated (i.e. music events/ theatre) when they received the personalised email. What the respondents had not realised was that they had indeed received the full festival brochure with some highlighted information.

The unwillingness of the festival organisers to consider testing a fully customised brochure also demonstrates a degree of scepticism on the part of producers towards brochure customisation. Although the organisers were concerned with the festival's rising marketing costs, they were worried that a fully customised brochure would reduce the visibility of some events and hence, negatively affect ticket sales. The festival organisers appeared to associate the provision of more information with improved marketing efficiency and increased attendance figures. The organisers of larger festivals could have a very different approach to customisation but it is likely that they would also exhibit some apprehension about relinquishing control of their marketing efforts to a third party or the festival attendees themselves. The opportunity cost between printing/marketing costs and maintaining control of their marketing process could be a determinant factor of producer attitudes towards the different degrees of customisation.

On this occasion, customisation appeared to further empower the producer rather than the consumer, as there was a reluctance to relinquish control and allow the users to create their own, individual brochures. Enabling full customisation would ultimately require the reconfiguration of marketing and branding approaches, as the brochure user would be transformed into the *creator* (not just co-creator) of their own festival images, experiences and consumption of place. The fully customisable brochure would turn the tables on the mediation process itself by placing the user at the centre and thus enabling self-mediation and self-interpretation of the brochure. Such changes would question the very essence of the tourist brochure, as a promotional tool that influences image formation, destination choice and consumption of place (Molina and Esteban 2006).

Image Creation in Festival Brochures

Like other tourism products, festivals are intangible and their brochures create expectations about the festival experience, ambience and interactions with other festivalgoers. Selling the festival experience can be a challenge and the brochure can have a significant impact on creating expectations about the festival experience. Promotional media produce the scripting of the festival; that is how the festival is to be consumed by the attendees, and also direct and mediate their gaze (Urry and Larsen 2011). Consequently, festivalgoers also make their decisions based on the messages they have received by such media (Wang et al. 2012). Nonetheless, 'image' construction and festival consumption is not only produced through brochure images, text and illustrations. The festival experience is constructed through learning, understanding and feeling the visited spaces and the culture that is embedded in these. Previous engagement with the festival through marketing media, past attendance and word-of-mouth will create certain expectations of festival experiences and interactions. Image consumption and the festival experience are thus influenced by the different types of festival engagement and not just the brochure.

The case festival's choice of text and images in their brochure reflected the multiculturalism of the local community and the social mobility and population restructuring trends that characterise it. As such, there was specific programming for the local Polish community and the festival organisers also helped local Muslim women to put together women-only events that were not formally advertised in their brochure. The use of specialised themes and the existence of exclusive programming was a reflection of the festival's commitment to the area's local populations and their needs.

When the users of customised brochures were questioned, their expectations of the festival, what it signifies and its image associations came to the forefront. One respondent commented '(I) thought the concept was excellent and I was really impressed that [name] Festival was using technology in this way. As a marketing activity I thought it was brilliant and made [sic] left me with a great impression of the festival and their partners' (Female, 29, postgraduate).

This quote clearly demonstrates how engagement with the festival is modified through the customised brochure; how the expectations and images associated with this particular festival are reconfigured, and how the festival experience is further mediated through the customised brochure. An unexpected positive outcome was that the brochure customisation projected an image of a festival that is contemporary and current due to it embracing modern technologies. Moreover, customisation created positive image and brand associations of the festival in the mind of some respondents because of its engagement with innovative technology. These findings suggest that even partial customisation can enhance and extend the mediated gaze by allowing for greater flexibility and creativity in the brochure creation on the part of the users.

In addition, the information that was gathered through the personalised email could provide further insights on the popularity of particular types of events. Customisation could then also aid the organisers in improving the visibility of shows and performances that might have otherwise been buried in the brochure.

Interestingly, the positive image associations are not only restricted to the festival organiser but also its partners. In previous studies the role and influence of third party producers such as designers and photographers on the design of tourist brochures were studied and their influence was significant (Scarles 2004). The festival partners in this study were a local university and the company that produced the customised campaigns, and their logos had appeared in the back covers of the customised brochure. As the standard brochure had already been created before the customisation campaign had been agreed, these festival partners had no influence over the design or presentation of the customised brochure other than in ensuring the customised brochure looked as good as the standard brochure. Nonetheless, it would appear that they also benefited through the publicity effort and by having their names associated with this innovation. In this respect, the extensions that customisation could generate in terms of image building and brand awareness could be significant for third parties and not just the festival organisers. The benefits of customisation to other festival stakeholders could also be an influential factor in the decision to run customised marketing campaigns, if a substantial positive outcome could be demonstrated.

Customer Customisation Sensitivity in the Festival Brochure

The different ways in which respondents use the festival brochure as an information and inspiration source, the expectations they have of the content and purpose of the brochure and the ways in which they process information also surfaced. Some of the respondents commented on the information overload that they experience when using festival brochures and how customisation could create time benefits for them: 'A lot of the time there can be a feeling of "information overload" with regard to festival brochures and I can end up feeling overwhelmed and often giving up. The customised brochure took the hard work out of it and saved a lot of time too!' (Female, 39, postgraduate).

Information overload could lead to disengagement with the festival, but the customisation of the brochure could allow those festival attendees who are short of time or patience to more easily identify the events and performances that are interesting to them. Moreover, in a city like Edinburgh, there is an abundance of festivals, which could fuel the 'information overload' feelings of festivalgoers. In this respect customising the brochure even partially could enable the festival organisers' marketing message to stand out from the competition.

Although several respondents commented positively about their experience of customisation, they also suggested that they liked having the option to see the rest of the brochure:

> I liked the customised brochure. It saved me time wading through all the stuff that I wouldn't be interested in. I would like access to the full brochure as well though, as I don't trust a computer/another person to completely decide on what I would like. I might surprise myself if I look through the full brochure and find something that I wouldn't instantly think would be my cup of tea. (Female, 33, university)

Mistrust about relinquishing control to another party, or worse – a computer, to make decisions on one's behalf is implied in this quote, reflecting findings from previous research on how diverse the experiences and perceptions of technology could be (Larsen et al. 2006, Gretzel and Jamal 2009). Moreover, brochures are not just information media but a source of inspiration so text, images and layout could have significant implications for the festival consumption too.

'It's a great idea but I worry that I will miss out on finding shows that I would not normally attend and discovering new things' (Female, 41, postgraduate). In other words, the use of the brochures is not always targeted, but rather festivalgoers wish to experience things that will take them out of their comfort zone, stumble upon new experiences and explore the different possibilities that the festival offers. Gretzel's (2011) assertions of the importance of uncertainty and inspiration in tourism decision-making and experiences, which is often ignored and misunderstood when electronic media are created, were also confirmed by customised brochures. Vogt and Fesenmaier (1998) argued that tourists carry out information searches not just to find specific information but for stimulation, entertainment and to satisfy their social needs. Rather than having firm ideas about what they are interested in and what they are looking for, some festival attendees select their events based on how these are presented in the brochure and could be enticed to attend a different range of events, if the brochure promotes these in a persuasive manner. There is currently limited awareness of how festival brochures influence decisions to attend a festival and there is also 'limited research on how tourists express their information needs and respond to information offers' (Gretzel 2011: 770).

Brochure customisation might necessitate the re-thinking of how information is presented, how brochures are laid out and the information needs of the brochure users. The type of brochure and the level of customisation will affect the quantity and quality of information that is then provided. Each configuration of the brochure will result in a different, personal 'image' of the destination or tourism product, which will be conditioned by the individual's personal attributes, previous experiences and expectations of the tourist experiences.

The size of the festival also determines the length of the brochure. As the case study festival was of short duration and had a relatively small number of events, some respondents were not sold on the necessity of customisation:

> I don't think there was [*sic*] enough events to warrant a customised version. I like to see everything, afraid that I'll miss something – and something that might take me out of my comfort zone. I wouldn't get a chance to do this if all I received was all I 'usually' enjoy. (Female, 39, postgraduate)

It is implied that larger festivals, and consequently, larger brochures may warrant a customisation campaign rather than the case study event. Consequently, attitudes to customisation will vary depending on personal preferences and attitudes towards technology and availability of information, the use of brochures for information and/or inspiration purposes, as well as the length and complexity of the standard festival brochure.

It is worth noting that despite a degree of uncertainty regarding the usefulness of the customised brochure, 88 per cent of the survey respondents were positive to the idea of future customisation campaigns, which would suggest a mainly positive experience with the customised brochure.

It is possible that there will be a breakeven point where the costs and benefits of customisation are equal. An awareness of the customisation requirements of different market segments would allow the tourism providers to establish what level and type of customisation they prefer. Rather than replacing the full brochure, a customised version could be offered in parallel for those users that experience information overload or are time poor to identify preferences for each.

However, for any of this change to take place the tourism providers would have to be willing to take risks and embrace the opportunities that customisation creates. As the case study demonstrated, there was a reluctance on the part of the festival organisers to try out full customisation. This attitude is perhaps indicative of the resistance that other tourism providers might display unless the benefits of brochure customisation become more visible and quantifiable. In order for this to be achieved, more research on the customisation potential of brochures is necessary, as well as on the information needs and brochure use of tourists.

Conclusion

The purpose of this chapter was to examine consumers and tourism providers' attitudes towards customised brochures and explore the ways through which customisation may alter the mediation process. Brochures are a key medium through which tourism providers mediate the tourism experience and allow the user to imagine and consume the destination before the actual visit (Scarles 2004, Long and Robinson 2009, Tressider 2010, Ye and Tussyadiah 2011). The literature review established that they remain popular with tourism providers and consumers alike despite their description as static and passive media and the increased fascination with electronic media, online experiences and moving images.

Using data from a case study of festivalgoers to an Edinburgh festival, it was argued that new technologies could reconfigure how information is presented in brochures by allowing the brochure user to select the type and volume of information they receive. Consequently, customised brochures could also enable interactive consumption of the destination and tourism products, and facilitate new ways of experiencing and imagining the destination and associated products. It was suggested that the mediation potential of customised brochures could be substantial and such customisation could revolutionise how destinations are packaged and marketed.

The survey findings suggested that the brochure users responded differently to customisation. The expectations and prior experiences of the festival; their images of the festival and how these are generated; the engagement with technology and their preferences for more or less information will affect the extent to which they prefer brochure customisation. Personal preferences, time availability, information processing capacity and the use of the brochure as a source of inspiration could be some of the factors that affect the users' levels of *customer customisation sensitivity* (Hart 1995). The findings indicated that there is some customer sacrifice gap with existing festival brochures and that there are variations in customer customisation sensitivity.

These issues would have to be studied systematically and in different contexts, as the demographics of festival audiences are varied. The survey findings echo Gretzel's (2011) claims that utilising technological innovation effectively requires a profound understanding of the psychology of tourists, the social structure within which tourism is experienced, the tourists' relationships and use of technology and the language of tourism, all of which is currently lacking. However, the study also demonstrated that a profound understanding of the psychology of tourist providers towards technological innovation would also be useful.

Full brochure customisation could give more power to the visitor by allowing for self-mediation to take place; by allowing the visitor to select the messages, visual or otherwise, that they wish to consume to enliven the imagination process. Ultimately though there would be some resistance from tourism providers as full customisation could lead to a loss of control in terms of the projected images. A key challenge to the process of customisation is then to further ascertain the attitudes of tourism providers towards it.

Brochure customisation might be particularly suited for delivery on mobile media and platforms (i.e. smartphones, tablet PCs & pads) which have more limited capacity for viewing images and large files, and where the message needs to be more targeted and selective to stand out.

The adoption of customisation in the marketing of destinations and tourism products and services through brochures and other media, could reconfigure the current discussions about marketing, image creation and the significance of visual media for tourism. Whereas a large part of the literature has discussed how the destination and experiences are mediated by stakeholders through the visual images, the use of colour and text in tourist brochures (Scarles 2004, Hillman 2007, Long and Robinson 2009) customisation could place the visitor in the driving seat of the image formation process. Depending on the level and type of customisation, the brochure user could then become a *co-designer* or even *creator* of the brochure, and more knowledge could be generated about the information needs and brochure requirements of different users, if the reservations of the tourism providers could be surpassed.

The expansion of brochure customisation will ultimately herald a re-conceptualisation of layout and design, debates on how information is presented, and what type of information could and should be personalised. Moreover, the use of image and text in the brochure and the messages the organisers wish to convey may also need to be re-considered. This could be a significant factor affecting the production of fully customisable brochures.

In the case study festival the size of the festival brochure was an influencing factor on how the festival attendees perceived the value and relevance of the customised brochure. A small scale festival would wish to maximise the publicity of its events so may wish to limit the extent of individualisation and maintain control of its marketing and branding. For larger festivals such as the Edinburgh Fringe that include thousands of performances, the relevance and value of customisation could be more significant as a means of personalising the interactions with the festival, and creating a more unique image and message before the experience takes place. Brochure customisation may thus be more desirable for informational rather than promotional or lure brochures (Getz and Sailor 1993), or for brochures which are lengthy and detailed. At the same time though, more research is needed on the way festival attendees use the brochures for inspiration, as well as for information seeking purposes.

The next stage of research would be to explore how different tourism providers feel about brochure customisation. It is anticipated that their attitudes towards customisation will be conditioned by the size of the organisation they manage, the complexity and length of the brochure they produce as well as their own attitudes towards technological innovation. Further research should also be carried out with the users of brochures in a variety of contexts to begin to determine individual characteristics and attributes that may influence their approach to customisation. Such research would help to further refine how the personalisation of brochures influences the consumption of places and how places are imagined and consumed through this dynamic medium.

References

Álvarez, L.S., Diaz Martín, A.M. and Vásquez Casielles, R. 2007. Relationship marketing and information and communication technologies: analysis of retail travel agencies. *Journal of Travel Research*, 45(4), 453–63.

Aram, S. 2011. International tourists' image of Zhangjiajie, China: content analysis of travel blogs. *International Journal of Culture, Tourism and Hospitality Research* 5(3), 306–15.

Buhalis, D. 2003. *eTourism Information Technology for Strategic Management*. London: Pearson.

Chiou, W.-B., Wan, C.-S. and Lee, H.-Y. 2008.Virtual experiences vs brochures in the advertisement of scenic spots: how cognitive preferences and order effects influence advertising effects on consumers. *Tourism Management*, 29(1), 146–50.

Edelheim, J.R. 2007. Hidden messages: a polysemic reading of tourist brochures. *Journal of Vacation Marketing*, 13(1), 5–17.

Fink, J. and Kobsa, A. 2002. User modelling for personalised city tours. *Artificial Intelligence Review*, 18(1), 33–74.

Fotis, J., Buhalis, D. and Rossides, N. 2011. Social media impact on holiday travel planning: the case of the Russian and the FSU markets. *International Journal of Online Marketing* 1(4), 1–19.

Franke, T. 2003. Enhancing an online regional tourism consulting system with extended personalised services. *Information Technology & Tourism*, 5(3), 135–50.

Getz, D. and Sailor, L. 1993. Design of destination and attraction-specific brochures. *Journal of Travel &Tourism Marketing*, 2(2–3), 111–31.

Gilmore, J.H. and Pine II, B.J. 1997. Four faces of mass customization. *Harvard Business Review*. Jan–Feb 1997, 91–101.

Gration, D., Raciti., M and Arcodia, C. 2011. The role of consumer self-concept in marketing festivals. *Journal of Travel & Tourism Marketing*, 28(6), 644–55.

Gretzel, U. 2011. Intelligent systems in tourism: a social science perspective. *Annals of Tourism Research*, 38(3), 757–79.

Gretzel, U. and Jamal, T. 2009. Conceptualising the creative tourist class: technology, mobility and tourism experiences. *Tourism Analysis*, 14(4), 471–81.

Gretzel, U., Fezenmaier, D.R., Formica, S. and O' Leary, J.T. 2006. Searching for the future: challenges faced by destination marketing organisations. *Journal of Travel Research*, 45(2), 116–26.

Hart, C.W.L. 1995. Mass customisation: conceptual underpinnings, opportunities and limits. *International Journal of Service Industry Management*, 6(2), 36–45.

Hart, C.W. 1996. Made to order. *Marketing Management*, 5(2), 10–23.

Hays, S., Page, S. and Buhalis, D. 2012. Social media as a destination marketing tool: its use by national tourism organisations. *Current Issues in Tourism*. [DOI:10.1080/13683500.2012.662215]

Hillman, W. 2007. Travel authenticated? Postcards, tourist brochures and travel photography. *Tourism Analysis*, 12(3), 135–48.

Holloway, C. and Humphreys, C. 2012. *The Business of Tourism*. Harlow: Pearson Education.

Huffman, C. and Kahn, B.E. 1998. Variety for sale: mass customisation or mass confusion? *Journal of Retailing*, 74(4), 491–514.

Jansson, A. 2007. A sense of tourism New media and the dialectic of encapsulation/decapsulation. *Tourist Studies*, 7(1), 5–24.

Jennings, G. and Weiler, B. 2006. Mediating meaning: perspectives on brokering quality tourist experiences, in *Quality Tourism Experiences*, edited by G. Jennings and N. Nickerson. Oxford: Butterworth-Heinemann, 57–80.

Jiang, P. 2002. Exploring consumers' willingness to pay for online customisation and its marketing outcomes. *Journal of Targeting, Measurement and Analysis for Marketing*, 11(2), 168–83.

Johansson, M. and Kociatkiewicz, J. 2011. City festivals: creativity and control in staged urban experiences. *European Urban and Regional Studies*, 18(4), 392–405.

Larsen, J., Axhausen, K.W. and Urry, J. 2006. Geographies of social networks: meetings, travel and communications. *Mobilities*, 1(2), 261–83.

Lee, Y-K., Lee, C.-K., Lee, S.-K. and Babbin, B.J. 2008. Festivalscapes and patrons' emotions, satisfaction and loyalty. *Journal of Business Research*, 61(1), 56–64.

Loh, S., Lorenzi, F., Saldaña, R. and Lichtnow, D. 2004. A tourism recommender system based on collaboration and text analysis. *Information Technology & Tourism*, 6(3), 157–65.

Long, P. and Robinson, M. 2009. Tourism, popular culture and the media, in *The Sage Handbook of Tourism Studies*, edited by T. Jamal and M. Robinson. London: Sage, 98–114.

Månsson, M. 2011. Mediatised tourism. *Annals of Tourism Research*, 38(4), 1634–52.

Migas, N., Anastasiadou, C. and Stirling, A. 2008. individualized tourism brochures as a novel approach to mass customization. *Journal of Hospitality & Leisure Marketing*, 17(1–2), 237–57.

Molina, A. and Esteban, A. 2006. Tourism brochures usefulness and image. *Annals of Tourism Research*, 33(4), 1036–56.

Norrie, M.C., Palinginis, A. and Signer, B. 2005. *Content Publishing Framework for Interactive Paper Documents*. Proceedings of the 2005 ACM symposium on Document engineering, Bristol, UK, 187–96.

PODI. 2004. *Bermuda Department of Tourism Direct Mail Program* [Online] Available at http://www.podi.org [accessed: September 20 2007].

Prentice, R. and Andersen, V. 2003. Festival as creative destination. *Annals of Tourism Research*, 30(1), 7–30.

Ricci, F. and Werthner, H. 2002. Case base querying for travel planning recommendation. *Information Technology & Tourism*, 4(3–4), 215–26.

Rowley, J. 2002. *E-business Principles and Practice*. New York: Palgrave.

Rumetshofer, H., Pühretmair, F. and Wöß, W. 2003. Individual information presentation based on cognitive styles for tourism information systems, in *Information and Communication Technologies in Tourism (ENTER 2003)*, edited by A. Frew et al. New York/Wien: Springer-Verlag, 440–49.

Scarles, C. 2004. Mediating landscapes: the processes and practices of image construction in tourist brochures of Scotland. *Tourist Studies*, 4(1), 43–67.

Sigala, M. 2006. A framework for developing and evaluating mass customization strategies for online travel companies, in *Information and Communication Technologies in Tourism* 2006, *Proceedings of the International Conference in Lausanne, Switzerland*, edited by M. Hitz, et al. New York/Wien: Springer-Verlag, 112–24.

Tressider, R. 2010. What no pasties!? Reading the Cornish tourism brochure. *Travel & Tourism Marketing*, 27(6), 596–611.

Tussyadiah, I.P and Fesenmaier, D.R. 2009. Mediating tourist experiences: access to places via shared videos. *Annals of Tourism Research*, 36(1), 24–40.

Urry, J and Larsen, J. 2011. *The Tourist Gaze 3.0*. London: Sage.

Vogt, C. and Fesenmaier, D.R. 1998. Expanding the functional tourism information search mode. *Annals of Tourism Research*, 25(1), 551–78. Wan, C.-S., Tsaur, S.-H., Chiu, Y.-L. and Chiou, W.-B. 2007. Is the advertising effect of virtual experience always better or contingent on different travel destinations? *Information Technology and Tourism*, 9(1), 45–54.

Wang, D., Sangwon P. and Fesenmaier, D.R. 2012. The role of smartphones in mediating the touristic experience. *Journal of Travel Research*. 51(4), 371–387. [DOI: 10.1177/0047287511426341].

Ye, H. and Tussyadiah, I.P. 2011. Destination visual image and expectation of experiences. *Journal of Travel & Tourism Marketing*, 28(2), 129–44.

Yüksel, A. and Akgül, O. 2006. Postcards as affective image-makers: an idle agent in destination marketing. *Tourism Management*, 28(3), 714–25.

Zhou, Z. 1997. Destination marketing: measuring the effectiveness of brochures. *Journal of Travel & Tourism Marketing*, 6(3–4), 143–58.

Chapter 9

The Mediatisation of Culture: Japanese Contents Tourism and Pop Culture

Sue Beeton, Takayoshi Yamamura and Philip Seaton

In its truest sense, media 'mediates' messages between the sender and receiver, providing not only a language with which to communicate, but also a framework within which to place various communications and understand the tourist experience. Furthermore, the mediating and meaning-making role of media also motivates people to travel in general and to specific places, or in search of specific physical and/or emotional experiences. This is nicely illustrated in Laing and Frost's recent publication on *Books and Travel* (2012), where they consider the role of books in relation to inspiring travel, not only physically in the footsteps of the writers or their storylines, but also metaphorically in terms of the Hero's Journey, which many tourists tend to emulate in their internal dialogue and reminiscences. They argue that the books people have read 'culturally acclimatised [them] to aspects of travel, before they even set foot outside their front door...[and] have deep and nuanced effects on the traveller' (Laing and Frost 2012: 1–2). They conclude by arguing that media, in the form of literature, 'is a powerful agent for cultural change...through its influence on our ideas of travel, the way we experience travel and potentially on travel behaviour, including motivations' (Laing and Frost 2012: 193).

In this chapter, we look at the growing influence of popular culture on tourism in Japan, particularly in relation to film as an exemplar of today's popular cultural expression (Butler 1990). By applying the concepts of 'soft power' as introduced by Nye (1990a, 1990b) to popular culture and tourism, we illustrate its significance as a tourism generator and meaning-maker. We also argue that the attraction of film and popular culture is greater than the sum of its parts, imparting a sense of purpose to tourists following the path of the meanings (or content) inherent in popular culture.

It has certainly been noted that tourists are often attracted to a place due to the influence of the popular culture of the day, particularly since the age of mass media and (mass) tourism. The concept of the 'tourist gaze' as introduced into the tourism discourse by John Urry (1990) is becoming ever more mediated, with the mass media providing much of the gazing framework, interpretation and personal meaning for the individual as well as the mass tourist (Beeton et al., 2005). Jansson (2002: 431) further supports this, observing that 'the tourist gaze has become more and more intertwined with the consumption of media images'. However, even prior to that time, the popular media such as art and literature was already a powerful tourism attractor, with young English 'gentlemen' touring Europe on the Grand Tour of the eighteenth and nineteenth centuries in order to view and experience the great works of art and literature first hand (Hibbert 1969; Turner and Ash 1975; Towner 1985). This was not merely an artistic aesthetic upon which to gaze, but also the narratives in epic poems, literature and even art, played a major role in exoticising the Other, especially the 'Far East'. As Löfgren notes, these tourists were motivated by a search for the picturesque, 'a certain way of selecting, framing, and representing views' (Löfgren 1999: 19). Many European lay anthropologists, adventurers and travellers were also attracted to 'The East' desirous of experiencing the exotic cultures of the day, bringing back styles that became so popular in the modern design of the early twentieth century.

Such embedded narratives can be conceptualised as providing 'content' to the touristic attractiveness of places and images. The notion of 'contents tourism' (*kontentsu tsūrizumu*) is particularly Japanese, with broader research into this phenomenon to date facing a language/interpretation barrier, with key concepts or research findings struggling to make their way from Japanese into English or other languages, despite over a decade of research into the phenomenon in Japan. While this has been referred to as 'content' tourism, by the Japanese Ministry of Foreign Affairs (MOFA 2006a) along with some scholarly publications (for example Otmazgin and Ben-Ari 2012), it is more accurate to refer to it in the plural, as 'contents'. This is not only because it is closer to the Japanese pronunciation, but also because it better represents the plurality of contents (narratives, characters, locations, soundtracks and so on) in any given work that may create fan affinity with the work or actually induce tourism.

However, the rise in the West of interest in all aspects of Asian popular culture and a growing understanding of its nature presents opportunities for us to study this phenomenon from a broader, yet more inclusive, cultural perspective. Similar to the processes witnessed as a result of the *Hallyu* (Korean Wave) in Japan's east Asian neighbour (see Kim et al., 2007; Kim and Wang 2012), 'contents tourism' encompasses cultural elements of popular culture and their relationship to tourism. As a team of Australian, Japanese and English researchers and authors, we straddle the western, European and Asian divide; remaining heavily influenced by Hollywood and European media, yet having also experienced a growing Asian cultural perspective as a backdrop to our lives. While growing up loving the US Westerns and cartoons, those in the 'West' were also introduced to some Japanese anime (Japanese animated stories shown on film and television, as well as via the Internet) from an early age through TV series such as *Kimba the White Lion* (1965) and *Astro Boy* (1964). However, anime is not analogous to the western, 'Disney', interpretation of 'animation' as fantasy; rather it is a complex and detailed cultural form of expression, often being used to represent real places (and people) in minute detail.

Consequently, this chapter attempts to synthesise the Japanese as well as English language literature regarding the links between pop culture contents and tourism, and thereby provide a more nuanced understanding of media-induced tourism in the twenty-first century, which the nations of East Asia will play a huge role in shaping.

'Pop Culture' and Soft Power in Japan and Asia

While the actual term *pop culture* (as opposed to *popular* culture) did not join the public lexicon until the rock 'n' roll era of the late 1950s (Kennedy and Kennedy 2007), earlier forms of art and literature fit a broad understanding and use of that term today. Nevertheless, there are those who differentiate between 'high' and 'low' culture and 'high' and 'low' art, with the 'lows' tending to refer to the popular or 'pop' elements and being in some way inferior to the higher forms of art and culture (Wheeller 2009).

However, as Wheeller (2009) notes, this is a very limiting perspective to take when considering tourism, with Beeton (2005) arguing that even what we now consider to be 'high' art of the past was, more often than not, the popular culture of the day. For example, the works of Shakespeare are now considered to be a form of 'high' art, yet his plays were more often than not treated as one-off (or limited) performances primarily for a 'general' public (Patterson 1989). A contemporary example is the raising of Jack Kerouac's *On the Road* from a cult-based beat novel to a guide and road map for tourists as evidenced in the popular travel media (see Associated Press 2007, Reid 2012).

In 2012, the Australian Prime Minister, Julia Gillard, announced an Asian focused policy initiative in the White Paper *Australia in the Asian Century*, further acknowledging Australia's place and role in the Asia-Pacific region, now and into the future (Commonwealth of Australia 2012). Yet, many young Australians would be surprised that we need to articulate such a policy. They are already familiar with much of Asia's contemporary popular culture, from the Korean *Hallyu* and K-Pop to Japanese anime, manga and even J-Pop, converging with tourism to create what in Japan has become known as 'contents tourism'. As noted in the White Paper:

> Intraregional tourism has boomed and popular culture is now shared across Asia as more people throughout the region and the world discovered Japan's pop music and manga, Hong Kong cinema, South Korea's television soaps and India's Bollywood films. (Commonwealth of Australia 2012: 46)

If we were not already aware of the love for, and fascination with, Asian pop culture in Australia, recent articles in our national newspapers on the phenomenon, along with the success of blockbuster exhibits such as *Game Masters* at the Australian Centre for the Moving Image (ACMI 2012), reinforce this; all of which appears to be exacerbated by social communication and technology. The fascinating global rise of Korean pop star, PSY (Park Joe-sang), and his Gangnam dance style is more than simply a fleeting fad, with it becoming the most viewed YouTube clip of all time (at the end of 2012). While he may fade from the public consciousness, the pop culture of South Korea continues to become more and more embedded in Western as well as Asian cultures. Furthermore, the J-Pop of Japan is also moving beyond Asia, with stars such as the fashion blogger Kyari

Pamyu Pamyu's breakout hit *PonPonPon*, which has been described as 'making *Gangnam Style* look like an elderly Sting taking a long lunch' (Bayley 2012).

So, what has this to do with tourism? As with the points made in the opening section concerning the role of popular culture in our early travel, a case can be made that today's pop culture is also a powerful motivator, contributor and mediator of the tourism experience, as eloquently illustrated in the work of Iwashita (2006: 59), when she states that '...popular cultural forms of the media can promote, confirm and reinforce particular images, views, and identities of destinations in a very powerful manner', along with that of Karpovich (2010), Kim (2010), Croy and Heitmann (2011), among others. Furthermore, when we combine a range of senses such as the audio with the visual, the result can be outstanding, both in terms of our experience of the pop cultural phenomenon and then even more so during an experience at a site, be that physical, metaphorical or imaginary.

If we look at this in relation to film and TV, the relationship becomes even clearer. From late last century, numerous studies have looked at the relationship between movies, TV and tourism in relation to Hollywood and Europe including Tooke and Baker (1996), Riley, Baker and Van Doren (1998), Beeton (2000, 2001, 2005, 2006, 2010), Croy (2010), Reijnders (2011) and Connell (2012). Following on from this work, we are beginning to see commentators from Asia considering this relationship in terms of inter-Asian as well as international tourism, such as Kim et al. (2007) and Kim and Wang (2012). This emerging literature regarding Asia not only allows us to see different case studies of film-induced tourism, but also to develop new theoretical insights into the phenomenon informed by particular conditions in Asia.

One particularly important characteristic in this regard is the discourses of power within film-induced tourism in Asia. While the Western relationship between film and tourism is typically thought of in terms of a global consumer culture and analysed in isolation from broader geopolitical discourses (with the exception perhaps of critical noises about the 'cultural imperialism' inherent in Hollywood's global reach from observers such as Hayward 2000, Beeton 2008 and Mintz and Roberts 2010), in Japan, film-induced tourism is an important element of the debate about how pop culture affects contemporary regional politics and relations.

Such discourses developed after Nye (1990b) introduced the notion of popular culture as a form of 'soft power'. *Soft power* is distinguished from *hard power* – military and economic power that can force other countries to obey – in that the former can be defined as the kind of power that enables a state to build favourable international relations based on the confidence of the international community and influence therein. Such confidence and influence can be enhanced through other countries' support to, understanding of, or sympathy with culture, political values and policies of the state. Joseph Nye, professor at the Harvard Kennedy School, first conceptualised soft power in his book *Bound to Lead*, published in 1990. This concept was further refined in his subsequent book, *Soft Power*, published in 2004.

Since then, the popularity of Japanese pop culture across Asia has been frequently seen as a positive form of 'soft co-optive power' which counterbalances or coexists with negative forms of 'hard command power' (whether present geopolitical and/or economic rivalries, or insensitive official handling by the Japanese government of 'history issues', namely the legacies of Japanese militarism in the twentieth century). An influential article by American journalist Douglas McGray titled 'Japan's gross national cool' (McGray 2002) then helped to trigger an active policy of cultural diplomacy. In a key speech on the issue, Aso Taro (then Foreign Minister but later Prime Minister) urged content industry practitioners to 'join with us in polishing the Japan "brand"' (Ministry of Foreign Affairs 2006a). The appeal of cultural diplomacy in Japan is that, given the restraints on Japanese military and diplomatic power since its defeat in World War II, cultural power or 'soft power' enables Japan to exert a presence on the world stage beyond simply its economic presence.

But, the soft power discourse precipitated by Nye's and McGray's work, and its manifestation within Japanese policy under the banner of 'Cool Japan' or cultural diplomacy, opens up a complex debate about the real nature and effectiveness of soft power (see for example Press-Barnathan 2012, Bouissou 2012). Glen Fukushima (2006: 18), for example, questions whether the popularity of a nation's pop culture really translates into soft power:

> Japanese no doubt find it gratifying to see that karaoke is the rave in certain parts of Asia, sushi restaurants can be found in Europe, and manga is being read by youth in the United States. But does this really mean that Japan is therefore more respected, trusted, or admired by others, or that it has greater influence on the thinking and behavior of others?

Fukushima breaks the debate down into those who argue Japan should enhance its soft power through cultural diplomacy, and those who argue that Japan achieves considerable soft power via its pop culture whether Japan likes it or not. As the citation above indicates, ultimately Fukushima is suspicious of the real extent of 'soft power' generated by popular culture and calls on Japan to develop 'a grand strategy to win friends, gain supporters, and influence world opinion' (ibid.: 20).

The need for a grand strategy becomes particularly important when one considers that international opinions of Japanese pop culture are not always positive. Indeed, the use of pop culture diplomacy, or defining the national brand in terms of pop culture, may be considered a double-edged sword. According to the definition of pop culture of the Ministry of Foreign Affairs (2006b: http://www.mofa.go.jp/mofaj/annai/shingikai/koryu/h18_sokai/05hokoku.html), pop culture is 'culture produced in the course of the daily activities of ordinary people' and is 'culture that has been refined through people's daily lives; and it is through this culture that the sensitivity and spirit of the Japanese people is communicated, and a portrait of the nation is presented' [author translation]. According to this perspective, *ukiyo-e*, pottery, the tea ceremony and other art forms now considered quintessential examples of Japanese traditional culture were expressions of the pop culture of the time.

Yet, such promotion of pop culture diplomacy can be criticised for an uncritical assumption that pop culture automatically has positive connotations for those abroad. The strategy can easily backfire where there is the potential for confusion between fiction and reality. For example, if a fictional character such as Doraemon is sent on an ambassadorial mission rather than a real human being, it may simply end up in fictional diplomacy – some empty smiles and handshakes that make attractive media copy, but which do little to address substantial issues (or perhaps even cause resentment that the empty smiles and handshakes belittle those more substantial issues). And while much Japanese pop culture comprises beautifully crafted illustrations/animation, inventive storylines and appealing characters, some manga and anime contain explicit sex and violence, which has created something of a notorious international reputation for the genres (Ravitch and Viteritta 2003, Wong 2007). When communicating the 'sensitivity and spirit of the Japanese people', Japan as the land of explicit sex and violence is surely not the nation branding the Ministry of Foreign Affairs has in mind. Therefore, the precise nature of the power of popular culture in Japan and its effectiveness or appropriateness in nation branding is still an issue of considerable debate. Yet, what is clear is that the power of pop culture contents to induce tourism is increasing and gaining ever more attention in media and scholarly circles. And given the examples of Asian popular culture that have made considerable impacts outside the region (such as Korean rapper PSY), interest in this phenomenon will simply continue to grow.

From Film-induced Tourism to Contents Tourism

Film-induced tourism has been variously defined and described as movie-induced tourism (Riley et al. 1998), cinematic tourism (Tzanelli 2010), film tourism (Roesch 2009), set jetting (Grihault 2007), TV tourism (Reijnders 2011) and so on. Beeton (2000) initially applied the term 'film-induced tourism' to encompass the range of terms that have emerged over the past 15 years. For this chapter, we continue to apply Beeton's inclusive and broad use of the term 'film' to cover fictional movies and TV series as well as animation, but we also are expanding the whole concept into 'contents tourism'.

Japan has a vibrant and extremely creative film industry. Hundreds of feature films are produced each year, mainly by the major studios such as Toei, but also by independent production companies. Japanese anime films, of which those produced by Studio Ghibli and Oscar-winning director Miyazaki Hayao are merely the tip of the iceberg, have achieved global recognition and a massive international fan base. Japanese television dramas may reach domestic audiences of 10 to 20 million people and achieve popularity abroad, too, particularly in Asia. National and local governments in Japan have realised the potential of film-induced tourism. At a national government level, the Japan National Tourism Organisation (JNTO) has produced anime maps in English and other languages to guide fans to anime locations (Japan Anime Map 2011). At the end of 2012, the webpage also has a link called 'Pilgrimages to Sacred Sites', which leads to an interactive map covering cinema as well as anime. Hokkaido (where two of the authors of this paper are based) is the location for two movies on this map – *Love Letter* (1995) and *If You Are the One* (2008) – which stimulated film-induced tourism among Korean and Chinese tourists respectively. These movies also feature on a dedicated film tourism page in the official tourism website of the Hokkaido government, *Visit Hokkaido: Hokkaido in a movie and a drama* (sic) (2011). TV series also play a major touristic role, with the locations of dwellings from the TV series *From the Northern Country* (1981–2002), including Goro's Stone House and the Recycled House, along with a dedicated museum remaining strong tourist attractions around the Furano district today.

Elsewhere across Japan, local authorities are realising the potential of film-induced tourism, too. As in many Western countries, Japanese local authorities these days frequently have film commissions to attract filmmakers and provide support on location. The national organisation is the Japan Film Commission (http://www.japanfc.org/en/index.php) established in 2009 as successor to the Japan Film Commission Promotion Council. Their website provides links to the many regional film commissions throughout the country. Furthermore, employees are assigned to the task of ensuring their town does not miss out on the potential benefits of film making and its associated tourism. This is particularly the case when the locations are assured national attention through being the setting for a major cinematic or television production. For example, after Japan's public broadcaster NHK (Nippon Hōsō Kyōkai) announced in June 2011 that Aizu-Wakamatsu would be the location for part of the 2013 Taiga Drama about the life of Niijima Yae (the 'Bakumatsu Joan of Arc' who fought in the defence of Aizu-Wakamatsu Castle during the Boshin War, 1868–9), the decision was widely welcomed as providing a much-needed boost to Fukushima prefecture after the 11 March 2011 earthquake and nuclear disaster. Taiga Dramas run for a whole year on Sunday evening primetime and typically generate large tourism booms in the sites featured in the drama (see Seaton forthcoming). That September, Aizu-Wakamatsu city announced that it was setting up a project team and would be opening exhibits to coincide with the drama (Fukushima Minyu Nyūsu 2011). Preparing to take advantage of film-induced tourism is now 'standard operating practice' in Japan.

Film-induced tourism in Japan, therefore, exists in a form easily recognisable from the key theoretical work in the English-language literature. However, within Japanese-language scholarship and official government reports, discussion of film-induced tourism has taken on a slightly different character to its English-language equivalents. There are some young Japanese scholars working to apply the main theoretical concepts from the English-language literature to the Japanese case – for example, Kimura's (2011) work on film location tourism – but the buzzword in the Japanese academy, and the term adopted by the Japanese government in its official promotional strategies regarding film-induced tourism, is the aforementioned 'contents tourism'.

As noted in the introduction of this chapter, the term 'contents tourism' is a Japanese concept that has been in use for over ten years, referring to all aspects of pop culture in relation to tourism. The concept of contents (*kontentsu*) in relation to theme and narrative in popular culture emerged in scholarly and business circles in the 1990s. Following the emergence of the concept, scholars started reconsidering early forms of tourism in Japan and arguing that what is now called contents tourism has actually existed for centuries. Masubuchi (2010: 29), for example, gives the example of visits to sites immortalised in the poetry of Matsuo Bashō (1644–94) during the Edo period as an early form of contents tourism.

'Contents' as a concept made its way into the official language of the Japanese government's tourism strategy in a 2005 report published jointly by the Ministry of Land, Infrastructure, Transport and Tourism (MLITT), the Ministry of Economy, Trade and Industry, and the Agency for Cultural Affairs. The report defined the essence of contents tourism as follows: 'the addition of a "narrative quality" (*monogatarisei*) or "theme" (*teemasei*) to a region – namely an atmosphere or image particular to the region generated by the contents – and the use of that narrative quality as a tourism resource' (MLITT et al. 2005: 49). The different forms of contents tourism were broken down in the following way:

This table contains many of the familiar elements from the film-induced tourism literature, but, as already stated, cuts across particular media forms to focus on the narratives: *monogatarisei* (narrative quality) is the key word in the contents tourism literature. In this context, Horiuchi (2010) presents a simple model of the three main players in contents tourism, in which, interestingly, films or other media forms are not mentioned by name at all, but subsumed within a generic 'contents businesses' (*kontentsu sangyō*).

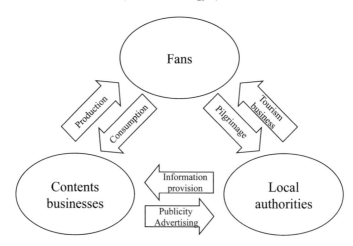

Figure 9.1   The players in contents tourism

Source: adapted from Horiuchi 2010: 62.

Note: Horiuchi's model refers specifically to history fans and the so-called 'history boom', the tourism generated by representations in the media of popular historical figures from the samurai period (broadly speaking the twelfth century to the 1870s). In the diagram, 'history fans' has been changed to 'fans'. [Translated by the authors.]

Table 9.1 Forms of contents tourism

	Type of Contents	
	Films, TV Dramas, Novels	**Manga, Anime, Games**
Displays or exhibitions of the contents	– Museum about the writer – Exhibits of the sets or props used during production	– Museum about the writer or producer – Exhibits about the characters
Preservation or construction of sites that contribute to the use of contents	– Preserving locations – Preserving sets used in filming	– Erecting monuments in stations or high streets
Holding events related to the contents	– Film festivals – Talks by directors, actors and writers; accompanied tours – Cosplay events for fans and *otaku*	– Talks by directors, voice actors and writers; accompanied tours – Cosplay events for fans and *otaku*
Performances for enjoying the contents	– Accompanied tours with directors, actors and writers	– Putting anime characters on public transport
Sale of spin-off goods or product branding	– Using images from the contents on local products – Using the contents in local area branding strategies	
Information provision	– Publicity through various media: television, newspapers, magazines, etc. – Publicity on the Internet – Local information provision through weblogs	
Human resources	– Training volunteer tour guides – Encouraging the participation of locals as extras during filming – Holding competitions to develop a new generation of creators – Supporting local people working in creative media	– Supporting the local people working in creative media

Source: MLITT et al. 2005: 50. [Translated by the authors.]

Yamamura (2011: 50–53), meanwhile, introduces the concepts of the 'media mix' and 'multi-use' to highlight how the distinctions between different media forms are broken down as the same contents appear across different forms. He identifies three important periods:

1. *The 1990s*: The development of the media mix – Characters and narratives appear much more in different forms including anime, manga, novels and games.
2. *The early 2000s*: The Internet as media – The rise in blogging and Internet use expanded the role of contents production and development into the domain of all people, particularly fans who used their sites to generate their own interpretations of contents.
3. *The later 2000s*: The region as media and site of interaction – Tourist sites, like other forms of media, are thought of as a vessel that transfers contents from producers to consumers, yet they also become places where people who share an interest in the same contents may come together as tourists and fans in a real rather than virtual community.

When fans start uploading their home-produced videos incorporating elements of the original contents to YouTube, or produce their own online guidebooks/ weblogs to disseminate information about locations to other fans, or set up cosplay events (via social networking sites) at which the fans assemble 'in character', or produce fanzines for sale at comics markets, they have assumed an active role in both the evolution of the contents and the touristic behaviour they drive. Fans become 'prosumers' (Yamamura 2011: 48), producers and consumers, whose fandom and online activities work to create the very contents that stimulate their own and others' desires to visit the sites that they consume as tourists. Within specialised communities of fans, the contents they produce and disseminate among themselves are typically the trusted sources of information accessed prior to any touristic activity, rather than the information disseminated by official local tourism boards trying to promote visitation to their community. Fans/tourists many even forge strong links with local communities and act as volunteer guides, thereby completely turning traditional notions of 'host' and 'guest' on their heads.

In this context, it is appropriate to think of regions and tourist sites as media. If media is defined as something that 'mediates' messages between a sender and a recipient, a museum panel or monument performs precisely the same function as a newspaper article or documentary. What distinguishes a newspaper and a museum panel, however, is where the onus lies for actually being able to access the information via the media. In the vernacular usage of 'media' (television, newspapers and so on), the onus is on the producer to place the product in the hands of the consumer during the course of daily life: to place the book on a shelf in a local bookshop, or put the film onto the TV screens of people in their homes. In other words, the physical product is able to be 'sent' to the consumer. While the consumer may still play some active role in obtaining the product, it is very different to the more intangible tourist experience that cannot be experienced at home. In that situation, the onus is on the tourists to physically visit the tourism site in order to experience it, on what is usually a conscious break from their normal daily routines.

Yet, just as the Internet has collapsed distinctions between 'producer and consumer', so too has it collapsed the distinction between 'media' and 'tourist sites' by unifying the act of consuming media products with the act of visiting (web)sites. Furthermore, the virtual communities created when fans chat in online chatrooms become real communities of people when they converge on the geographical locations special to them (a practice in Japan known as *ofu-kai* or 'offline meetings'). All these issues that arise at the intersections between 'media' and 'tourism', and the multifaceted role of the Internet in connecting the 'film' and 'tourism' elements of 'film-induced tourism', constitute the very essence of the contents tourism literature.

A further key issue in contents tourism concerns the transition that has to be made from an appreciation of the contents to an appreciation of the locality related to the contents. Unless this transition is made, fans do not convert their media experiences into touristic ones. In many of the early Japanese case studies of Japanese contents tourism – such as *Lucky Star* (Yamamura forthcoming a), *K-On* (Okamoto forthcoming) and *Sengoku BASARA* (Yamamura forthcoming b) – forging a strong and mutually beneficial relationship between the fans and the community is crucial to the success of the contents tourism strategy.

The development of these ideas within tourism studies has taken place against a backdrop of considerable changes in the natures and practices of tourism. The tourism sector in Japan has gone through a number of stages in its development. Very broadly speaking, the Japanese tourism sector has gone through three major phases in recent decades (adapted from Ishimori and Yamamura 2009: 9):

1. *Mass Tourism* (1960s–70s): In this period, tourism was driven by tour operators; 'tour companies' enabled 'customers' to visit sites; tourism assets were seen as a source of profit-making opportunities; and the contents driving any media-induced tourism were national media events in a period of limited numbers of television channels, radio stations and cinema studios. This might also be called 'industrial society' tourism.

2. *New Tourism* (1980s–90s): In this period, the focus was more on the local communities possessing tourism resources; 'hosts' welcomed 'guests' into their communities; policy was directed to creating resorts to activate those local resources; and the contents driving any media-induced tourism were diversifying with increased options for media consumption, particularly in the form of private viewing (namely videos in which viewers choose the time and place of their viewing). This might also be called 'destination' or 'community-based' tourism.

3. *Next Generation Tourism* (2000s onwards): In this period, tourism is driven by lifestyles; individuals undertake more independent travel; economic transactions are between individuals in a touristic space; and the contents

driving any media-induced tourism are chosen largely by individuals from a vast range of media and Internet-based options. This might also be called 'information age' tourism.

'Contents tourism' has particularly come to the fore in the Next Generation or 'Information Age' phase. This does not mean that the characteristics and practices of touristic behaviour evident in previous generations have disappeared, but merely that new trends are laid on top of older practices resulting in a massive diversification of the options available to tourists and therefore greatly increasing complexity in tourism behaviour.

But in the information age stage, issues of communication and media are intertwined with tourism at all stages of the process. The processes of the mediatisation of culture, therefore, comprise two parallel processes occurring in tourist sites: first, the tourist sites themselves become media sites in which meanings are transmitted from the creators of the spaces and monuments (either the original creators or those who have converted a pre-existing site into a tourist site), and second, the act of visiting those sites is itself mediatised by the recording and dissemination of experiences via media (such as blogs) which are available to an ever-increasing global population, in this age of smart phones and high-speed WiFi. In this sense, contents tourism gives birth to even more contents that create for every tourist site an ever-changing milieu of travelogs, blogs and other forms of contents that will inform or induce the travel experiences of the next wave of visitors.

Conclusion

In this form of mediatised tourism and culture, young people in the digital generation will inevitably play a central role in further developing the practices of next-generation tourism. Entrusting the future to today's youth might cause consternation in some circles, but this has been the case for centuries, and certainly the existing evidence from Japan is not necessarily a cause for concern. Many young traveller-fans in Japan have already illustrated that in concert with local communities, a mutual, healthy respect for media contents often translates into a healthy respect among tourists for the communities that they visit. This is the experience in a number of towns across Japan that have witnessed contents tourism booms.

Genuine fans of an anime are far more likely to post on Facebook a photo of themselves posing in front of a key location from the anime than to deface it with graffiti, and codes of conduct even extend to erasing personal information such as car number plates from uploaded photos (Okamoto forthcoming 2013). When affinity with and respect for the contents has been converted into similar feelings toward the local community where those contents were set, communities have often benefitted from high levels of repeat business among traveller-fans, and even active participation in community promotion and development (such as fans of the anime *Lucky Star* taking part in Haji festival of Washinomiya Shrine, or returning to favourite restaurants in the town where over repeat visits they have built up a rapport with the owner – see Yamamura forthcoming a). In this sense, many young people who have become contents tourists have shifted their mindset from tourism as a form of consumption to tourism as a lifestyle and a way to provide additional meaning to their lives.

So, when we travel, we tend to take all of these cultural references with us, which in turn inform our travel experiences, presenting a multi-faceted 'language' which we use to interpret them. This in itself provides many guidelines for those involved in presenting or creating tourism experiences – while we are certainly not all fans of specific genres of movies or other forms of pop culture, we are, in the main, fascinated by their role in today's society, and often seek further understanding of them in relation to the cultures we experience through our travel.

However, 'contents tourism' is not only a form of tourism for young people in Japan, with older visitors continuing to demonstrate a fascination with their own (and others') versions of popular culture and the layers of meaning this can provide. By looking at popular cultural tourism in terms of its content and meaning, we can take the notion of 'contents tourism' beyond Japan, using it as a framework from which to consider the relationship between tourism and culture of the day in other cultures and parts of the world.

References

Associated Press. 2007. 'On the Road' with Jack Kerouac: Retrace famed author's steps on the 50th anniversary of his masterpiece, NBC News. com http://www.msnbc.msn.com/id/20977397/ns/travel-destination_travel/t/road-jack-kerouac/, [accessed: 20 December 2012].

Bayley, J. 2012. Ears tuned to the East. *The Age*, October 28: www.theage.com.au.

Beeton, S. 2000. It's a Wrap! What happens after the film crew leaves? An examination of community responses to film-induced tourism *TTRA National Conference – Lights! Camera! Action!*, Burbank, CA, 127–36.

Beeton, S. 2001. Smiling for the camera: the influence of film audiences on a budget tourism destination. *Tourism, Culture & Communication*, 3(1), 15–26.

Beeton, S. 2005. *Film-Induced Tourism*. Clevedon: Channel View Publications.

Beeton, S. 2006. Understanding film-induced tourism. *Tourism Analysis*, 11(3), 181–8.

Beeton, S. 2008. Partnerships and social responsibility: leveraging tourism and international film business, in *International Business and Tourism: Global Issues, Contemporary Interactions*, edited by Tim Coles and C. Michael Hall. London: Routledge, 256–72.

Beeton, S. 2010. The advance of film tourism. *Tourism and Hospitality Planning & Development*, 7(1), 1–6.

Beeton, S., Bowen, H. and Santos, C. 2005. State of knowledge: mass media and its relationship to perceptions of quality, in *Quality Tourism Experiences*, edited by G. Jennings and N. Nickerson. Oxford: Elsevier Butterworth-Heinemann, 25–37.

Bouissou, J-M. 2012. Popular culture as a tool for soft power: myth or reality? Manga in four European countries, in *Popular Culture and the State in East and Southeast Asia*, edited by N. Otmazgin and E. Ben-Ari. Abingdon, Oxon: Routledge, 46–64.

Butler, R.W. 1990. The influence of media in shaping international tourist patterns. *Tourism Recreation Research*, 15(2), 42–63.

Commonwealth of Australia 2012. *Australia in the Asian Century*. Licensed from the Commonwealth of Australia under a Creative Commons Attribution 3.0 Australia Licence.

Connell, J. 2012. Film tourism – evolution, progress and prospects. *Progress in Tourism Management*, 33(5), 1007–29.

Croy, G. 2010. Planning for film tourism: active destination image management. *Tourism and Hospitality Planning & Development*, 7(1), 21–30

Croy, G. and Heitmann, S. 2011. Tourism and film, in *Research Themes for Tourism*, edited by P. Robinson, S. Heitmann and P.U.C. Dieke. Wallingford: CAB International, 188–204.

Fukushima, G. 2006. Japan's 'Soft Power', *Japan Foreign Trade Council Newsletter*, July/August 2006. http://www.jftc.or.jp/shoshaeye/contribute/contrib2006_078b.pdf [accessed: 12 December 2012].

Fukushima Minyu Nyūsu. 2011. Wakamatsu ni taiga dorama 'Yae no sakura' no tenjikan setsuritsu e. 14th September 2011. http://www.minyu-net.com/news/news/0914/news7.html [Accessed: 26 September 2011].

Grihault, N. 2007. *Set-Jetting Tourism – International*. London: Mintel International Group.

Hayward, S. 2000. Framing National Cinemas, *Cinema and Nation*, edited by M.H. Jort and S. Mackenzie. London: Routledge, 88–102.

Hibbert, C. 1969. *The Grand Tour*. London: Putnam.

Horiuchi, J. 2010. Rekishi kontentsu no juyō ni kansuru jittai chōsa: 'Shinsengumi' kontentsu ni kansuru chōsa hōkoku. *Japanese Association for Contents History Studies Annual Conference 2010*. 61–71.

Ishimori, S. and Yamamura, T. 2009. Jōhō shakai ni okeru kankō kakumei: bunkashiteki ni mita kankō no gurōbaru torendo. *JACIC Joho* 24(2): 5–17. http://eprints.lib.hokudai.ac.jp/dspace/bitstream/2115/39125/1/JACIC_Vol94_ishimori-yamamura.pdf (accessed: 12 December 2012).

Iwashita, C. 2006. Media representation of the UK as a destination for Japanese tourists: popular culture and tourism. *Tourist Studies*, 6 (1), 59–77.

Jansson, A. 2002. Spatial phantasmagoria: the mediatization of tourism experience. *European Journal of Communication*, 17(4), 429–33.

Japan Anime Map, 2011. http://www.jnto.go.jp/eng/animemap/index.html [accessed: 11 December 2012].

Karpovich, A.I. 2010. Theoretical approaches to film-motivated tourism. *Tourism and Hospitality Planning & Development*, 7(1), 7–20.

Kennedy, M. and Kennedy, J.B. 2007. *The Concise Oxford Dictionary of Music*. 5th edition. Oxford University Press, Oxford.

Kim, S. 2010. Extraordinary experience: re-enacting and photographing at screen tourism locations. *Tourism and Hospitality Planning & Development*, 7(1), 59–75.

Kim, S. and Wang, H. 2012. From television to the film set: Korean drama *Daejanggeum* drives Chinese, Taiwanese, Japanese and Thai audiences to screen-tourism. *International Communication Gazette*, 74(5), 423–42.

Kim, S.S., Agrusa, J., Lee, H. and Chon, K. 2007. Effects of Korean television dramas on the flow of Japanese tourists. *Tourism Management*, 28, 1340–53.

Kimura, M. 2011. Eiga satsueichi ni okeru kankō genshō no kanōsei ni kansuru ichikōsatsu: satsueichi kanren jōhō ni shōten wo atete. *Journal of Contents Tourism Studies*, 2. http://eprints.lib.hokudai.ac.jp/dspace/bitstream/2115/44703/1/HUS CAP02kimura.pdf [accessed: 11 December 2012].

Laing, J. and Frost, W. 2012. *Books and Travel. Inspiration, Quests and Transformation*. Bristol: Channel View Publications.

Löfgren, O. 1999. *On Holiday: A History of Vacationing*. Berkeley: University of California Press.

Masubuchi, T. 2010. *What is Contents Tourism? Monogatari wo tabi suru hitobito*. Tokyo: Sairyusha.

McGray, D. 2002. Japan's gross national cool. *Foreign Policy*, 130, 44–54.

Ministry of Land, Infrastructure, Transport and Tourism et al. 2005. Eizō tō kontentsu no seisaku katsuyō ni yoru chiiki shinkō no arikata ni kansuru chōsa hōkokusho. http://www.mlit.go.jp/kokudokeikaku/souhatu/h16seika/12eizou/12eizou.htm [accessed: 26 September 2011].

Ministry of Foreign Affairs. 2006a. A New Look at Cultural Diplomacy: a Call to Japan's Cultural Practitioners. Speech by Foreign Minister Aso Taro at Digital Hollywood University. http://www.mofa.go.jp/announce/fm/aso/speech0604–2.html [accessed: 11 December 2012).

Ministry of Foreign Affairs. 2006b. 'Poppu karuchā no bunka gaikō ni okeru katsuyō' ni kansuru hōkoku. http://www.mofa.go.jp/mofaj/annai/shingikai/koryu/h18_sokai/05hokoku.html [accessed: 11 December 2012].

Mintz, S. and Roberts, R.W. 2010. Introduction: the social and cultural history of American film, in *Hollywood's America: Twentieth-Century America through Film*, 4th edition, edited by S. Mintz and R.W. Roberts. Chichester: Wiley-Blackwell.

Nye, J.S. 1990a. *Bound to Lead: The Changing Nature of American Power*. New York: Basic Books.

Nye, J.S. 1990b. Soft power. *Foreign Policy*, 80, 153–71.

Nye, J.S. 2004. *Soft Power: The Means to Success in World Politics*. New York: PublicAffairs.

Okamoto, T. forthcoming. Otaku tourism and the Anime Pilgrimage Phenomenon in Japan.

Otmazgin, N. and Ben-Ari, E. (eds) 2012. *Popular Culture and the State in East and Southeast Asia*. Abingdon, Oxon: Routledge.

Patterson, A.M. 1989. *Shakespeare and the Popular Voice*. Oxford: Basil Blackwell Inc.

Press-Barnathan, G. 2012. Does popular culture matter to international relations scholars? Possible links and methodological challenges, in *Popular Culture and the State in East and Southeast Asia*, edited by N. Otmazgin and E. Ben-Ari. Abingdon, Oxon: Routledge, 29–45.

Ravitch, D. and Viteritta, J.P. 2003. Toxic lessons: children and popular culture, in *Kid Stuff: Marketing Sex and Violence to America's Children*, edited by D. Ravitch and J.P. Viteritta. Baltimore, MD: Johns Hopkins University Press, 1–18.

Reid, R. 2012. Jack Kerouac's US Road Trip, *BBC Travel*, 12 September, 2012, http://www.bbc.com/travel/feature/20120913–jack-kerouacs-us-road-trip, [accessed: 20 December, 2012].

Reijnders, S. 2011. *Places of the Imagination: Media, Tourism, Culture*. Farnham: Ashgate.

Riley, R., Baker, D. and Van Doren, C.S. 1998. Movie Induced Tourism. *Annals of Tourism Research*, 25(4), 919–35.

Roesch, S., 2009. *The Experiences of Film Location Tourists*. Clevedon: Channel View.

Seaton, P. forthcoming. Taiga Dramas and Tourism: Historical Contents as Sustainable Tourist Resources.

Tooke, N. and Baker, M. 1996. Seeing is believing: the effect of film on visitor numbers to screened locations. *Tourism Management*, 17(2), 87–94.

Towner, J. 1985. The Grand Tour: a key phase in the history of tourism. *Annals of Tourism Research*, 12, 297–333.

Turner, L., and Ash, J. 1975. *The Golden Hordes: International Tourism and the Pleasure Periphery*. London: Constable.

Tzanelli, R. 2010. *The Cinematic Tourist*. London: Routledge.

Urry, J. 1990. *The Tourist Gaze: Leisure and Travel in Contemporary Societies*. London: Sage Publications.

Visit Hokkaido: Hokkaido in a Movie and a Drama (sic.), 2011. http://en.visit-hokkaido.jp/events/movie/index.html [accessed: 11 December 2012].

Wheeller, B. 2009. Tourism and the arts, in *Philosophical Issues in Tourism*, edited by J. Tribe. Bristol: Channel View Publications, 191–210.

Won, K.S. 2007. A study of anime's success factors in the USA and its suggestions. *International Journal of Contents*, 3(1): 29–33.

Yamamura, T. 2011. *Anime, manga de chiiki shinkō*. Tokyo: Tokyo Hōrei Shuppan.

Yamamura, T. forthcoming a. Contents Tourism and Local Community Response: *Lucky Star* and Collaborative Anime-Induced Tourism in Washimiya.

Yamamura, T. forthcoming b. Revitalization of Historical Heritage Using Pop Culture in Japan: Shiroishi City and the Game/Anime *Sengoku BASARA*.

Chapter 10
Developing the E-Mediated Gaze[1]

Peter Robinson

Introduction

This chapter reflects upon and develops the conceptual model presented by Robinson (2012), which proposes an e-mediated tourist gaze, exploring the ways in which tourism images are produced digitally and shared with global audiences through forums, image sharing websites and Google Earth. It considers the role of technology in the development of the tourist gaze, and develops a discussion which begins by considering the relationship between visuality and tourism, and then explores the geo-spatial nature of images and the ways in which they are accessed and understood in order to mediate, or rather in this instance, e-mediate, the construction of destinations and places in relation to tourist activity. Robinson (2012) notes that numerous authors have explored the relationship between tourism and visuality across a range of disciplines, including Baudrillard (1988), Debore (1983), Emmison and Smith (2000), Hamburger (1997), Haraway (1991), Mirzoeff (1998), Mitchell (1998), Pink (2001), Rose (2001), Shohat and Stam (1998), Urry (1990), and Virilio (1994). However, much of this research has, focused upon either the collection of photographs and postcards, or the presentation of images in travel brochures and marketing materials, carefully selected by those responsible for promoting a destination.

This chapter explores the role of technology in the tourist gaze, and considers current research around the mediation of place through technology. There is a clear lack of empirical research to explore how the gaze, and its relationship to semiotics and tourist behaviour, has been influenced, manipulated or altered by technological innovation (Robinson 2012). As a result, the chapter also considers the complex relationships which exist within and between new technologies and the gazes that they offer. The ability to view destinations online, with photos, street views and links to a range of information sources, offer an opportunity to view images of the tourist destination which result from the collection and display of images captured at different times, by different people, through different lenses, as opposed to the 'official' lens of the destination management organisation which adopts its own semiotic language and content in order to define the destination. This

---

1 This chapter draws upon and develops work published in Robinson, P. (2012), The e-mediated (Google Earth) gaze: an observational and semiotic perspective, *Current Issues in Tourism*, 15(4), 353–67.

creates an official and an unofficial representation of place which is much more complex as a result of the instantaneous and infinite scope of digital technologies, and the ability to share these globally with other Web 2.0 literate Internet users. As a result, the chapter concludes by highlighting contemporary issues in the creation of place and self through digital technologies.

Visuality in Tourism

As Robinson (2012) reflects, the fundamental principles of visuality in developing representations of place are discussed by Boorstin (1964), who developed the notion that what can be understood through visual media is only the first stage in understanding the relationship between image and self. Berger (1972) suggests that visuality is a key tool in our understanding and construction of the spaces that we inhabit. The fact that we travel to other places to inhabit them for temporary periods of time, means that visuality plays an even more important role in helping us construct and give meaning to these places which we visit as tourists. Harper (2000) supports this further, stating that our understanding of the world emerges from the things that we gaze upon and Larsen (2006: 241) observes that tourism and photography are 'modern twins':

> at a time when steamships and railways made the world physically more within reach photographs made it visually at hand [and] photography soon became a ritual practice of tourism and photographic objects roamed the globe, which, in turn, engendered a train of ideas, objects places, cultures and people.

Crouch and Lübbren (2003: 11) explain that 'the individual does not merely inhabit space, landscape or visual culture, but dwells in relation to them, in a process [of] becoming', and posit that this is achieved as 'the self and object are refigured in the process of encounter and performance'. *The Tourist Gaze*, the seminal work by Urry, (1990, 2002, Urry and Larsen 2011), explores the idea that tourism has a fundamentally visual character and the third edition (2011) explores visuality within photography, digitisation and performance. These ideas seek to explain tourism within a cultural framework, consider the importance of image within tourism and explore the relationship which exists between place, image and people as a central theme.

The relationship that exists between photography and tourism is predicated by the importance of visuality within tourism, and has a long tradition. Butler (1990) investigated this, and concluded that literary and artistic traditions of the eighteenth and nineteenth centuries have been superseded with new forms of visual media including television, film and photography. Thus he highlights that image has always been key to understanding other places, travelling to see otherness and identifying the sites that are worthy of being seen. Bourdieu (1990) provided a structuralist account of the social role of photography, suggesting that it defines social relations, plays a key role in social integration and family membership and provides a method for tangibly recording important occasions and events, narrativising individual lives. These factors, although family orientated, have considerable relevance to tourist activity. As many important events are marked by travel, holidays and being away from home, so these images also come to form a key component in the way that landscapes are understood and viewed away from the site where the image was originally recorded (Robinson 2012).

During the latter part of the twentieth century and into the twenty-first century, access to the Internet spread rapidly, as did the creation of virtual spaces which could be used, accessed and shared. Shaw et al. (2000: 276) suggest that whilst tourists may have some sense of place from images and information they have seen online, 'increasingly, people travel to actual places to experience virtual places…tourists increasingly are being drawn to places that have been popularised by literature, television and film and a number of studies explore such influences' suggesting that online sources did not replace real travel, or create a virtual tourism, but instead helped consumers to make travel decisions. In the second edition of *The Tourist Gaze* (2002) Urry observed that technology would change some of the accepted notions of visuality in tourism research. In *The Tourist Gaze 3.0* (2011: 181) a decade later Urry and Larsen note that 'photographs are now widely produced, consumed and circulated upon computers, mobile phones and via the Internet, especially through social networking sites', and recognise that 'digitisation and internetisation mean that photographs travel faster and cheaper… can be easily (re)distributed to significant others at-a-distance or exhibited in virtual space. Holiday photographs can be consumed without being co-present with the photographer' (ibid.: 181). This is achieved through email, file sharing sites, social media, online photo galleries, Google Earth and Web 2.0. Such rapid growth makes the subject ripe for investigation, as it changes the nature of the production of tourism and tourism places. As Crouch and Lübbren (2003: 12) suggest 'the production of tourism is in part a process of encounter, with space, landscape and its visual cultures of representation. Being a tourist is to produce, not only to consume, landscape, place and visual material'.

The production of tourism images by tourists has been an essential feature of the Circle of Representation (Albers and James 1988, Hall 1997, Jenkins 2003) which explains how images are projected into society by marketers, and subsequently reproduced through tourist photographs of the same iconic sites. These images are then shared with friends and family and perpetuate a constant representation of place within society. It is important to see this hermeneutic circle as a continuous circuit where images are perpetuated and therefore, over time, change and influence the representation and perception of tourist destinations. Indeed, Urry (2002) suggests that images from a range of sources create, over time, a self-perpetuating system of illusion which influences travellers' expectations of a particular site. However, digital images potentially change this, because no longer does the focus need to be on particular sites due to a limited quantity of camera film, or because of the processing costs. No longer are individual collections restricted to slide shows and photo albums. They are instead circulated within a wide cultural context, identifying the shared cultural meanings produced when images are collected from a number of similar sites and distributed through different channels of communication to influence individuals within different societies. The hermeneutic circle suggests that images are tracked down and recaptured, and the resulting photographs are displayed to show others that the visit has been made. As Urry (1990: 139) observes, 'tourism itself becomes a search for the photogenic...a strategy for the collection of photographs'.

The Circle of Representation further demonstrates the ways in which images are understood within a society and then by individuals from within society who may make different judgements based upon their personal experiences. Robinson (2012) suggests that tourists still tend to take photos that they have already seen in the brochures (often with family members included in the image, discussed by Haldrup and Larsen (2003) in *The Family Gaze*), which, it is argued, proves that a visit was made to a place identified as worth seeing. As Sontag, (1979: 9), explains 'photographs will offer indisputable evidence that the trip was made... and fun was had'. Urry and Larsen (2011: 187) note, however, that whilst the hermeneutic circle does provide an explanation of the relationship between image and culture, it is also crucial to recognise that 'tourist photographs can violate existing place myths and contribute to new ones while commercial photographs mirror photographs by tourists', so that in the same way people consume places by visiting them, they also consume them by recording them and the photograph is the tangible proof of the experience. Scarles (2009) also supports this, noting that photography is a complex fusion of predictable and reactionary practices which are conflicted between an acceptable/ethical image and the thoughts at the precise moment when the photograph is taken. This sense of immediacy is heightened by the ability to record images endlessly using digital cameras and mobile phones. This consumption of images and representations of first hand visual experiences supports the network of resources that facilitate the tourist gaze in the first place, including transport and accommodation. The visual sense helps to organise the experience, to identify what to see, what is worth seeing and what is being seen.

Mediation

Mediation describes the way in which people relate to information about a destination, and the way in which they use information from a range of sources to develop an idea, or perception, of the destination. Chalfen (1987: 98), for example, explains that whilst 'photographs offer us mediated reconstructions of portions of the visible environment [they] do not offer us a documentary account of exactly what the worlds looked like; collections of snapshots do not provide viewers with a magical mirror of the past and present "true" situations'. Robinson (2012) notes that the collection of images, or consumption of place through photography, locates individual values and beliefs and offers some tangible ownership of what are otherwise just memories of people and places. Urry (1990: 86) furthers this discourse, considering that:

> Much of what is appreciated is not directly experienced reality itself but representations, particularly through the medium of photography…while earlier forms of visual image reproduction, like sketches, may have conditioned the way that particular places or views are seen today, the influence of photography had caused an explosion in the production and propagation of visual images.

This idea of 'seeing' or 'gazing' has always been a part of tourist culture, but it was Urry (1990: 2) who defined it as an activity which 'presupposes a system of social activities and signs which locate the particular tourist practices' and it therefore offers a tool through which an image can be deconstructed into its component signs and signifiers, allowing the researcher to understand the foci of the image that the tourist is seeking to view once the image is captured and stored. The sites and peoples identified as worthy of viewing are generally those which have been defined by a history of tourism activity (sites which have been made famous through historic tourism), and those which are considered exotic or unusual, usually identified by travel experts, explorers or the communities who inhabit these places – in all cases some form of visual media is involved in the promulgation of the images of these sites and, therefore, their transformation into sights. MacCannell (1976: 44) helps to clarify these ideas further by explaining that such sites are sacralised, and developed the 'sight sacralisation' model to illustrate how a place becomes a tourist sight. Initially '…the sight is marked off from similar objects as worthy of preservation', using official designation schemes. MacCannell refers to this stage as 'naming' where the site is given an identity or brand. Other stages encompass:

- Framing & elevation
  - Putting on display, on pedestal, or open for visitation – the site is open for the public to visit.
  - Protecting or enhancing – the site is managed to preserve it in a specific state or time period.
- Enshrinement
  - The site is identified as 'special', as a place to visit.

Urry has further clarified these ideas (1990: 172) by noting that 'the tourist gaze is a mix of different scopic driven by which things of significance in history/culture/nature/experience are identified, signified and totalised'. Complex relationships are also bound up in the notion of the tourist gaze, not least because the gaze can be described as a form of voyeurism, can be gender oriented and can place local communities and people as the subjects of the gaze. Urry (1990) suggests that these can be discussed as romantic, collective, spectatorial, environmental and anthropological gazes. Recent research has explored these typologies further, and new ideas have emerged which link gaze to behaviour more closely. This research often takes the form of a type of gaze, examples include: the travel glance (Larsen 2001), the family gaze (Haldrup and Larsen 2003), the aerial gaze (Strain 2003), and the mutual gaze (Maoz 2006), the e-mediated gaze (Robinson 2012), or as the gaze applied to specific places, such as Malta (Black 1996) and or specific contexts, such as railways (Halsall 2001). The gaze, then, is essential to understanding the idea of mediation, of giving meaning and narrative to a place and consequently leading to its consumption though tourism. Rose (2007) discusses the use of photographs as mechanisms for the capture of texture – that convey the sense of place, in a way that words cannot.

Technology as a Mediator

At the start of the twenty-first century most people collecting photographs still relied on film cameras. As a result, care was needed to select the sites to be recorded and the number of images that could be captured was limited by the size of films and the cost of processing. Good quality cameras were relatively expensive and therefore the ability to record well defined images was relatively restrictive. Urry and Larsen (2011) suggest that this analogue photography was aimed at a future audience, yet the ability to share photos instantaneously entirely transforms this notion of temporality. The increased importance of place within popular culture (film especially) and the subsequent impact of film tourism and the framing of self within the gaze at film locations, illustrates Urry's view (2002: 151) that tourism vision is increasingly media-mediated, that the 'mediatised gaze' celebrates, as Larsen explains (2006: 247) 'places made famous in media worlds of popular culture'. It is entirely possible then, as Urry and Larsen (2011: 187) observe, that the 'photographs [taken] by "fellow tourists" may come to choreograph cameras [as] much as "professional" images and TV programmes'.

Technology has, however, changed the way in which these processes occur, because the global spread of digital images gives these myriad collections of individual pictures a far greater presence alongside the official marketing media, an idea discussed by Urry and Larsen (2011) as the afterlife of photos – where images may be used as posters, as pictures, as decoration in the home and are also passed from person to person as a tangible object, sometimes at the point of production. Digital photography changes entirely the ideas around the recording and sharing of images. Robinson and Andersen (2002: 44) state that tourism is 'defined by setting and meanings that are socially coded and understood within spatial and temporal boundaries', yet digital photography is temporally different as images can be recorded, viewed, edited and shared instantaneously (Jansson 2007). There is no time lag between taking the image and receiving the processed photograph. The images become almost 'live' in nature, where the quality of the image can be checked as soon as it is captured, and it can be deleted and taken again, and again, until perfection is achieved (Urry and Larsen 2011). The ability to edit and alter the digital image further can fundamentally change the composition of the image and its meaning.

Digital photography allows the user to delete and retake pictures, as many times as desired, such that the commodity becomes instantaneous, (Bell and Lyall 2005, Larsen 2006). Larsen (2006) questions how this changes the way photographs are recorded, surmising that these new technologies, including camera-phones, blogs, emails and so on 'timelessly transport images over great distances. The new temporal order of tourist photography seems to be "I am here" rather than "I was here"', (Bell and Lyall 2005, cited in Larsen 2006: 255). In terms of travel De Botton (2003: 223) states that 'technology may make it easier for us to reach beauty, but it has not simplified the process of possessing or appreciating it'. It has, however, made it much easier to share it! Urry and Larsen (2011: 59) note that 'the internet became in some ways more open, collaborative and participatory...where connected individuals not only surf but can make things through editing, updating, blogging, remixing, posting, responding, sharing, exhibiting, tagging and so on... Web 2.0 highlights how consumers have become part of the production process'.

Table 10.1 considers the range of tools which facilitate the e-mediation of tourist gazes. This table demonstrates the scope and opportunity offered by new technologies where, by contrast, only a decade ago photography (postcards, travel brochures, newspapers and tourist photos) and film were the only forms of visual mediation, and these were exclusively temporal in nature, published after the image was recorded.

Table 10.1   Visual mediators

Hard Mediators

Mediator	*Explanation*
Mobile Phones Portable Computers (laptops, tablets)	These technologies allow users to record and distribute photos digitally, and instantaneously
Digital Cameras Digital Camcorders	Digital cameras allow the user to see the image immediately, to change colours and formats and to delete and record images continuously, as both still pictures and moving images
Computers	A computer acts as a hub for managing social media (as do mobile phones and portable computers) and offers advanced software which can change and manipulate images

Soft Mediators

Mediator	*Example*	*Explanation*
Web 2.0	Facebook, Bebo	Social networking sites which host photo galleries, which allow people in images to be tagged and shared, and offers the opportunity for friends to view each other's pictures online

Mediator	Example	Explanation
User Generated Content	Trip Advisor	Review sites where users can leave comments, and photos, relating to their personal travel experiences
Virtual earth applications	Google Earth (via Panoramio – see below)	Allows images to be tagged, positioned where they were taken, viewed by users worldwide and provides links to websites. Official tourist boards are also producing tours and fly-throughs on Google Earth
Galleries and Photo Upload Sites	Flickr, Panoramio	Websites where individuals can have accounts and can upload images, share images and allow images to be added to other users public themed albums

Robinson (2012) explores the gaze through an observational and semiotic analysis of tourist images published on Google Earth. To a large extent the findings reflect the observations made by MacCannell (1976) and Culler (1988), identifying that digital tourist practices remain closely linked to the consumption of signs and, therefore, the idea of the tourist as semiotician remains unchanged. Largely the images focus upon recognised tourist sites in large numbers. Of particular note in the analysis was the absence of any pictures of people, suggesting that there is a differentiation between personal pictures, which carry meaning for the photographer beyond the view, and are therefore perhaps less willingly shared than those images of a particular place. There is, therefore, a clear divide in the gaze which is selected for public consumption.

Robinson (2012) notes that whilst the semiotics, the signs and icons of the destination remain unchanged in the e-mediated gaze (MacCannell 1976, Culler 1988), the ability to globally share images democratises personal photography and the added 'reality' of these non-official photographs may subsequently convey additional new meanings about specific spaces (Larsen 2006). This suggests then that the ideas around tourism, visuality and photography remain the same, but the mediation for the viewer of the photo (or indeed the aerial view or the street view) is more highly influenced by the 'honesty' of the tourist photo as opposed to the official photo which fits well with the increased use of TripAdvisor and other forms of user-generated content.

However, this projected image may be contested not by the images, but by the posting of the image. Robinson (2012) observes that images are uploaded by individuals who are known only by an alias or user name, so that there is no simple way to identify which images are posted by locals and which by visitors to a destination, which also creates methodological challenges for research. As noted, people are rarely pictured within the Google Gaze, the anonymity of the photographer is preserved further. This contradicts the idea that ownership of the images ascribes a notion of success as a tourist (Taylor 1994), although does support the assertion that little is known about why tourists collect images

(Haldrup and Larsen 2003) and could be more about a sense of using caution when sharing personal pictures in public forums. There appears to be a different form of behaviour when an image is shared online, compared to that employed when an image is shared on Facebook for friends and an invited audience to see and to comment upon, which is more akin to the photo album, where the owner of the image asserts some control over who can view the pictures. These issues represent a further development of the difficulties outlined by Cohen (1995), Feighley (2003) and Foster (1988) in seeking to understand the reasons that certain images are selected, although this now extends from the point of recording to the point of public sharing, (Robinson 2012), which may occur simultaneously.

The increased versatility of new technology leads then to a democratisation of tourism image, and to contested issues around the nature and form of the lens through which virtual tourism is explored, and suggests a liminality to the divide between a virtual world and a real experience, where these imagined mobilities and time spent as a virtual dweller then inform the decisions made regarding the selection of real experiences, and further defines the expectations of the traveller, based upon their virtual experiences. Ingold (2001) suggests that dwelling and landscape are intertwined, and that the temporality of the changing landscape is even more entwined. Cloke and Jones also support this idea, observing that temporality is essential to understand the nature of dwelling as a 'time-deepened experience' (2001: 654) and they observe that dwelling describes the 'ongoing togetherness of beings and things that make up landscape and places, and which bring together nature and culture over time' (2001: 651). This embodiment of people and place plays out in the narrative around the temporality of images, the point when images were recorded show a point in time, images of beings and things, and the virtual dweller resides in that space. Thus the virtual space becomes embodied and is further explored through a virtual gaze.

The Virtual Gaze

The principles of virtual reality and the software and headsets that were needed were developed in the latter part of the twentieth century, and tourism was quickly identified as an activity that could be replicated to create the sensation and visualisation that the user was sitting on a beach that was in reality several thousand miles from where they were enjoying the virtual experience. Whilst the fully immersive, headset wearing non-travelling tourist may have disappeared, the shared images propagated online by travellers have helped render these worlds as virtual spaces, resulting in a virtual space through which the gaze can be mediated within most tourism destinations around the world.

The development of StreetView on Google Earth also allows users to explore a virtual world, and to arguably dwell within it. Whilst such virtual experiences may make accessing places easier, it does not replicate the sensual experiences or connections with locals which define the destination. The purely visual nature of the experiences makes it a more valuable resource to research and assess a destination before an actual visit is made, rather than to replace the real experience, and as a result is being adopted more by marketers keen to use it as a promotional tool. This 3DVT (3-Dimensional Virtual Tourism) experience brings new meaning to the idea of armchair tourism and allows users to gaze at a place before they visit, whilst reserving hotel rooms, looking at online reviews, choosing what to visit and sharing ideas and suggestions online. Urry (2002) has also demonstrated the inseparability of image and tourism through what he has called 'imaginative mobility' which is clarified by Larsen (2006: 242) as 'armchair travel through books, images and television'. This distinction between virtual and corporeal travel is also considered by Urry and Larsen (2011: 23) in explaining that 'we distinguish between virtual travel through the internet, imaginative travel through phone, radio and TV, and corporeal travel…but there are complex intersections between these different modes of travel that are increasingly de-differentiated from one another'. This suggests that the Internet still remains a source for inspiration and ideas, rather than a replacement for the act of travel.

The Aerial Gaze

As Robinson (2012) identifies, the revolution in Web 2.0, together with GPS has revolutionised the way that travellers interact with maps, and the ability to view layers over electronic maps now offers users the opportunity to gain different perspectives. Google Earth, and a number of other online mapping providers, offer an opportunity to enjoy an aerial view, or a bird's eye view, of a destination. These are often linked to mapping software, and can be used as satellite navigation systems. Satellite imagery provides an aerial gaze, which Strain (2003: 35) suggests:

> moves towards an abstracted knowledge, representative of what Fabian calls anthropology's belief in "geometric qua graphic-spatial conceptualisation" as the most "exact" way of communicating knowledge that is at least authoritative as that of the resident, if not more so [and tourist attractions after similarly structured] to give the sightseer multiple perspectives on a single object.

Strain (2003: 36) contends that 'tourists also clamour to transcend this localised [on the ground] perspective and get a privileged view from above…the aerial gaze places the viewer outside and above the locale, separated from the action and progression of the narrative'. This privileged view is further enhanced by the ability on Google Earth to choose from sets of aerial photography from the past, enabling users to explore temporality within the gaze. The fact that the gaze can be explored through mobile technologies, and can be used for navigation and to see inaccessible views, changes entirely the way that travellers interact through mobilities and temporality.

The Shared Gaze

To understand why travellers choose to share their pictures it is essential to understand what photography means for those who collect the images (Robinson 2012). Markwell (1996: 132) notes that 'the ability to select particular images to photograph provides tourists with a degree of control over the tangible evidence they bring back from their experience' whilst, and as discussed previously in this chapter, Stalker (1988) observes that these collections of snapshots build up to create an almost official narrative of an individual's life, recording happy and positive experiences whilst ignoring those less favourable moments, reflecting back on the earlier notion that images are taken to record key events and celebrations. As Horne (1992: 112) comments, 'it was the camera that invented most of the sights we (as tourists) were expected to see' and 'one of the rituals of tourism is "doing" the particular sights already defined by professional photographers... and photographing these sights in the same way as they have already been photographed in the travel literature preferably with your companions in front of them' (also see Larsen 2006). Indeed, the promulgation of images on Google Earth around specific tourist sites is evidence of this.

The Shared Gaze (Robinson 2012), however, moves beyond the image as mediator, as it forms a part of the mediation alongside sources from review sites, wikis and other publicity created online content. Urry and Larsen (2011: 55) discuss how VisitBritain ask users to upload reviews, photos and videos to its multimedia platforms, yet this propagates 'an international division of tourist sites [where] Britain came to specialise in history and heritage, and this affects what overseas visitors expect to gaze upon and what attracts British residents to spend time holidaymaking within Britain'. However, the evidence presented here suggests that this will not change in the future because these are the imaged commodities which are used to sell the tourist product 'Britain'. What may change is the way that people find out about a destination as:

> travellers post stories and blogs, images about their experiences, and make recommendations which may be used by travellers who then elect not to engage with official communication at all – these are often believed to be more honest than the official communications of the destination. Electronic word-of-mouth entirely renegotiates the way that trusted recommendations work. (Urry and Larsen 2011: 59)

The E-mediated Gaze

Attention now turns to the e-mediated gaze (Robinson 2012). Urry (2002: 70–71) suggested that the:

digital convergence and interactivity of multiple media constitutes an enormously powerful force, the "social" consequences of which are unpredictable...because these electronic technologies are embedded in complex sets of socio-spatial practices [and this] depends upon the ways that they transform the dwelling practices of millions of people in diverse societies engaging in various kinds of social practice.

Urry (2002: 74) also identified that 'in cyberspace people do not dwell within a particular place although of course there are some markers of where users should gather, such as sites, nodes, home pages and so on'. Franklin (2001: 120) argues 'the potential tourist [can] do on the Internet what the travel agent used to do and indeed to access in a way some sense of what the tourist gaze will be like if you go there'. Robinson (2012) suggests that whilst new media may well influence the gaze, it is unlikely to reveal anything new about the places that tourists already visit because of the careful selection of accepted images that are already in existence and shared by travellers online, which all replicate each other in basic content analysis, just as illustrated in the Circle of Representation. In *The Tourist Gaze 3.0*, Urry and Larsen (2011) pay particular attention to the role of technology, but focus attention on the ability to record and select images at the point of consumption, suggesting that it is, therefore, the digital camera first and foremost which dictates the flexibility of the images that are captured, and potentially allows the perfect image of a site to be chosen from many pictures recorded at the same time, with no concern for the cost of developing analogue pictures...Without digital technology the photograph would, like the painting (Berger 1972), remain a production for future consumption, and primarily a private item. The instantaneous ability to collect images and to place them in the public domain often makes the image a short-term, transitory, and ephemeral item, appearing at the top of a Facebook home page for a while before being replaced by another image, or another post. The picture is soon lost to obscurity, yet is also in the public domain, where it may be used and reused, and potentially abused beyond the knowledge of the person who captured it, its original meaning, context and importance lost (Urry and Larsen 2011).

    The opportunities provided by the Internet for the public display of photographs for anyone to see perhaps best demonstrates Urry's (2002: 69) observation that 'the public sphere has been turned into a visible public stage transforming the possibilities of social interaction and public dialogue'. Computers, and Internet enabled mobile technologies especially allow 'distant events personalities and happenings [to be] mundanely brought into the living room...we imagine ourselves sharing events, experiences, and personalities with many others, with whom we constitute certain kinds of communities' (ibid.: 69). Mobilities, therefore, become instantaneous, making it 'possible to sense the other, almost to dwell with the other, without physically moving either oneself or without moving any physical objects' (Urry 2002: 70). Larsen (2006: 241–2) identifies that 'contemporary tourism is intrinsically constructed culturally, socially and materially through images and performances of photography and vice versa. The tourism industry invests enormously in photographic images to choreograph desirable "place myths", desiring bodies and photogenic places'. Yet, in this new era this is challenged by the tourist themselves. The e-mediated gaze, therefore, could be argued to be not one type of gaze, but a conglomeration or multiplicity of gazes, which are only possible as a result of technology, and which are heavily influenced by the technology. Table 10.2 illustrates this composition of the e-mediated gaze.

Table 10.2   The e-mediated gaze

The E-mediated Gaze	
The Virtual Gaze	Collections of images, Birds Eye Views and street level views, and indeed transitory possibilities within these views, all create a virtual world, where it is possible to dwell, to spend time and to 'see' places which exist before travelling to visit them
The Aerial Gaze	The ability to look down upon places, proffered by the accessibility of satellite imagery and mapping. In Google Earth this is combined with the ability to access other gazes, and to read reviews and opinions about the destination, Strain (2003)
The Nostalgic Gaze	Online communities, dedicated forums and websites offer travellers the opportunity to gaze upon images of places which no longer exist, and to share these nostalgic experiences with others, through the public sharing of images. Such images add new meaning to existing places, and can be seen as temporally placed images offering opportunities to further construct a sense of place through history, (Robinson 2012)
The Prohibited Gaze	The aerial gaze offers a privileged view of places, but there are also groups of urban explorers who visit (or trespass) in order to visit defunct historic sites, disused leisure parks and old industrial buildings. These groups or 'urbexers' also build their communities through online image sharing, and add a new virtual gaze for others to look in upon (Robinson 2012)
Westernised Gaze	Digital camera ownership is predominant in developed countries and thus any travel photos of developing countries shared online are likely to present a 'westernised' gaze, which may lead to an organic development of the representation of a destination, rather than an image induced through marketing activity (Awaritefe 2004). Alneng (2002) observes a distinct difference between the Tourist-as-Westerner and the relatively immobile non-Westerners who become the focus of the tourist gaze.

Conclusion

This chapter has demonstrated the importance and role of technology in the mediation of tourism places. There are many potential areas for future research, and whilst the evidence presented in this chapter would suggest the basic notions of visuality in tourism remain unchanged, there are many human factors which dictate the way in which images are treated. Technology offers opportunities to capture images and to circulate these to a global audience as they happen. There is no necessity for emotional reflection once an image has been recorded, and the image may be seen as almost valueless, something to share briefly on a social networking site, or to post on a blog. Yet there clearly are personal considerations – images of family and friends caught in a family gaze (Larsen 2006) are the staple diet of social media sites, but are absent from travel sites, where it is the tourist site that is central to the gaze.

These images narrate the story of a specific space and may, over time, create their own tourist sites (Urry 1990, 2002), although such is the importance of a defined tourist site, and so caught up are those sites in the Circle of Representation, that whilst tourist photography may challenge accepted ideas about a place, it is essentially unlikely to change them (Robinson 2012). Mobile technology also places no limit on how and where other people access images, and so a traveller can dwell in one environment, whilst gazing at another, or gazing upon the activities of friends and family, almost as a live activity, happening elsewhere in the world. As Urry (2011: 23) notes 'the last two decades have seen remarkable "time-space" compression as people across the globe have been brought closer through various technologically assisted developments. There is increasingly what Bauman describes as the shift from a solid, fixed modernity to a more fluid and speeded-up liquid modernity (2000)', one in which travellers are fully engaged.

References

Albers, P. and James, W. 1988. Travel photography: a methodological approach. *Annals of Tourism Research*, 15, 134–58.

Alneng, V. 2002. The modern does not cater for natives. travel ethnography and the conventions of form. *Tourist Studies*, 2(2), 119–42.

Awaritefe, O. 2004. Motivation and other considerations in tourist destination choice: a case study of Nigeria. *Tourism Geographies*, 6(3), 303–30.

Baudrillard, J. 1988. *The Consumer Society: Myths and Structures*. London: Sage.

Bell, C. and Lyall, J. 2005. 'I Was Here': pixilated evidence, in *The Media & The Tourist Imagination: Converging Cultures*, edited by D. Crouch et al. London: Routledge.

Berger, J. 1972. *Ways of Seeing*. London: BBC.

Black, A. 1996. Negotiating the tourist gaze: the example of Malta, in *Coping with Tourists: European Reactions to Mass Tourism*, edited by J. Boissevain. Oxford: Berg.

Boorstin, D. 1964. *The Image: A Guide to Pseudo-Events in America*. New York: Harper & Row.

Bourdieu, P. 1990. *Photography: A Middle-brow Art* [English translation]. Cambridge: Polity Press.

Butler, R.W. 1990. The influence of the media in shaping international tourist patterns. *Tourism Recreation Research*, 15(2), 46–53.

Chalfen, R. 1987. *Snapshot Versions of Life*. Ohio: Bowling Green State University.

Cloke, P. and Jones, O. 2001. Dwelling, place, and landscape: an orchard in Somerset. *Environment and Planning A*, 33, 649–66.

Cohen, C. 1995. Marketing paradise, making nation. *Annals of Tourism Research*, 22, 404–21.

Crouch, D. and Lübbren, N. 2003. *Visual Culture and Tourism*. Oxford: Berg.

Culler. J. 1988. *Framing the Sign: Criticism and its Institutions*. Oxford: Basil Blackwell.

De Botton, A. 2003. *The Art of Travel*. London: Penguin Books.

Debore, G. 1983. *Society of the Spectacle*. Detroit: Black and Red.

Emmison, M. and Smith, P. 2000. *Researching the Visual: Images, Objects, Contexts and Interactions in Social and Cultural Inquiry*. London: Sage

Feighley, W. 2003. Negative image? Developing the visual in tourism research. *Current Issues in Tourism*, 6(1), 76–85.

Foster, H. (ed.) 1988. *Vision and Visuality*. Seattle, WA: Bay Press.

Franklin, A. 2001. The tourist gaze and beyond. An interview with John Urry. *Tourist Studies*, 1(2), 185–96.

Haldrup, M. and Larsen, J. 2003. The family gaze. *Tourist Studies*, 3(1), 23–46.

Hall, S. 1997. *Representation: Cultural Representations and Signifying Practices*. London: Sage.

Halsall, D. 2001. Railway heritage and the tourist gaze: Stoomtram Hoorn–Medemblik. *Journal of Transport Geography*, 9(2), 151–60.

Hamburger, J.F. 1997. *Nuns as Artists: The Visual Culture of a Medieval Convent*. Berkeley and Los Angeles: University of California Press.

Haraway, D. 1991. *Simians, Cyborgs, and Women: The Reinvention of Nature*. New York: Routledge.

Harper, D. 2000. Reimagining visual methods: Galileo to neuromancer, in *Handbook of Qualitative Research*, edited by N.K. Denzin and Y.S. Lincoln. London: Sage, 176–98.

Horne, D. 1992. *The Intelligent Tourist*. McMahon's Point: Margaret Gee Publishing.

Ingold. T. 2001. *The Perception of the Environment: Essays in Livelihood, Dwelling and Skill*. London: Routledge.

Jansson, A. 2007. A sense of tourism: new media and the dialectic of encapsulation/decapsulation. *Tourist Studies*, 7(1), 5–24.

Jenkins, O. 2003. Photography and travel brochures: the circle of representation. *Tourism Geographies*, 5(3), 305–28.

Larsen, J. 2001. Tourism mobilities and the travel glance: experiences of being on the move. *Scandinavian Journal of Hospitality and Tourism*, 1(2), 80–98.

Larsen, J. 2006. Geographies of tourist photography. Choreographies and performances, in *Geographies of Communication: The Spatial Turn in Media Studies*, edited by J. Falkheimer and A. Jansson. Gøteborg: NORDICOM, 243–61.

MacCannell, D. 1976. *The Tourist: A New Theory of the Leisure Class*. New York: University of California Press: Schocken Books.

Maoz, D. 2006. The mutual gaze. *Annals of Tourism Research*, 33(1), 221–39.

Markwell, K. 1996. Dimensions of photography in a nature based tour. *Annals of Tourism Research*, 24(1), 131–55.

Mirzoeff, N. 1998. *The Visual Cultural Reader*. London: Routledge.

Mitchell, D. 1998. Writing the western: new western history's encounter with landscape. *Ecumene*, 5(1), 7–29.

Pink, S. 2001. *Doing Visual Ethnography*. London: Sage.

Robinson, M. and Andersen. H.C. (eds) 2002. *Literature and Tourism: Essays in the Reading and Writing of Tourism*. London: Thomson.

Robinson, P. 2012. The E-Mediated (Google Earth) Gaze – An Observational and Semiotic Perspective. *Current Issues in Tourism Research*, 15(4), 353–67.

Rose, G. 2001. *An Introduction to the Interpretation of Visual Materials*. London: Sage.

Rose, G. 2007. *An Introduction to the Interpretation of Visual Materials*. 2nd edition. London: Sage.

Scarles, C. 2009. Becoming tourist: renegotiating the visual in the tourist experience. *Environment and Planning D: Society and Space*, 27(3), 465–88.

Shaw, G., Agarwal, S and Bill, P. 2000. Tourism consumption and tourist behaviour: a British perspective. *Tourism Geographies*, 2(3), 264–89.

Shohat, E. and Stam, R. 1998. Narrativizing visual culture: towards a polycentric aesthetics, in *The Visual Culture Reader*, edited by N. Mirzoeff. New York: Routledge, 27–49.

Sontag, S. 1979. *On Photography*. New York: Farrar, Strauss and Giroux.

Stalker, P. 1988. Can i take your picture?: the strange world of photography. *New Internationalist*, 185(July), 4–6.

Strain, E. 2003. *Public Places: Private Journeys. Ethnography, Entertainment and the Tourist Gaze*. London: Rutgers University Press.

Taylor, J. 1994. *A Dream of England: Landscape, Photography and the Tourist's Imagination*. Manchester: Manchester University Press.

Urry, J. 1990. *The Tourist Gaze*. London: Sage.

Urry, J. 2000. *Sociology beyond Societies: Mobilities for the Twenty-First Century*. London: Routledge.

Urry, J. 2002. *The Tourist Gaze*. 2nd edition. London: Sage.

Urry, J. and Larsen, J. 2011. *The Tourist Gaze 3.0*. London: Sage.

Virilio, P. 1994. *The Vision Machine*. London: British Film Institute.

Chapter 11

Souvenir or Reconstruir? Editing Experience and Mediating Memories of Learning to Dive

Stephanie Merchant

Introduction

At a time when audiovisual technologies significantly infiltrate tourist practices and experiences, the structure and content of personal and collective memory is becoming evermore mediated and transmogrified (Bolter and Grusin 1999, Jansson 2007, Tussyadiah and Fesenmaier 2009). As such, tourists' future understandings of self and place are entering a slippery realm where reality and imagination combine in the construction of virtual histories, ever in process yet never fully loyal to the original instance of experience. This digitisation (particularly due to the speed of image processing, the simplicity of editing and the volume of imagery capable of being captured since the advent of memory card storage) of the tourist gaze has resulted in increased attention being given to technological mediators such as digital cameras and camcorders by tourism scholars (Tussyadiah and Fesenmaier 2009).

In this chapter I explore how video technologies can alter tourists' understandings of underwater space and the memories they develop of embodied actions and experiences, acquired whilst SCUBA diving on holiday. It is becoming common practice for learner divers to be filmed in the most popular diving resorts, such as Koh Tao and Phuket, Thailand, particularly during the final stages of the PADI's, Open Water course. These tourists are subsequently offered a souvenir DVD of their time learning to dive, which they can then take home to show their families and friends or to upload on to social networking sites such as Facebook. It is argued that people have a vested interest in such objects as 'they come to serve as material triggers of personal memories' (van Dijck 2007: xii). The mediated memories triggered by souvenir DVDs though are not mere extensions of the brain, rather they are the products of a 'complex interaction between brain, material objects and the cultural matrix from which they arise' (van Dijck 2007: xii).

Whilst learning to become an underwater videographer and simultaneously carrying out participant observation I was educated in the intricate ways in which acts and processes of mediation permeate the production method of the souvenir DVDs. Thus consequently, I was left to consider what the implications of 'interfering' with personal memory might entail for tourists' conceptualisations of identity and space.

In this chapter I initially provide an overview of existing research, which has taken the role of photography and videography seriously in relation to tourist activities. I then go on to outline the history of where philosophers from Descartes (Sutton 1998) to Bergson (2004) and Deleuze (2003), believe memory to be located, moving chronologically from a 'static, files in the mind' theorisation to an approach that emphasises the ongoing process of becoming *in conjunction with* stimuli from cultural artefacts, such as DVDs (Marks 2000), and the present. By acknowledging that matter 'informs' recollection, the chapter will be set up to consider what enlacing these elements mean for memory, when their materiality (screen, DVD etc.) is not only an instigator for remembering but also transformative in itself (Damasio 1999).

Following this the chapter will be concerned with the precise ways the tourists' original experiences were altered in the production process. Thus, I will consider editing from several angles. Firstly by looking at the way certain filmic styles were encouraged by the videography company that I worked for. The camera's perspective will be analysed to consider what aspects of the encounter are lost/ gained for the tourists when the shots are framed by an 'outsider' who cannot capture their point of view, but whose artistic subjectivity and recording skill is framed by their (my) own personal experience. Thereafter, I will outline the technological means by which images are 'improved' to become visually more stunning and vivid than the often dark and almost monochrome blue scenes that are seen in situ by the tourists. Then, the chapter will address the mediation process from the perspective of the tourists themselves. Following Barthes (1981), I will consider the various means by which the tourists perform and present themselves whilst being filmed, in order to show that the learner divers want to see themselves, and be seen by others, at a later date, in a certain light (for example as adventurous, skilled, happy, etc.).

Having covered these themes the chapter will conclude by asking what these mediatory acts and processes mean for individual and shared constructions of tourist space and identity. I will argue that the souvenir DVDs encourage the creation of a 'virtual consciousness', where memories are informed by technologies that picture a place that never looked so polished and of a person (whether it be of the self or others featured in the films) who (at times at least) was/were acting for the camera.

Image Capturing and Tourist Practices

For the most part, it is photography which has received considerable attention within touristic studies of identity and place, rather than videography. This is likely due to the relatively new status of filmic equipment and production facilities as accessible to the general population. However, the increase in purchases of video cameras led Tagg (1982) and Stallabrass (1996) to declare that videography has followed photography as 'on the one hand democratizing aesthetic production and, on the other, colonising an ever-expanding range of spaces and experiences' (Crang 1997a: 363). The additional advantage of videography though, is that it also allows what Crang (1997b) describes as 'levity and enjoyment' to be captured, and I would add here sound, motion and a sense of chronology, whilst also adhering to Sontag's utilitarian notion of the images existing of proof that 'the trip was made, the project was carried out, the fun was had' (Sontag 1977: 8).

Dating further back, the picturing practices of photography have been argued to be inextricably linked with tourist activities since the first Grand Tour (Albers and James 1988, Cohen et al. 1992, Crang 1997a, Feighey 2003, Garlick 2002, Griffin 1988, Markwell 1997). Indeed, Belk and Hsiu-yen Yeh (2010) argue that photography and tourism owe the success of each to the other. Heidegger goes so far as to say that the enframing powers of technology were the key characteristic in the turn to modernity, 'the conquest of the world as picture' (1977: 134), a way of 'revealing the world in which everything within it comes to be seen as, "standing-reserve", that is, as something that "stands by", as a resource, rationally ordered and ready to be exploited' (Garlick 2002: 293). Thus, resources can become knowable and systematised, as Sontag states 'through being photographed, something becomes part of a system of information, fitted into schemes of classification and storage' (1977: 156). This way of thinking about visual imagery, perpetuated the myth that photography is a realist medium, a representative of truth and science (Slater 1995). By extension then, photographic practices positioned tourists as disconnected and disengaged from the people and landscapes which they came across, with the camera epitomising the occularcentric and objective nature of their travel experience (Adler 1989, Urry 1992).

Whilst the study of photography and tourism has been prolific and sustained, actual studies that analyse tourist-produced imagery until late, have been rare. As Garrod (2009) has explained, studies of images tended to concentrate on those produced by professional photographers which appear in brochures, posters, postcards etc. (for example Dann 1988, Edelheim 2007, Hunter 2008, Pike 2002, Scarles 2004). In recent years studies concerning the specificities of tourist-produced imagery, have opened up theorisations of how and why tourists engage with the practice of photography and/or videography. Indeed research has begun to explore the ways in which tourists produce and consume touristically through photography (Caton and Santos 2008, Haldrup and Larsen 2004, Larsen 2006, Scarles 2009). This chapter sits somewhere in between both such approaches, as on the one hand, analysis is of professionally produced imagery, but on the other, this footage is of the tourists themselves. Consequently, the chapter cross cuts the aims of previous research, attempting to deconstruct the image-making processes which contribute to the production of the underwater souvenir DVD (processes which are common within broader tourism film productions such as adverts, documentaries and interactive entertainment stations), whilst also taking into account the potential for memory manipulation such media may have on tourist divers, which I would argue could be synonymous with people's personal (holiday or everyday) filmic productions. In line with this, within a tourism context Larsen has argued that 'instead of understanding photographs as reflections or distortions of a pre-existing world, photography can be understood as a technology of worldmaking' (2006: 78).

Considering why people choose to capture their experiences and extending the argument above, that visual practices allow for an ordering of understandings of place and people, Garlick (2002) has noted that, whilst picturing practices dislocate visual stimuli from the sites in which they were first conceived, they become re-ordered into sites of self-representation, contributing to the construction of memory and self-identity. Thus Garlick (2002) links photography to the Foucauldian concept of one's 'life as a work of art'. Pictures, and more recently footage of holiday activities, can be captured and brought back for a number of reasons, but existing research has pinpointed two in particular, which I later argue are not mutually exclusive, yet result in a tension over meaning construction in the production process. On the one hand then, images are taken and brought home for public viewing, either to pass around hard copies or to show footage to friends, or more recently by uploading these on to social networking sites such as Facebook, Flickr and YouTube. This fits with Garrod's (2009: 347) contention that photos (and by extension film) become part of a hermeneutic cycle of 'tourism (re) production, in which tourists seek to acquire photographic images of the place they are visiting so that they can prove to others that they have been there'. However, this is a notion which has been deconstructed of late, with the tourists themselves being written back into the story as embodied active agents within the context of image production (Haldrup and Larsen 2004).

As such the agency of the tourist in the notion of 'narrative construction' becomes of importance and feeds back into Foucault's idea of the life as a work of art. In Foucault's words 'arts of existence' are 'those reflective and voluntary practices by which men [sic] not only set themselves rules of conduct, but seek to transform themselves, to change themselves in their singular being, and to make their life into an oeuvre that carries certain aesthetic values and certain stylistic criteria' (Foucault 1992: 10–11). In other words, not only is an idealised self-image constructed and manipulated to present to others, but also for the self. Keep-sakes or souvenirs become the instigators of memory work concerning past activities, and on holiday these may allow for a certain 're-configuring' of the self, due to increased freedom and an escape from lifestyle constraints of the home (Urry 1992). The prefigured scene can be transformed into a souvenir in times to come (Crang 1997a). This is not just a retrospective use of the imagery then, but informs its very construction. Memories and their 'tone' are not merely *captured* in the process of taking a photo or video but are often *created* in the very act. Whilst this may change the way we think about tourist performance and imagery, it does not necessarily reflect insincerity in image production. What it does do though, is further infiltrate the practice of image capture within the tourist practices and performance, rendering the various stages of capture and production as impossible to think about in isolation. This highlights that photo-(or video-)graphy is a social performance in itself not a way of transparently capturing the tourist performances taking place the other side of the viewfinder (Crang 1997a, Crang 1997b, Edensor 2001, Haldrup and Larsen 2004, MacCannell 1979).

Before turning to the precise ways in which the alterations and mediations noted above are made, I first move on to provide a background to theoretical understandings of memory.

Situated Memory?

In John Sutton's (1998) book *Philosophy and memory: Descartes to Connectionism*, the author outlines a timeline of conflicting theorisations of memory's location. It is argued that throughout the nineteenth century, the locus of memory was for the most part believed to rest solely within the mind, stored in a manner similar to the files in a filing cabinet, ready to be retrieved upon being stimulated by an object or image, or more simply, upon the request of the thinker. These stored memories were considered to be hermetically sealed from the changing world in which the perceiver was living, stable in the face of time and unchanging with context. However, in the twentieth century conceptualisations began to shift and in doing so highlighted the interconnectedness that exists between time, context and memory. Bergson's work in this domain was particularly important in changing previous ways of thinking about memory. In *Matter and Memory* (2004) Bergson explains that in perceiving matter we do not simply perceive an object in its present state. By contrast, we mix in with our perception the myriad recollections, which we have gained previously, making our understandings complicated deeply by the temporal, 'enriching' perception of the present yet making it vastly subjective. Thus, memory is seen to be an ever evolving, inter-subjective thread which confirms and simultaneously troubles our understanding of the past, at once alluding to encounters which took place but conflating the details of this particular past with those of subsequent pasts, as well as the present. Drawing on Bergson, van Dijck (2007: 30) explains this more clearly, stating that 'the present dictates memories of the past…the brain does not store memories but recreates the past each time it is invoked [so that] "the memory of the past serves as a base"'. Incorporating and building upon Bergson's work, Deleuze (2003) tells a similar story of the intersubjective nature of perception and memory although he relates this specifically to the receipt and visualisation of cinematic images. Deleuze (2005: 334) argues that,

> Instead of a continued memory, as function of the past which reports a story, we witness the birth of memory, as function of the future which retains what happens in order to make it the object to come of the other memory…[M]emory could never evoke and report the past if it had not already been constituted at the moment when past was still present, hence in an aim to come. It is in fact for this reason that it is behaviour: it is in the present that we make memory, in order to make use of it in the future when the present will be past.

Therefore, we have moved from thinking about the past as being firm and steady, to instead thinking about it as being fractured; 'from a history sought in the continuity of memory to a memory cast in the discontinuity of history'. This troubles our conceptualisations of 'what has been, can, and should be remembered' (Hoskins 2001: 334).

In this chapter I want to think of memories in this way. Not as a collection of static files in the mind, but rather I want to think about a re-collection as something which is 'rewritten each time' it is intentionally sought, or brought to the fore subconsciously (van Dijck 2007: 32). However, whilst this 'rewriting' may enrich our understanding of the way we perceive the *present*, at the same time it troubles the extent to which we can rely on personal memory to gain realistic accounts of the past. If we intersect here a further mediating player, that of visual media (in this case souvenir DVDs of learning to dive), the blurring of memory, reality and digitally altered imagery would make for a recollection which is even further removed from the original experience, as the merging of 'external' and 'internal' images converge into experience (van Dijck 2007: 125).

The fluid and fluctuating nature of memory is something which psychologists have devoted considerable time and effort to comprehend (Johnson et al. 1988). Whilst a number of scholars, including myself, have highlighted the benefits of using visual imagery to bring to cognition elements of 'genuine' experience which previously eluded research participants (Merchant 2011, Pink 2006, Scarles 2004, Spinney 2006), of more relevance to this chapter is the work emanating from psychology which explicitly troubles the role visual media plays in contributing to significant memory *alterations* over time. Such work builds on earlier studies, which used narratives of plausible events instead of visual images in their research design (Hyman and Billings 1998, Hyman and Loftus 1998, Neisser et al. 2000, Weiser 1990, Williams and Banyard 1998). Irrespective of the method though, psychologists have gone so far as to demonstrate that not only are research participants capable of recollecting 'aspects' of previous experience that are incorrect or fabricated, but with the aid of visual images, the participants can even fabricate complete events or believe themselves to have attended events fabricated by the researchers (Loftus and Pickrell 1995, Wade et al. 2002). In fact, it has been argued that memory performance, upon receipt of misleading information can cause between a thirty and forty per cent deficit in accuracy (Loftus and Pickrell 1995). This type of memory alteration has been labelled 'retroactive interference', the act of altering memory formation after the event (as opposed to 'proactive interference' in which memory is disrupted by events that occurred previous to experience).

It is argued that people 'tend to think of photographs as frozen moments in time, place faith in them and see them as reliable representations of the past' (Wade et al. 2002: 597). Over the last 20 years in particular, witnessing and producing visual images has become particularly commonplace, at times even overwhelming, within our daily encounters. Since the 'digital turn' this has been intensified further still (Laurier et al. 2008). Outside of the touristic literature reviewed above, Hoskins similarly (2001) explains that; the desire to capture and store memories electronically, in order to complement our own memory capabilities, whilst not always necessarily the main reason for engaging in photographic and videographic activities, is a process that has increased in demand, particularly over the last ten years. In conjunction with this is the increased availability of relatively cheap and accessible image manipulation and film editing software, that further disrupts our understandings of the real and the altered.

It is argued that photographs require less 'constructive processing than do narratives to cultivate a false memory' (Wade et al. 2002: 602). If this is true, and research findings seem to corroborate with this theory, then surely, by extension, watching a film of a holiday experience in which you feature would prove an even more trustworthy medium of representing past experiences of space and self. As Loftus and Pickrell (1995: 725) state:

> After receipt of new information that is misleading in some way, people make errors when they report what they [originally] saw…the new, post-event information often becomes incorporated into recollection, supplementing or altering it sometimes in dramatic ways. New information invades us, like a Trojan horse, precisely because we do not detect its influence.

Whilst the souvenir DVDs I produced of tourists were not of a fabricated event, they were filmed to certain aesthetic trends of the time. Films were heavily edited and visually modified to produce a product that would emphasise the 'positive' aspects of learning to dive, and to downplay the 'negative' aspects of learning to dive (including the scenery, bodily movements and personal interactions). Before moving on to consider what the consequences of such editing practices might be, I will firstly outline the various ways in which these were carried out, in addition to troubling the performative actions and behaviours of the learner divers themselves.

Filming Styles

Whilst learning to become an underwater videographer I was instructed to shoot, edit and represent the tourists and the underwater world in a very contrived manner. Each aspect of the process is repeatedly rehearsed. The structure of each film is virtually identical yet for the tourists their 'individual' DVD seems personally tailored, as they are unaware of the videographer's training experiences or the production process. Producing films in this manner is essential if one is to meet the course requirements of the certification company, who have developed over time and decided upon what they believe to be the optimal aesthetically pleasing approach to film production. These aesthetic codes are the culturally constructed ideals of the time (2010), as James Moran notes, 'movie technologies can hardly be separated from social contexts…in conjunction with the technical tools we use to capture. The movie camera, the video camera, and more recently the digital camcorder' are thus inseparable from tourist life (in van Dijck 2007: 123).

However, they are essentially a compromise between the videographer's capability, creativity, time constraints, the sophistication of the camera equipment and editing suite, the 'performance' of the wildlife, weather conditions and the tourists themselves, as well as the structure of the PADI Open Water course. Upon passing from the 'trainee' stage to the 'employee' stage of a videographer's 'career', further demands are put on the quality of the visual output and there is even less freedom to experiment as time constraints are further intensified (typically one film of around 20 minutes is to be shot, edited, produced and screened within a twenty four hour period).

Within the broader film framework, further stylistic approaches were encouraged. 'Footage' refers to the raw unedited material, which is recorded by the camera. This footage is divided into 'shots', normally of between 2–10 seconds (longer shots are frowned upon as a viewer's attention will typically diminish after 12 seconds), which are combined to create a sequence. Videographers are encouraged to mix up the range of these shots to tell a story in a visually interesting way. For example, a sequence could start with a very wide shot of two divers swimming over a reef. It could then cut to a long shot of the divers, with one of them pointing at something on the reef. This could then cut to an over the shoulder shot of the diver, with the camera focused on a small crab (the subject being pointed at). Before returning to a long shot of the divers swimming away again, there could be an extreme close up of the crab. Thus contrary to filming in a fluid and continuous way that is more akin to human perception, the film is made to look more interesting, by leaving out the in-between (so called 'boring') moments of perception. The film still alludes to the sequence of events, which led up to the climax of the encounter (discovering the crab), but the time invested in the search for something to look at is portrayed proportionally condensed compared to the time spent gazing at the crab. Similarly, once the sequence is over, no more filming will be necessary until the next exciting or interesting event/discovery occurs, whereby once more the videographer will set the scene with a long shot, move in to frame the key subject, perhaps cut away to something being looked at or adding to the event, returning to the subject before filming a further long shot of the subject leaving the scene.

An element of these shots which is decided upon by the videographer is the movement of the camera throughout. Too many static shots are considered dull, but integrating them in to the sequence an 'appropriate' number of times will make the film easier to watch. Furthermore, panning is deemed unattractive underwater yet tracking is argued to make for an engaging visual encounter. Certain camera angles are equally important in constructing the overall 'style' of the film. Eye level and low-level angles are deemed more aesthetically pleasing underwater, as they set coral and divers against the blue of the sea and can silhouette divers with a background of sun. These angles alter our perception of the true density of coral, but make for more interesting scenes in comparison to a bird's eye view which flattens the topography of the ocean floor, yet highlights the sheer, sprawling volume of coral.

Here then, there are further trade-offs to be weighed up, with the outcome not being representative of 'real-time' perception. It is considered better practice to picture coral set against the deep blue background of the ocean than to represent it as the majority of learner divers (the prospective DVD buyers) would see it: from above, mostly looking straight down. Whilst this may not be the case for more experienced divers who have fine-tuned their buoyancy control and are therefore more capable of meandering through the contour changes of the reef, it is the case for the majority of learner divers who swim over the coral for fear of getting too close.

Adding the occasional Dutch tilt[1] can give a film a more contemporary feel and when combined into a tracking or flyover shot can break up the monotony of continually shooting movement horizontally. These techniques allude to the freedom of movement offered by the viscosity of the water, as to pull them off successfully and smoothly the videographer must roll, stretch and tilt their body significantly. Similarly though, picturing the ocean from such 'artistic' angles, is not reflective of the views witnessed by the learners.

Despite the fact that these aesthetic interventions do not accord with the unmediated visual experience of real-time perception, within the broader sequence structure of the film set out above, these stylistic approaches would be used for specific shots. For example, the opening shot would normally be a close up shot of the dive school sign, which then zoomed out to capture the whole school. Whilst filming the divers walk down the jetty and onto the dive boat, the company would ask that the videographer follow the group, framing them in the centre of the shot whilst adding a continuous Dutch tilt from one side to the other. The final shot was similarly beyond the freedom of expression of the videographer as he/she/ me would be required to pan across the group, who would be sat next to each other, arm in arm at the videographer's request. As the camera panned to each individual they were encouraged to wave/smile/pull a face as the camera lingered on them at a jaunty angle. Such techniques were deliberately staged to leave the viewers convinced of the friendly atmosphere and light-hearted nature of their time of learning to dive. This tactic indeed worked for the most part, with divers seeming nostalgic upon watching the last scenes of the film. Sarah, a 23 year old learner from the UK, noted for example, 'Aaaaahhh, I'll miss you guys!' and Andrea exclaimed 'oh, that's it! I don't want to go home now'. However, the tension between the structured and predetermined stylisation of the footage seems almost at odds with the notion of nostalgia. Defined as a subjective sentimental longing for a past event or place, it is surprising that watching an almost generically arranged film has the potential to induce such feelings. Yet the tourists seem unaware of the production line nature and construction of not only their DVD but indeed their entire learning to dive experience (or if they are aware of this then they actively go along with the act). This may raise ethical issues surrounding the extent to which relations with videographers, other divers and dive staff are genuine and whether the selective

---

1   A shot which is framed at a slight angle.

attitude towards what is captured is representative of tourist experience or rather becomes a work of aesthetic appreciation in which tourists feature.

The Editing Room

Once the morning or afternoon of filming was complete, the following stage in the production process was to digitally edit the footage. If the above rules had been stuck to this process would be much easier, as there would be less of a need to sift through 'irrelevant' footage or to salvage quality footage from erratic shots. Editing is an artistic and technical process that requires manipulating shots into an order that enhances the quality of the visual output. Shots may be deleted, added, rearranged. For example, if a number of scenery shots have been filmed on the boat in a row, they might be used to separate the sequences of each diver 'gearing up'. Similarly, if footage of an eel or ray hiding under a rock is too dark to be digitally adjusted, older footage of the same species might be used so as not to disappoint the divers who often express excitement at the prospect of being able to re-witness certain creatures. For example Alex commented upon re-surfacing after his second dive; 'did you get the ray? You got so close, I'd like to see it close up, I was too scared of its tail though'. This is perhaps the most ethically dubious element of the film making process[2] as scenes that were never seen are integrated seamlessly amongst those that were, significantly challenging the perceptive skills of the viewers. Personally I felt uncomfortable with such splicing activities but equally I felt that leaving out the footage of the most rewarding sightings would disappoint the tourists.

The ease with which the divers bought into such alterations either demonstrates their desire to believe in the supposed 'quality' of their experience and/or the trick of 'blind' trust they hold in the videographer. Here then not only is the temporal aspect of the footage re-arranged, but the images are also colour corrected. The camera has a red filter that covers the lens in an attempt to maintain the variety of colours that people are used to seeing in underwater documentaries and films. However, as the depth of the filmed dives varies this can lead to variations in colour intensity throughout the captured footage. To a certain extent, colours can be put back in to the images or taken away to maintain a 'realistic' looking white balance, and so the levels of the footage are played with to achieve this.

The human eye though, is neither equipped with a red filter, nor capable of these sophisticated alterations. Thus, the images that are witnessed post this stage of editing were rarely originally perceived to be so colourful in real time experience. By contrast, the deeper one dives, the more blue the scenery becomes, as the other colours of the spectrum are gradually filtered out. Divers would rarely comment on this (apparently not so) striking alteration to visual perception. This

---

2 However, such occasions did seem rare and were largely due to the failure of an intern to capture good quality shots in the first place, rather than representing the general ethos of the company.

could be a consequence of the proactive interference that watching underwater films and documentaries has on the divers as well as the retroactive interference caused to their memory by watching their souvenir DVD. In other words, 'the here and now' is considered to play as much a part in future recollections as the 'there and then' (Hoskins 2001: 335, see also Barthes 1981).

In addition to these alterations further inputs supplement the visual images. Transitions, which seamlessly blur one underwater encounter into the next, allow sudden changes of scenery and activity to wash over the viewer, disguising the extent to which real-time experience has been cropped. Textual headings of dive site locations, fish names, dates etc. are added to remind the learners, when in some distant time in the future they will no longer be able to pin point the specific details of the course. A further yet significant contextualising element is the sound track to the film with a selection of upbeat, strongly affective tunes such as Temper Trap's *Sweet Disposition*, The Red Hot Chilli Pepper's *Can't Stop*, Coldplay's *Clocks* and Jose Gonzalez's *Heartbeats* to name but a few favourites. Faster paced songs are used for the land/boat sequences to gee up the audience and end on a high, with relaxed and calming songs being used for the underwater scenes. Like the footage the soundtrack is also edited, 4–5 songs cut and arranged to make the film seem longer (and hence better value for money), but equally they change up the pace to maintain the attention of the viewer/listener and the energy of the film.

Performing Tourists

As I detailed in the second part of this chapter in relation to Foucault's notion of the 'self as a work of art' (Rabinow 1991), it is not just the prerogative of the videographer to try and polish the film to the highest possible aesthetic standards. The learner divers themselves, aware of the gazing eye of the camera, often equally contribute to this process quite openly. In *Camera Lucida*, Barthes (1981) analyses the difficulty people have in confounding a variety of self-images into a single 'image' or representation. The moment a person feels the camera focusing upon them there is a conflicting desire to acquire a representation that at once captures an essence of reality, but this should also capture the subject in a favourable light so as to ensure that the resultant memory objects will invoke positive recollections and be seen by friends and family favourably. Thus, the aim is to merge one's 'idealised self-image' with one's 'public self-image'. In order to carry this out divers would act for the camera when they realised they were being filmed. Divers would wave, blow bubbles or make comic bodily movements. On the boat they would smooth down their hair when they saw me reaching for the camera or for example would 'hide', look away or wave me off when they were having dive related issues they did not want captured. Common acts would include 'thumbs up' gestures, performing summersaults, blowing bubble rings, or in one instance comically looking terrified and pointing behind the camera as if a shark were approaching. Barthes (1981: 10) explains his own experiences of being pictured in a similar fashion 'once I feel myself observed by the lens, everything changes:

I constitute myself in the process of "posing", I instantaneously make another body for myself, I transform myself in advance into an image'. Barthes (1981: 11) continues 'I lend myself to the social game, I pose, I know I am posing, I want you to know that I am posing, but (to square the circle) this additional message must in no way alter the precious essence of my individuality'.

van Djick, (2007: 101) referring to process of photography comments, 'when a picture is taken, we want those photographs to match our idealised self-image – flattering, without pimples, happy, attractive – so we attempt to influence the process by posing, smiling or giving instructions to the photographer'. Thus, the camera's presence not only alters future memories through its mediatory technological apparatus, but it also encourages the learner divers to alter their real-time behaviour, *in order to* make the future memories more pleasurable and exciting. This is further intensified by the commonplace usage of visual productions as media of communication. Indeed sometimes, this is the primary role of the DVDs, as opposed digital re-memory/embodying aids, their use is solely to portray the 'pleasurable' and 'exotic' experience of learning to dive to friends and family. Thus, 'hyper-mediation creates a new vulnerability…a haunting anxiety for missing the "right" opportunity for communication, and simultaneously the touristic experience itself' (Jansson 2007: 16). The very act of having a camera present shapes the tourist's performance into acts of self-presentation; the camera constructs the arena for acting and observing, 'sacrificing the immediacy of experience and orienting activities to (future, distant) viewers' (Crang 1997a: 365). Consequently, future memory can be determined as much by the divers' imaginative capacities for action as the videographer's 'tools for reconstruction' (van Dijck 2007: 123).

Discussion

In response to Jansson's (2007) call for further research on the nexus between tourism, media, communication and geography, here I have tried to render visible the often unconsidered aspects of visual media production that result in, not only visual images themselves, but also by extension, the construction of alternate realities of place, performance and identity by tourists and tourist workers. The connectionist approach to the study of memory advocated throughout this chapter refutes the notion that 'memories are images of lived experiences stored in the brain that can be recalled without affecting their content' (van Dijck 2007: 41). Furthermore, it highlights that mediatory technologies, whilst acting as stimulants for recollection, actually inform and construct memories rather than transmitting realistic snippets of past experience. That is not to say that all recollection instigated by film is false or of fictitious events, nor that film is incapable of allowing for an embodying of the sights, sounds and actions presented on the screen. Rather, it is to say that the slippery nature of memory is formed in conjunction with the retroactive influence of the film, which when shot for a particular purpose (to be sold) is accompanied with a set of experience and place enhancing techniques.

From brighter, more colourful images, to seamlessly integrated never before seen creatures, footage is cropped, sped up and made to shine. As Loftus and Pickerell (1995: 725) have argued, 'nearly two decades of research on memory distortion leaves no doubt that memory can be altered via suggestion. People can be led to remember their past in different ways', and indeed these remembrances will be contingent upon the contexts in which they are taking place. In other words, 'the here and now' is considered to play as much a part in future recollections as the 'there and then' (Barthes 1981, cited in Hoskins 2001: 335).

Thus, there is a tension here surrounding the discontinuity between the DVD as *souvenir* and the DVD as an economically driven, artistic production. The term *'souvenir'* is French and literally refers to the act of remembering. The Oxford English Dictionary (2011) refers to a souvenir 'as something (usually a small article of some value bestowed as a gift) which reminds one of some person, place, or event'. In other words, the purpose of a souvenir is to bring back to consciousness the details relating to a particular experience. Those purchasing a dive encounter souvenir DVD, do so to be reminded of the scenery, the people, the animals, the culture and the forms of embodiment, which they were exposed to throughout their PADI Open Water course and their time on the island of Koh Tao. Thus, it would follow that they would desire visual imagery that is 'as close' to their real-time encounter as possible. Or do they? It has been argued that the 'post-tourist' is often perfectly aware of the lack of authenticity in many tourist activities and happy to go along with the pretence (Urry 1992, Wang 1999). But if the 'charade' is entertaining with desirable outcomes then is authenticity even a relevant frame of reference? (Hughes 1995).

Whilst authenticity is not at odds with the intentions of those producing the DVDs, it is equally not in sync either. As Laurier et al. (2008: 9) argue, 'the concerns film editors are orienting to as they assess footage, set edit points and so on are of a filmic order rather than an epistemic one'. The filmmakers know that tourists do not want to be reminded of negative experiences, and they will only buy DVDs that show the above elements of experience in a favourable manner. Thus it is in the interest of the filmmaker to rely on artistic style, the digital techniques of footage alteration and the manipulability of memory to their advantage. This is further complicated by the fact that, for the divers the DVDs have two roles; the first as memory aids and the second being communication aids; to share their experience with others not present at the time. This aspect of communication can involve 'sharing' the footage with a much wider audience than was possible 15 years ago, as digital memory objects can now become networked in minutes. In this case the aim of the videographer fits well with the desires of the diver, who is less concerned with accuracy than with perpetuating an idealised representation of place, atmosphere and bodily skill. This may be particularly true due to the demographic and activity being analysed in this chapter (almost exclusively gap year students, travelling around the world before or after going to university).

As already noted, the 'idealised self-image' comes in to play at this point as divers consciously manipulate their behaviour and attitude when in front of the camera. As van Dijck (2007: 127) argues 'the act of memory...is already anticipated at the moment of shooting' and consequently, filmed dives always involve 'remembrance, fabrication and projection' (2007: 123). However, the argument here is that; even if the divers recognise the mediatory influence the videographer has had on the production process of film, and similarly recall the way in which they acted up for the camera, for the first 1,2,3...6 times they watch their souvenir DVD, the active practice of forgetting the additional (personal) information, eventually serves to confound the mediated re-presentation with personal recollection. Thus self-editing out 'reality' whilst becoming increasingly vested in the 'produced'.

In addition, whilst for the divers themselves there is the problem of the relatively fast deterioration of personal memory (in contrast to the mediated memories), for those who witness Koh Tao's dive sites in the first instance on the screen (family, friends, social network users and YouTube browsers), awareness of the extent to which the images are altered from reality is even more uncertain *from the first observation*. Thus, as Hoskins (2001) argues, the medium actually becomes the memory. The viewers lose the 'intrinsic dynamic that exists...at the instantaneity of' the live encounter (Hoskins 2001: 342). Neither featured nor unfeatured spectators will be capable of retrieving the 'fullness' of the moment. As such, 'even electronified memories, although reframed, re-interpreted and enhanced over time, are always incomplete' (Hoskins 2001: 342). Jansson (2007:14) argues that visual media such as these DVDs then, digitally altered and rearranged, become 'scripting devices' which are based on an 'idealised framework for a touristic memoryscape' which are subsequently consumed by the public.

Thus, souvenir DVDs trouble the relationship that the individual diver has with the underwater seascape, but they equally construct Koh Tao into a magical tourist destination for those yet to visit. For the divers, previous experience becomes highly selectively remembered so that the seascape itself is recalled imaginatively as a tropical wonderland, saturated with colour, packed with activity and wildlife. Everyone is happy, everything goes to plan and everyone gets along in an overtly enthusiastic and outgoing manner. Discoveries are made one after another, new skills are always successfully demonstrated, qualifications are always achieved and at the end of the day the sun always sets majestically into the ocean's horizon. Thus, as van Dijck (2007) argues, moving images, edited, re-arranged, clipped, saturated and framed in a certain style can become contradictory and inconsistent signifiers of a relation *to* and a version *of* tourist space, that was never realised yet is processually remembered and shared with others.

References

Adler, J. 1989. Travel as performed art. *American Journal of Sociology*, 94(6), 1366–91.

Albers, P.C. and James, W.R. 1988. Travel photography – a methodological approach. *Annals of Tourism Research*, 15(1), 134–58.

Barthes, R. 1981. *Camera Lucida: Reflections on Photography*. New York: Hill and Wang.

Belk, R. and Hsiu-yen Yeh, J. 2010. Tourist photographs: signs of self. *International Journal of Culture, Tourism and Hospitality Research*, 5(4), 345–53.

Bergson, H. 2004. *Matter and Memory*. London: Macmillan.

Bolter, J. and Grusin, R. 1999. *Remediation: Understanding New Media*. Cambridge, MA: MIT press.

Caton, K. and Santos, C. 2008. Closing the hermeneutic circle? Photographic encounters with the Other. *Annals of Tourism Research*, 35(1), 7–26.

Cohen, E., Nir, Y. and Almagor, U. 1992. Stranger–local interaction in photography. *Annals of Tourism Research*, 19(2), 213–33.

Crang, M. 1997a. Picturing practices: research through the tourist gaze. *Progress in Human Geography*, 21(3), 359–73.

Crang, P. 1997b. Performing the tourist product, in: *Touring Cultures: Transformations of Travel and Theory*, edited by C. Rojek and J. Urry. London: Routledge.

Damasio, A. 1999. *The Feeling of What Happens: Body and Emotion in the Making of Consciosness*. Orlando, FL: Harcourt.

Dann, G. 1988. Images of Cyprus projected by tour operators. *Problems of Tourism*, 3(41), 43–70.

Deleuze, G. 2003. *Cinema 2: The Time Image*. Minneapolis: University of Minnesota Press.

Deleuze, G., 2005. Cinema *1: The Movement Image*. London: Continuum.

Edelheim, J.R. 2007. Hidden messages: a polysemic reading of tourist brochures. *Journal of Vacation Marketing*, 13(1), 5–17.

Edensor, T. 2001. Performing tourism, staging tourism. *Tourist Studies*, 1(1), 59–81.

Feighey, W. 2003. Negative image? Developing the visual in tourism research. *Current Issues in Tourism*, 6(1), 76–85.

Foucault, M. 1992. *The History of Sexuality: Volume Two*. Harmondsworth: Penguin.

Garlick, S, 2002. Revealing the unseen: tourism, art and photography. *Cultural Studies*, 16(2), 289–305.

Garrod, B. 2009. Understanding the relationship between tourism destination imagery and tourist photography. *Journal of Travel Research*. 47(3), 346–58.

Griffin, M. 1988. Snapshot versions of life – Chalfen, R. *Journal of Communication*, 38(3), 174–6.

Haldrup, M. and Larsen, J. 2004. The family gaze. *Tourist Studies*, 3(1), 23–46.

Heidegger, M. 1977. The age of the world picture, in: *The Question Concerning Technology and Other Essays*, edited by W. Lovitt. New York: Harper Torchbooks, 115–54.

Hoskins, A. 2001. New memory: mediating history. *Historical Journal of Film, Radio and Television*, 21(4), 333–46.

Hughes, G. 1995. Authenticity in tourism. *Annals of Tourism Research*, 22(4), 781–803.

Hunter, W.C. 2008. A typology of photographic representations for tourism: depictions of groomed spaces. *Tourism Management*, 29(2), 354–65.

Hyman, I.E. and Billings, F.J. 1998. Individual differences and the creation of false childhood memories. *Memory*, 6(1), 1–20.

Hyman, J.I.E. and Loftus, E.F. 1998. Errors in Autobiographical Memory. *Clinical Psychology Review*, 18(8), 933–47.

Jansson, A. 2007. A sense of tourism: new media and the dialectic of encapsulation/decapsulation. *Tourist Studies*, 7(1), 5–24.

Johnson, M.K., Oltmanns, T.F. and Maher, B.A. 1988. Discriminating the origin of information, in *Delusional Beliefs*, edited by T.F. Oltmanns and B.A. Maher. Oxford, England: John Wiley & Sons, 34–65.

Larsen, J. 2006. Picturing Bornholm: producing and consuming a tourist place through picturing practices. *Scandinavian Journal of Hospitality and Tourism*, 6(2), 75–94.

Laurier, E., Strebel, I. and Brown, B. 2008. Video analysis: lessons from professional video editing practice, *Forum Qualitative Sozialforschung/ Forum: Qualitative Social Research*, North America.

Loftus, E. and Pickrell, J. 1995. The formation of false memories. *Psychiatric Annals*, 25(12), 720–25.

MacCannel, D. 1979. Staged authenticity: arrangements of social space in tourist settings. *American Journal of Sociology.* 79(3), 589–603.

Marks, L. 2000. *The Skin of the Film*. London: Duke.

Markwell, K. 1997. Dimensions of photography in a nature-based tour. *Annals of Tourism Research*, 24(1), 131–55.

Merchant, S. 2011. The body and the senses: visual methods, videography and the submarine sensorium. *Body & Society*, 17(1), 53–72.

Neisser, U., Libby, L.K., Tulving, E. and Craik, F.I.M. 2000. Remembering life experiences, *The Oxford Handbook of Memory.* New York: Oxford University Press, 315–32.

OED. 2011. *Oxford English Dictionary*.

Pike, S. 2002. Destination image analysis – a review of 142 papers from 1973 to 2000. *Tourism Management*, 23(5), 541–9.

Pink, S. 2006. *The Future of Visual Anthropology: Engaging the Senses*. Oxford: Taylor Francis.

Rabinow, P. (ed) 1991. *The Foucault Reader: An Introduction to Foucault's Thought*. London: Penguin Books.

Scarles, C. 2004. Mediating landscapes. *Tourist Studies*, 4(1), 43–67.

Scarles, C. 2009. Becoming tourist: renegotiating the visual in the tourist experience. *Environment and Planning D: Society and Space*, 27(3), 465–88.

Slater, D. 1995. Photography and modern vision: the spectacle of 'natural magic, in *Visual Culture*, edited by C. Jenks. London: Routledge, 218–37.

Sontag, S. 1977. *On Photography*. London: Penguin.

Spinney, J. 2006. A place of sense: a kinaesthetic ethnography of cyclists on Mont Ventoux. *Environment and Planning D: Society and Space*, 24(5), 709–32.

Stallabrass, J. 1996. *Gargantua: Manufactured Mass Culture*. London: Verso.

Sutton, J. 1998. *Philosophy and Memory Traces: Descartes to Connectionism*. Cambridge: Cambridge University Press.

Tagg, J. 1982. The currency of the photograph, in *Thinking Photography*, edited by V. Burgin. London: Macmillan, 110–41.

Tussyadiah, I.P. and Fesenmaier, D.R. 2009. mediating tourist experiences: access to places via shared videos. *Annals of Tourism Research*, 36(1), 24–40.

Urry, J. 1992. The tourist gaze 'revisited'. *American Behavioral Scientist*, 36(2), 172–86.

van Dijck, J. 2007. *Mediated Memories in the Digital Age*. California: Stanford University Press.

Wade, K., Garry, M., Don Read, J. and Lindsay, D. 2002. A picture is worth a thousand lies: using false photographs to create false childhood memories. *Psychonomic Bulletin & Review*, 9(3), 597–603.

Wang, N. 1999. Rethinking authenticity in tourism experience. *Annals of Tourism Research*, 26(2), 349–70.

Weiser, J. 1990. More than meets the eye: using ordinary snapshots as tools for therapy, in *Healing Voices: Feminist Approaches to Therapy with Women*, edited by T.A. Laidlaw and C. Malmo. San Francisco: Jossey-Bass, 83–117.

Williams, L.M. and Banyard, V.L. 1998. *Trauma & Memory*, London: Sage.

Chapter 12

The Mediation and Fetishisation of the Travel Experience

Michael Salmond

Introduction

Over the past twelve years I have been creating a body of digital media artwork, which has been influenced by the travel experience. In this chapter I will be discussing my video artwork, which has coalesced around two related concepts. One is how we as travellers consciously or sub-consciously mediate our expression of travelling through various recording devices and how such mediation influences our understanding of the travel experience. The other is how the travel experience is influenced by particular considerations of traveller identity. My work aims to encourage its audience to question their own expectations and assumptions of travel as well as their expectations of my work as a mediated travel experience. Although my work is driven by my own experiences as a traveller, it does not aim to be autobiographical, but rather to provide an additional perspective, essentially creating two lenses through which the travel experience has been mediated. The positionality of the artist clearly influences created work in some capacity (England 1994) but my aim is to record without editing or an additional selection of what aspects to include or exclude. In this way, I am attempting to minimise my influence (although I acknowledge I cannot completely erase it) and position the audience as traveller allowing them to select which aspects of the journey to focus on. There is a duality in creating the work; I am an artist and a tourist so the process becomes reflexive. I am as much the subject of my work as those I see as subjects, but this does not interfere with the concepts at the heart of the work. In this way my work contrasts with other researchers working in tourism for whom maintaining a separation between an identity as a researcher and a tourist is important (Ness 2002, Nunez 1989). The videos I have created are not about myself as traveller or focused on the space or geography. The concept is to examine the performativity of the tourist and reflect their approaches towards mediating their experiences. The work invites audiences to reflect on their own experiences as tourists and in how they share and recall those events.

Mediation of travel is not a new phenomenon; artists and travellers have captured elements of the 'foreign' experience for many years through painting, poetry or travel writing. Through this process, travellers either consciously or subconsciously create particular identities for peoples and places (Pratt 1992).

What is new is the scale by which almost anyone can share, send and publish their accounts of travel from almost anywhere in the world, often instantly by texting images, blogging travel narratives or updating social media websites such as Facebook and Twitter. As media devices become increasingly ubiquitous at home, they become a key part of our lives and as such, our travel experience (Greenfield 2006). In essence, as tourists recording our travels, we become stars of our own reality show enhanced by a new level of self-awareness brought about by social media technologies implying a willing audience. As we record and distribute our memories and experiences, we employ those media as vehicles for defining and constructing both personal and cultural identity (Bolter and Grusin 2000, Larsen 2005). At the individual level the process of recording, choice of subject and method of dissemination helps to (re)create a personal identity. These personal identities then reflect and reinforce particular identities for cultural groups, which influence both hosts and guests (Smith 1989). These identities are carried through travelogues in video, text and images that broadcast the traveller's thoughts and feelings without any process, need for editing or compliance with a media demographic. Increased economic security expanded the numbers of individuals able to travel and, in more recent times, the access to cheaper and more immediate technologies has widened the scope of mediated travel experiences. Today, we are all travel journalists, presenters and critics, and the travels become virtualised as they are re-experienced through recorded media. In recent years it is the immediacy of this dissemination of travel experience that has accelerated. Travellers are able to record an event and post it online to an audience at home almost in real-time.

How travellers see, interact and then comment on their environment is in part influenced by the technologies now employed by travellers and tourists. The concept of the 'tourist lens' (Urry 2002) suggests that tourists sub-consciously situate particular places and cultures through the process of 'viewing' them as different. Similarly, the concept of the lens can be extended to the physical lenses and screens tourists use to communicate their experiences. The mediated surface of the recorded experience created in real time and space serves as a memory and tangible proof of an event; this process has become a conceptual base for my work. The 'lens' is now far more ubiquitous than ever before. Technology enables those with camera phones, WiFi enabled smartphones, tablet devices and cheap palm-sized video cameras to record and mediate their lives in numerous different ways. As with daily life, for many travellers the immediate experience is undermined by the need to record and disseminate it. This aspect of the travel experience can be traced as a common thread across travel narratives, both literary and visual. Many of the artists who deal with tourism as a premise (Parr 1990, Riedler 2005a and 2005b, Struth 2004a and 2004b, NL Architects 2003 and 2007, Barrada 2002a and 2002b, Ryu 2005, and Monk) focus on the tourist individual or group as subject. The work I have created examines the touristic experience itself, albeit in an abstracted, mediated, even virtualised way. The video work I discuss in this chapter puts the audience into the traveller's point of view, the camera lens becomes their own eye and frames their experience of these collected travels. The choice of technology used to communicate the work is tied to travel experience. The projected image itself harks back to the days before video cameras and the advent of the Cine-Film camera and projector and 'home-movies'. Although the video work may now be presented in much higher definition, on much larger screens with audio, the premise is still the same. The audience is being invited to watch vacation footage, and listen to the experience unfold, thus creating their own experience of travel from the presented details, which in turn feeds into the wider discourses of travel.

The Tourist Identity

The language and discourses of travel influence individual experiences. How individuals label and define themselves when travelling is part of the creation and recreation of the individual. In this way, the process of travelling becomes a performance whereby the traveller is enacting the role of a tourist by following expected behaviours (Edensor 2000). Whether the individual chooses to call oneself a traveller or a tourist is a process of self-identification with a particular identity. These layers of identity inform the tourist/traveller in everything they record: what to record, how to record and the language used to describe events. The identity of the tourist is one of someone who records the easily recognisable landmarks, high profile events or stereotypical cultural practices as proof of their being in a foreign land for their audiences (MacCannell 1999). In contrast, the traveller will deny the recording of these tourist tropes and instead seek out the unusual and frequently the mundane in order to reinforce their identity as different from the tourist. In this way, the traveller is seeking to create a different identity for oneself by seeking out the 'real' aspects of the host culture (Richards 1997). The language used by travellers frequently evokes the sense of difference utilising phrases such as 'off the beaten track' or 'authentic' or 'real' suggesting that their experience is somehow deeper, more meaningful and more adventurous than those of their fellow 'tourists'. Striving for authenticity, for the perfect undiluted travel experience, is at the heart of the performance of travel. In various locations tourism is frequently staged with specific performances and settings created for tourist consumption (Cohen 1988, Britton 1991). This staged nature of tourism has led to the desire for the experience of the 'authentic' within tourism with tourists deliberately avoiding the 'staged' authenticity of the repeated, cliché experience (MacCannell 1999). New narratives of experiencing the 'real' location and interacting with 'real' communities have led to the desire for the ultimate real and authentic through experiences with gritty and unpleasant daily life (Hutnyk 1999). Even when going 'off the beaten path' and to 'places no other tourist goes' individuals are still performing the role of tourist. The accoutrements of travel are often the recording devices, the video and SLR camera (Hutnyk 1996) signifying the individual as a 'tourist'. In order to avoid such identification and to create an identity as a 'traveller', many choose to consciously resist the draw to record and document their experiences (Mowforth and Munt 2003). However, even when refusing to record their travels, they remain tourists; out of place and out of synch with the local population. It is this language of tourism and the performance of the tourist ideal that underpins aspects of my work. Often the traveller will produce an internal and external narrative of their experiences, this narrative or 'Chronotope' (Fornais et al. 2007) is drawn from the discourses of travel in travel books, advertisements, wider media etc. These discourses feed into and influence their experience; where they go and what they do and ultimately what they record and broadcast to others.

The use of technology when travelling is not examined directly in my work, but my work is influenced by the use of technology and the ways in which technology becomes an integral part of our lives. Technology becomes an outward separation of traveller versus tourist. Our use of media devices has become more common and media allows its users the solidification of an experience, it becomes tangible after the event through the practice of creating a virtual world or simulation via recorded media (Lovejoy 2004). The process of digitisation and remediation creates a simulacra of peoples and/or places that is then distributed as a form of reality. The video, social media site or blog are virtual realities, one that are both abstract and real. Recording images, video and text and the act of creating a digital artefact is creating an experience (Bolter and Gromala 2003). The advent of mobile media devices, connectivity and social media has increased the recording of daily life, and in doing so has created a new virtual platform where the minutiae of people's lives are played out (Shaviro 2003). It is not dissimilar from the recording of events (weddings, parties, children growing up and so on) that occurred in previous decades, but new technologies enable wider distribution and make the content far more accessible. When on vacation or experiencing any form of travel, there is a conscious rise in media capturing. People tend to use Twitter or Facebook far less to record their meals when at home, immediately they travel every meal and minor event becomes worthy of sharing with an audience. In this way the tourist/traveller is exoticising the Other, identifying difference and creating the identity for both self and other (Said 1996). When one travels nothing is mundane, every tree, every bus and coach is different aesthetically and experientially. For tourists, the everyday and mundane becomes exotic, as it is perceived as different (Nash 1989). Through the recording of every experience while travelling, the tourist/traveller also reinforces one's own identity.

The recording and preservation of the travel experience is fixed in the idealised performance of what it is to travel. In some cases it would seem some people do not even wish to be aware of the event as it unfolds but are more comfortable viewing events through a distanced mediated camera and then eventually a television. This could be a reaction to the media saturated environment, or that the camera gives a different sense of immediacy and importance both to the recorder and the event. There is a sense that the tourist recording an event is a scribe, a documentarian, and a filmmaker. Once the footage is captured many feel the need to share their images, text and audio with friends, colleagues and relations as evidenced through the frequent use of social media sites. Through sharing, others connect with this version or account of the tourist experience and are afforded an illustration of the subjects and objects in the recordings. As an artist it has always seemed strange to me that others would be interested in such an abstract image, of seeing people they know in a place they have never been. Following on from still images and written accounts, we now have video and film recording, which allows for a new way of recording the travel experience. The travel video is the first reality television show; it is a window into the tastes and recreational habits of others. It is also, as Rosalind Krauss postulated in 1976, a narcissistic viewpoint when the artist (or in this case tourist), is at the centre of and the subject of the video or image. Travel video itself is an edited record of leisure moments that often centre on the positive aspects of travel. The happiness and the good times, in building positive memories, reinforce the positive aspects of tourism and infers the negative side of everyday existence.

Mediation of Memory

The video as artefact is a frustrating reflection of a period of time, even if it is reinforced with other media writing and souvenir ephemera. The video is another reality and one that eventually overwrites the memory of that past experience as it becomes more immediate and accessible. Increasingly technology is utilised as the repository for memories, the recollection of an event is now less and less likely to be stored biologically. Instead the memory is mapped to digital devices, which become memory objects (van Dijck 2007). In effect the mediated travel memory becomes a simulacra of the event, a virtualised version. When viewing edited footage of travels of the individual self what we observe is a different version: a simulation, a digital clone, a time traveller and one who is less recognisable to the present as time goes on. What begins to inform my art work and thought process is that the video is often seen as the most engaging and accurate representation of the travel experience. Instead the travelogue video is a selective slice of time that is a constrained re-imagination of events replayed as a form of truth. As audiences view my work they bring with them their own assumptions of what they will see. Through this process, they recreate their own understandings of peoples and places through viewing the videos and (hopefully) questioning the expectations they had. People see a part of my past which then becomes a part of their connotated perception (Barthes 1977). The understanding is that this is an edited highlight or show reel of that past but because of the nature of the gallery-space it is now important and immediate. When the record of travel is shown it becomes tangible again, and creates a temporal reality for the period of the show. As each audience experiences the work it creates a bridge between my memory and their own, based on what they see and experience. It becomes part of a feedback loop of realities converging and colliding. In part this is achieved by making the work the 'hero' of the exhibition space. By projecting the video footage in much larger-than-life aspect ratios and sizes it heightens the sense of immediacy: the audience being able to immerse themselves more fully in the footage even though it is so exaggerated. Bolter and Grusin (2000) define the immediacy of video and the extension of sharing that experience online or in digital form as 'hypermediacy'. Hypermediacy is not so much someone who is immersed in the content of the media but one who is interrelated and connected through media tropes and cultural norms. So even someone who has never visited Japan or Hong Kong can connect to the works because of the nature of the medium they are created in.

The heightening of the travel experience is not just explained with higher definition video and better quality footage. The sharing of memories has also changed along with digital technology. Because of social media platforms (Facebook, Twitter, Foursquare etc.), the digital tourist no longer sends physical postcards or hand written letters. Instead they write reportage style blogs, online diaries and upload images in a constant stream of travelogue updates. They are remembering and creating the event while it is occurring, there is less space for recollection and contemplation, digital media encourages a heightened sense of now and performing for an audience. For some tourists recollection and reporting has always been an important part of travelling, every Facebook update and Tweet is a form of performance art by and for the masses.

Hybrid Journeys (2008–2012)

My travelogue works began with a piece, which has now become a series called hybrid journeys. The name of the series evokes the dual nature of travelling and

Figure 12.1   Hybrid Journeys 9 (installed in gallery)

Figure 12.2   Hybrid Journeys 9 (detail)

identifies how experiences can perform multiple functions. In 'Hybrid Journeys 9' (2012), I present a collection of nine places recorded from tourist bus journeys in Singapore; Berlin, Germany; Kuala Lumpur, Malaysia; Las Vegas, Nevada, USA; London, UK; New York City, USA; Budapest, Hungary; Hong Kong, China and Tokyo, Japan. The run time of the video depends on the gallery setting but is usually on a twenty-three minute loop. The work can be extended into a forty-five minute version, a variety of edited forms of the 'Hybrid Journey 9' have been shown nationally and internationally.

   The starting point of the 'bus' series came from travelling on a bus in Hong Kong on a route frequently used by tourists to the city, connecting the airport with major locations for tourist hotels. However, this bus was also used by locals as a mode of transport and the presence of tourist items such as suitcases and backpacks was incongruous to the presence of local items such as shopping bags and other non-travel related ephemera. In addition, there was a difference between the clothing worn by tourists; causal and comfortable compared to the business attire worn by the locals. This all suggested difference between the tourists and the locals and made the space of the bus a more complex hybrid space which is repeated in many locations around the world. This one recorded journey was the catalyst for an artistic exploration surrounding the space that the tourists inhabit and perform in. The Hong Kong part of the hybrid journey series began as a regular tourist video, but this subconscious drive to record this hybrid journey led

Figure 12.3 Hybrid Journeys 9 Detail – Hong Kong (still)

me to seek out similar journeys in other locations. An accident of placement of the camera became integral to the work that followed.

Placing the camera at the top deck and front window of the bus created a challenging perspective, one that was the basis for the on-going works. The 'first person' point of view, of being able to see through the camera's eye as if sat on the seat, created a visual dichotomy and in effect a virtual experience. You, as the viewer, were 'sat' on the bus and travelled along with the camera as rider, which created an obvious frame for the recorded experience. The point of view also divorced any sense of the body of the traveller, erasing any particular race, gender or cultural identity, creating a void, which could be filled by the individual audience member and a contemporary mediated body for the audience to inhabit (Lovejoy 2004). When viewed, the audience sees only what the camera or traveller would see from a fixed perspective. This positioning of the camera views the landscape of the location, rather than the people (making an ethical choice not to include individuals without consent but also to disassociate the individual and 'foreigner' from the frame and to concentrate on the space and passage through it). The audience is cut off from outside stimuli experienced at the street level in the same way as the original traveller. There is no outside sound or smell that intrudes into this space, no wind, rain, heat or chill. The audience is in a metal box following a set path down a road inside the metallic frame of the vehicle as occurred in the original production. The video and collection of the bus's passage through the landscape becomes a metaphor for the travel experience, you are at once there and not there, you are included and excluded. There is a distancing that most tourists

Figure 12.4   Hybrid Journeys 9 Detail – New York City (still)

feel, of being in an environment but cut off from it, removed by the process of the mediation, but it maintains an electronic aura of the experience (Lunenfeld 2000). The disconnect occurs in part due to cultural unfamiliarity, custom, language or by deliberate attempt on the part of the tourist to be distanced so as to see the locals as 'other' and more 'exotic'. However the electronic mediation reconnects an audience through the television screen or projected video. A different geography as viewed through the familiarity of the electronic image enables the audience to connect with elements that are more familiar; public transport, cars, architecture, nature and so on. It is at once familiar and unfamiliar and this generates a connection between the traveller experience and the gallery audience.

The bus journeys operate in a disconnected and connected space and as the work expanded, the focus altered to highlight the identity of a bus that is for tourists alone. They move the tourist around the geography of the city or environment but, like the projected video in a gallery, the bus travellers are always distanced from it. This is mirrored in what the series became, an interaction with tourist routes on buses, or buses that serve no purpose for transport in the traditional sense of public service. In effect the tourist bus is an 'anti-bus', it is a created space that further separates the traveller from the foreign environment. The tourist bus often has its own presenter, voiceover or canned narrative describing landmarks and histories in a script that is performed daily and routinely to participants seeking the same experiences as others. The tourist bus frequently serves no public transport need, but instead is a way for tourists to get an overview of a place, which becomes an integral shared experience along with other tourists. It is a diesel driven moving theme park within a city; a product developed for no other need than those of the tourists or traveller. The tourist bus is focused on communicating the prescribed identity for a place, one which is frequently defined and/or reinforced through created travel brochures, advertisements or descriptions crafted by state and business actors (McGregor 2000, Robinson 1999). In this way, the bus journey is providing a controlled dose of a particular identity for a place, edited and presented in a condensed form. The choice to travel on a tourist bus also reinforces the individual identity as a tourist rather than a traveller. In some cases (although rarely) a tourist route may be used by a mix of locals and tourists, one which functions for both hosts and guests (Smith 1989). In this hybrid environment the identifier between the hosts and guests is frequently the use of the camera. This technology has also changed as part of the time frame of the production. In the early iterations the camera was, at best, a low fidelity VHS-C camera that many tourists would have access to. As the time has gone on so has the resolution of the footage, what was once VHS, standard quality footage has now become high definition, digital widescreen aspect footage. Although not addressed directly in the artwork, the change in video media is as much a marker of the passage of time as the subjects and environments in the footage.

Weather's Here, Wish You Were Lovely (2008) and Travelschism (2006)

In a related work 'Weather's Here, Wish You Were Lovely' created in 2008, I explore the expectations of the travel experience. The title is a direct reference to the 'humorous postcards' of the 1930's and 1960's by publishers such as Bamforth and Co., Davidson Brothers and J. Salmon, before the Internet rendered them somewhat obsolete. Since owning a video camera, I have always travelled with one and as an artist (and tourist) I frequently recorded aspects of my journeys. One of these processes has been the recording of travelogues, which were recounts (sometimes daily) of experiences whilst travelling. The perspective in the video is that of a camera directed at me as I talk towards it, my position and framing suggesting a 'presenter'. The style of these travel diaries follows similar themes seen in travel narratives on TV and was later to be seen in reality shows such as *Big Brother*. It is the form of a video diary and was originally intended to be just that, the footage would be for personal recollection and an aid to framing the experience as time passed.

The recordings present an insight into the frustrations, which occur when travelling, from the detailing of small difficulties, to the disappointment of experiencing a travel environment, which differs from a subconscious expectation of a place. The whole 'Weather's Here' piece is edited together from 12 different trips, none of which were ever intended for public view. The piece accidentally conforms to the remix and share generation, the knowledge that there is an audience out there for everyone and that every camera is an opportunity for a voice to be heard, with websites such as YouTube providing that access (Lessig 2008). The final work is an assembly and runs for 45 minutes in edited form, the unedited form runs for over six hours. Unintentionally in keeping with the YouTube or online video ranting, the work creates an uneasy, hard to watch, 45 minute long 'moan' about being in some of the most fantastic places on earth. 'Weather's Here, Wish You Were Lovely' is not just an anti-postcard it is an anti-travel brochure in video form.

'Weather's Here' also illustrates how my memory of an experience was usurped by the reality exemplified through the recording of the experience, creating almost a glitch between my memory and the real experience. In a similar vein my work 'Travelschism' (2006) explores memory and recollection and the shifts between the two as a focal point for representing the slippage between memory and digitised recording of an event. As I record video digitally it is visually perfect, the experience of pulling away from a train station as recorded through the eye of my camera is exactly the same as it was when I was there. Of course the camera can only record images and sound, but even so this is how many people remember their vacations, a smell or tactile trigger may bring back a memory, but it is often vague. There is a gap between the vague recollection of today and that of the past (Halbwachs 1992), although we may change the video, memory remains immune to atrophy and change. In the video the conductor is always on the exact same spot where he was in 2001, the speed of the train does not change, neither does the weather nor condition of the window the video camera is seeing out of. This is how we remember now; these digital tools are extensions of our memory in HD, computers mean we can record our lives and never need to forget (Mayer-Schönberger 2012). The digital technology allows us to recall instantly, in millions of pixels, a time in space of our travels. Our physical memories do not work

Figure 12.5   Travelschism (still)

Figure 12.6   Travelschism (still)

like this, they are muddy, they are vague, and they are messy. In some cases our memory is flawed and what we remember conflicts with what actually occurred and we may have gaps of partial memory, or areas which are completely missing.

'Travelschism' attempts to recreate via electronic means a physical memory of a train journey. It is messy, it has glitches and it was surprisingly hard to create digitally because the nature of the technology is designed to reproduce copies of itself perfectly. Digital remembers everything, every copy and every generation flawlessly. The aesthetic of this video is an intersection point, using digital technologies to attempt to describe the physical world, by recording the imperfect physical. Memories are abstractions of the event and so I am using software algorithms to generate the level of abstraction in order to reproduce the recollection process as much as possible. Using the algorithms I have little or no control over the final outcome, which reflects the lack of control over any total recall of any event or experience. The video piece is an abstraction and is time-based but is an attempt to recreate recollection. It is in juxtaposition to an abstracted image created by a painter or sculpture, which are entirely intentional and planned. 'Travelschism' is code-based and by nature its aesthetic is uncontrolled and randomised. We do not remember sequentially as characters do in movie flashbacks, we recollect elements, feelings, nuances and fragments all the while being in the present and still taking in information. It is this feedback loop of recollection, fragmentation and situating it in the present that underpin this work. It has become an important lynchpin piece in my series on recollection, remediation and memory.

Figure 12.7   White Wall (brochure print)

White Wall (2008) and Thai Market (2010)

In a departure from the landscape and place oriented works, the video work 'White Wall' is an exploration of the voyeuristic nature of tourism. It is in part a focus on the 'othering' of local populations (drawing from the concept of Other as discussed by Edward Said) as well as a reflection on why we travel at all. In the video the fixed point of view is of a wall that is description-less and without feature. There is no sense of place, space or cues as to location. The only cue as to locale is the predominance of Asian subjects as they walk to and fro across the camera's field of view.

The location is a shopping district in Tokyo, but the camera is disassociated from any visual trappings one would associate with such a place. There is just a white wall, no store fronts, no consumer ephemera. The camera's viewpoint is occupied by locals and tourists, some here to shop for the day, others here to observe difference. For many of the western tourists a major retail street is the familiar but when in the social context of a country like Japan it becomes totally unfamiliar. The short film records a space that exists purely in the camera, devoid of any peripheral information (it was shot outside a café) and context, so therefore appears to be just people exiting and entering the frame. The interest comes not

Figure 12.8   White Wall (still)

from seeing the locals, as you would expect from a tourist video, but from the viewing of the tourists as subjects. These are the people who stand out, and this reverses the sense of 'othering' in that it is the non-local population who are held up as other, not the local from the tourist point of view. These are the subjects who are identified as different, even when trying to blend in with their environment. When projected into a large exhibition space as with the other video pieces, 'White Wall' becomes a heightened exaggerated spectacle of enormous people walking to and fro, the subjects are in public spaces going about their lives and it is the normalcy and mundanity of the actions and subject matter that gives the work when projected, a symbolic or transformative presence. Mark Wallinger deals with similar subject matter in one of his works; 'Threshold to the Kingdom' (2002). It is a slowed down fixed camera of people coming through an arrival gate at an airport and is described as '...the slowing down of reality, a familiar scene gains a symbolic meta-level upon which the cycle of life is debated' (Martin 2006). This video reframes the traveller as hero, as adventurer, as well as narcissist and these themes are becoming more and more central in my work. With 'White Wall' my attention has begun to focus less on the space of tourism and the spectacle of it, and instead is examining the tourist as subject and their relationship with their performance and understanding of tourist created environments.

Other artists have drawn from similar themes within their artwork. For example Reiner Riedler staged a series of photographs of 'fake holidays' in which he documents tourists behaving as tourists, often in their own country. Riedler also examines industries who have created tourism spaces that are truly artificial

Figure 12.9   Thai Market (still)

such as indoor Ski parks. This form of 'fantasy travel' is a truly post-modern spectacle, people can now visit a recreation of a set of a science fiction show (the promenade from *Star Trek Deep Space 9* at a casino in Las Vegas), or go skiing in an 'authentic' alpine setting inside a massive warehouse in Japan. The more fake the manufactured tourist landscape, the more real it seems to become as a tourism destination, from Las Vegas as a spectacle destination, to old movie sets and restored architecture. There is a freedom to the truly invented destination, the theme park for example, because there is no authenticity to seek for the traveller. There is no purpose, no history to seek out, no indigenous population to record or interact with. These invented spaces are the purest of tourist environments. However, even within these created environments there are frequently gaps, or glitches, which allow for the 'real' to leak in. To paraphrase Debord the collection of images and their socialised relationship (via sharing, YouTube and blogs) invents the spectacle and this becomes the tourist attraction (Debord 2002). The more focused these images, the more of them there are, and the more certain the catalogued space is to become a spectacle worth tourist attention. These invented spaces cross between virtual as they exist, both in the digital space and the real as they have a physical location. These concepts have informed a new work 'Thai Market' (created in 2012). This video piece is a reflection on the authentic tourist space and also on its artificiality that occupy the same space. Footage was shot on location on Bangkok's Khao San Road, in what used to be a street with some market stalls and hostels and has now become a tourist location in its own right. The video 'Thai Market' follows a series of western travellers and tourists as they roam up and down the street in what almost appears to be a psychologically caged environment. The landscape they are experiencing is limited to this one street and the same individuals will wander back and forth as if the process of walking the road was the experience of their travel. The tourists appear as animals being steered along the road, the local market stall and café owners take on the appearance of game wardens occasionally herding the tourists up and down the street or in and out of market stalls. The initial reason for the road as a service market has become usurped and a more experiential place has been created. Tourists who are not staying on Khao San Road will come from elsewhere to visit the location where other tourists stay. It is a theme park environment that exists purely to serve the tourist and yet is not controlled by one business or company. Areas like Khao San Road exist all over the world and share many of the contexts of 'invented' physical spaces that serve the tourists and also suggest questions over the authentic travel experience.

Conclusion

This chapter has situated my work within the broader literary and visual works related to tourism and mediation. When creating art, it is more of an emotional, visceral response that drives the creativity, it is important to situate the work within a larger, deeper context based on where that creative response comes from. The creation of these works means coming to terms with the fact that the maker is a subject as well as a curator of the travel experience being recorded. Issues of authenticity and truth in making have arisen in the aftermath of showing the works. It has become harder to make artwork about travel and tourism from a reactive or naïve point of view following the creation of these pieces. Originally the visuals and aesthetics were often made through the lens of exoticisation focusing on the new and the unfamiliar. Since showing the works the methodology has become more deliberate and knowing. When visiting any city the first point of call is to any tourist route buses and the focus is on adding the video to the 'Hybrid Journey' series. As the creator there is more distance from the subject and landscapes than when the process began. The tourists, locations and conveyances are now my subjects and canvas. Due to the nature of the work it has become impossible to be a tourist or traveller; instead I have become a pseudo-documentary artist always looking to grow my body of work.

The accident or honesty of a situation or recorded event that originally drove my work is now replaced with a deliberate creative process. When your work is focused on tourism, the mind's internal camera becomes more obsessed with the potential for any location or experience to become the framework for a new series. It means that I can no longer film myself talking into a camera as I did with 'Weather's Here' because it would no longer be an authentic unconscious work. In some ways it is the amateur going professional, the hobby becoming the business. So as this body of work has grown over the past ten years, I have become more interested in the discussion of what being a tourist/traveller means. The videos look less at the landscapes and spaces tourists inhabit and have become more focused on the identity and awareness of the tourist and how they mediate and express their experiences to others. In this way, I hope my work encourages a more reflective experience when travelling and when 'viewing' other peoples and place.

References

Barrada, Y. (Artist) 2002a. Women at Window [Photo]. From the series: The straight project, 1999–2003.

Barrada, Y. (Artist) 2002b. Bay of Tangier [Photo]. From the series: The straight project, 1999–2003.

Barthes, R. 1977. *Image, Music, Text*. London: Fontana Press.

Bolter, J. and Grusin, R. 2000. *Remediation, Understanding New Media*. Cambridge, MA: MIT press.

Bolter, J. and Gromola, D. 2003. *Windows and Mirrors: Interaction Design, Digital Art, and the Myth of Transparency*. Cambridge, MA: MIT Press.

Britton, S. 1991. Tourism, capital and place: towards a critical geography of tourism. *Environment and Planning D: Society and Space*, 9(4), 451–78.

Cohen, C. 1988. Authenticity and commoditization in tourism. *Annals of Tourism Research*, 15(3), 371–86.

Debord, G. 2002. *The Society of the Spectacle*. translated by K. Knabb. Canberra, Australia: Hobgoblin Press.

Edensor, T. 2000. Staging tourism: tourists as performers. *Annals of Tourism Research*, 27(2), 322–44.

England, K. 1994. Getting personal: reflexivity, positionality, and feminist research. *Professional Geographer*, 46(1), 80–90.

Fornas, J., Becker, K., Bjurstrom, E., and Ganetz, H. 2007. *Consuming Media Communication, Shopping and Everyday Life*. London: Berg.

Greenfeild, A. 2006. *Everyware: The Dawning Age of Ubiquitous Computing*. Berkeley, CA: New Riders.

Halbwachs, M. 1992. *On Collective Memory*, translated by L. Coser. Chicago, IL: University of Chicago Press.

Hutnyk, J. 1996. *The Rumour of Calcutta: Tourism, Charity and the Poverty of Representation*. London: Zed Books.

Hutnyk, J. 1999. Magical mystery tourism, in *Travel Worlds: Journeys in Contemporary Cultural Politics*, edited by R. Kaur, and J. Hutnyk. London: Zed Books, 94–137.

Krauss, R. 1976. Video: the aesthetics of narcissism. *October*, 1: 50–64.

Larsen, J. 2005. Families seen sightseeing: performativity of tourist photography. *Space and Culture*, 8(4): 416–432.

Lessig, L. 2008. *Remix: Making Art and Commerce Thrive in the Hybrid Economy*. London: Bloomsbury Academic.

Lovejoy, M. 2004. *Digital Currents: Art in the electronic age*. 3rd edition. New York: Prentice Hall.

Lunenfeld, P. 2000. *Snap to Grid: A User's Guide to Digital Arts, Media and Cultures*. Cambridge, MA: MIT Press.

MacCannell, D. 1999. *The Tourist: A New Theory of the Leisure Class*. Los Angeles: University of California Press.

Martin, S. 2006. *Video Art*. London: Taschen

Mayer-Schönberger, V. 2012. *Delete: The Virtue of Forgetting in the Digital Age*. Princeton, NJ: Princeton University Press.

McGregor, A. 2000. Dynamic texts and tourist gaze: death; bones and buffalo. *Annals of Tourism Research* 27(1): 27–50.

Monk, J. (Artist) #129, MALTA £189 [Photo]. From the series: Holiday Paintings, 1992–2000.

Mowforth M., and Munt I. 2003. *Tourism and Sustainability: Development and New Tourism in the Third World*. London: Routledge Press.

Nash, D. 1989. Tourism as a form of imperialism, in *Hosts and Guests: The Anthropology of Tourism*, edited by V. Smith. Philadelphia: University of Pennsylvania Press, 37–52.

Ness, S. 2002. *Where Asia smiles: An ethnography of Philippine tourism*. Philadelphia: University of Pennsylvania Press.

NL Architects. (Artist) 2003. Cruise City [Photo]. From the series: Virtual Realities, 2003–2008.

NL Architects. (Artist) 2007. Plugin City [Photo]. From the series: Virtual Realities, 2003–2008.

Nunez, T. 1989. Touristic studies in anthropological perspective, in *Hosts and Guests: The Anthropology of Tourism*, edited by V. Smith. Philadelphia: University of Pennsylvania Press, 265–80.

Parr, M. (Artist) 1990. The Matterhorn [Photo]. From the series Small World, 1987–1994. Collected and Published (1996, 2007), revised edition. Stockport: Dewi Lewis Publishing.

Pratt. M. 1992. *Imperial Eyes: Travel Writing and Transculturation*. New York: Routledge.

Richards, G. 1997. The social context of cultural tourism, in *Cultural Tourism in Europe*, edited by G. Richards. Wallingford: CABI International.

Riedler, R. (Artist) 2005a. Schilift [Photo]. From the series Fake Holidays, 2004–2009. Munich, Germany: Moser Verlag.

Riedler, R. (Artist) 2005b. Indoor Pool: Tropical Islands [Photo]. From the series Fake Holidays, 2004–2009. Munich: Moser Verlag.

Robinson, M. 1999. Cultural conflicts in tourism: Inevitability and inequality, in *Tourism and Cultural Conflicts*, edited by M. Robinson and P. Boniface. Wallingford: CABI Publishing, 1–44.

Ryu, H-Y. (Artist) 2005. Flughafen [Photo]. From the series: Audiences.

Said, E. 1996. *Orientalism*. New York: Random House Inc.

Shaviro, S. 2003. *Connected: or What it Means to Live in the Network Society*. Minneapolis: University of Minnesota Press.

Smith, V. (ed) 1989. *Hosts and Guests: The Anthropology of Tourism*. Philadelphia: University of Pennsylvania Press.

Struth, T. (Artist) 2004a. Audience 8 (Galleria dell'Accademia) Firenze [Photo]. From the series: Audiences.

Struth, T. (Artist) 2004b. Audience 1, Firenze [Photo]. From the series: Audiences.

Urry, J. 2002. *The Tourist Gaze*. London: Sage Publications.

van Dijck, Jose. 2007. *Mediated Memories in the Digital Age*. Stanford, CA: Stanford University Press.

Wallinger, M. (Artist) 2002. Threshold to the Kingdom [Video]. From the series: Audiences.

Chapter 13

Being a Tourist or a Performer? Tourists' Negotiation with Mediated Destination Image in Popular Film

Maltika Siripis, Caroline Scarles and David Airey

Introduction

This chapter is set in the context of the relationship between media and tourism consumption. Specifically, it deals with film which it is claimed has a significant influence in encouraging tourism at destinations because of its visual primacy and its power to reach wider audiences (Butler 1990, Riley and Van Doren 1992, Tooke and Baker 1996). Urry's tourist gaze (1990 and 2000) and the influence of visual media, including film, on tourism are rooted in a commonality between the film industry and the tourism industry. Both involve the exploitation of places and visual consumption by both film audiences and tourists alike. In the tourism industry, a tourist destination is a raison d'être of tourism (Boniface and Cooper 2009). In the film industry, after the decline of the studio era in the 1960s, central primacy has been afforded to the actual locations, in many cases tourist destinations, within which filming now takes place. This development in the film industry has further inter-linked these industries. Tourist destinations and film locations are no longer mutually exclusive, but rather exist within the same spatial locations.

Film is an aspect of visual culture and popular media that provides repertoires of images and creates narratives of place which frame travel styles and tourists' behaviour at destinations (Adler 1989, Edensor 1998, 2000). Mercille (2005) and Iwashita (2006) argue that film directly influences tourists' expectations of patterns of behaviour. In other words, tourist practices at destinations are influenced by these images and narratives derived from travel media, including popular media. Tourists can be viewed as subjects under the influence of these travel discourses (Adler 1989, Edensor 2001). In unpacking the relationship between the visual consumption of place through film and subsequent tourist performance at destinations, this chapter aims to further investigate the influence of popular film on tourists' interpretations of films and their subsequent behaviour as tourists. It specifically explores issues of tourists' self-awareness at film locations and their responding travel practices within these environments. The chapter then explores the role of tourists as performers before moving on to examine tourists' negotiated image of Thailand as a consequence of their interpretation of film. It draws on published literature as well as on the findings from a research study into the relationship between the film *The Beach* and tourism in Thailand (Siripis 2011). The research involved the respondents watching the film and reporting on the tourist cinematic experience as well as their experience at the actual film location in Thailand.

A Tourist and a Performer

To discuss the concept of being a tourist or a performer, it is essential to consider the concept of staging tourism. The term 'stage' is used in tourism practices by MacCannell (1976), who applies Goffman's (1959) concept of the front region and the back region to touristic spaces. MacCannell (1976) states that the front region is the meeting place of hosts and guests or customers and service personnel, whereas the back region is an area where members of the 'home team' retire between performances to relax and to prepare. The tourism industry therefore produces the link for guests who are motivated by a desire to see 'life as it is really lived' (ibid.: 94). Against this background, the growth of mass tourism has brought with it not only the expansion of front region tourism spaces but it has also promoted the avenue of the back regions to the tourist gaze. Hence, the back region needs to be de-mystified. The result of this is what MacCannell (ibid.) refers to as staged authenticity. According to this concept, most tourists who visit film locations are considered serendipitous film tourists whose motivation is based on novelty and social interaction as distinct from general film tourists whose motivation is based on novelty and nostalgia for films (Macionis and Sparks 2009). This chapter seeks to further develop the subtleties and complexities of this relationship in order to understand the plurality of emergent tourist behaviour at destinations.

Indeed, acknowledging MacCannell's concept of staged authenticity, Edensor (2000) provides an alternative approach to understanding tourist practices. He argues that tourism itself can be classified as a form of performance; a dramaturgical series of active expressions and doings that become manifest through strategic 'stage-management' (ibid.: 323). According to Adler (1989), travel styles and tourist practices are framed and influenced by different discourses which provide practical orientations and cultivate subject positions, specifying what actions should take place at particular places and times. Agreeing with Adler (1989), Edensor (1998, 2000) suggests that features of touristic performance include temporal and spatial dimensions, social and spatial regulation, and touristic performance.

According to both approaches, it is difficult to differentiate between tourists and performers. Tourists are either portrayed as spectators who are drawn to tourist destinations and film locations to gaze at spectacular scenery and to witness the film set as a tourism attraction. Or, film tourists are called performers at tourist destinations, particularly film destinations. They participate in film tourism activities, for example taking photographs with the film set, posing and acting like the film stars. Macionis (2004) proposes a typology of film tourists identifying three types. Serendipitous film tourists are tourists who happen to be on a location that is portrayed in the film. General film tourists are drawn to the film set as part of tourism activities. Specific film tourists actively seek to see places they have seen on the screen. Connell (2012) argues that film tourists are mostly incidental as tourists may visit the film locations during the course of a holiday as they have emerged as tourist attractions. Therefore, as Adler (1989), Edensor (2001) and Perkins and Thorn (2001) suggest, films create supporting travel discourses that both mobilise and influence tourists' travel practices at destinations.

Crouch et al. (2005) and Moore (1993) maintain that media audiences or tourists are active media receivers, who in turn become active producers of meanings of the media being consumed. Once the media audience transforms themselves into tourists, MacCannell and MacCannell (2001) suggest that tourists decode both visual signs and text at the destination and are aware of the obscurity of the staged destination. Tourists have the second gaze which turns back onto the gazing subject and an ethical responsibility for the construction of their own experience as they refuse to leave the construction to the corporation, the state or the apparatus of touristic representation. The possession of the second gaze implies that tourists oversee the staged authenticity of a tourist destination. However, at the destination tourists are aware that they are on the stage and perform according to the staged environments. They 'look for the unexpected, not the extraordinary, objects and events that may open a window in structure, a chance to glimpse the real' (ibid.: 36). A study of tourists' actual practices at the film location is based on tourists renegotiating with, and a move away from, tourism producers, as Edensor (2000 and 2001) suggests, as directors of the performance.

Film, Tourist Gaze and Tourist Imagination

For tourism, the most significant influence of film is the popularisation of destinations (Kim and Richardson 2003, Mercille 2005). Film can represent locations and portray tourist practices in various ways dependent on storylines, characters and genres. Most research into the influence of film on tourism, for example Riley and Van Doren (1992); Tooke and Baker (1996); Riley et al. (1998), suggests that popular film has an influence on tourists' perception of destinations that feature in films, which results in increasing numbers of tourist arrivals at locations associated with films. The research presented here goes further to suggest that film also has an impact on tourists' behaviour and consumption. This part of the chapter explores further the influence of film on tourists' behaviour which includes how film influences the tourist gaze and tourist imagination.

Film is thought to enhance the audience or tourist's construction of the gaze because visual representation is predominant. Mulvey (1989) summarises the relationship between visual pleasure and narrative cinema in that the elements of film create a gaze, a world and an object, thus producing an illusion cut to the measure of desire. Bearing this relationship in mind, when the audience or potential tourist watches a film scene which consists of a film star's performance, setting, sound and narrative, they capture the gaze derived primarily from visual pleasure. The development of cinema presentation also reinforces the power of film to shape the tourist gaze which as Urry (1990) suggests, is constructed through signs. Accordingly, film language is operated by the systems of signs which, in a motion picture, are mostly the sounds and acting of film stars. Film signs can be classified into two parts, namely *the signifier* and *the signified*. The signifier is the physical form of the sign, for instance the image or photograph, and the signified is the mental concept of the physical form (Turner 1993). In film viewing, the audience gets messages through a number of signs and codes which are film elements (Heath 1981, Monaco 2000). As performed through embodied visualities, such elements of film allow audiences to move beyond the primacy of the visual as the scenes presented stimulate fascination, fear, anticipation, and intense pleasure for film audiences and tourists alike. The film elements appeal to tourists' senses of hearing, smell, and sight (Crawshaw and Urry 1997). The landscapes and townscapes in films are iconised in an extraordinary aura by the elements and process of film-making. Filmic icons relate to the process of cinematic on-site consumption (Riley and Van Doren 1992, Riley et al. 1998). They are presented in realistic ways that enable audiences to believe that they are really present at the film location. As a consequence, these filmic icons have become attractions that pull tourists to visit these film sites.

The other significant concept underlining the tourist gaze is tourist imagination. Urry (1990: 13) suggests that 'people's basic motivation for consumption is not therefore simply materialistic. It is rather that they seek to experience "in reality" the pleasurable dramas they have already experienced in their imagination'. Film influences tourist imagination in two principal ways: the elements of film and the cinematic experience. The elements of film, namely cinematography, film stars, scenery and storyline, offer the audience the pleasure of looking, which enhances the tourist imagination. Film audiences, as Turner (1993) suggests, react to the cinema image as if it were real. He further explains that this blurring of boundaries between the imaginary and the real is at the heart of the cinema experience. The film image or the imaginary signifier refers to the fact that reality in the film image is always absent and present only in the audience's imagination.

Acland's (1998) study of the Image Maximum (IMAX) technology and tourist practices reveals that IMAX screen technology increases the power of film to reduce the distinction between the screen world and the real world. IMAX technology provides the audience with the experience of being there or getting there. The audience or tourist imagination can be enhanced by the hyper-real motion pictures that are exhibited by IMAX screen technology which produces images so real that they offer an illusion of material presence and create the sensation of movement for audiences. Thus, audiences transcend the confines of their physical self; mobilising the possibility of self as an alternative, imagined other with a foundation in that which is viewed and enlivened onscreen.

Such transcendence is mobilised as film provides a realistic image and narrative style in which the audience or would-be-tourists develop a self-identification with film character and situation. In tourism practices, the self-identification of the audience or the tourist reinforces the tourist imagination as well as influencing the tourist's behaviour. Turner (1993) suggests that the film experience is heightened in cinemas where audiences sit in comfortable seats and focus their attention on the screen. The film experience encourages the audience to identify with situations and heroes/heroines in films. The tourist imagination entails both understanding and feeling about the world, which recognises utopian aspiration at the level of the individual. They react as if they were the narrator of the film. As audiences fail to distinguish between their own eyes and projection apparatus, the camera lens becomes tourists' eyes as they gaze upon the unfolding scenes as if they were holding the camera. Thus, such compression of distance between self and other mobilises audiences to identify with every character depicted on the screen. However, in actual film watching, each individual audience may react in different ways depending upon audiences' background, which associates them with situations in the film.

The utopian aspiration of imagined and imaginative travel is suggested by the vision of a world re-formed in the image of the media or tourist promotion (Crouch et al. 2005). Films are engaged in facilitating an emotional disposition, combined with imaginative and cognitive activity which can potentially be converted into tourist activities. A film such as *The Beach* (Boyle 2000) heightens audiences' imagination through the main character, Richard's (Leonardo DeCaprio), journey to the pristine beach featured in the film, Maya beach in Thailand. The film enhances the tourist imagination of a perfect tropical beach, which results in actual tourist behaviour. Nonetheless, the actual impact of film on tourist practices is still debatable. These are some of the questions among a range that could be asked; Do tourists act and perform according to the media representation? Do tourists who visit the destinations associated with films consider themselves tourists or performers?

The Beach and Tourism

The Beach has been utilised as a case of the influence of film on tourism in two different aspects; destination marketing and tourists' behaviour. First, Grihault (2003) studied the phenomenon of film tourism and the influence of *The Beach* on destination marketing activities after the film's release. This involved inviting the media to visit the location and generating collaborative campaigns with the film company. It has been reported that The Tourism Authority of Thailand (TAT) heavily advertised its attractions during release of *The Beach*, including joint activity with 20th Century Fox to make the most of further popularity of Thai beaches. The TAT invited UK journalists and travel agents to join the familiarisation trip as well as financing a holiday prize on a BBC television game show with a quiz theme around *The Beach*. The study suggests that film has a significant influence on destination marketing as it draws tourist attention to the film location. Within the study of film and destination marketing, Warnick et al. (2005) further investigated the effects of *The Beach* on the image of Thailand among college students, who are main targets of the film. Their findings suggest that the film did not affect the likelihood of the college students to visit Thailand and it also noted that it represented the dark side of tourism in Thailand. This points both to the fact that the film has a minimal impact on the image of Thailand and that destination marketers should be careful about using it as a promotional tool due to its disturbing message.

The later research studies of *The Beach* focus on the film and tourists' consumption of places. Tzanelli (2006) investigates the effects of *The Beach* as popular culture on tourists' gaze on Thailand. The study focuses on how Thailand was represented in the film as well as how audiences or would-be-tourists perceived it. It is suggested that *The Beach*'s film elements have been structured and directed to resonate with a new wave of backpacker tourists in Thailand and their conflict with the hostile environment in Thailand (Tzanelli 2006). *The Beach* and the tourist gaze were revisited in the study by Law et al. (2007) of interconnections between film and tourism. The study suggests that film viewing itself can be considered a form of tourist practice. The film gaze is 'bound up with processes of material landscape transformation' (ibid.: 159).

According to these research studies, *The Beach* is used to demonstrate the influence of film on tourism in two different approaches. The research on which this chapter is based revisits the influence of *The Beach* on tourism, but in doing so rather focuses on tourists' view and interpretation of the film and on the process of their negotiation in the film representation.

Study Methods

The study adopted a case study approach employing multi-methods to gain in-depth information such as people's insights and interpretation. A semi-structured interview technique was used with photo and film elicitation in order to obtain respondents' interpretations of, and reactions to, the film. Film elicitation involves projection of the entire film, or particular film sequences, to respondents. The use of multi-methods allows respondents to compare their actual experiences with imaginary ones. The research respondents were residents of the UK who had seen *The Beach* and who had travelled or were planning to travel to Thailand. By the time of the final interview they had all visited Thailand. Ultimately 40 interviews were conducted. The strategies to recruit potential respondents were placing advertisement posters in public places and using snowballing sampling strategy. The 40 respondents were interviewed and asked to watch some sequences of *The Beach* together with the researcher. The interviews were carried out in various locations both in the UK and in Thailand during 2009.

Being a Tourist or a Performer? An Awareness of One-self

Adler (1989) maintains that travel is a performed art whose styles are framed and influenced by different discourses. These discourses impart practical orientation, cultivate subject position and specify what actions should take place at particular places and times. A tourist destination therefore exists as a performance stage upon which tourists are directed to perform by a range of agents within the tourist experience: tourism developers, tour operators and travel agents, to name but a few (see also Crang 1997). Narratives of places, particularly mediated representations of destinations substantially affect tourists' behaviour at the destination (Edensor 1998, 2000, 2001). Among those agents, film as a popular medium has the power to create a story and myth of a place (Selwyn 1996, Iwashita 2006). Indeed, Law et al. (2007: 149) suggest that a popular film such as *The Beach* 'engenders a place mythology around the filming sites' and articulates tourism practices in the film locations. These practices include using the film as an unconventional destination marketing promotion tool and presenting alternative travel patterns in Thailand for tourists who want to move away from the staged tourist areas. The film makes the film site a new stage for tourists. According to these theories, tourists have traditionally been viewed as passive and likely to succumb to media and the developers of tourist areas, tour operators and travel agents. However, this chapter argues that tourists are active and aware of being subject to the influence of media and stage managers.

I'm a Tourist!

The information from tourists interviewed reveals that their practices and behaviour at the destination (Thailand) were not influenced by *The Beach*. Tourists felt that they considered themselves as tourists who had different travel practices to the young backpackers portrayed in the film. It is apparent that tourists were conscious of the difference between being tourists and backpackers. As a consequence of this realisation, tourists did not associate themselves with the characters in the film and negotiated to behave differently from mediated tourist practices, as Jane and James observed:

> We were tourists in the hotels and we booked a tour out, whereas now we tend to go on adventure group holidays where there are 8 to 16 people with a tour guide and a local guide. Sometimes, we stay in the local houses as well, that's how we will absolutely go there. We didn't have that community sort of spirit like in the film.

Chris, another respondent also stated his motivation for travelling to Thailand, which was different from that of the backpackers, as he revealed:

> I didn't personally because I didn't come here as a backpacker, you know, I
> came here to visit my mum. You know, so I saved my money and when I came
> here I knew I was going to have a comfortable time and it was going to be a more
> high end holiday rather than just getting by with a backpack.

Most respondents identified themselves as tourists whom Urry (1990) calls
post-tourists; they denied that the film narrative, which features stories of young
backpackers, had an influence upon their behaviour at the destination. In this case,
tourists can also differentiate between tourists and backpackers. They considered
themselves as tourists due to their motivation which was for having a relaxing
holiday experience in visiting Thailand. Indeed, those interviewed reflected
their self-awareness and their image of Thailand as a tourist destination. Their
negations indicated that the film had a minimal influence on their behaviour and
their image of the destination. Their preferred practices on holiday in Thailand
were influenced by the places' environment and commercially established images,
for example from travel brochures, travel websites and postcards that they bought
before their visit. Their major motivations to visit Thailand were to have relaxing
holidays on beaches. This corresponds with the research of McCabe and Stokoe
(2004) who suggest that tourists' behaviour is influenced by places, particularly
their physical characteristics, and that a 'tourist place' must have describable
features with which people can identify themselves. In this case, respondents
identified themselves as tourists who desire to have a relaxing holiday on tropical
beaches not as backpackers who longed for adventure and excitement.

Indeed, the respondents' reflections indicate that they did not associate the
meaning of Thailand as a tourist destination with *The Beach*. This was because
their original intentions to visit the country were not based on the fact that it was
featured in *The Beach*. This supports Crouch et al. (2005) who argue that tourists
also make meanings of the space by their practices, their expressions, and their
interpretation of mediated representations.

> I don't know, I've not been one of them who have done it but I think because you
> have got a city and beautiful scenery as well. There's an appeal in the film to go
> to the south and north. I don't know. I think people just really want to travel and
> spend quite a bit of time in Thailand. (John)

From respondents' reflection of themselves as tourists, they challenge
Macionis's (2004) definition of a film tourist whose major motivation is to seek
new experience from film tourism activities. The respondents admitted that they
were simply ordinary tourists at the film location. The film did not have any
influence on their motivation nor their behaviour. Their main motivation to visit
the destination and film location was primarily to have a travel experience and
holiday in Thailand. Film location, according to their general opinion, is only
part of the destination's attractions. Maya Beach was considered to be a beautiful
tourist attraction in its own right. In fact, the beach has been popular among

international tourists and had already been heavily promoted by the TAT and local tour operators before the release of *The Beach*. Being featured in the film helped to popularise it and reinforce its beauty.

Nonetheless, the tourists' description of themselves as ordinary tourists prompts their negation of being performers and at staged tourist attractions. Adler (1989) and Edensor (1998, 2000, 2001) maintain that tourists are comparable to performers at tourist sites. Tourist practices at the destination are influenced by the site's narratives, story and physical environment. This relationship is reversed in the case of *The Beach* and Thailand. The film itself portrays popular tourist practices which have already been evident at the destination, for example the hedonistic lifestyles and the backpackers' experiences. The existence of these practices and the tourism situation in Thailand inspired the author to write the original novel which was then interpreted by the film director. The film locations were well known tourist areas which already ranked amongst the main tourist attractions in Thailand. *The Beach* visualises these practices by exaggerating them as extreme practices of young travellers. Most respondents did not believe and did not perform those practices. At a destination, they performed practices with origins in existing travel discourses. These performances are part of a wider mediation process that includes the originating moments and experiences within which the film had its origins.

This finding of the study reported on in this chapter suggests that tourists themselves were not aware of their secondary status as performers at the destination. The temporal and spatial nature of their behaviours was determined by their holiday and their knowledge of Thailand as a well-established tourist destination, particularly in terms of its beautiful beaches. Their practices at the destination were influenced by their desire for this type of holiday experience. Therefore, tourists pursued typical tourist practices in Thailand that they had learned about from tourist brochures and anecdotes from friends and relatives, as Jeff revealed: 'For my generation we would want the golf courses, the nice restaurants, the culture, the temples and the canal trips in Bangkok; that sort of thing would interest us'.

Tourists are not totally controlled and influenced by those mediated practices. It is believed that at the destination, there have been a number of tourist practices provided by stage managers and tourism agents for tourists (Crang 1997, Edensor 2000). They can select to perform according to their lifestyles and the activities that are offered at the destination during the time they visit. The above quote illustrates the respondent's preferred choices of tourist practice, according to his particular lifestyle. For example, although this particular quote suggests the preference of a keen golfer, other respondents preferred family holiday activities at peaceful beaches. The tourists interviewed suggested that the mediated tourist practice in *The Beach* is different from most tourists' image of holiday experiences and lifestyles. Therefore, they did not choose to perform in a similar way to these mediated tourist practices.

Tourists' Negotiation Process

Crouch et al. (2005: 12) suggest that the tourist is an active and imaginative media receiver who '…acts, ignores, rejects, reacts or negotiates the communicated'. Tourists realise that film exists as another mediated representation of the destination image, the cultural identity and potential tourist practices that exist at a destination. In the particular case of *The Beach* and Thailand, they are not convinced that the mediated representations of place are absolute; providing insight into an experience free from the influence of both individual and collective variables in consumption practice. The tourists interviewed considered that *The Beach* only offers a partial representation of Thailand. This indicates that their collective memories and knowledge of the destination are fundamental in the process of negotiating with the film. When encountering visual representations of a destination in the film, the tourists' first reaction to the mediated representations is to compare their existing knowledge of the location, particularly that gained from their actual experience at the destination, with the mediated representation. The comparison leads to a process of negotiation between the film representation and their existing image of the film location. Respondents suggested that the mediated landscapes and scenery were the most accurate features in comparison to their knowledge. The depicted landscapes of Thailand's beaches and capital city, as featured in *The Beach*, are the most accurate in comparison to their existing images and previous knowledge of Thailand. Tourists' images of Thailand, based on their own visits to Thailand are similar to the representation in *The Beach*. They considered that Thailand's beaches (and not only those in the southern part of the country, as featured in *The Beach*) and Bangkok are beautiful and welcoming. As Ed described it:

> I knew the island that they referred to and there's the scene at the beginning which I know that it was in Khao San Road, Bangkok. Obviously I knew that the secret beach did not exist but the physical location obviously did. I've been to many beautiful islands and seen equally beautiful places so it didn't seem unrealistic for me.

This respondent's visual image of Thailand corresponded strongly to the representation of the landscape and townscape in *The Beach*. These visual representations, regardless of storyline and character, are realistic and reinforce the strongest competitive elements of Thailand as a tourist destination, the warm and beautiful tropical beaches and the exotic capital city. These aspects provide tourists with both relaxing and adventurous travel experiences, as Linda reflected: 'it shows that it's very beautiful and quiet, an untamed place that you can explore'. Nonetheless, representations in the film mostly over-emphasised predominant attributes of the locations. Although their dominant image of Thailand is one of warm and sunny beaches, several tourists also remarked that beaches in Thailand offer modern tourist facilities and are well developed for tourists, Sam suggested:

'Yeah… because I think a few years ago, places like Koh Pha-ngan, are like idyllic and relaxing, but now, there are so many people going there. It is not like that anymore, it's so busy, isn't it?' This quote demonstrates the tourist's awareness of the extent of development of the tourist industry in Thailand. Tourists' negotiated image of Thailand to representations in *The Beach* is of a modern tourist destination where unspoiled and idyllic places, as depicted in the film, no longer exist. This idea is reflected in Joe's comment:

> Yeah, it's really good for tourism but that's all there is. It's like Phi Phi, 5 years ago, it was a really nice island, like untouched, and no-one was there. Now they have knocked down all the trees, built diving shops, restaurants, internet café every other shop, internet, restaurant, diving shop. It's stupid, it's just ridiculous. It's like people get here and it's all in your face, you just want to go, we don't care. It's just a party. Thailand is just one big party.

This respondent's view confirms that *The Beach* tends to portray a tourist's search for authenticity in a destination and illustrates it by offering two contrasting types of holiday experience. On the one hand, is an imaginative holiday experience at a newly discovered attraction; on the other is a prosaic holiday experience in one of the main tourist areas of Thailand. His view reflects the destination's lack of authenticity as a result of the invasion of the mass tourist industry. Most respondents realised that there is little possibility for finding authenticity at the destination; the over-development of tourist facilities has already destroyed it. This contradicts the message in *The Beach*. Respondents appreciated that the representation of the destination in the film is too idealistic and impossible to achieve in a modern, highly tourist-oriented destination such as Thailand.

Tourists can differentiate between the reality of the place and mediated representations. The tourists' negotiation process underlines tourists' awareness of themselves at a tourist destination. The negotiation process takes place when tourists decode messages of the film. Tourists use their collective knowledge and images of the destination to argue, react and finally negotiate the message of the film. As a consequence, tourists develop more sophisticated images of a destination. The process also suggests that the film has minimal influence on tourists' images of the destination and their behaviour at the destination.

Conclusion

This chapter has focused on the process of tourist negotiation to the mediated representation and their self-awareness when encountering a film. It began by considering the influence of film on the tourism industry. In the tourism industry, popular films are often used as part of destination marketing. Being a part of popular culture as well as popular media, film is a powerful marketing tool that can influence consumers' behaviour. The case of *The Beach* and Thailand provides a different perspective on the influence of film on tourists' behaviour. Against the concept of tourists as performers, tourists are not totally influenced by media which are supporting travel discourses. On the contrary, they are aware of their selves as tourists and that they are subject to the influence of stage managers. The negotiation process discloses tourists' ability to differentiate between the reality of the tourism industry and the mediated representation. Tourists are not passive media receivers or passive performers at the destination. When they watched the film, tourists interpreted the meaning of the film using their own experiences and knowledge of Thailand. They did not totally believe the media but were partially influenced by the visual representation of the destination. Tourists not only negotiate with the meanings of the representation but also negotiate the pattern of practices at the destination. The degree of tourists' negotiation to the mediated is also subjective. Some tourists are not interested in visits to the film locations because they feel that the film lessens the authenticity of the destination. Tourists' negotiation to the mediated practices revealed their preferred practices, which were collectively influenced by other media, for example travel brochures and the anecdotes of family and friends, which are still important influences on their behaviour.

References

Acland, C.R. 1998. Imaxtechnology and the tourist gaze. *Cultural Studies*, 12(3), 429–45.

Adler, J. 1989. Travel as performed art. *The American Journal of Sociology*, 94(6), 1366–91.

Boniface, B. and Cooper, C. 2009. *Worldwide Destinations: The Geography of Travel and Tourism*. 5th edition. London: Elsevier.

Boyle, D. 2000. *The Beach*. Figment Film and 20th Century Fox.

Bulter, R.W. 1990. The influence of the media in shaping international tourist patterns. *Tourism Recreation Research*, 15(2), 46–53.

Connell, J. 2012. Film tourism – evolution, progress and prospects. *Tourism Management*, 33(5), 1007–29.

Crang, P. 1997. Performing the tourist product, in *Touring Cultures: Transformations of Travel and Theory*, edited by C. Rojek and J. Urry. London: Routledge.

Crawshaw, C. and Urry, J. 1997. Tourism and the photographic eye, in *Touring Cultures: Transformations of Travel and Theory*, edited by C. Rojek and J. Urry. London: Routledge.

Crouch, D., Jackson, R. and Thompson, F. (eds) 2005. *The Media and the Tourist Imagination: Converging Cultures*. London: Routledge.

Edensor, T. 1998. *Tourist at the Taj: Performance and Meaning at a Symbolic Site*. London: Routledge.

Edensor, T. 2000. Staging tourism: tourists as performers. *Annals of Tourism Research,* 27(2), 322–44.

Edensor, T. 2001. Performing tourism, staging tourism: (re)producing tourist space and practice. *Tourist Studies*, 1(1), 59–81.

Grihault, N. 2003. Film tourism – the global picture. *Travel & Tourism Analyst*, 5, 1–22.

Heath, S. 1981. Film/Cinetext/Text, in *Articles in Screen reader 2: Cinema & Semiotics*, edited by B. Brewster et al. London: Villies Publications.

Iwashita, C. 2006. Media representation of the UK as a destination for Japanese tourists: popular culture and tourism. *Tourist Studies*, 6(1), 59–77.

Kim, H. and Richardson, S.L. 2003. Motion picture impacts on destination images. *Annals of Tourism Research*, 30(1), 216–37.

Law, L., Bunnell, T. and Ong, C. 2007. *The Beach*, the *Gaze* and film tourism. *Tourist studies*, 7(2), 141–64.

MacCannell, D. 1976. *The Tourist: A New Theory of the Leisure Class*. London: MacMillan Press, Ltd.

MacCannell, J. and MacCannell, D. 2001. Tourist agency. *Tourist Studies*, 1(23), 23–37.

Macionis, N. 2004. Understanding the film-induced tourist, in *International Tourism and Media Conference Proceedings*, 24–26 November 2004, edited by W. Frost et al. Melbourne: Tourism Research Unit, Monash University, 86–97.

Macionis, N. and Sparks, B. 2009. Film-induced tourism and incidental experience. *Tourism Review International*, 13, 93–101.

McCabe, S. and Stokoe, E.H. 2004. Place and identity in tourist accounts. *Annals of Tourism Research,* 31(3), 601–22.

Mercille, J. 2005. Media effects on image: the case of Tibet. *Annals of Tourism Research,* 32(4), 1039–55.

Monaco, J. 2000. *How to Read a Film: The World Of Movies, Media, Multimedia*. 3rd edition. Oxford: Oxford University Press.

Moores, S. 1993. *Interpreting Audiences: The Ethnography of Media Consumption*. London: Sage Publications.

Mulvey, L. 1989. *Visual and Other Pleasures*. Hampshire: Palgrave.

Perkins, H.C. and Thorns, D.C. 2001. Gazing or performing? Reflections on Urry's *Tourist Gaze* in the context of contemporary experience in the Antipodes. *International in Sociology*, 16(2), 185–206.

Riley, R.W. and Van Doren, C.S. 1992. Movies as tourism promotion: a 'pull' factor in a 'push' location. *Tourism Management*, 13(3), 267–74.

Riley, R., Baker, D. and Van Doren, C. 1998. Movie-induced tourism. *Annals of Tourism Research*, 25(4), 919–35.

Selwyn, T. 1996. *The Tourist Image: Myth and Myth Making in Tourism*. Chichester: John Wiley & Son.

Siripis, M. 2011. The role of film in mediating destination image and tourist practices: *The Beach* and Thailand. Unpublished PhD Thesis, Guildford: University of Surrey.

Tooke, N. and Baker, M. 1996. Seeing is believing: the effect of film on visitor numbers to screened locations. *Tourism Management,* 17(2), 87–94.

Turner, G. 1993. *Film as a Social Practice.* 2nd edition. London: Routledge.

Tzanelli, R. 2004. Construction the 'Cinematic Tourist': the 'Sign Industry' of *The Lord of the Rings. Tourist Studies*, 4(1), 21–42.

Tzanelli, R. 2006. Reel western fantasies: portrait of a tourist imagination in *The Beach. Mobilities*, 1(1), 121–42.

Urry, J. 1990. *The Tourist Gaze: Leisure and Travel in Contemporary Societies.* London: Sage.

Urry, J. 2000. *The Tourist Gaze: Leisure and Travel in Contemporary Societies.* 2nd edition. London: Sage Publication Ltd.

Warnick, R.B., Bojanic, D.C. and Siriangkul, A. 2005. Movie effect on the image of Thailand among college student travellers, in Proceeding of the 2005 *Northeastern Recreation Research Symposium*, April 10–12, edited by J.G Peden and R. Schuster. Available at: http://www2.tat.or.th [accessed: 2 December 2011].

Chapter 14

The Hollowed or Hallowed Ground of Orange County, California

Chris Lukinbeal and Ann Fletchall

Introduction

In this chapter we explore the disjuncture of virtual and actual tourism and how expectations can lead to different experiences. We do so by drawing on tourist experiences (including one of the author's) in Orange County, California, the spectacular setting of seminal television shows *The OC, Laguna Beach: The Real Orange County* and *The Real Housewives of Orange County*. We argue that cinematic and televisual places are hyperreal simulations, where the virtual, actual, and experiential combine in new ways to create meaningful connections. These places are created by haptic experiences, but as the actual becomes further entwined with the virtual, we wonder where this may lead the tourist experience: to a hollowed or hallowed ground?

Optical and Haptical Film Tourism

A tourist is frequently defined as a person who travels for pleasure (Leiper 1979, Smith 1994, Hunt 1991). But with film tourism, travel is actual and virtual, or more frequently, a combination of both. Rather than a binary or dialectic, actual and virtual tourism melds with the cinematic and televisual experience. Along these lines, Bruno (1997) argues for a shift in film theory, one that moves us away from optics and sight, to haptic and site. A focus on optics renders the filmic tourist as either occupying a reel or real space, producing an indexical relationship between image and reality. This is related to ocularcentrism and the privileging of the visual as opposed to the embodied visualities of the visual encounter. Optical models help us to understand how ways of seeing are naturalised, but it reduces spectatorship to a disembodied gaze which is unfit 'to account for the types of displacement that are represented, conveyed, and negotiated in the moving image' (Bruno 2002: 16). Through a focus on optics, a film tourist is either an immobile *sight*-seer of a reel landscape, or a *site*-seer of a real landscape seeking the pleasures of the reel. Positioned by optics, film-induced tourism is an attempt to visit a place and experience and extend the pleasure gained from a film or television show. Where much attention has been paid to *sight* and the indexical relation of image and reality, we argue that spectators haptically engage in mobile *site*-seeing as peripatetic voyagers, inhabiting and participating in spatio-visual encounters.

A haptical understanding focuses on embodied site-seeing where 'the film "viewer" is a practitioner of viewing space – a tourist' (Bruno 1997: 17). With film, space is framed for viewing, perusing, and wandering. This is not a re-production or a re-presentation of an ontologically given real space, but a space co-constituted by the spectator and the narrative trajectories of a film. Haptical perception is a 'kinaesthetic, embodied vision, a "cross-modal" activity where the world is made meaningful to us not only by vision, but also in cooperation with other sensorial meaning' (Laine 2006: 94). Haptics is related to vision, but is more a 'mode of bodily consciousness' (Laine 2006: 99) as it 'establishes a relationship between touching and looking, skin and images' (Laine 2006: 95). A haptical engagement moves 'beyond the inside/outside division, locating us as touching and being touched in the cinematic experience. Furthermore, skin gives shape to our affective engagement with the film, "spreading" affect over our entire body' (Laine 2006: 96). Rather than an indexical relationship between subject/object, inside/outside, through one's skin 'it is no longer quite clear where the outside of things is found' (Laine 2006: 96). As such, the concept of skin and hapticality positions film, space, and spectator in terms of 'touch, rendering and shaping' (Laine 2006: 100).

The spectorial experience of cinema and television resonate a kinaesthetic and emotional affect. Emotion is 'the act of being moved' (Harris and Sørensen 2010: 149) towards or away from us (Ahmed 2004). The etymology of emotion, according to the Oxford English Dictionary (2011, http://www.oed.com/), is 'a moving out, migration, transference from one place to another.' Through cinema and television we are more than motionless voyeurs gazing at moving images across a screen. Cinema and television offer a form of tourism that is a corporeal experience, where hapticality is not simply an 'add on' to the visual (cf. Laine 2006), but rather, an affective engagement, an e-motion that transforms scopophilia into topophilia allowing the spectator to pleasurably wander (Fletchall et al. 2012).

While it may seem reasonable to position haptics with emotion, affect, and non-representational theories and align optics with representational theory, this would reify a binary logic, which obfuscates rather than enlightens. Though human geographers have explored issues surrounding emotion (like Tuan 1974, 1976, Relph 1977, Ley and Samuels 1978) and the body (Porteous 1986a, 1986b) recent interest in emotion may be traced to Anderson and Smith (2001). Emotion and affective research can be differentiated in terms of representability, with emotion focusing on expression whereas nonrepresentational theory emphasises inexpressible affects (Pile 2010). Research on emotion and affect has emphasised the proximate, ethnographic inquiry, and the body. Affect has become a test for delimiting the terrain of non-representational theory (Pile 2010), but a focus on affect in geography often overlooks the longstanding emphasis in film theory on haptics and the optical unconscious (see Doel and Clarke 2007, Carter and McCormick 2006, Aitken 2006). Although geographic theory and film theory share much in common, the emphasis on nonrepresentational theories in geography tends to reinforce and reify the problematic theoretical, methodological, and normative distinction between primary/secondary experience, firsthand/secondhand experience, and real/representation which has been much debated in media geography (Aitken and Dixon 2006, Lukinbeal and Zimmermann 2006, Lukinbeal 2004a, Dixon and Grimes 2004, Cresswell and Dixon 2002, Kennedy and Lukinbeal 1997, Burgess 1990). How we confront and move beyond these binaries is of importance (Dixon and Grimes 2004, Cresswell and Dixon, 2002) for as Aumont (1992) explains (cit. Doane 2003: 96):

> What we call representation is nothing other than the more or less complicated history of resemblance of its hesitation between two poles, that of appearance, of the visible, of the phenomenon, of the representative analogy, and that of interiority, of the invisible, or of the beyond-the visible, of the being of expressive analogy.

Or as Dewsbury et al. (2002: 438) puts it: 'Non-representational theory takes representation seriously; representation not as a code to be broken or as an illusion to be dispelled rather representations are apprehended as performative in themselves; as doings. The point here is to redirect attention from the posited meaning towards the material compositions and conduct of representations'.

Place as Emotional Resonance

If the modality of film tourism is an embodied e-motion then we must move away from our fixed notions of place as structured by absolute location. Place is a nexus of 'spatio-temporal events' (Massey 2005: 130) that is called forth through practice and performance, gatherings, and encounters. Cinematic and televisual places are where things, thoughts, memories and emotions collide to produce meaningful experiences (Escobar 2001). Tuan (1977: 4) suggests that 'places are centers of felt value' to which Bruno (2007: 38) adds that through moving images, places are an 'intimate exploration – a screen of personal and social, private and public narratives', a 'map of intersubjective views. A haptic architexture. A topophilic affair. A place for the love of place. A site of close picturing for undistanced *emotion*. A museum of emotional pictures.'

Place thus takes on many forms, not all of which are material or based on absolute location. As Fletchall et al. (2012: 17) argue, 'place is an expression of emotional resonance, a product of our imagination, memories and image-events from television and cinema.' To make this claim they draw from André *Malraux's* (1967) concept of the *musée imaginaire* as central to place-making where: 'we... carry around with us a *musée imaginaire* in our minds, drawn from experience (often touristic) of other places, and knowledge culled from films, television, exhibitions, travel brochures, popular magazines, etc. It is inevitable...that all of these get run together' (Harvey 1990: 87, cf. Jencks 1984).

The *musée imaginaire* is a metacinema (McHugh 2009), an 'emotional map...we experience, on topophilic grounds, an architecture of inner voyage, a geography of intimate space. Filmic site-seeing is immersed in the geopsychic act of interfacing affect and place' (Bruno 2007: 39). It fills the lacuna of material engagement with place (Jhally and Lewis 1992), allowing us to journey and site-see through film and television. This is:

> An "art of memory", [where] film itself draws memory maps. In its memory theater, the spectator-passenger, sent on an architectural journey, endlessly retraces the itineraries of a geographically localized discourse that sets memory in place and reads memories as places. As this architectural art of memory, filmic site-seeing...embodies a particularly mobile art of mapping: an *emotional* mapping. (Bruno 2007: 23–4)

Emotional and Geographical Realism

How a spectator understands realism can set up expectations for how they will experience film tourism. Both geographic realism and emotional realism come into play when we tour the cinematic/televisual landscape. Realism has three connotations in film theory: as indexical, perceptual (impression of reality), and reality-effect (affecting spectators) (Nagib and Mello 2009). Geographic realism is a narrative technique that appropriates social-spatial meanings onto a location's sense of place (Lukinbeal 2004b, 2006). But a location filmed and a location depicted in a film or television show does not have to have a one-to-one relation; places can double or stand in for other locales. As Lukinbeal (2006: 339) notes, 'geographic realism is subjective and fluid, not objective and factual.' Therefore 'with cinematic landscapes, form does not follow the function of a site's everyday use; form follows the functional needs of the script' (Lukinbeal 2012: 180). This can lead to unmet expectations about a place seen in a film or television show as geographic realism functions primarily as an optical referent. In other words, a place filmed is not bound by absolute location, and when tourists seek out the place filmed in its absolute location, they are often confronted with the paradox of two places sharing one location: the everyday functional place and the filmic place. This disrupts the tourist pleasure when the sights/sites of the cinematic/ televisual scene are visited in the hope of extending these transient encounters and affective engagements. Here the virtual meets the actual, where the site filmed is not the place one has emotionally invested and inhabited. The experience of film-induced tourism only vaguely resembles the spectatorial experience, which often leads to disappointment.

Where geographic realism works to construct a filmic landscape that is meaningful to the narrative and the viewer, emotional realism works through the optical unconscious provoking 'tension, contestation, and emotional responses because it does not separate subject (the viewer) from object (the content and form of the visual/audio)' (Lukinbeal and Zimmermann 2008: 21). The optical unconscious highlights 'the conviction that the world is not a ready-made that can be counted on and reflected upon. It is an event, a happenstance, a taking place. What takes place, however, is not arbitrary, as eventfulness is increasingly *anticipated* by a plethora of more or less imperceptible "performative infrastructures"' (Doel and Clarke 2007: 898).

With emotional realism, spectators identify with characters and their situations as 'popular pleasure is first and foremost a pleasure of recognition' (Ang 1985: 20, paraphrasing Bourdieu). According to Ang (1985: 61), this emotional realism is measured by the ability of a film or television show to evoke emotions, to recognise and take part in a 'complex of meanings' that penetrates the 'imaginative world' and 'connects up with one of the ways in which [spectators] encounter life.' Ang (1985: 83) goes on to argue that in the case of fans of the television show *Dallas*, 'imagination is an essential component of our psychological world, the pleasure of *Dallas*...is not a *compensation* for the presumed drabness of daily life, nor a *flight* from it, but a *dimension* of it...a life without imagination does not exist' (Ang 1985: 83). Through emotional realism, spectators forge new meaningful engagements with spatio-temporal events, effectively participating in place-making. But more than place-making is occurring here, as Bruno (2007: 39–40) notes:

> Cultures and individuals fixate on specific landscapes for different reasons and reactively pursue them. A traveler seeking a particular landscape may go there, even filmically, to be replenished, restored, held, and fed. In the hub of traveling and dwelling, we are absorbed in the stream of emotions and experience an embracing affective transport.

While emotional realism works to replenish the traveller, it also allows him or her to disengage from the effects of emotional entanglement. Travellers are simultaneously insiders and outsiders of these places, these 'dreams of presence' (Rose 2002: 547).

Touring *The OC*

Americans were introduced to Orange County in 2003 when a television show called *The OC* debuted on Fox. This was the tale of a troubled youth, Ryan, who was taken in and given a new life in the home of a wealthy Newport Beach family. Through its four-season run, viewers experienced *The OC* as an emotional roller coaster ride. With Ryan as our anchor and window to the world of the Orange Coast elite, we experienced teenage angst, heartbreak, marriage and divorce, drug and alcohol abuse, and death – the typical overwrought world of the primetime soap (e.g. *Dallas, Dynasty, Beverly Hills 90210*). Not only was *The OC*'s storyline emotionally wrenching, but it depicted Orange County as a series of stunning landscapes of water, sun, wealth, and beauty. This double dose of high drama and spectacular scenery made the show a big hit (at least in its first season) and was integral in transforming Orange County's image from bastion of suburban conservatism to trendy coastal paradise (Fletchall et al. 2012).

The following year, in a bid to capitalise upon *The OC*'s popularity with its target audience, MTV created a reality show set in Orange County, titled *Laguna Beach: The Real Orange County*. This show purported to document the lives of real teens from this latest 'it' setting; although many scenes were apparently staged, *Laguna Beach* more than made up for lack of action with its devotion to showcasing the physical beauty of this decidedly quaint coastal town. As McCarthy (2004) explains:

> …many scenarios are clearly staged for the camera. We see teenage boys squirm and mumble as they endeavor to carry on a group conversation on a set topic: will they stay in touch after graduation? And we witness both ends of telephone conversations, a strategy that signals the show's commitment to narrative form and continuity over the pretense of spontaneous action. These staged moments position the teenage cast as improvising actors rather than sociological subjects. Together with the show's lush cinematography, they forge a connection between *Laguna Beach*'s "real Orange County" and the dramatic show it aims to supplement: Fox's lavishly shot teen soap hit *The OC*.

Laguna Beach landed MTV high ratings for a cable network during its two successful seasons.

On the heels of *Laguna Beach* and the reality TV craze, in 2006 came Bravo's *The Real Housewives of Orange County*. This show capitalised on Orange County's televisual appeal and popularity, but focused on slightly older women who lived in a gated community in inland Orange County. Although lower-budget, with less attention paid to producing iconic coastal Orange County scenery, the show struck a nerve with viewers. Of this Orange County-based trio, it is the only one that survives to this day, having aired eight seasons (at the time of writing) and multiple spin-offs.

As explained above, through emotional realism, viewers can forge a strong connection with the characters and lifestyles presented in these shows. We would argue that television more than cinema forges an ongoing emotional connection that allows for place-making to occur. In the past one could point to cinema's superior aspect ratio (widescreen) which allows for geographic realism to feel infinite in its horizontality. However, with the rise of high definition widescreen TVs, television now has much the same ability. Further, where a film is viewed once or twice, the episodic nature of television invites spectators to return over a period of years, forging a deep emotional bond, a regular routine of engagement which strengthens place-making.

Television critics have expressed the affective nature of these shows: '*Laguna Beach*...is the sort of place that people who have never been to Southern California imagine it should look like' (Steinhauer 2006); another describes the Orange County of these shows as looking like 'some landlocked Midwesterner's dream vision of Southern California' (Gallo 2003). As one reviewer observes: 'The current fascination with Orange County taps the need Americans seem to have to create a bubble in which playful adolescent fantasies can act themselves out in the sun, removed from any real-world complications...' (Williams 2004). Respondents to surveys taken by the authors echo these sentiments in their descriptions of Orange County as seen on TV:

> 'A place where people live next to the beach and live a luxurious life' (Davis, C. 2008. Personal communication, June 12).

> 'The best place in the world to live' (Sorenson, D. 2008. Personal communication, June 12).

> 'A beautiful place, for beautiful people' (Michaelson, R. 2008. Personal communication, June 12).

> 'To be and have great things you should live in Orange County' (Brenner, B. 2008. Personal communication, June 20).

> 'Makes it look beautiful and perfect – an attraction for anyone watching' (Dwyer, K. 2008. Personal communication, June 20).

> 'OC is portrayed as the most beautiful, richest, paradise on earth' (Peters, R. 2008. Personal communication, June 20).

Several survey responses reported by Fletchall et al. (2012) express a deeper experience within the world of televisual Orange County:

> 'It's fun to imagine you're a part of [the show]' (ibid.: 99).

> '[The shows] make you feel you want to live in Orange County' (ibid.: 101).

> 'We all wished we lived there because it is so pretty. We wish we were in the show' (ibid.: 101).

> '[Laguna Beach] is amazing! I would do anything to be there!' (ibid.: 101).

Each of these shows portray Orange County as both a visually and emotionally engaging place, its lifestyle and scenery dangled as a tempting lure to draw viewers into the televisual world. Much like touristic experience in Orange County, these viewers have enjoyed meaningful trips to a place called *The OC*.

As the survey responses suggest, *The OC, Laguna Beach*, and *The Real Housewives* connected with viewers on an emotional level, as all popular shows do, providing an outlet for our emotions and an escape from everyday life (cf. Ang 1985). What these shows added to the mix, however, was a particular focus on place. Considered both separately and as a body of work, the shows started with an actual place, and from it, via the television screen (i.e. framing, editing, generic conventions), created a virtual world, *The OC* – an Orange County comprised solely of beautiful people, picturesque beaches, and riveting drama. In the words of another survey respondent, 'I know Orange County like I see it in *The OC*, with the beautiful houses and the beach, nice cars, hot surfers' (quoted in Fletchall et al. 2012: 103).

Touring Orange County

Given that *The OC* and Orange County share the same name, it is no wonder that devoted fans of these shows would seek to find *The OC* in Orange County. Such tourists would hardly be the first. From Ramona-seekers in Southern California at the turn of the century (DeLyser 2005) to *Sex and the City* bus tours of Manhattan one hundred years later (Gill 2009), media depictions of place have captivated and lured many seeking to extend their mediated experience, to mobilise their virtual/actual place-making through an actual/virtual tour. These experiences can be quite fulfilling, as Torchin (2002) describes the Manhattan Television Tour as an experience which thrives on blurring the boundary between the televisual and 'real' world. On the tour, guests are shuttled around the city to glimpse what would otherwise be ordinary New York buildings, but for their use in establishing exterior shots of popular TV shows (stops include the *Friends* apartment building and *The Cosby Show* brownstone). Drawing from Rojek (1997), Torchin (2002: 251) applies the concept of 'dragging' to the tour: signs, symbols, and images in movies and TV 'are dragged onto the physical landscape and the physical landscape is then reinterpreted in terms of [these] cinematic events.' In other words, place unfolds as an amalgam, simultaneously real and mediated. Place emerges, not only by our presence in it, but with fragments and figments of our *musée imaginaire* and the thrill of association with the more exciting, simulated world of TV. Through all of these, reality is enhanced, and 'the everyday world of New York City is reconfigured as interesting' (Torchin 2002: 248).

Similarly, some visitors to the set of Britain's long-running soap, *Coronation Street* remember a highly fulfilling experience of being on the *actual* street:

> From the moment I put my foot on the Street I feel like a star. I start my walk down the Street...I look through ALL the windows and through ALL letter boxes. I touch the stone cladding of number 9. I feel so happy and trouble free

when I walk down the Street…It is the best thing and most wonderful thing I have ever done. (Couldry 1998: 103)

However, such trips can be equally frustrating when high expectations of glamour and geographic realism are not met. For example, Jackson (2005) describes her visit to Los Angeles:

> Visiting the Chinese Theatre brought the realization that whenever this location is filmed…we see the stars, the red carpet, and the adoring crowd. Yet, immediately adjacent was wasteland, fronted by old railings sporting tacky advertisements, a bleak contrast to the TV-transmitted glitzy glamour…We made sense of most places by comparing them to screen images, being surprised at our own naivety, having failed to appreciate how extensively our imaginations had been fueled by the "metaphoric construction of ideas and desires". (Jackson 2005: 186, quoting Crouch and Lübbren 2003)

Given that *The OC* is a re-imagining of grounded place, visitors to Orange County have surprisingly little to see once they arrive (besides Disneyland, located in a more diverse part of the county not included in television portrayals). They are hindered by the fact that *The OC* wasn't even filmed in Orange County, but on a soundstage and various locations in Los Angeles, and also that it is impossible for most fans to gain access to gated communities in which cast members of the

Figure 14.1 *Friends* **apartment building**

Figure 14.2   Laguna Beach High School

reality series live. Laguna Beach tourists make do by gawking at the high school where cast members are assumed to attend (although no filming took place there) and browsing the shops and boutiques featured on the show. To appease visitors to Newport Beach, the visitors' bureau developed a map directing tourists to local spots which *inspired* locations used in *The OC*. There is also a plaster cast of cast members' handprints on display at a local RV resort (Fletchall et al. 2012).

Figure 14.3   Handprints of *The OC* cast as displayed at Newport Dunes Waterfront Resort

Figure 14.4   Newport Coast McMansions

Conclusion

It was little surprise to the authors that their foray into TV-induced tourism via the 'OC Experience' bus tour of Newport Beach was fraught with disappointment. The tour went to many scenic spots and even included a harbour cruise, and a trip to a fancy shopping mall, but precious little of *The OC* was experienced. The closest we came to television was driving through an upscale 'McMansion' development to see homes purportedly used as filming locations on the series. When comparing our televisual experience of Orange County to riding on a bus on a freeway through traffic, our experience in the actual could not compare to the virtual. Where we had felt an emotional connection to characters in the shows and a strong desire for *The OC* lifestyle, the magic was missing when we actually visited Orange County. Our television screens had been filled with ocean views and mansions, but the average visitor to Orange County sees much more blight, views obstructed by strip malls, and lacks access to a private yacht. The disconnect between the televisual and actual place is best described by Gill's (2009: 53) critique of the women on the *Sex and the City* bus tour: 'The storyville they're looking for doesn't exist and never did, and trying to search for the literal in literature inevitably kills the object of affection, murders the fiction stone-dead...'

Through an optical understanding of cinema and television, tourism situates an indexical relationship between places filmed and places in film, between the disembodied voyeur and the tourist seeking *The OC* in Orange County. Cinema and televisual tourism is not about re-presentations, but simulations, a constant interjection of figuring and figuring out, a 'radical negation of the sign as value'

(Baudrillard 1994: 6) rather than a 'sign of reality' (Aitken and Zonn 1994: 20). Simulation kills absolute realism, it 'envelops the whole edifice of representation itself as a simulacrum' (Baudrillard 1994: 6) leaving only a hollowed ground, the negation that an absolute location is equivalent to its representation. Indexicality murders the sign and our mediated tourist experience; it kills the 'object of our affection' (Gill 2009: 53) by limiting the sign to reality, whereas the simulation requires the referent to be left open and relative, a happenstance, a haptical engagement, an e-motion of eventfulness that allows for places to be forged on hallowed ground.

References

Ahmed, S. 2004. *The Cultural Politics of Emotion*. London: Routledge.

Aitken, S. 2006. Leading men to violence and creating spaces for their emotions. *Gender, Place and Culture*, 13(5), 491–507.

Aitken, S. and Dixon, D. 2006. Imagining geographies of film. *Erdkunde*, 60(4), 326–36.

Aitken, S. and Zonn, L. 1994. Re-presenting the place pastiche, in *Place, Power, Situation and Spectacle: A Geography of Film*, edited by S.C. Aitken and L.E. Zonn. Lanham, MD: Rowman & Littlefield, 3–25.

Anderson, K. and Smith, S. 2001. Editorial: emotional geographies. *Transactions of the Institute of British Geographers*, 26(1), 7–10.

Ang, I. 1985. *Watching Dallas*. London: Methuen.

Aumont, J. 1992. *Du Visage au Cinema*. Paris: Editions de l'Etoile/Cahiers du cinema.

Baudrillard, J. 1994. *Simulacra and Simulation*. Ann Arbor: University of Michigan Press.

Bruno, G. 1997. Site-seeing: architecture and the moving image. *Wide Angle*, 19(4), 8–24.

Bruno, G. 2002. *The Atlas of Emotion: Journeys in Art, Architecture, and Film*. New York: Verso.

Bruno, G. 2007. *Public Intimacy: Architecture and the Visual Arts*. Cambridge, MA: The MIT Press.

Burgess, J. 1990. The production and consumption of environmental meanings in the mass media: a research agenda for the 1990s. *Transactions of the Institute of British Geographers*, 15(2), 139–61.

Carter, S. and McCormack, D. 2006. Film, geopolitics and the affective logics of intervention. *Political Geography*, 25(2), 228–45.

Couldry, N. 1998. The view from inside the 'simulacrum': visitors' tales from the set of *Coronation Street*. *Leisure Studies*, 17(2), 94–107.

Cresswell, T. and Dixon, D. 2002. Introduction: engaging film, in *Engaging Film: Geographies of Mobility and Identity*, edited by T. Cresswell and D. Dixon. Lanham, MD: Rowman & Littlefield, 1–10.

Crouch, D. and N. Lübbren (eds) 2003. *Visual Cultural and Tourism.* Oxford: Berg.

DeLyser, D. 2005. *Ramona Memories: Tourism and the Shaping of Southern California.* Minneapolis: University of Minnesota Press.

Dewsbury, J-D., Wylie, J., Harrison, P. and Rose, M. 2002. Enacting geographies. *Geoforum*, 33(4), 437–40.

Dixon, D. and Grimes, J. 2004. Capitalism, masculinity and whiteness in the dialectical landscape: the case of Tarzan and the tycoon. *Geojournal*, 59(4), 265–75.

Doane, M. 2003. The close-up: scale and detail in the cinema. *Difference*, 14(3), 89–111.

Doel, M. and Clarke, D. 2007. Afterimages. *Environment and Planning D: Society and Space*, 25(5), 890–910.

Escobar, A. 2001. Culture sits in places: reflections on globalism and subaltern strategies of localization. *Political Geography*, 20(2), 139–74.

Fletchall, A., Lukinbeal, C. and McHugh, K. 2012. *Place, Television, and the Real Orange County.* Stuttgart: Franz Steiner Verlag.

Gallo, P. 2003. The OC. *Variety* [Online, 3 August]. Available at: http://www.variety.com/index.asp [accessed: 6 January 2008].

Gill, A. 2009. The out-of-towners. *Vanity Fair*, January, 52–3.

Harris, O. and Sørensen, T. 2010. Rethinking emotion and material culture. *Archaeological Dialogues*, 17(2), 145–63.

Harvey, D. 1990. *The Condition of Postmodernity.* Cambridge, MA: Blackwell.

Hunt, J. 1991. Evolution of travel and tourism terminology and definitions. *Journal of Travel Research*, 29(4), 7–11.

Jackson, R. 2005. Converging cultures; converging gazes; contextualizing perspectives, in *The Media and the Tourist Imagination: Converging Cultures*, edited by D. Crouch, R. Jackson and F. Thompson. London: Routledge, 183–97.

Jencks, C. 1984. *The Language of Postmodern Architecture.* London: Academy Editions.

Jhally, S. and Lewis, J. 1992. *Enlightened Racism: The Cosby Show, Audiences, and the Myth of the American Dream.* Boulder, CO: Westview Press.

Kennedy, C. and Lukinbeal, C. 1997. Towards a holistic approach to geographic research on film. *Progress in Human Geography*, 21(1), 33–50.

Laine, T. 2006. Cinema as second skin. *New Review of Film and Television*, 4(2), 93–106.

Leiper, N. 1979. The framework of tourism: towards a definition of tourism, tourist, and the tourist industry. *Annals of Tourism Research*, 6(4), 390–407.

Ley, D. and Samuels, M. (ed.) 1978. *Humanistic Geography: Prospects and Problems.* London: Croom Helm.

Lukinbeal, C. 2004a. The map that precedes the territory: an introduction to essays in cinematic geography. *GeoJournal*, 59(4), 247–51.

Lukinbeal, C. 2004b. The rise of regional film production centers in North America, 1984–1997. *GeoJournal*, 59(4), 307–21.

Lukinbeal, C. 2006. Runaway Hollywood: Cold Mountain Romania. *Erdkunde*, 60(4), 337–45.

Lukinbeal, C. 2012. 'On Location' filming in San Diego County from 1985–2005: how a cinematic landscape is formed through incorporative tasks and represented through mapped inscriptions. *Annals of the Association of American Geographers*, 102(1), 171–90.

Lukinbeal, C. and Zimmermann, S. 2006. Film geography: a new subfield. *Erdkunde*, 60(4), 315–26.

Lukinbeal, C. and Zimmermann, S. 2008. A cinematic world, in *The Geography of Cinema – A Cinematic World*, edited by C. Lukinbeal and S. Zimmerman. Stuttgart: Franz Steiner Verlag, 15–23.

Massey, D. 2005. *For Space*. London: Sage Press.

McCarthy, A. 2004. *Laguna Beach. FlowTV* [Online, 3 December]. Available at: http://flowtv.org/?p=667 [accessed: 16 August 2011].

McHugh, K.E. 2009. Movement, memory, landscape: an excursion in non-representational thought. *GeoJournal*, 74(3), 209–18.

Nagib, L. and Mello, C. 2009. *Realism and the Audiovisual Media*. New York: Palgrave Macmillan.

Pile, S. 2010. Emotions and affect in recent human geography. *Transactions of the Institute of British Geographers*, 35(1), 5–20.

Porteous, D. 1986a. Bodyscape: the body-landscape metaphor. *The Canadian Geographer*, 30(1), 2–12.

Porteous, D. 1986b. Intimate sensing. *Area*, 18(3), 250–51.

Relph, E. 1976. *Place and Placelessness*. London: Pion.

Rojek, C. 1997. Indexing, dragging, and the social construction of tourist sights, in *Touring Cultures: Transformations of Travel and Theory*, edited by C. Rojek and J. Urry. New York: Routledge, 52–74.

Rose, M. 2002. Landscape and labyrinths. *Geoforum*, 33(4), 455–67.

Smith, S.. 1994. The tourism product. *Annals of Tourism Research*, 21(3), 582–95.

Steinhauer, J. 2006. Real 'OC' starts objecting to its MTV portrayal. *New York Times* [Online, 8 November]. Available at: http://www.nytimes.com/2006/11/08/us/08laguna.html [accessed: 16 August 2011].

Torchin, L. 2002. Location, location, location: the destination of the Manhattan TV tour. *Tourist Studies*, 2(3), 247–66.

Tuan, Y. 1974. *Topophilia: A Study of Environmental Perception, Attitudes, and Values*. Englewood Cliffs, NJ: Prentice-Hall.

Tuan, Y. 1976. Humanistic geography. *Annals of the Association of American Geographers*, 66(2), 266–76.

Tuan, Y. 1977. *Space and Place: The Perspective of Experience*. Minneapolis: University of Minnesota Press.

Williams, A. 2004. The county formerly known as squaresville. *New York Times* [Online, 10 October]. Available at: http://www.nytimes.com/2004/10/10/fashion/10ORAN.html [accessed: 16 August 2011].

Chapter 15

Maps, Mapping and Materiality: Navigating London

Catherine Palmer and Jo-Anne Lester

This chapter focuses on materiality as a way of mediating tourist experiences of place. We argue that 'flat' visual images of destinations and activities, such as brochure images and photographs may encourage individuals to engage in tourism but these images tell us nothing about the actual experience of tourism. In effect, people do not experience images, they experience other people and the materialities of place; architecture as buildings, parks and cities; doorways and staircases, paths and rivers; buses and trains, rocks and sand. Of course images can be evocative and thought provoking and they can trigger positive and negative memories, our world is after all a visually rich environment. However, we do not experience the world through images, we *find* the world through them. We find the buildings, monuments, landscapes and things that are confined within the image and use them to navigate our way around and towards them. Our argument here is influenced by the anthropologist Tim Ingold's work on walking and seeing, where he states that the very idea of image as representation needs to be rethought. For Ingold (2011a: 197) images are 'place holders' for things in the world and travellers watch out for these things, and take direction from them, '[c]an it be that images do not stand for things but rather help you find them?'

The images associated with tourism may tell us what to look for, but it is our encounters with the material reality of what we find that mediate the experience of tourism. Hence it is not the image *per se* that matters but the direction it gives to tourists on what to find and how to find it. As Crang (1999: 252) illustrates by reference to photography '[t]he snapshot like all souvenirs, is not simply a pictoral form, but an object...that connects us to other times and spaces...its presence reminds us of a larger whole'. In finding the highlighted landmarks of tourism, individuals are brought into contact with the materiality of life in its broadest sense; life as mediated by the buildings and artefacts that have been brought into existence by human creativity. The coming together of image and materiality is illustrated by the use of maps to help direct individuals towards places, landmarks and 'things'. Maps are in themselves objects of the material world in that they are physical things produced for use by individuals in their everyday lives. The fact that maps can be accessed by digital means such as the Internet, mobile phones and tablets does not take away their essential *materiality* as part and parcel of the material world. Maps in this sense are what Salmond (2012: 214) refers to as digital 'surrogates' that not only stand in for the original object, but are also artefacts in their own right. Moreover, as anthropologists have shown, modern cartography is merely one way of navigating from place to place. Different cultures and groups may navigate by means of the stars or on the basis of inherited knowledge of how to get from one place to the next (Lewis 1976, Frake 1985, Widlok 1997, Ingold 2011b, Fagan 2012).

Furthermore not all maps are devised as orientation devices in relation to geography, landscape and topography. There are social maps depicting the spatial relations between people, place and problems such as crime, poverty, disease and prostitution; economic maps detailing the flow of capital, trade and commerce; and cultural maps that move beyond a focus on land to depict the relationships and linkages between people and such aspects as linguistic diversity, tangible and intangible resources such as archaeological remains, sacred sites, flora and fauna (Chambard 1980, Kodras 1997, Gilbert 2002a, Poole 2003, Fratianni and Marchionne 2012). While acknowledging such complexities, for the purposes of this discussion our focus rests on those maps generated as part of a contemporary leisure/tourism agenda. Such a focus links in with current debates about the role of maps, mapping and map-making in tourism (Del Casino and Hanna 2000, Farias 2011, Hanna and Del Casino 2003a, Roberts 2010, Rossetto 2012).

Whether held in the head or in the hand all maps serve a similar function, they are place finders and place holders for accessing particular perspectives and experiences of the world. They are therefore deeply embedded in the social, cultural, political and historical contexts within which they are produced (Black 1997, Withers 2000, Wood 2010). Indeed, Ingold (2011b: 219) argues that because '...locations have histories' then individuals orientate themselves in relation to place history rather than in terms of spatial coordinates. While Ingold refers specifically to the ways in which indigenous native inhabitants come to know and to understand where they are, his point is instructive for people more used to the textual and technological tools of modern cartography. In this context, such people are, of course, tourists. We argue that modern cartographic techniques enable individuals to orientate themselves through a fusion of history, location and self as it is impossible to separate one from the other. This is because the self is always somewhere and is always conditioned by what has gone before through the influence of past experience (Morgan and Pritchard 2005, Rossetto 2012). The point here is that maps, as material objects, do not solely mediate the movement of people from one place to the next, they also mediate a connection between people, place and history. In this way they illustrate the merging of mind and world (Herva 2010, Ingold 2011b) through the maps ability to bring forth knowledge of the world as a means of helping individuals to find where there are. For example, when we look at a map of London we mentally decipher the symbols and pictures in terms of what we already know about the roads and landmarks of London. In doing so we connect with London on the basis of how familiar we are with the city. Familiarity feeds into a sense of self because it connects or disconnects us to particular places (Palmer 2003, McCabe and Stokoe 2004, Prentice and Andersen

2007). By looking at a map of London we can connect to a sense of self as being British, whereas in looking at a map of Paris we recognise the other that which we are not.

Maps therefore enable us to explore who we are in relation to where we are both in time and space. So, when Cosgrove (1999: 1–2) argues that '[t]o map is in one way or another to take the measure of a world...', mathematically, spiritually, politically and morally he is, in effect, pointing to the cosmological function of maps. By using a map individuals are linking in with a particular way of understanding and relating to the world around them. Such a point is illustrated by Herva's (2010: 336) discussion of maps and magic in Renaissance Europe where she argues that, '...maps were magical not by virtue of some special designs and symbols, but because their representational content connected them causally with the relationally constituted cosmos of the Renaissance'.

Maps then are emotionally charged artefacts because of their ability to connect or disconnect individuals to places and people, to past events and future possibilities. By looking at a map we not only orientate ourselves geographically, we also connect where we are to whom and what we know, to where we have been and where we imagine ourselves moving towards. Such connective possibilities enable an individual to locate him or herself in relation to a sense of self and to connect this self with wider understandings of identity linked to place, region or nation (Hanna and Del Casino 2003b).

The function of maps, therefore, goes far beyond enabling individuals to find places and things in terms of mere location, they connect individuals to the environment by encouraging movement in, across and around the environment. Maps thus bring us into the environment and they bring us into the world rather than separate us from the world. This is because we use maps to relate to and understand where we are physically and through the imagination. By looking at a destination point on a map we imagine ourselves getting there by moving along a particular route. In this way we experience the world through the coming together of materiality and movement.

Materiality and Movement

Whilst noting the link between maps and movement, Ingold (2011b: 242) suggests '...the world of our experience is a world suspended in movement, that is continually coming into being as we – through our movement – contribute to its formation...'. He then goes onto argue that the cartographic world is a lifeless world, still and silent, devoid of sunlight, clouds and birds. While this is an interesting observation, it ignores the fact that maps are used by people who are *in* the environment and are therefore subject to the vagaries of the environment – wind and rain, sleet and snow, sunshine, moonlight, heat and cold. A map may be a lifeless object, but its function is to support movement, such as that associated with tourism, where maps of destinations and places of interest facilitate the movement of people from one place to the next. A map is brought to life in the moment, it is picked up, read and used to move individuals from place to place both physically and in the imagination.

A focus on movement takes us away from a static narrow view of mediation within tourism studies to one that recognises the importance of *moving around* the places, people and 'things' that provide the focus for tourism. Such a view adds life to tourism by highlighting the interplay between movement and materiality as people navigate themselves from one place to the next through the movement of bodies, arms, feet, organs and blood. Such embodied movement is triggered by an individual's engagement with the material world through the medium of the map. A map thus brings the body into the world and as our knowledge of the world is continually evolving as we move about in the world then this turns a map into what Cosgrove (1999: 2) refers to as '...the spatial embodiment of knowledge...'. However, it is more than this, it is also a means by which the world is made known through the body's engagement with the world as it follows the paths, legends and 'clues' offered by the map. Thus maps enable the world to be lived in, to be embodied. Sara Cohen's (2012: 135) research on urban musicscapes in the English city of Liverpool provides a useful illustration of how maps connect people to material environments through movement. Part of her research involved musicians producing hand-drawn maps tracing the routes and paths taken by them to sites they considered significant in relation to their own music-making. In drawing the maps the musicians talked about what they were mapping, they reminisced about the disappearance or relocation of specific music venues and discussed the people and moments linked to particular sites. Analysis of the musicians' maps highlighted how they experienced and embodied the urban material environment through a combination of moving and talking '...although the hand-drawn maps... took the form of dots and lines, the stories told by the musicians helped to flesh out those patterns, bringing them to life and making them fluid' (Cohen 2012: 138).

This example further illustrates the ability of maps to mediate an embodied human-environment relationship. For tourists, a text or digital map provides signs and symbols, lines and patterns to direct the eye from map to landscape. The mind thinks, the voice speaks, the body moves and a process of engagement or dwelling-in-the-world occurs that is deeply embedded in movement. In tourism, the map mediates movement and tourist maps are as ubiquitous as the act of photography, they are an ever-present comfort blanket suggestive of safe passage through unfamiliar territory. Maps of destinations, maps to and around sites and attractions are the means by which tourists *move* whether walking, driving or cycling and this moving goes hand in hand with talking, thinking and doing. As tourists move to locate the landmarks indicated on the map, they are, according to Rossetto (2012: 6), dwelling in the map because they experience not just the places they were looking for they also experience the map, 'maps mediate people's experience of space as spaces mediate people's experience of maps'. Such a view is interesting because it opens up the possibility of there being a different type of relationship between maps and tourism where maps are more than visual representations of space – see Hadlaw's (2003) 'reading' of Beck's iconic London Underground map which ignored rather than represented geographic realism. In this revised view of tourist maps the map becomes an active device for embedding person in place and place in person. When we talk about maps we are referring to more than representational devices for understanding particular spaces. The urban environment we are experiencing also serves as a map helping people orientate and navigate themselves towards their destination. Hence we look out for features such as buildings, monuments, statues, and retail outlets to help us to 'know' which turning to take and which road to cross.

We illustrate the ideas set out in the preceding discussion through an account of our experiences of navigating London through a combination of maps, materiality and movement. Our approach is located within and alongside the work of various authors who have each, in their own way, contributed to a dialogue between maps, mapping and materiality; for example Roberts' (2012) spatial anthropology, Wood's (2012) anthropology of cartography and Rossetto's (2012) autoethnography of Berlin's cartography.

The Big Egg Hunt: Our Personal Narrative

Our focus on materiality and movement is the city of London and in particular our participation in *The Big Egg Hunt*, a charity fundraising event (sponsored by the jewellers Fabergé) that took place over six weeks in the spring of 2012. The egg hunt was just one event in a year that included the London 2012 Olympics and the Diamond Jubilee celebrations for Queen Elizabeth II. Our discussion of mapping, movement and materiality and their influence upon mediated experience is illustrated by a visit to London in search of two hundred and ten, metre high giant egg sculptures created and decorated by celebrities, artists, architects, jewellers, fashion designers and companies.

Our trip to London in search of the eggs was prompted by an interest in how such objects mediated the tourist experience, for example how people might interact with the eggs in terms of moving around them, talking about them and photographing them. However this chapter is primarily concerned with the process of mediation that underpins the finding of the eggs. The focus is, therefore, on the concept and experience of maps, mapping and navigation in relation to materiality. Specifically, we are interested in how such elements of the material world mediate the experience of place. The egg hunt provided the impetus for the research but the eggs are merely one part of the overall encounter with materiality. By materiality we mean the eggs as landmark beacons, the ephemera of maps and brochures together with the attendant architecture, buildings, transportation networks, open spaces and monuments that helped to mediate our day.

Our perspective draws from the principles of autoethnography and reflexivity and thus links in with on-going debates about acknowledging the situated and contextualised nature of research generally and particularly in terms of tourism

(Sparkes 2000, Morgan and Pritchard 2005). Indeed, Pink (2008) notes that as researchers we cannot disentangle ourselves from the people and the experiences we seek to investigate. In a similar vein to that of Rossetto (2012) our personal narrative provides a collective account of our experiences of the above examples of materiality and the ways in which they mapped and mediated our day. Whilst we acknowledge the individual and subjective nature of experience, for the purposes of this account we present a set of collective reflections gathered in real time on the day to include our memories of the day. We do not separate out our reflections because we are highlighting the co-construction of knowledge that occurs during a shared social experience (Chronis 2005, Morgan and Pritchard 2005, Pink 2008, Rickly-Boyd 2010). As both tourists and researchers what we present here will inevitably encompass elements of selectivity but this merely reflects the fact that lived experience is selective, premised as it is on memory and recall, remembering and forgetting.

Advertised as the largest ever Easter egg hunt, the eggs were located in twelve 'egg zones' around Central London. The zones were St Christopher's Place, Mayfair, Knightsbridge and Sloane Square, Green Park, St James's Park, Piccadilly, Trafalgar Square, Carnaby Street, Covent Garden, Southbank, The City, and Canary Wharf. Interestingly, the eggs were displayed in various ways; some were located in the open at ground level, some were placed on top of walls or floated on water, while others were suspended from ceilings or located inside department stores, shopping arcades and hotels. The event culminated in all the eggs being brought together at one location, Covent Garden, for a final viewing before being sold at auction. The egg auction and the associated merchandising – which included small replica eggs on sale at the egg hunt shop in Covent Garden – raised over £1 million for the charities involved. The 'interactive' egg hunt was mediated by a combination of SMS technology, individual egg zone maps available from the Internet, cryptic clues to help individuals locate each egg, and a 'cheat sheet' accessible via Google

Figure 15.1   Egg sculpture, *Egg Hog* by Victoria Scott

Figure 15.2   Egg plinth instructions

maps. The official website includes full details together with examples of the zone maps referred to here (www.thebigegghunt.co.uk).

The zone maps provided directions to each area but did not give the precise location of the eggs. If people were unable to solve the cryptic clues then the cheat sheet provided access to Google maps where the precise location of each egg could be found. Once located, the plinth upon which each egg sat contained a unique keyword, which could be texted via SMS to provide one competition entry to win the Fabergé *Diamond Jubilee Egg* valued at £100, 000. The eggs could also be located via Facebook by scanning a code on the plinth and a colour brochure of all the eggs was available for purchase. This brochure provided details of the artist, individual or group who had designed and produced each egg. This combination of search methods is why the organisers referred to the egg hunt as interactive.

It is clear from these brief details that what we are discussing is not only one particular experience of movement and materiality, it is also a partial experience because the Egg Hunt was limited to a specific part of London. London is not, of course, a singular city, as the contributors to the book by Gilbert (2002b) illustrate there are many different *Londons* reflecting the city's complex history and its diverse contemporary economic, social and cultural geography. London has been described as a living breathing body, as both having and being a personality and as possessing particular features and characteristics (Eade 2000, Ackroyd 2001, Reed 2002). In this respect our egg hunt experience is defined by an absence of London in that the event was concentrated and targeted on central London rather than the whole of London. This absence is not just in terms of the events lack of engagement with other parts of the city it is also because our visit took place during the day and London by day is very different to London by night.

A Day Out

Our search for the eggs begins with a commonplace experience, a train journey along a familiar route ending in our arrival at a station we had used many times before, namely London Victoria. As we step down from the train we fall into the routine of ticket barriers, crowds, the sights and sounds of the station. There is little need for discussion, decision-making or negotiation in relation to where we are heading as past experience guides our exit from the station. Our strides towards the platform exit barriers are quick and purposeful – tickets at the ready. Busy train stations are not always conducive to walking 'together', however the occasional cursory glance ensures that we are both in sight of one another. We move through the barriers swiftly with a sense of expertise and intuition born not only from past experience but also from the learned cultural knowledge that explains the working mechanics of the train station. Once through the barriers, tickets safely stowed away in our pockets, we join the natural flow of the crowd heading across the station concourse in the general direction of the London Underground. Despite the many interruptions to our pace caused by other travellers crossing our path, or by having to circumnavigate a stationary person, or to avoid colliding with a piece of luggage, navigating ourselves across the concourse is an almost subconscious and relatively uneventful pursuit.

Our train journey into London Victoria station had given us plenty of time to decide on which part of London we would head to first in search of the eggs. The process of deciding incurred several considerations: limitations of time, our familiarity with London, and importantly the maps and information we had pre-printed from the website advertising the big egg hunt; the small pocket sized street map of London and the underground 'tube' map we had in our possession. During the day we also acquired the official egg hunt brochure providing further information on the eggs.

Our egg hunt route is initially determined by our point of arrival in London, coupled with the fact that both of us have the physical mobility to utilise London's underground system. Our knowledge of the underground map means that we are well versed in navigating the schematic. Victoria station is easily located, positioned as it is north of the River Thames at the horizontal intersection between the vertical light blue Victoria line and the horizontal green and yellow District and Circle lines. We decide that a short journey via either the Circle or District line, followed by the Northern Line would take us to Charing Cross station, a short walk from Trafalgar Square. At this point, our decisions are not based on any knowledge of distance or any precise calculations of time, but rather on our experiences and knowledge of the underground network. This knowledge overlaid our general observations in relation to the number of stops required and our impression of distance ascertained from the map (i.e. does its 'look' a long distance on the diagrammatical representation of the journey).

As we move down into the underground we instinctively draw upon a cultural awareness that enables us to know and conform to the tacit etiquette that dictates

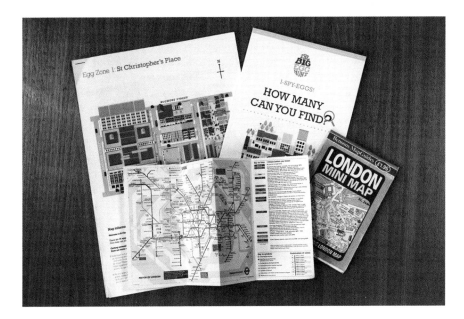

Figure 15.3   Maps and materiality

Sources: The Big Egg Hunt brochure reproduced with permission of Action for Children; Tube map reproduced with permission of Transport for London © Transport for London; and London Mini Map cover image included by permission © Fernando Benito & Pedro Benito, 2012.

which side of the escalator is for standing and which side is for walking, and whether to walk on the right or left side of the corridors and tunnels. In this way we pass quickly through the barriers taking us towards the District and Circle lines running east. We already have our tickets, so we manage to avoid the congested purchasing areas and find ourselves pausing for some minutes on the platform awaiting the arrival of a tube train. Travelling on the tube, a journey through a tunnelled network masks conceptions of distance and location in relation to actual places above ground. For us it is a mechanistic process, a linear journey in the sense that we are travelling (and consequently following) the lines of the tube map, passing through its matrix of grids that bear no relation to the actual contours of the land. As we sit on the swaying train the various stops are displayed on the side of the carriage. We monitor and mentally discard the names of the stations as we pass through them. During this journey the physical urban space of inner London is not at the forefront of our consciousness, it sits above our heads an imagined place of familiar sites, activities, people and events that we associate with London as a capital city.

The functionality of the journey and our fixation with reaching our destination mean that we subconsciously blank out our corporeal embodied experience of the tube. We experience a blurred form of embodiment seemingly out of time and space. We are enclosed underground and at that particular time of day (mid-morning) we have avoided the levels of congestion that can occur on the network during busier times. It is still busy, with the noises unique to the underground system created by the trains on the tracks, the brakes as they come to a standstill and the opening and closing of the doors. These mechanical noises are accompanied by tannoy announcements that are often difficult to understand. As we wait for the next train to arrive we look down at the tracks, we read the advertising posters on the tunnel walls, we observe people as they pass by and those that stand in front of us. Eye contact is avoided and the absence of the usual smells and odours from the close body contact associated with the 'rush hour' reinforces our sense of blurred embodiedness. The absence of any fresh airflow and exposure to the natural elements is a continual reminder of the underground nature of our journey and further emphasises our experience of space as closed and confined. We chat and laugh together quietly.

Our bodies feel and move with the rhythms and tempo of the tube train, we experience variances in speed, the jolts and shudders, the screeching of the breaks. We engage in quiet snippets of 'commentary' with each other punctuated by moments of silence. We are both conscious of the presence of other people in close proximity to ourselves. We constrain our usual levels of conversation (both in terms of content and volume) preferring to remain relatively inconspicuous and immersed in the fabric of the 'people-scape' (such positioning feels safer on the tube). Perhaps the spatial environment heightens awareness of our own sensorial responses, resulting in a subliminal redirecting of our own consciousness towards the banality and functionality of the journey.

Reaching Charing Cross station we leave the train and make our way to the exit where our attention is captured and thus diverted towards a public display of tube art and in particular to a series of abstract works (re)presenting the schematic of London's underground network.

As we take a small pause in our journey these artworks add an interesting layer to our use of maps to navigate our journey towards the eggs. We muse on the different ways in which London can be characterised through such representations of the underground. For example one of us had recently purchased the underground film map which provides different imaginings of London by 'renaming' the existing tube stations as films, TV shows, actors, producers and cinematographers and so forth linked to popular media and film. During the day trip we purchase yet another depiction of London's underground – the Olympic underground map, presumably produced in celebration of the city's hosting of the 2012 summer Olympics.

Eventually we find ourselves in Trafalgar Square, for both of us a place of familiarity. In particular, for one of us the square conjured up childhood memories – a place triggering associations with the classic children's film *Mary Poppins* and a song from the film, called *Feed the Birds*. Although not the place actually depicted in the film, we briefly talk about the memories and stories linked to this film including the recollection of a photograph one of us has of herself as a child in the square feeding the pigeons. Our visit to Trafalgar Square is temporarily turned

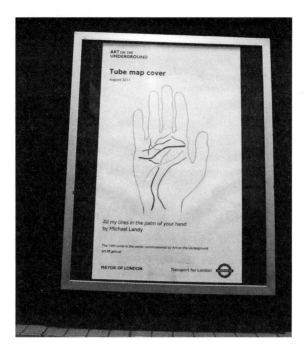

Figure 15.4   Tube map poster art

Source: Reproduced with permission of Transport for London © Transport for London.

into a space of adventure and intrigue because our purpose is to follow the clues in search of the eggs. In complete contrast to the relative darkness and enclosed space of the underground system, the day is beautifully sunny and warm. As we cast our gazes around the busy square, we do so with earnestness and with a sense of expectation, however our expressions soon turn quizzical as we expected the eggs to be clearly visible in relation to the familiar architecture of the square. Our pace quickens as we move around the square, glancing here and there, surveying the space. We refer to our paperwork, the maps and the information on the eggs. We refer to the treasure hunt clues to help us find the twelve eggs located in this zone. We look for the first egg linked to a statue of Oscar Wilde by following the clue on the Zone map, 'Oscar Wilde was a master of the English Language, and once you find his statue you won't need to be a master egg hunter to find this fast-moving egg'. But we fail to find the statue or any of the eggs. This is interesting in light of our sense of familiarity with Trafalgar Square, clearly we did not know the space as well as we had thought. The maps, on this occasion, brought disorientation rather than clarity to our wanderings.

Slightly perplexed we sit on the stone benches in the square to check our information. One of us has an iPhone so we access the webpages which we find challenging given the size of the screen and the effect of the bright sunshine on our ability to read the information. Confused and slightly frustrated we make a phone call to someone who we know will be able to assist us in locating the statue and the egg. We knew that the eggs were due to be moved to what at the time had been advertised as a 'secret' location and we had planned our trip ahead of this date to enable us to experience the actual egg hunt. As it turns out we soon discover that the entire collection of eggs has already been re-located to the 'secret' location, Covent Garden, where they are exhibited en masse.

So with the knowledge that all the eggs are now in Covent Garden, and before we decide upon our next course of action, we take some minutes to think through our situation. Initially we are disappointed and deflated, however our mood quickly changes as we comprehend the opportunity presented to us. Rather than spending an entire day searching out a limited number of eggs we realise we will be able to encounter all the eggs in one zone. In being redirected in this way our hunt results in a spectacle of materiality. As we sit in the square musing on our predicament, we become more consciously aware of the weather-environment and its impact upon our experience. The weather reminds us of the bodily nature of existence, we feel part of life as our senses react to the elements around us, a warm and sunny day. We choose not to use the tube again because the underground separates us from the sensory experience of life lived above ground by protecting us from the elements. We prefer instead to walk above ground to make our way to Covent Garden.

We have subsequently reflected on whether we would have done so if we had been on our own – or whether there is something to be said for the companionship in walking and talking, perhaps enjoying the idleness of such activity. Walking with someone enables a different form of contemplation, different rhythms as you slow down, halt, engage in the act of purposeful observation and talking. There is a different dynamic here, there is negotiation, shared viewing, interaction and emotion (such as smiling or laughter).

Encountering the Eggs

There is no formula or pre-subscribed way of navigating Covent Garden, it is not a space or tourist attraction with a single entrance, to the contrary you can approach its Piazza from numerous directions. Although the road leading down from Covent Garden tube station is typified by a defined and often heavy two-way flow of people coming and going we enter at the opposite side to this flow. Covent Garden is a cosmopolitan and therefore very popular place in Central London. It is always busy, a place of many activities – market stalls, indoor and outdoor (with partial overhead covering); drinking and eating outlets; street entertainment and busking; various gift and souvenir shops. This space also hosts London's Transport Museum and the Covent Garden Opera House. It is also situated amid the theatre district of London's West End.

Reaching Covent Garden, we are caught up in the thrill and spectacle of 'The Grand Egg-stravaganza!' (The Big Egg Hunt Brochure). It does not take us a long

Figure 15.5   Suspended egg sculptures inside Covent Garden

time to orientate ourselves amid the chaotic and busy space and to realise that
the Piazza has been turned into a huge open-air exhibition of over two hundred
unique and beautifully decorated ornate eggs. There is no natural flow of people,
individuals and groups pass through or navigate the space with seeming purpose,
others meander and engage in a serendipitous exploration of the space. As always
the Piazza is crowded, full of the hustle and bustle of activity, what is different
on this occasion however is the presence of the eggs. As we move through the
Piazza we look around us and notice other people like ourselves being directed
by these material objects. We observe people searching out the eggs, looking,
gesticulating, touching, stroking and photographing the eggs – the eggs act like
beacons signalling their location, demanding the visitor's attention.

We become part of the crowd engaging in a visually rich and tactile experience.
The egg and its positioning structure the extent to which 'we' and 'others' can
get close to and touch each egg. The eggs are variously positioned, some are
suspended up high and out of reach, and some are enclosed in glass display units,
while others openly invite the audience to actively engage with the egg.

We are part of the flow of people, looking up, down and around – talking,
pointing and waiting to get close to the various exhibits. We observe how many
times visitors wait for people to move on from one egg to another so that they can
take up the best vantage point, choreographing the taking of photographs in what are

Figure 15.6   Egg sculptures outside Covent Garden

relatively small and crowded spaces. We too join in with this activity endeavouring to capture the best shots and to effectively 'collect' as many of the eggs as we can. We also observe people looking for the eggs in the egg hunt brochure, reading up about them and recording each find by making a note in the brochure.

Many of the eggs are located out in the open alongside the Piazza where they are lined up in rows wide enough to enable people to walk around and between them. While under cover in the Piazza we forget about the weather, but once we move outside to see the display we realise that it is raining. We struggle to hold the umbrella, to take photographs and look at each egg all in one go. The weather is part of the experience, it cannot be ignored, and it is as much a mediator of our material journey as are the maps, eggs, architecture and brochures that feature more readily in accounts of engagement with the material world. The rain came at the end of a tiring day so we decide to head home, but instead of walking we retrace our steps back underground, back through the ticket barriers, back over ground and eventually back onto home space.

Concluding Reflections: Materiality and Movement as Mediation

In this chapter we have argued that schematic devices such as maps, the urban environment and the egg sculptures are all forms of materiality that collectively mediate our experiences of the world. They are all 'maps' providing information to enable people to situate and navigate themselves around particular spaces. Crang (1994) makes a similar point about the heritage, which he describes as an object that operates like a map directing people to a particular view of history. Yet this heritage object does not exist in isolation, '[h]eritage is not an object seen as existing independently of how it is experienced' (Crang 1994: 342). We cannot, therefore, divorce the maps we use, whether metaphorical, conceptual or physical, from the actual experience of being in the world, from moving, walking, talking and doing. The notion of 'active doing' has been discussed by various authors in relation to understanding the nature of lived experience generally and specifically in terms of materiality and movement (Crang 1997, Ingold 2004, 2011a, Scarles 2009). Our narrative account is an illustration of active doing where the physical, the conceptual and the virtual coalesce to structure and mediate lived experience. Physical in terms of maps, brochures, egg sculptures, buildings and trains; virtual in the form of information delivered by iPhone and Internet; together with the information we have stored away in our subconscious, are not just navigational aids, they are the means by which we embody the world through movement.

Our narrative embodiment of place has a starting point and the starting point of any journey reliant upon maps and other material devices plays a significant part in shaping the journey because of their ability to influence decisions linked to such aspects as the necessary mode of transportation and the amount of time available relative to the distance to be travelled. Likewise the direction of travel is linked to the starting point, whether to move east or west, to turn left or right. But where is the starting point? For our narrative we chose the point at which we set out physically on the day but we actually started before this in terms of researching the event, the trip, timings and so on. So by taking our departure as the starting point we are highlighting the moment at which we chose to physically *join* the map and how it then helped to shape our journey as an 'embodied doing' through the city.

It is important here to note the role of talking in mediating how we move, how we navigate our way. Navigating is about more than compass points, it is about talking and moving, strolling, paying attention to the rhythm and flow of the body in response to external stimuli such as the train, the weather, and each other. Walking is an important part of the embodiment of place and although there is a growing body of literature on the role and significance of walking (Pinder 2001, Ingold 2004, Ingold and Lee Vergunst 2008, Pink 2008), our purpose is not to unpick the nature of walking *per se* as it is merely one form of movement. As our narrative illustrates we moved from one place to the next by both walking over-ground and via underground trains and our experiences on each train also involved movement as we were rocked to and fro by the train's own movement along the track. This coming together of materiality (the train) with movement mediated our experience of the city. However, there is another important aspect structuring our experience and that is the weather. The weather is frequently ignored in discussions of maps as part of the material world. Indeed, Ingold (2011b) argues that the weather is conspicuous by its absence in accounts of the engagement between people and aspects of the material world. Yet we both made frequent references to the weather as we looked for the eggs. We should not, therefore, ignore the physicality of the environment when seeking to explore how materiality mediates the tourist experience.

What we have shown here is that maps and mapping operate at various levels and exist in different forms, and that when we talk of materiality in terms of navigating and moving we should not confine ourselves to objects. The weather, too, mediates movement as it causes us to change direction, to slow down or speed up our pace, or move to a different place entirely. Our personal narrative demonstrates how we connect with places through active engagement with different forms of materiality including the weather. It has also demonstrated how we *find* the world through maps, materiality and movement.

References

Ackroyd, P. 2001. *London. The Biography*. London: Vintage.

Black, J. 1997. *Maps and Politics*. London: Reaktion Books.

Chambard, J-L. 1980. *Atlas D'Un Village Indien. Piparsod.Madhya Pradesh [Atlas of an IndianVillage, Piparsod, Madhya Pradesh]*. Paris: Ecole des Hautes Etudes en Sciences Sociales.

Chronis, A. 2005. Coconstructing heritage at the Gettysburg storyscape. *Annals of Tourism Research*, 32 (2), 386–406.

Cohen, S. 2012. Urban musicscapes: mapping music-making in Liverpool, in *Mapping Cultures*, edited by L. Roberts. Basingstoke: Palgrave Macmillan, 123–43.

Cosgrove, D. 1999. Introduction: Mapping Meaning, in *Mappings*, edited by D. Cosgrove. London: Reaktion, 1–23.

Cosgrove, D. 2008. *Geography and Vision. Seeing, Imagining and Representing the World*. London: I.B. Tauris.

Crang, M. 1994. On the heritage trail: maps of and journeys to olde Englande. *Environment and Planning D: Society and Space*, 12 (3), 341–55.

Crang, M. 1997. Picturing practices: research through the tourist gaze. *Progress in Human Geography*, 21 (3), 359–73.

Crang M, 1999. Knowing, tourism and practices of vision, in *Leisure/Tourism Geographies: Practices and Geographical Knowledge*, edited by D. Crouch. London: Routledge, 238–56

Del Casino, V.J. and Hanna, S.P. 2000. Representations and identities in tourism map spaces. *Progress in Human Geography*, 24 (1), 23–46.

Eade, J. 2000. *Placing London: From Imperial Capital to Global City*. Oxford: Berghahn.

Fagan, B. 2012. *Beyond the Blue Horizon. How the earliest mariners unlocked the secrets of the oceans*. New York: Bloomsbury Press.

Farias, I. 2011. Tourist Maps as Diagrams of Destination Space. *Space and Culture*, 14 (4), 398–414.

Frake, O. 1985. Cognitive maps of time and tide among medieval seafarers. *Journal of the Royal Anthropological Institute* (N.S.), 20 (2), 254–70.

Fratianni M. and Marchionne F. 2012. Trade costs and economic development. *Economic Geography*, 88 (2), 137–63.

Gilbert, P.K. 2002a. The Victorian social body and urban cartography, in *Imagined Londons*, edited by P.K. Gilbert. Albany, NY: State University of New York Press, 11–30.

Gilbert, P.K. (ed.) 2002b. *Imagined Londons*. Albany, NY: State University of New York Press.

Hadlaw, J. 2003. The London Underground map: imagining modern time and space. *Design Issues*, 19 (1), 25–35.

Hanna, S.P. and Del Casino, V.J. (eds.) 2003a. *Mapping Tourism*. Minneapolis: University of Minnesota Press.

Hanna, S.P. and Del Casino, V.J. 2003b. Introduction: tourism spaces, mapped representations, and the practices of identity, in *Mapping Tourism*, edited by S.P. Hanna and V.J. Del Casino. Minneapolis: University of Minnesota Press, ix–xxvii.

Herva, V.-P. 2010. Maps and magic in Renaissance Europe. *Journal of Material Culture,* 15 (3), 323–43.

Ingold, T. 2011a. *Being Alive. Essays on Movement, Knowledge and Description*. London: Routledge.

Ingold, T. 2011b [2000]. *The Perception of the Environment* (with new Preface). London: Routledge.

Ingold, I. 2010. Footprints through the weather-world: walking, breathing, knowing. *Journal of the Royal Anthropological Institute* (N.S.), 20 (1), S121–S139.

Kodras J. 1997. The changing map of American poverty in an era of economic restructuring and political realignment. *Economic Geography*, 73 (1), 67–93.

Lewis, D. 1976. Observations on route finding and spatial orientation among the Aboriginal peoples of the Western Desert region of Central Australia. *Oceania*, 46 (4), 249–82.

McCabe, S. and Stokoe, E.H. 2004. Place and identity in tourists' accounts. *Annals of Tourism Research,* 31 (3), 601–22.

Palmer, C. 2003. Touring Churchill's England: rituals of kinship and belonging. *Annals of Tourism Research,* 30 (2), 426–45.

Phillips, A. 2005. Cultural geographies in practice. Walking and looking. *Cultural Geographies*, 12 (4), 507–13.

Pinder, D. 2001. Ghostly footsteps: voices, memories and walks in the city. *Ecumene, a Journal of Cultural geographies* 8 (1), 1–19.

Pink, S. 2008. An urban tour. the sensory sociality of ethnographic place-making. *Ethnography*, 9 (2), 175–96.

Poole, P. 2003. *Cultural Mapping and Indigenous Peoples*. UNESCO Report 159090. http://www.unesco.org/new/en/unesco/resources/online-materials/publications/unesdoc-database/ [accessed: 5 December 2012].

Prentice, R. and Andersen, V. 2007. Interpreting heritage essentialisms: familiarity and felt history. *Tourism Management*, 28 (2007) 661–76.

Reed, A. 2002. City of details: interpreting the personality of London. *Journal of the Royal Anthropological Institute* (N.S.), 8 (1), 127–41.

Rickly-Boyd, J. 2010. The tourist narrative. *Tourist Studies*, 9 (3), 259–80.

Roberts, L. 2010. Dis/embedded geographies of film: virtual panoranas and the touristic consumption of Liverpool waterfront. *Space and Culture*, 13 (1), 54–74.

Rossetto T. 2012. Embodying the map: tourism practices in Berlin. *Tourist Studies*, 12 (1), 1–24.

Salmond, A. 2012. Digital subjects, cultural objects: Special Issue Introduction. *Journal of Material Culture*, 17 (3), 211–28.

Scarles, C. 2009. Becoming tourist: renegotiating the visual in the tourist experience. *Environment and Planning D: Society and Space*, 27 (4), 465–88.

Sparkes, A.C. 2000. Autoethnography and narratives of self: reflections on criteria in action. *Sociology of Sport Journal*, 17 (1), 21–43.

Widlok, T. 1997. Orientation in the wild: the shared cognition of Hai‖om Bushpeople. *Journal of the Royal Anthropological Institute* (N.S.), 3 (2), 317–32.

Withers, C.W.J. 2000. Authorizing landscape: 'authority', naming and the Ordnance Survey's mapping of the Scottish Highlands in the nineteenth century. *Journal of Historical Geography*, 26 (4), 532–54.

Wood, D. 2010. *Rethinking the Power of Maps*. New York: Guilford Press.

Wood, D. 2012. The Anthropology of Cartography, in *Mapping Cultures*, edited by L. Roberts. Basingstoke: Palgrave Macmillan, 280–303.

Chapter 16
Mediating Tourism: Future Directions?

Jo-Anne Lester and Caroline Scarles

Introduction

The ways in which we navigate and negotiate our presence and experiences in an increasingly technologically advanced world is through complex, diverse and often chaotic mediating processes channelled by various forms of media. Undeniably, globalisation and the role of media technologies have impacted upon processes of knowing, comprehension and communication at both societal and individual levels. Indeed, spaces and practices of everyday life are mediated not only through the physicality and materiality of our surroundings, but also through virtual media spaces. The ways in which individuals and societies experience and internalise these encounters affect their understandings, perceptions and imaginings of the world.

Forms of media have long been recognised for their constituting power to construct and convey particular discourses and depictions of people and places of travel and tourism, as well as their propensity to influence and construct tourist and traveller experiences (see for example Dann 1996, Wang 2000). Indeed Burgess and Gold (1985: 1) once posited '...a geography of the media must address the question of the ideology of places as well as focusing on their qualities and the emotional experiences that they generate'. Yet arguably, in the context of tourism, the research agenda has been relatively slow to develop, particularly in terms of mediated experiences. In the context of popular media at the time, Burgess and Gold (1985: 2) reflected on the status afforded to such media, urging that 'popular media, such as newspapers, music and film, be considered just as legitimate an expression of culture as literature, sculpture and the theatre'.

The notion of tourism as an institution and its mediating power is not a new concept (see Urry 1990, Morgan and Pritchard 1998) with the connections between media and tourism having received greater attention in recent years (see for example Jansson 2002, Crouch et al. 2005, Beeton et al. 2006, Jansson and Falkheimer 2006, Månsson 2011). Indeed, Beeton et al. (2006) remind us that tourism and media have much in common historically, having followed similar trajectories in their development. Reflecting specifically on social, economic and technological advancements of the twentieth century and the globalisation of both tourism and media, Beeton et al. (2006:157) in their introduction to a special issue in *Tourism and Media into the 21st Century* asserted that during this time,

[b]oth tourism and media became commonly prefixed by *mass*, and both
were often criticized for being so. Both shaped cultures, drove globalization,
eroded traditions, inspired people, and provoked arguments about authenticity/
accuracy. Some saw tourism and media as having moral responsibilities; others
saw mainly profits. And both were connected, continually influencing the other.

Beeton et al. (2006) went on to highlight that despite these comparisons
and connections, the interactions between tourism and media has received
limited academic attention. At the same time, scholars were calling for greater
interdisciplinary cooperation between tourism and media studies (Mazierska
and Walton 2006). In addition to those mentioned above, there have been
some significant contributions to researching media, mediation and the tourist
experience, although these have amassed around particular forms of media, most
notably those that are visually orientated (see Crouch and Lübbren 2003, Burns
et al. 2010a, 2010b) and film specifically (see Beeton 2010, Connell 2012) with a
developing research agenda and interest in social media (see for example Sigala
et al. 2012). However, despite these significant contributions, the relationships
between tourism, media and the tourist experience continues to be relatively
under-researched, most notably so amid the immense development in mediating
technologies within postmodern societies more generally.

Couldry's (2012) insightful work, *Media, Society, World*, brings to the fore
the many advancements in media, particularly those in wealthier societies, and
in so doing highlights a number of significant shifts in mediating practices that
include (among others) intensifications in volumes of information disseminated
through an increasing array of mediating platforms; upsurges in speed and reach
of information; mobility of media and mediating practices; and the interactivity
and immediacy inherent in particular mediation processes. Importantly, a focus
on the interplay between media and processes of mediation move beyond our
understandings of the ways in which we 'engage with', 'experience' and 'exist
in' a media infused society (see Couldry 2012), but lie also with the mediatisation
of society in terms of how society and culture is affected by media (Hjarvard
2008). Indeed, if we adopt Hjarvard's (2008: 106) assertion that, '[t]he concept
most central to an understanding of the importance of media to culture and society
is mediatization', and that '...an understanding of the importance of media in
modern society and culture can no longer rely on models that conceive of media as
being separate from society and culture' (ibid.), then to refer to the mediatisation
of tourism recognises both the continued importance of, and inextricable links
between, media and tourism.

Such observations hold particular resonance for this volume. Variously the
collection brought together in this publication embraces 'media' in different ways
to explore a range of mediating practices; such practices enshrine, infuse and
construct particular tourism activities thereby influencing that of 'being a tourist'.
Drawing on an eclectic mix of media, in both traditional and newer forms, this
collection demonstrates the breadth of perspectives that encapsulates the notion

of mediating tourism, thus contributing to the growing literature in this area. In doing so, they collectively raise some interesting questions, whilst simultaneously revealing gaps in existing understandings of a complex area, and in so doing highlight the rich expanse of unchartered territory to be explored. Certainly, given the social and cultural significance and influence of media within societies generally (Couldry 2012), a continuation in media-related research in tourism is essential. Reflecting upon the key theoretical advancements proposed within this publication, the aim of this concluding chapter is to present a research agenda for future work on media, mediation and the tourist experience.

Research Agenda

Askew (2002:2–3) talks of the 'entanglement of media and society' which is an apt expression when considering ways to engage with and to express the complex and undoubtedly infinite terrain within which to advance academic inquiry in this area. Indeed Månsson (2011: 1649), in her reflections on progressing research into mediatising tourism, acknowledges the continuing convergence of different media forms and tourism consumption making reference to '…opening Pandora's Box, with layers and layers of new challenges and/or possibilities'. Consequently, it is not the intention here to provide a neatly framed research agenda, but rather to present a set of reflections and thoughts that will contribute to focusing attention on the many opportunities that exist for research and researchers in this and related areas of inquiry. In helping to navigate the 'entanglements' the following will be loosely structured around mediascapes; representation; enacting tourism; and virtual mobilities.

Mediascapes

The collection of chapters in this volume draws on a range of media forms, for example: brochures, e-brochures, film, television, the Internet, video, video technologies, photographs, social media sites, and features of the material world. The nature of our encounters with such media varies depending on how we interface with these, for example virtually and/or physically as illustrated in promotional material and brochures, which exist both in print and electronic forms (see Wilkes, Anastasiadou and Migas this volume). It is perhaps interesting to also observe the several contributions to this volume that focus on film and other forms of audio-visual data (see O'Connor and Kim, Curtin, Beeton et al., Siripis et al., Lukinbeal and Fletchall). This is perhaps reflective of the burgeoning research agenda within tourism, which as highlighted previously, has traditionally focused on image and representation, drawing on visually rich promotional media with a growing recognition and inquiry into other mediascapes such as film.

Such reflections align with Askew's (2002) observations that, in general, visual media has dominated academics attention rather than those that are aural. In the context of tourism, Beeton et al. (2006) made a similar observation regarding the range of media warranting attention, studies in their special issue included written and aural media in addition to visual media. Moreover, literature (see Herbert 2001, Robinson and Anderson 2002), guidebooks (see Bhattacharyya 1997, Gilbert 1999, McGregor 2000) and music (see Gibson and Connell 2005, Dawe 2007) are types of media texts, which in varying ways have been utilised to further understandings of the relationships between media and tourism. Walter's (1998) polemic on the impact of electronic guides in a tourist attraction is an early example of inquiry into the role of technologies and the tourist experience.

These observations aside, we call here for a greater engagement with a fuller range of media forms and mediascapes that not only attend to the visual nature and orientation of media, but also extend beyond those recognised primarily for their visual qualities (these of course remain important), to embrace aural and text-based media, advancing our understandings of the role of these in mediating tourism and tourist experiences.

Moreover we also call for greater acknowledgement of materialities of mediation in the context of tourist experiences. In this collection, Beeton et al.'s chapter presents the notion of sites of tourism as media, stating '[i]f media is defined as something that "mediates" messages between a sender and a recipient, a museum panel or monument performs precisely the same function as a newspaper article or documentary' (148). They subsequently question the role of the producer and consumer in the exposure to different forms of media, arguing that in the case of the former (i.e. the sites of tourism) engagements are largely dependent upon the action of the tourist. Palmer and Lester's study (this volume) engages with how the built environment and aspects of materiality narrates and mediates everyday lived experience and consequently that of being a tourist. Whilst acknowledging the evocative power of images, they rather provocatively assert '...that "flat" visual images of destinations and activities, such as brochure images and photographs may encourage individuals to engage in tourism but these images tell us nothing about the actual experience of tourism' (237). Indeed, a recent example of a study of postcards illustrates a shift from focusing on the notion of visual representations to their material significance. Whilst acknowledging the propensity of their 'images and texts [to] trigger imaginative travel' (Andriotis and Mavrič 2013: 36), framed by Urry's (2000 and 2007) New Mobilities Paradigm, Andriotis and Mavrič (2013: 36) posited '...that postcards are themselves travelling objects that necessitated systems of photography, production, dissemination and literacy in order to travel'. Consequently, space exists for research that acknowledges the tangible, physical, object and material world and their mediating significance.

Placing attention on tourism's object and material world, highlights not only the mediating role and symbolic significance of such ephemera, but also orientates attention to the symbiotic relationship between media forms and the necessary systems, processes and actors that support their mediating functions.

To draw on Couldry's (2012: 35) broader definition of media '...encompassing not just traditional media (television, radio, press, film) but all the other media platforms, mobile or fixed, through which content of any sort – both institutionally and individually produced – is now accessible or transmissible', highlights the significance of mediating technologies and their role in mediating tourist experiences.

Scope also exists to reconnect the research agenda in focusing on forms of media and their multi-sensory qualities. Such positioning invites further exploration into the embodied and sensory engagements with particular forms of media – smell, touch, sound (Rodaway 1994) and their mediating power to advance inquiry into the links between such media and the range of sensory experiences and mediating practices they engender (see Marks 2000, 2002, Bruno 2002, Barker 2009). Tourism literature has seen a move to reconceptualising the tourist gaze both in terms of its sensory qualities beyond those attributed to the visual (see Crouch and Lübbren 2003, Haldrup and Larsen 2003, Bærenholdt et al. 2004, Scarles 2009, 2010). It is not just the sensory qualities of media that warrant attention but also the context in which these exist or are experienced which is significant. Indeed, as introduced in the chapter by Lukinbeal and Fletcher (this volume), such orientations bring to the fore the spatial conditions in which mediating practices occur. For example in the context of film viewing, Zonn (2007:64) reminds us:

> Watching a film at the local multiplex, in front of your own 42" flat screen TV, on a DVD player at 35,000 feet, or through the windshield of your car are place-based experiences that can become subtle yet integral and even defining features of our daily lived practices.

Moreover it is the interplay of different types of media that beckons greater consideration given the intertextual nature of different forms of media as well as the often simultaneous consumption of a range of media. Indeed, advocating the appropriateness of the term 'media tourism', Reijnders (2011: 234) in his study into *Dracula*, Transylvania and the popular imagination also acknowledges the influence of literature and film in such cases: '...recognising the many-sided and historical back-ground of the phenomenon'.

Representation

While the above highlights the value in exploring forms of media that move beyond their representational qualities, in this collection Wilkes' chapter, concerned with the politics of representation, outlines a number of reasons why it remains necessary to question and critique the mediation of particular dominant representations and discourses. Of particular note is the ways in which these are often presented, and thus received, in the absence of their historical and political contexts. Continuing to question tourism representations is important particularly amid the context of the multiplicity of media, mediating technologies and the volume of information readily accessible through a range of media. Such societal conditions increasingly have the potential to widen the disconnect between representations and their contextual foundations. Indeed, the sheer volume of information readily available through a myriad of communication interfaces could almost be characterised as 'sound-bites', snippets of data that we receive, often within relatively short periods of time and in close succession. In the context of the Internet, as a virtual platform for knowledge seeking and dissemination, Scherle and Lessmeister's chapter (this volume) concludes with the argument that '[t]he oversupply of information, services and offers is probably the biggest challenge for the virtual tourist' (100).

In the context of globalisation and hypermobility through innovative networks of communication, the opportunities to engage with individuals and different user groups not only to explore a fuller range of understandings and interpretations of particular discourses, but also to elicit greater appreciations of how these have been realised warrants much more attention within academic inquiry. Consequently, exploring the politics of representation needs to extend beyond the authorial voice of the researcher to elicit the views of other audience/stakeholder groups to greater effect. In this collection, O'Connor and Kim's chapter signposts this issue, with Hoffman and Kearns and Siripis et al. making a response. In order to develop a greater understanding from the perspectives of other stakeholder groups, both their studies shifted the focus from the researcher's readings and interpretations of particular discourses of media texts, to those of residents of a destination in the first case and tourists to a destination in the second. In both cases, the findings of their research went some way to dispel commonly held assumptions regarding the influence of mediated discourses on different stakeholder groups.

Within tourism the circle of representation, at one level of abstraction, provides a useful conceptual framework in which to situate and identify the various stages in which the travel experience and being a tourist can be mediated, both at a societal and an individual level (see Jenkins 2003). However, an acknowledgement within tourism inquiry currently exists that repositions this process as more complex, nuanced and fluid, with a shift in emphasis that moves away from the traditional positioning of the tourist as 'passive' (see for example Månsson 2011). Rather, tourists become active agents of 'doing' (Franklin and Crang 2001). Also critical of traditional understandings of the circle of representation and notions of agency, as outlined in the introduction to this book, this collection of chapters has endeavoured to deconstruct traditional linear dichotomies of producer and consumer, and reconceptualises media and mediation in the tourist experience as a series of non-linear, dynamic and immanent practices and processes (Scarles and Lester, this volume). Bell's chapter responds specifically highlighting the role of the tourist in the cycle of knowledge production. Beeton et al., in the context of Japanese 'contents tourism' and pop culture, refer to fans as 'prosumers', in that '...producers and consumers, whose fandom and online activities work to create the very contents that stimulate their own and others' desires to visit the sites that they consume as tourists' (148). Moreover Siripis et al.'s chapter challenges the power of popular film and the notion of tourists as passive receivers of a film's mediating messages. The results of their study caused them to conclude that tourists '…are aware of their selves as tourists and that they are subject to the influence of stage managers. The negotiation process discloses tourists' ability to differentiate between the reality of the tourism industry and the mediated representation. Tourists are not passive media receivers or passive performers at the destination' (220). However, this is an area that would benefit from further empirical inquiry that challenges and tests the circle of representation.

This volume has elicited, not unsurprisingly, the role and advancements of technology in the processes of mediation (see Scherle and Lessmesiter this volume) and advances in digital technologies and image capture/display (see Robinson, Salmond, Merchant this volume). In doing so questions surrounding notions of agency surface, which further challenge the once accepted concept of the dominance of institutions and producers of information and their influence on the more passive and dis-empowered consumer. To this end, the speed of technological invention and innovation, as well as the many potential user groups, beckons continued exploration into issues of power, distributions of power, the producer and consumer interface. As such, there exists much opportunity to empirically investigate, through a range of tourist settings and situations, the concept of the tourist as a co-producer and his or her role in (re)mediating the experiences of tourism and being a tourist. It is through continued inquiry in this area that we can obtain greater insights into the significance, consequences and impacts of these processes and relationships.

Enacting Tourism

In terms of tourism and performance, there is much scope for further research into how people interact with the natural, material and virtual worlds, and in particular the fusion of these 'worlds' in mediating experience (see Palmer and Lester this volume). For example, advancements in technologies and innovations in handheld mobile devices such as smart phones and iPads are significantly changing the ways in which individuals visually capture and consume their travel experiences. There also exists a corporeal element in these interactions to be observed and understood. As an illustration, during one of the author's recent travels to a popular Italian town in the Mediterranean, frequented by visitors for its stunning coastline views, she could not help but look on with intrigue and at the time with some sense of bemusement regarding the ways in which people 'visually' captured the panoramic with iPads. Indeed, the level of choreography between self and others during these performances was evident. So too was the 'disposable' nature of the images moments after they were captured; these hand-held devices being able to display larger and clearer pictures enabling immediate onsite viewing and approval/disapproval of the photographs taken. Such cursory observations raise issues in terms of the role of mediating technologies in the construction and conspicuous display of self-identity, inviting further inquiry into such mediated experiences and the burgeoning research agenda in this area (see Larsen 2005, Palmer and Lester 2007, Robinson and Picard 2009, Scarles 2012).

Tourists' experiences amid an increasingly mediatised and simulated world continue to raise questions surrounding concepts of authenticity (Wang 1999, 2000, Jansson 2002, Beeton et al. 2006, Tzanelli 2006, Law et al. 2007, Lau 2010). Concepts of reality and the obscuring of boundaries between the real and the imagined amid the increasingly simulated nature of tourism has received significant academic attention, for example Urry (1990: 85) comments '[e]verything is a copy, or a text upon a text, where what is fake seems more real than the real'. Moreover, Jansson (2002: 437) reflects specifically on the mediatisation of tourism stating, '[d]ue to the mediatization of tourism, there can hardly exist any realistic hedonism in the true sense of the word'. He also observes the increasingly simulated nature of tourism where '…tourism catalogues, travel magazines and Internet sites are not only simulations of reality, they are simulations of already simulated environments' with '[m]ediated images…thus becoming the "originals" against which experiences of simulated landscapes and socioscapes are measured' (ibid.: 439). Consequently, he concludes '…the concept of "authenticity" [as becoming] gravely problematic' (ibid.). These observations are grounded in postmodernist thinking, as Hjarvard (2008: 110) presents '[s]ome see mediatization as an expression of postmodern condition, in which media give rise to a new consciousness and cultural order'. Hjarvard (2008: 110) goes on to credit significant connections between mediatisation and postmodernism to the early work of Baudrillard (1994),

> …who perceives the symbols or signs of media culture – images, sound, advertisements, etc. – to form simulacra, semblances of reality that not only seem more real than the physical and social reality, but also replace it. It is like a map of the world that has become so vivid, so detailed and comprehensive that it appears more real than the world it was created to represent.

Such observations resonate with Månsson's (2011: 1649) work on mediatising tourism, in which she continues to question 'what is authentic'. Furthermore the concept of authenticity emerges in various guises throughout this collection (see for example O'Connor and Kim, Siripis et al., Lukinbeal and Fletcher), affirming and adding to the on-going attention that the concept receives within tourism inquiry. Certainly, the concept of authenticity remains complex, subject to differences in usage, interpretation and comprehension, and undoubtedly the debates surrounding authenticity and what is meant or deemed to be authentic will continue. However, rather than becoming entangled in these on-going debates regarding conceptualisations of authenticity specifically, and particularly in the context of the above observations regarding postmodernism and mediated realities, we advocate a shift in focus to one of greater empirical inquiry in pursuit of understanding individual and collective experiences of 'doing' tourism (Franklin and Crang 2001). Focusing on the relationships between media, tourist performances and experiences, the research agenda in this area needs to continue to foster greater understandings of individual interpretations and appreciation of what is authentic in relation to their experience. Such inquiry has the propensity to elicit much greater appreciations of the role of media, impacts and influences on tourists' expectations and experiences (see Lukinbeal and Fletcher this volume). This is particularly important given the continued mediatised nature of tourism and its associated activities. In particular, the advances in digital technologies foster greater interactivity and the virtually situated nature of experiences have the potential to mobilise unique and different ways of experiencing the world.

Virtual Mobilities

The contributions in this volume demonstrate the continued role of media in mobilising the gaze generally with Robinson's chapter (this volume) bringing to the fore the increasingly virtualised nature of lived experience. Concepts of travelling or being mobile in different spaces is not new (see Prideaux 2002) and whether referred to as virtual tourism, cybertourism or mind travel (Löfgren 1999, Prideaux 2002, Guttentag 2010, Urry and Larsen 2011), the ways in which we orientate ourselves in the 'worlds' of travel and tourism are increasingly sophisticated and far-reaching. Indeed virtualised technologies have the potential to mobilise aspects of lived experience, as Moreno (2007:41) asserts, '[in] many ways the Internet (chat rooms, online gambling, search engines, pornography, and MySpace) and digital media sources (DVDS) now allow us to dwell: we can belong to virtual social networks. We can navigate our bodies in virtual spaces'. Whilst we may accept that concepts of dwelling are not confined to the physical world, what matters is the extent to which we understand various practices, attitudes and motivations for engaging in different forms of lived experience in the context of travel and tourism.

Ascertaining such insights are arguably compounded by varying attitudes towards such technological innovations (see Scherle and Lessmeister, Anastasiadou and Migas this volume), with Anastasiadou and Migas's study highlighting the need to engage in research that develops a greater understanding of the psychology of both tourists and tourist providers in relation to technology usage. Whilst earlier conceptualisations of virtual tourism posed questions about replacing traditional forms of travel, such a situation has yet to be realised (see Prideaux 2002), as such there is no suggestion that travel experiences in the corporeal physical sense will be superseded by virtual mobility (Urry 2002). Rather, increasingly sophisticated, simulated and interactive virtual spaces provide not only different forms of virtual mobilities but also a space through which individuals are able to present themselves and their travel experiences to others. For example, we are now confronted with a plethora of possible platforms upon which we can share, exhibit and express self-authored and selected insights of our travel experiences (i.e. Myspace; YouTube; Facebook; Google imaging; Shutterfly, Flickr). Consequently there is scope to reflect and build upon existing inquiry on media, such as photographs and albums (see Sontag 1979, Hirsch 1981), to further explore how greater access to globalised, technologically advanced virtual spaces are fundamentally altering the ways by which knowledge, experiences, opinions and memories can be collated, archived, communicated, disseminated, manipulated and re-mediated. Such virtualised spaces beckon greater empirical inquiry that explores the concept of self-authoring and the potential for biographical constructions of place through virtual encounter.

Concluding Reflections

Whether from the perspective of tourism as a significant global economic sector, or from that of conceiving tourism as a socio-cultural phenomenon, the symbiotic relationship between media and tourism necessitates continued attention. Such inquiry needs to recognise not just the range of mediated touristic practices but also, and importantly, to focus on developing a greater understanding of the potential impacts and consequences of the inextricable links between media and tourism.

The works presented in this collection respond to those scholars who have previously advocated the significance of such inquiry and to the calls to further advance the research agenda in tourism and media-related studies. Adding to the existing literature, this collection has brought together a set of studies by scholars residing in different parts of the world and from a range of disciplinary backgrounds. This has provided not only particular cultural and contextual appreciations of the relationships between tourism and media but also a range of subject based/theoretically orientated insights and perspectives.

What is clear, however, is that mediated tourist experiences unfold in complex, multifaceted, dynamic and fast changing settings. This leaves us is no doubt that the terrain for investigation remains multidimensional and cavernous, hampered by the speed at which forms of media and processes are developing and changing. Indeed, conditions of the postmodern era of the twenty-first century such as the amount and speed of accessing volumes of information, the constantly evolving technologies and what Couldry (2012:16) has described as '[w]ave upon wave of newly saturating media [which] has flowed over inhabitants of richer countries', are themselves conditions that challenges this field of investigation even for the most avid researcher.

We could argue that the recent interest in tourism and media derives from technological innovation and invention, with much of the recent inquiry oriented to what are often described as 'modern', 'postmodern', 'developed', 'richer' societies. Such a positioning beckons inquiry into the variances that exist in mediating technologies in different societies, including those that are less media saturated and technologically advanced, and any constraints to mediating practices that may exist in particular settings in the context of tourism experiences.

As such, there is much to embrace not just in relation to the many different forms of media, but also perspectives surrounding approaches to inquiry in the context of tourism. Such pursuit calls for greater interdisciplinary cooperation through which to investigate such phenomena and to further enrich and develop research in this area. Such endeavours will not only elicit other ways of conceptualising what to investigate but may also provide opportunities to utilise alternative methods of inquiry. The following is not intended to be an exhaustive list of possibilities, but rather a set of reflections by means of illustration.

From the contributions in this volume it would seem appropriate to focus further on consumption practices amid the increasing mediatisation of society in general and as a consequence, within the realm of tourism. There are many aspects of consumption that can frame inquiry in the context of media and mediating tourist experiences. A valuable line of inquiry is to unpack the nuanced nature of consumer culture and lifestyle choices. The ways in which people's tourism choices contribute to conceptions of self and other and constructions of self-identity (see Desforges 2000), and are framed by notions of conspicuous consumption (see Corrigan 1997) and taste (see Bourdieu 1984), is of interest. As reflected on above, there now exists a plethora of ways in which people can communicate/disseminate to far-reaching audiences their experiences of travel and tourism. It would also be interesting to investigate this activity from the perspective of those working in the tourism industry, particularly for those that travel away from home for this purpose, for example those living and working abroad for overseas tour operators.

There is scope to develop greater appreciation of the potential lifespan of technology and media products in the context of trends and fashion, not only linking into aspects of taste and identity but also to question the lifespan of particular forms of media, mediating practices and mediated experiences. Amid the increasingly disposable or replaceable nature of the world that we embody, innovations in concepts, such as Second Life, are also arguably subject to the same dynamics as their corporeal and tangible counterparts. However in contrast to the physical and material environment, virtual spaces of encounter are far more readily expendable. To this end, engaging with theories of consumerism and consumer culture may yield depths of understanding regarding particular types of mediated experiences and their longevity. In terms of consumer culture and media there is arguably a need to further develop our understanding of the extent to which various mediating practices augment or potentially replace traditional corporeal experiences of being a tourist.

Anthropological perspectives on the study of tourism continue to expand; there is value in exploring this strand of inquiry to obtain greater insights into the significance of mediating practices. This is particularly pertinent given the cultural significance of media on the everyday lives of people and societies. As noted, the shifts in tourism and mediating practices particularly in the context of the digital era provide many interesting areas to probe to deepen our understanding of the complexity and nuanced nature of tourist/traveller behaviour. For example, that which embraces creators, receivers and users of media to unpack the complexities and dynamics of power and agency, representations and constructions of self and other; the relationships between visitors and resident population/'guest' encounters; and rituals of use and behaviour. Indeed there is scope to further our understanding of tourists' engagements with mediating technologies and the interplay between what Scherle and Lessmeister (this volume) refer to as the media avant-garde versus the cultural pessimists in relation to innovations in technologies.

The significance of, and advancements in, digital technologies in tourism call for further development of insights into such technologies, their capabilities, constraints and limitations. To this end a greater appreciation and understanding of virtual and hybrid spaces of embodied experiences and how these are realised in the context of tourism would be of value. Such a quest holds potential for collaboration with those working in the realms of computer science; for example in the areas of digital technologies, 3-D technologies, virtual reality and the development of serious computer games. As an illustration, a recent exhibition entitled 'Reshaping History: a future for our past'[1] brought into sharp focus approaches and capabilities of 3-D technologies to interpret history. For example, one of the authors who visited the exhibition experienced a 3-D virtual encounter with history, that of the Egyptian temple Abu Simbel before it was taken apart piece by piece and moved to a new location. Such capabilities and scientific advances are potentially significant for tourism even if only to provide virtual and imaginative experiences with the past. Through processes of 3-D digital printing the exhibition also demonstrated how artefacts can be digitally reproduced and how these can be 'printed' in their tangible object form. In the context of the anthropology of objects, or the ephemera of souvenirs such technological advancements have the potential to yield practical application to tourism.

The collection of works in this volume extends and enriches the growing body of literature and research in the area of tourism media and mediating practices. Echoing the sentiments set out in the introduction to this collection these concluding reflections elucidate the continued importance of media in their many forms in the context of tourism. In so doing, the richness of these connections not only serves to illustrate the myriad of research opportunities to be pursued in this arena, but importantly the significance and value in doing so.

References

Andriotis, K. and Mavrič, M. 2013. Postcard mobility, going beyond image and text. *Annals of Tourism Research*, 40, 18–39.

Askew, K. 2002. Introduction, in *The Anthropology of Media, a Reader*, edited by K. Askew and R.R. Wilk. Oxford: Blackwell Publishing, 1–13.

---

1   Exhibition.3d-coform.eu (as at Dec 2012).

Bærenholdt, J.O., Haldrup, M., Larsen, J., and Urry, J. 2004. *Performing Tourist Places*, Aldershot: Ashgate.

Barker, J.M. 2009. *The Tactile Eye: Touch and the Cinematic Experience*. London: University of California Press.

Beeton, S. 2010. Introduction: The advance of film tourism. *Tourism Planning and Development*, 7(1), 1–6.

Beeton, S., Croy, G. and Frost, W. 2006. Introduction: tourism and media into the 21st century. *Tourism Culture & Communication*, 6, 157–9.

Bhattacharyya, D.P. 1997. Mediating India: an analysis of a guidebook. *Annals of Tourism Research*, 24(2), 371–89.

Burgess, J. and Gold, J.R. 1985. Chapter 1: Place, the media and popular culture, in *Geography, The Media & Popular Culture*, edited by J. Burgess and J.R. Gold. Beckenham: Croom Helm Ltd: 1–32.

Burns, P., Palmer, C. and Lester J. (eds) 2010a. *Tourism and Visual Culture: Volume 1 Theories and Concepts*. Wallingford: CABI.

Burns, P., Lester J. and Bibbings, L. (eds) 2010b. *Tourism and Visual Culture: Volume 2 Methods and Cases*. Wallingford: CABI.

Bruno, G. 2002. *Atlas of Emotion: Journeys in Art, Architecture, and Film*. London: Verso.

Bourdieu, P. 1984 [1979]. *Distinction: A Social Critique of the Judgement of Taste*. Translated by Richard Nice. London: Routledge & Kegan Paul.

Connell, J. 2012. Film tourism – evolution, progress and prospects. *Tourism Management*, 33, 1007–29.

Corrigan, P. 1997. *The Sociology of Consumption*. London: Sage.

Couldry, N. 2012. *Media, Society, World: Social Theory and Digital Media Practice*. Cambridge: Polity Press.

Crouch, D. Jackson, R. and Thompson, F. (eds) 2005. *The Media and the Tourist Imagination: Converging Cultures*. Contemporary Geographies of Leisure, Tourism and Mobility Series. London: Routledge.

Crouch, D. and Lübbren, N. (eds) 2003. *Visual Culture and Tourism*. Oxford: Berg.

Dann, G. 1996. *The Language of Tourism: A Sociolinguistic Perspective*. Wallingford: CABI International.

Dawe, K. 2007. Arcadia calling: Cretan music and the popular imagination. *Journal of Intercultural Studies*, 28(2), 227–36.

Desforges, L. 2000. Traveling the world, identity and travel biography. *Annals of Tourism Research*, 27(4), 926–45.

Franklin, A. and Crang, M. 2001. The trouble with tourism and travel theory. *Tourist Studies*, 1(1), 5–22.

Gibson, C. and Connell, J. 2005. *Music and Tourism: On the Road Again*. Clevedon: Channel View Publications.

Gilbert, D. 1999. 'London in all its glory – or how to enjoy London': guidebook representations of imperial London. *Journal of Historical Geography*, 25(3), 279–97.

Guttentag, D.A. 2010. Virtual reality: applications and implications for tourism. *Tourism Management*, 31(5), 637–51.

Haldrup, M. and Larsen, J. 2003. The family gaze. *Tourist Studies*, 3(1), 23–46

Herbert, D. 2001. Literary places, tourism and the heritage experience. *Annals of Tourism Research*, 28 (2), 312–33.

Hirsch, M. 1981. *Family Photographs: Content, Meaning and Effect*. Oxford: Oxford University Press.

Hjarvard, S. 2008. The mediatization of society: a theory of the media as agents of social and cultural change. *Nordicom Review*, 29(2), 105–34.

Jansson, A. 2002. Spatial phantasmagoria: the mediatization of tourism experience. *European Journal of Communication*, 17(4), 429–43.

Jansson, A. and Falkheimer J. 2006. Towards a geography of communication, in *Geographies of Communication: The Spatial Turn in Media Studies*, edited by J. Falkheimer and A. Jansson. Göteborg: Nordicom, 9–25.

Jenkins, O.H. 2003. Photography and travel brochures: the circle of representation. *Tourism Geographies*, 5(3), 305–28.

Larsen, J. 2005. Families seen sightseeing: performativity of tourist photography. *Space and Culture*, 8, 416–34.

Lau, R.W.K. 2010. Revisiting authenticity: a social realist approach. *Annals of Tourism Research*, 37(2), 478–98.

Law, L., Bunnell, T. and Ong, C.-E. 2007. *The Beach*, the gaze and film tourism. *Tourist Studies*, 7(2), 141–64.

Löfgren, O. 1999. *On Holiday: A History of Vacationing*. Berkeley: University of California Press.

Månsson, M. 2011. Mediatized tourism. *Annals of Tourism Research*, 38(4), 1634–52.

Marks, L.U. 2000. *The Skin of the Film: Intercultural Cinema, Embodiment, and the senses*. Durham and London: Duke University Press.

Marks, L.U. 2002. *Touch: Sensuous Theory and Multisensory Media*. Minneapolis: University of Minnesota Press.

Mazierska, E. and Walton, J.K. 2006. Tourism and the moving image. *Tourist Studies*, 6(1), 5–11.

McGregor, A. 2000. Dynamic texts and the tourist gaze: death, bones and Buffalo. *Annals of Tourism Research*, 27(1), 27–50.

Moreno, C.M. 2007. Affecting and affective social/media fields, *Aether: The Journal of Media Geography*, 1, 39–44.

Morgan, N. and Pritchard, A. 1998. *Tourism, Promotion and Power: Creating Images, Creating Identities*, Chichester: Wiley.

Palmer, C. and Lester, J. 2007. Stalking the cannibals: photographic behaviour on the Sepik River. *Tourist Studies*, 7(1), 83–106.

Prideaux, B. 2002. The cybertourist, in *The Tourist as a Metaphor of the Social World*, edited by G.M.S. Dann. New York: CABI, 317–39.

Reijnders, S. 2011. Stalking the count: Dracula, fandom and tourism. *Annals of Tourism Research*, 38(1), 231–48.

Robinson, M. and Anderson, H.C. (eds) 2002. *Literature and Tourism: Essays in the Reading and Writing of Tourism*. London: Thomson.

Robinson, M. and Picard, D. 2009. *The Framed World, Tourism, Tourist and Photography*. Farnham: Ashgate.

Rodaway, P. 1994. *Sensuous Geographies, Body, Sense and Place*. London: Routledge.

Scarles, C. 2009. Becoming tourist: renegotiating the visual in the tourist experience. *Environment and Planning D: Society and Space*, 27, 465–88.

Scarles, C. 2010. Where words fail, visuals ignite: opportunities for visual autoethnography in tourism research. *Annals of Tourism Research*, 37(4), 905–26.

Scarles, C. 2012. The photographed Other: interplays of agency in tourist photography in Cusco, Peru. *Annals of Tourism Research*, 39(2), 928–50.

Sigala, M., Christou, E. and Gretzel, U. 2012. *Social Media in Travel, Tourism and Hospitality: Theory, Practice And Cases*, Farnham: Ashgate.

Sontag, S. 1979. *On Photography*. London: Penguin Books.

Tzanelli, R. 2006. Reel western fantasies: portrait of a tourist imagination in *The Beach* (2000). *Mobilities*, 1(1), 121–42.

Walter, T. 1998. From museum to morgue? Electronic guides in Roman Bath. *Tourism Management*. 17(4), 241–5.

Wang, N. 1999. Rethinking authenticity in tourism experience. *Annals of Tourism Research*, 26 (2), 349–70.

Wang, N. 2000. *Tourism and Modernity: A Sociological Analysis*. Oxford: Pergamon.

Urry, J. 1990. *The Tourist Gaze*. London: Sage.

Urry, J. 2002. Mobility and proximity. *Sociology*, 36(2), 255–74.

Urry, J. and Larsen, J. (2011). *The Tourist Gaze 3.0*. London: Sage.

Zonn, L. 2007. Going to the movies: the filmic site as geographic endeavor. *Aether: The Journal of Media Geography*, 1, 63–7.

Index

THEORIZING MODERNISM

Essays in critical theory

Edited by Steve Giles

London and New York

First published 1993
by Routledge
11 New Fetter Lane, London EC4P 4EE

Simultaneously published in the USA and Canada
by Routledge
29 West 35th Street, New York, NY 10001

Editorial selection © 1993 Steve Giles. Individual chapters © 1993 the
respective authors

Typeset in Times by ROM-Data Corporation Ltd, Falmouth, Cornwall

Printed and bound in Great Britain by T. J. Press (Padstow) Ltd,
Padstow, Cornwall

British Library Cataloguing in Publication Data

A catalogue record for this book is available from the British Library

Library of Congress Cataloging in Publication Data

Theorizing modernism : essays in critical theory / edited by Steve Giles.
p. cm.
Includes bibliographical references and index.
1. Modernism (Literature) 2. Critical theory. I. Giles, Steve.
PN56.M54T44 1993
801' .95— dc20 93–3001
CIP

ISBN 0–415–07754–0